Mother Burslem

B.J.Hodgkiss

To my parents, born in the Victorian era, who sacrificed much in their dedication to their five offspring

I would like to extend my appreciation to the following who have provided me with knowledge, advice and facilities:

Kathy Niblett and her colleagues at the City Museum in Hanley.
The staff of the Reference Library in Hanley.
The staff of Burslem Library.
The staff of the William Salt Library, Stafford.
Edmund Yorke, Chairman of Wood and Sons, Burslem, who provided me with the interesting engravings incorporated in the book.
Paul Weston and his staff at The Burslem Community Development Trust.
John Potter of the Arnold Bennett Society who read my draft.
Lyndsey Clews who contributed a considered appraisal.

And to all the friends who gave advice and encouragement.

Finally my thanks to all the past authors whose books have provided both information and illustrations; I am in their debt.

CHURNET VALLEY BOOKS
1 King Street, Leek, Staffordshire, ST13 5NW. 01538 399033
www.thebookshopleek.co.uk

© B.J. Hodgkiss and Churnet Valley Books 2001
ISBN 1 897949 75 8

CONTENTS

The Turk's Head from Ward's History of Stoke on Trent

FOREWORD

To those not born in the 'Potteries' the title of my book may be misleading, since this is not the life of an individual but that of a community. I do not consider myself to be an historian; what I have written is more a review of the development of Burslem from a rural to an urban state. The appellation 'The Mother Town' is commonly used locally since Burslem was the first to develop manufactures the early days of the industrial revolution.

Burslem could be said to be typical of areas throughout Britain which mushroomed at that time, mainly producing specific products. Burslem achieved and maintained its eminence in ceramics for a long time, despite competition from Leeds, Bristol, London and elsewhere, and abroad, but failed ultimately to become the main civic and cultural centre of the city of Stoke on Trent, despite giving birth to the other townships which comprise the city.

My father was born in Burslem, but lived in Penkhull from the time of his marriage, and since my grandparents died when I was very young, apart from infrequent visits to a widowed aunt and cousins living in Cobridge, I doubt if I had been in the Burslem area more than a dozen times before I retired. But Burslem has always held an attraction for me. Apart from my family association, it had given birth to many interesting, indeed famous characters, among them Josiah Wedgwood and Arnold Bennett, both of particular interest to me. Bennett was a contemporary of my father, but older and I think that I am right in saying that he, like my father, won a scholarship to Kensington School of Art, Bennett however turning his talent to literature and continuing to live in London, whereas my father went on to become designer at the Wedgwood Etruria works for approximately twenty-five years.

Retirement gave me the opportunity of furthering my interest and the time to research the industrial, social, political, and religious influences of the period and how these were reflected in the growth of Burslem. I am appreciative of and indebted to many written sources, thereby indulging in reiteration on occasions, nevertheless I hope the manner of presentation will maintain the reader's interest.

We natives of the Potteries are proud of Burslem, and the Potteries as a whole, for the enterprise and artistic skills demonstrated in the past and to this day, and acknowledged throughout the world. To appreciate our heritage one has only to visit the Potteries Museum and enter this veritable Aladdin's cave where you will find yourself surrounded by priceless examples of local inspiration and artistic ability.

The manner in which the city developed has unfortunately influenced our physical heritage, and it would be difficult to claim that it reflects the artistic merits of the city's products, but a transformation has now been made with the removal of the most ugly elements from the Industrial Revolution, while carefully preserving examples of our history. The traveller who visits the district is assured of a welcome to view the old and the modern in the ancient art of the potter, and will surely leave with the feeling of a memorable and informative experience.

INTRODUCTION

Among the books to which I refer are many beautifully illustrated histories of potters and their products. These books are often voluminous and the culmination of a lifetime's study. The most comprehensive historical survey of this area is *The History of the Borough of Stoke on Trent in 1838* which includes chapters on Burslem. This work was originally issued in part form, in the earlier parts of which the author is shown as Simeon Shaw LLD, but when subsequently issued in book form it is attributed to John Ward and is usually referred to as *WARD's History of Stoke on Trent*. According to Ward, after the issue of part eight the printer refused to co-operate with Shaw, and Ward completed the remaining twelve parts. Ward also claims that he provided the information for the earlier issues, as you will see from the precised preface to his book which I include below. I have decided to quote Ward throughout, except on occasions where Shaw's name is definitely applicable.

Ward was a solicitor and leading citizen of Burslem. According to his obituary he died at the age of 88 in March 1870. Born in Slawston, Leicestershire, he served his clerkship in Cheadle, Staffordshire and was admitted in 1808. There were few solicitors in the pottery towns during their early growth and none at all in Tunstall.

He is said to have composed and published a poem on the staple manufacture of the district entitled *The Potter's Art;* and on the occasion of the death of Prince Albert he wrote a composition which he presented to Victoria. Apparently this was graciously received by Her Majesty - but there was no knighthood in return.

Ward it seems could be abrasive; he is assumed to have been the solicitor who was in frequent opposition to Thomas Jones, a Hanley lawyer, and the two are said to have rarely met in court without quarrelling, until the feud earned the caption 'Hanley law versus Burslem law". Jones was said to be voluble, Ward was pompous and dignified; he is said to have attempted to get Jones struck off, but Jones won on a counter charge which ended in a considerable financial loss for Ward.

Simeon Shaw came from Salford and, although a doctor of law, never appears to have practised law in this area. In fact it has been said that the LLD was added at a

THE

BOROUGH

OF

STOKE-UPON-TRENT,

IN THE COMMENCEMENT OF

THE REIGN OF HER MOST GRACIOUS MAJESTY

Queen Victoria,

COMPRISING

ITS HISTORY, STATISTICS, CIVIL POLITY, & TRAFFIC,

WITH

BIOGRAPHICAL AND GENEALOGICAL NOTICES OF EMINENT
INDIVIDUALS AND FAMILIES;

ALSO, THE

MANORIAL HISTORY OF NEWCASTLE-UNDER-LYME,

AND

Incidental Notices of other Neighbouring Places & Objects;

BY

JOHN WARD.

THE APPENDIX CONTAINS MANY ANCIENT AND CURIOUS CHARTERS
AND DOCUMENTS NEVER BEFORE PUBLISHED,

AND

THE WORK IS EMBELLISHED WITH A VARIETY OF PLATES.

LONDON:

PRINTED AND PUBLISHED BY W. LEWIS & SON, FINCH-LANE.

MDCCCXLIII.

1843

late date. Nevertheless, he was undoubtedly a scholar, but unbusinesslike, and was obviously the one who conceived the history project and canvassed successfully for contributors, among them Josiah Spode, Thomas Minton, Felix Pratt, Josiah Mayer, and Enoch Wood, all local celebrities with whom he claimed close friendship. It was probably inevitable that he approached Ward, who had a reputation for involvement in most family and business transactions in Burslem, but their personalities obviously clashed. That at least one of them was a sycophant is noticeable from the book - to quote only one example, with reference to a partner in a pottery business and most likely a contributor to the proposed history: *"He was esteemed for piety and philanthropy; for promoting the welfare of mankind and especially for ameliorating the condition of the poor, and his name will rank among the benefactors. Thus is his liberality known to all men as an excellent specimen of the followers of the meek and lowly Jesus".* The following is a precis of Ward's preface to *The History of Stoke-on-Trent* when it was first issued in book form. It gives the impression of Ward as a self-opinionated character:

JOSIAH WEDGWOOD ESQ.
F.R.S. & F.S.A.

Frontispiece in John Ward's History

"This work has been commenced under the sanction of another name, the individual who now avows himself as its author considers it necessary, for the purpose of justifying the claim he makes to its paternity, to give some explanation respecting the manner in which it was begun and carried forward, and at length arrived at its close; and having throughout the work assumed editorial dignity, and written in the first person plural, he will, in order to avoid ambiguity, descend to the familiar style and speak in his own person.

In the summer of 1838 Mr. Simeon Shaw, who had just before issued a prospectus of an intended History of the Borough of Stoke on Trent to be published in monthly parts, but had not then brought out a single number, called on me respecting his proposed work, when I told him I was in possession of a variety of materials, chiefly of an antiquarian character, relating to the northern portion of the pottery district, which might be serviceable for the commencement of his undertaking and which I had collected with a view of a similar history, should I ever find leisure to do so; I told him further, that I was quite willing to supply all I had in my possession, provided I were permitted to exercise a control over the publication, so long as I should furnish those materials I stipulated, in fact, that not a page of the Work should be printed whilst I remained connected with it, but what I should either write myself, or peruse in manuscript and approve. Mr. Shaw at once acceded to the rather arbitrary terms I propounded, and as he had some highly respected names on his subscription list, from whom he had promises of assistance, my idea was that, through their aid, he might be enabled to carry forward the work after it had passed the limits to which my attention was immediately directed. I was aware that a work of this sort was called for by the general voice of the district, and I was desirous of securing to it a respectability of character; flattering myself that the method and matter I should communicate to the early portions might induce competent persons to complete the undertaking upon the model I should lay down, but his style and mine did not at all harmonise, and the labour I experienced in adjusting the matter he supplied to my own philological standard was more than equal to that of the original composition".

SIMEON ACKROYD SHAW was the son of Edmond Shaw, mill owner, and his wife Betty (Ackroyd). Born in Salford, Lancashire, Shaw came to the Potteries to work as a printer and compositor for the "Potteries Gazette" and "Newcastle under Lyme Advertiser", but in 1818 he had established an "Academy for young Gentlemen" in Northwood, and a "Commercial Academy" in Piccadily, Hanley. He was said to be a linguist and wrote many books on a variety of subjects, among them the following:

> *Nature displayed. (six volumes 1823)*
> *History of Staffordshire Potteries. (1829)*
> *Books on Chemistry, Philosophy, and Grammar.*
> *Grammar of English Language.*
> *Wonders of Heaven and Earth.*

Despite the number of books he wrote, he earned a poor return in royalties. According to a relative he had a massive intellect and did intensive research in all branches of literature and science. He suffered a series of setbacks, but amidst it all he continued his research until his intellectual powers declined. He married twice, first to Elizabeth Simpson of Brownhills, who died in 1818 leaving him with five little children. Thirteen months later he married Harriet Marsh Broad of Burslem. She was eighteen years of age, and was said to have died in 1838 of typhoid fever leaving him with more children. His wife is buried in the grounds of Wolstanton Church, her name engraved on a tombstone which is shown in an etching of the church illustrated in Ward's history. One of his sons shocked Shaw when both he and his wife were converted to the Mormon faith and emigrated to Salt Lake City.

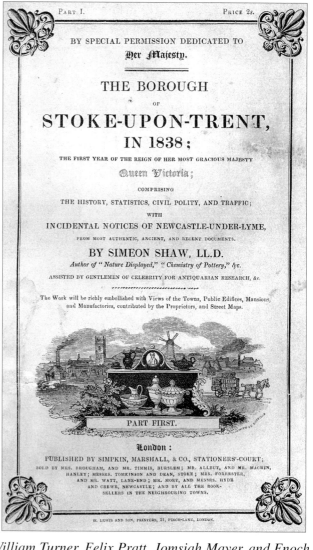

Dr Simeon Shaw with the 6 volumes of his
Nature Displayed behind him, and right, Part one
of the original Stoke on Trent history eventually
completed by John Ward

Shaw died in 1859 in the County Lunatic Asylum in Stafford, following increasing worries, both domestic and financial, coupled with overwork. He was buried in Bethesda churchyard in Hanley, his death certificate giving his age as 86, his funeral card as 75; it is likely that he was around 80.

One critic said of him: *"Although not a clever writer, he was a welcome gossip, and an intimate friend of Josiah Spode, Thomas Minton, William Turner, Felix Pratt, Jomsiah Mayer, and Enoch Wood. These were times of great potters who formed a constellation of remarkable brilliance in a sky of English ceramics."*

Perhaps an indication of the troubles that were to beset him is printed on the back of parts three and four of the first issues of the *History of Stoke on Trent*: *"with some surprise I have heard mention that for my present undertaking I have selected a very intricate subject, and the most inopportune time for its publication. To the accuracy of the remarks I shall demur."*

Scarratt, a local writer and a contemporary of both Shaw and Ward, made the following observations: *"Mr Ward's house has just lately been demolished. It stood next to the Riley's, and fronted fields in 1850 and backed on Furlong Parade. I saw Ward in 1854, I suppose he was a handsome man when young. He came on horseback to our school. His appearance was attractive, his stature small, with piercing black eyes and round face. He wore a black suit with a rather high-up neck cloth, stiff to the chin and spotless. Doctor Simeon Shaw was a tall man, rather thin, his attire was black with the usual swallow tail coat and not neat at all. The style of the two writers is quite observable, they were like two unequally yoked steeds".*

It is a pity that Ward's house has gone, but the adjacent Riley's remains in good condition and is currently used by the Education Authority.

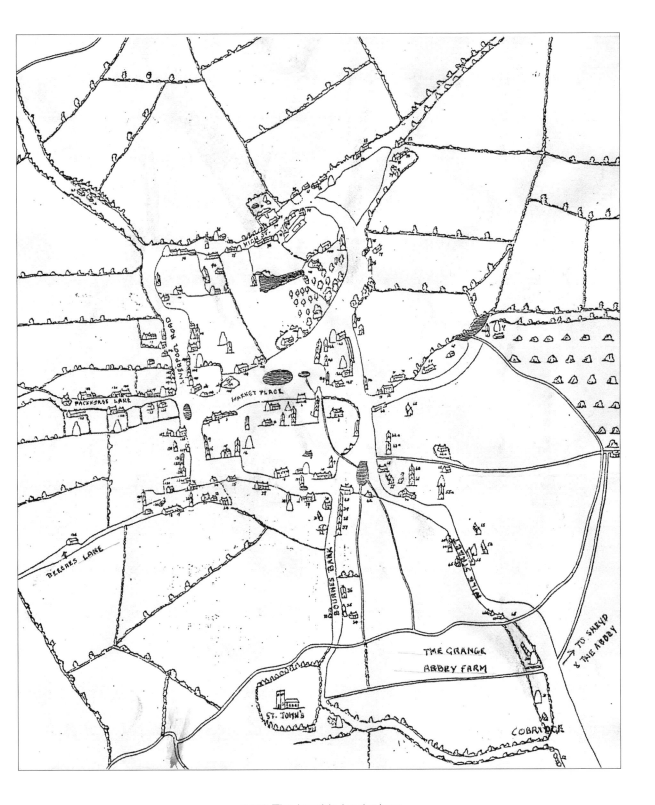

1720 The humble beginnings

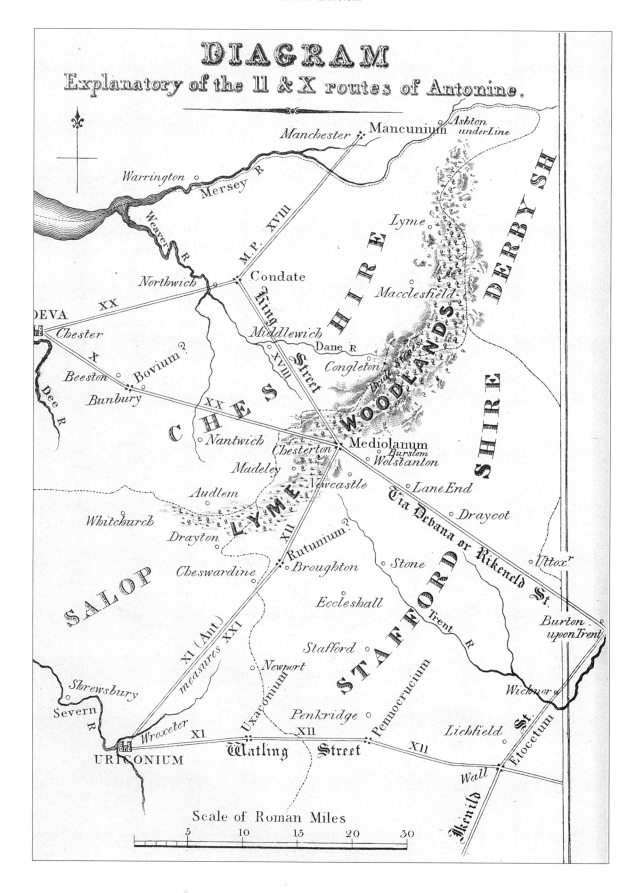

DIAGRAM
Explanatory of the ll & X routes of Antonine.

Scale of Roman Miles

CHAPTER ONE: Early Burslem

Origin of names. Antiquity of potters art. Farmers cum potters.

Place names mostly originated from physical and environmental factors. People similarly derived their names from areas in which they lived, or occupations in which they were involved. This district is no exception; there are Potters, Sneyds, Fentons, Hanleys - and although thin in the telephone directory, Burslems. Others have written that Burslem has had a number of names in its day. Among the earliest, in *Erdeswick's Antiquities*, is Baardardaslem, presumed to be of Saxon origin. Local historians have said it was known as Boars Lane, consequent on wild boar which pestered the neighbourhood. According to Scarratt, a local writer, it was called Barwardeslyme; in Domesday it is Barcardislem, generally interpreted as homes in or near Lyme Wood. There was in fact, to the north of Burslem, a King's forest, stretching from Leek to Audlem and known as Lyme Wood, consequently it is possible to visualise early Burslem as having an attractive setting, and accept as feasible the interpretation placed on the name. It is described in Domesday as Waste, which could be accepted as being unworked, and since agricultural value was important, it can be assumed that the income value was of low standing; in fact, again according to Domesday, the return from rents was of the order of one farthing per acre, and there was only one labourer per forty one acres in the county of Staffordshire. However it should not be overlooked that the county was at that time heavily wooded relative to its size, and this would limit the area available for cultivation.

In the England of Saxon times, Burslem was part of the kingdom of Mercia, and the area would have few cottages and no made roads. A cottage would be built of brick and wood and the roof thatched. If there was an upper floor, access would most probably be from outside the house. It is uncertain if at that time there would be a crude pottery kiln adjoining the house, such as existed in the 17th century. The occupants of the house would be peasant farmers, or associated with farming, and the pattern of life hardly altered after the Norman Conquest, except that all were then subjects of William.

These were feudal days, when people had to know their place in society; peasants were the humble strata, but they were largely allotted land sufficient for them to grow enough food for the family, in addition to which the peasant was called upon for unpaid services required by the lord of the manor.

Bordars and villeins were of a higher grade, but were still obliged to work a stipulated number of hours in the service of the lord. Freemen paid a tax to the lord in lieu of providing service. Thanes were of nobler vintage and formed the backbone of the army in Saxon times.

Following the Norman conquest, there was insurrection by the Saxon nobles in Mercia. Earl Edwin, godson of Godiva, succeeded to the throne of Mercia in 1062 and took part in this insurrection in 1071. William was on his way north at the time, to oppose a landing of the Danes in the Humber and their seizure of York, but was diverted to quell the revolt. Earl Edwin was forced to flee north with his followers by whom he was eventually slain. The whole of his domain was claimed by William, who awarded part to Norman nobles who accompanied him in the invasion. William's revenge for the insurrection of the Saxon nobles must have been savage and must have lain heavily on his conscience since it is said that his last words were:

I have persecuted the natives of England beyond all reason. Whether gentle or simple I have cruelly oppressed them. Many I unjustly disinherited, innumerable mutilated, perished by me through famine or sword. I fell on the English in the northern shires like a raving lion. I commanded their houses and their corn with all their chattels to be burnt without distinction, and great herds of cattle and beasts of burden to be butchered where they are found. In this way I took revenge on multitudes of both sexes by subjecting them to the calamity of cruel famine, and so became the barbarous murderer of many thousands both young and old of that fine area of people. Having gained the throne of that kingdom by so many crimes, I dare not leave it to anyone but God.

His dying bequest leaves us in no doubt that we should be a favoured community, but God failed to leave Mother Burslem head of the family and, instead of becoming the city of Barcardislem, with its

Arthurian overtones and the prospect of thousands coming to seek the Holy Grail, it became the City of Stoke on Trent, indeed a famed name but hardly as poetic.

It is rather late for claims, but Ward was of the opinion that the Burslem area was freehold before the Conquest, but the Earls of Audley usurped this right. One of a number of interesting deeds from an early date would seem to confirm this:

Year 1223. Grant by Henry de Audithleg to Richard de henleg for his homage and service, of the parts of Chelle, giving the bounds, namely from Snedehbroc by the sich ascending by the sich ascending to Assensaue, to the ditch of Chelle going down Blakesahe to the highroad going down to the highroad going down to the Holdeford in Stancotebroc, ascending to the Horestoneschoid going up to the Sneydbroc and up to the Sich at the spring of Chelle; excepting pannage for the pigs of his men in the wood of Sneyd; for the sum of two shillings to the quarter, and eight pence to the Hospital of Jerusalem for two parts of the assart of Suainnescroft warranty.

William de Auditheleg

Some areas, in or adjacent to Burslem, such as Chelle, Sneeze and Sich, are recognisable despite the spelling having altered over the years, and will be found mentioned in later chapters.

Man has used clay to produce artifacts throughout history; fragments of pottery with slip decoration found in south Japan are considered to be 5000 years old. Minoan potters in Crete were producing pottery in 2000 BC. The Egyptians, who themselves are said to have learned the art from the Phoenecians, used clay, not only for making useful and decorative objects, but also, prior to the introduction of paper, for correspondence. They used thin slabs of clay into which they cut cuneiform characters. The clay was then hardened and inserted into a clay envelope and sealed with wax before despatch. Both the Persians and the Chinese had long established pottery industries before the arrival of Christianity. According to Shaw, the Chinese went to great pains to keep the secret of their trade, but it is said that a missionary, using extreme cunning, gained knowledge of their materials and methods which he brought back to Europe. Travellers in the 19th century reported that in the province of Kian Si alone there were 500 kilns in use, and 800,000 people employed.

Probably from the Druidical age early Britains made cinery urns and food vessels. Shaw says that two hundred years before the Roman occupation there was an island off the mouth of the Thames, behind Margate sands, on the part called Queen's Channel. The island, which no longer exists, had on it a pottery producing roughly made earthenware and some pieces have been recovered in fishermens nets. The Roman occupation of Britain was firmly established in the first century AD and lasted for 400 years, and wherever they settled remains of pottery have been found. The Romans like the Egyptians probably learned the art from the Phoenicians who settled at the foot of Mount Vesuvius. They became known as

Celtic urn

Roman pot

Etruscans and their art has rarely been equalled - a viewpoint emphatically endorsed by Josiah Wedgwood.

Following the Romans, there were incursions by Jutes and Angles, and subsequently the Saxons who, by the year 580 AD had substantially conquered the whole of Britain. The Saxons must have found a country well stocked with pottery from the Roman era. They themselves used clay cinery urns, but their culinary vessels were mainly of wood and metal. They had particularly interesting drinking vessels made of glass or horn with a rounded base, which it would seem, once filled, had to be held until the contents were drunk. It has been suggested that the word tumbler is derived from this feature. The ornamentation of Saxon pottery was usually created by incision work in the friable clay state.

The Normans who succeeded the Saxons made pottery similar to the Romans. Some of it had a metallic glaze besides ornamentation. They were more adventuresome in design however. Jugs have been found made in the form of knights or of animals. These latter were similar to the milk jugs made in the form of a cow which were made in considerable quantity by the Burslem potters. Pilgrim bottles were an early pottery product which was widely used to carry liquid on a journey. These were commonly made in the form of a barrel with a handle which would also take a strap. One end of the barrel was flat but the other end moulded in the shape of a breast, perhaps a subtle way of indicating the purpose of the vessel.

It is rare to be able to claim that a firm foundation was based on clay, but this is nevertheless true of Burslem. Domesday referred to the land as 'Waste', but its value lay under the surface rather than on it! The period between Domesday and the visit of the historian Plott to the district in the 17th century embraced the Dissolution of the Monasteries and the Civil Wars, but neither appeared to have materially affected Burslem. When Plott published his history in 1686, Burslem appears to have been in a halfway stage between agriculture and industry. Plott described the area as *"one of scant houses and thatched buildings"*, and went on to say that *"it is the seat of the greatest pottery carried out in the county"*. There were some twenty farm buildings, each with an adjoining small kiln, and these holdings were known as *Sun Kiln Potteries*. He described the kilns as being about eight feet high, six feet across, bee-hive in shape, and surrounded by a protection wall of turves.

An early pottery (from Plott's *Natural History of Staffordshire*, 1686)
The clay is shown weathering in the foreground and pots are drying in the sun.

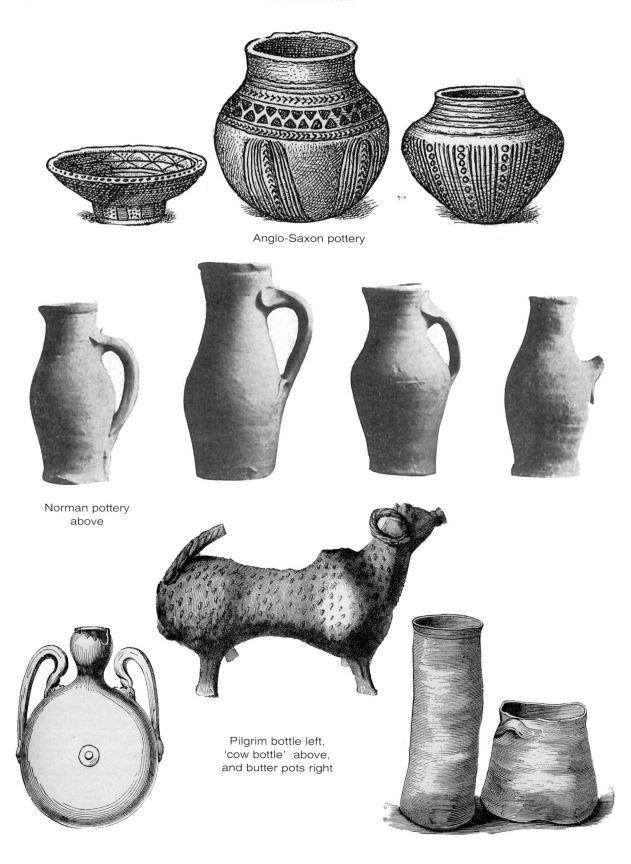

Anglo-Saxon pottery

Norman pottery
above

Pilgrim bottle left,
'cow bottle' above,
and butter pots right

Before the enclosure of lands, freeholders could, without molestation, dig clay or coal from any unenclosed or unenfranchised land, and both must have been freely extracted in and around Burslem. Digging was so widespread that there were numerous ponds, including two where the town now stands. One was in Market Square and one in Fountain Square, both presumably formed by clay extraction. There was a law prohibiting digging in roads without permission and failing to fill in the cavity *"on penalty of forfeit of six shillings and six pence"*. Difficulty would have been experienced at that time in distinguishing many roads, and if a seam of clay ran across it the temptation to go on digging would be overwhelming. John Wesley recounted falling from his horse into one of these holes *"deep enough to drown both horse and man"*. There are records of fines being imposed, one in 1692, when John Daniel and Richard Mitchell, both pottery owners, were fined for digging in the highway in Burslem.

In those days, preparation of clay commenced with it being stacked in the open to weather over an extended period. After weathering the clay was transferred to a pit lined with slabs, water was added to the clay and the whole agitated manually. This process was repeated until the pit was full. It was then left for the heat of the sun to evaporate the water, and it is from this that the title of Sun Kiln Potteries is derived. Plott remarked that Burslem had a variety of clays, both in colour and texture, and, *"when the potter has wrought the clay, either in hollow or flat ware, they set it abroad to dry in fine weather, or by the fire in foul, When they are dry, they 'stouk' them, i.e. apply handles or ears to such as need them. These also being dry, they slip and paint them with several sorts of slip as they design their work"*.

The ware produced in these Sun Kiln Potteries was mainly sold for domestic use and the process was very much a family affair, sons dug much of the clay, father was the potter, and the wife packed the crates which the packhorsemen would load on to their mules.

Production consisted mostly of bowls, cups, jugs, candlesticks, spill holders, and such like, but the quality was not to the liking of the gentry, who bought imported Chinese porcelain. In addition to domestic wares there was a growing demand for butter pots for the dairy trade. These pots, produced in common local clay and tubular in shape, held fourteen pounds of butter and were for use in wholesale dairy produce markets. They were one of the earliest items to become mass produced. They influenced the trend to factory building where division of labour could be applied to meet increasing demand. There was a large dairy produce market in Uttoxeter which attracted buyers from cities and towns, and this was supplied with butter pots from Burslem. As unfortunately happens, when business increased so did the use of unscrupulous practices, pots with good butter at the top and rancid butter at the bottom, or butter at the top and devoid of butter at the bottom. Transgression was not confined to the dairymen, pots were found with excessively thick bottoms, which cast doubts on the probity of the Burslem potters. The size of the problem can be judged by the reaction of the government, since they passed an act in 1661 to regulate trade practices, and worded it in a manner which emphasised their displeasure:

.......to regulate the abuse of the trade in the make of pot and false packing of the butter, which was before made good for a little depth at the top, and standing hollow at a great distance from the sides of the pot. The pot should not exceed six pounds in weight and contain at least fourteen pounds of butter. To prevent these little moorland cheats, than whom no people whatever are esteemed more subtle, every potter shall upon every pot which shall sell for the packing of butter, mark the just weight which shall be of every pot which is burnt, together with the first letter of his christian name and his surname at length upon pain of every pot one shilling.

A permanent official attended the market throughout the season armed with an instrument which checked the depth of the butter and the thickness of the pot bottom.

In a court case at Stafford in 1692, two Burslem potters were accused by Daniel Everard of Uttoxeter of *"unlawfully combining to double the price of their product, contrary to the law, and to the great prejudice of the county, and to the evil example of others"*.

It is important to bear in mind that a combination of farming and potting was a common practice in a great many counties, due to the seasonal nature of farming and the need for income out of season. If agriculture yielded a poor return in the Burslem area, then being so well endowed with both clay and coal, there was every incentive to expand the pottery side, indirectly aided probably by the enclosure acts.

A typical Cistercian abbey - much as Hulton Abbey would have looked before Henry VIII's dissolution of the monasteries

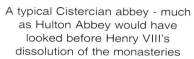

Early Staffordshire pottery, and earthenware gravestones from Burslem and Wolstanton

An early view of the Churchyard works

CHAPTER TWO: Early growth

The Plague. Subsequent growth of population. Increasing appeal of pottery. Magistrates and their responsibilities. Enclosure of land. Competition for labour. Early working conditions and practices.

Life in Burslem following the dissolution of the abbey at Hulton and up to the time of the Civil Wars, appears to have been little affected by the turmoil which surrounded Church, State and King. The two leading families in the Burslem area were the Biddulphs and the Sneyds, both of whom were Royalists. Biddulph Hall was surrendered to Sir William Brereton and sacked after an obstinate resistance during the Civil War. The hall, built in 1580 by Francis Biddulph, was left a partial ruin. Over the entrance is an interesting verse:

> Hence rebel heart, nor deem a welcome due
> From walls once ruined by a rebel hand
> Thrice welcome thou, if thou indeed be true
> To God, and the lady of the land

In 1652 the estate was sold by the Crown with the proceeds for the benefit of the navy. No attempt was made to rebuild but at a later date a farmhouse was built on the site, using debris from the hall.

Keele Hall, home of the Sneyd family, came through the wars relatively intact, but a heavy financial penalty was imposed for their royalist support, which impoverished the family.

A fear hung over the Burslem community - the threat of the Black Death which affected Stafford in 1604, 1610, and again in 1638. Its persistence caused the authorities in Stafford to employ wardens at the gates of the town to debar potential carriers. The plague finally struck Burslem in 1647, the infection brought by an Italian woman employed by the Biddulph family as tutor for their children. The family were living at the Grange, a Tudor house standing on farmland previously owned and farmed by the monks of Abbey Hulton, and situated in the Cobridge area of Burslem. The tutor was the first to succumb followed by several of the children. It spread to an area near the Grange and created terror among the local population who feared to go near, but left food and medicine outside the affected homes. The Biddulphs, a devout Catholic family, maintained a resident priest and he administered the last rites at the burials, not in the churchyard but in pits adjoining the Grange, and no record seems to have been kept of the number of victims.

As happened in other areas, an order was made by the magistrates at the Court of Sessions to all nearby parishes to contribute to a common fund to be used for the relief of stricken families. The monies were distributed by the overseers and church wardens, and the charges on the local district were as follows: These amounts were to be weekly for four weeks, after which they would be reviewed.

Burslem	£1. 0 0	Trentham	1. 3 4
Wolstanton	1. 5 0	Cheddleton	10 0
Stoke on Trent	1. 5 0	Audley	13 4
Norton in the Moors	10 0	Leek	1. 0 0
Newcastle	1. 0 0	Barlaston	13 4
Keele	13 4	Swinnerton	1. 3 4

Since so many references will be made to magistrates in following chapters it would be as well to define their position in the community. From the 14th century this was one of the most important public appointments. Ostensibly, it was made by the Privy Council and was one of the oldest posts in English history. It was invariably occupied by a man of means and in practice was an honorary appointment made by the High Sheriff. The success of the appointment relied in large measure on a conscientious approach, but was subject to scrutiny and a fine if a magistrate failed in his duties. He determined the wages to be paid to varying classes of worker. He was responsible for the upkeep of roads and bridges, for law and order, the functioning of the poor house and the supervision of the poor laws, and the licensing of public houses. With the rapid increase in population and the increasing movement of workers, it became an impossible burden, but he in turn devolved part of the work to local Overseers, mainly to collect and distribute poor relief. The Overseers were usually chosen from principal ratepayers of the area. The work was compulsory but, as with the Magistrate, honorary,

Local rates and taxes were levied as and when money was required for specific services, eg poor relief, roads, or as a poll tax, such as were levied specifically to pay for the wars with France and Spain in the latter half of the 18th and early part of the 19th centuries. Needless to say these latter taxes were as popular as the poll tax attempted in the late 20th century!

There was no great wealth in Burslem in the 17th century, the value of inventories at death rarely exceeding fifteen pounds. Few were described as 'gent', but a number as 'yeoman', and it is from these latter that most of the early master potters materialised.

Payments to the poor were at the discretion of the commissioners and were arbitrary. In 1723, however, an act of parliament obliged all parishes to provide a workhouse, and this reduced the responsibility of the overseers but devastated family life. The original workhouse, or poorhouse as it is also termed, was situated at Greenhead, and had many uses over the years.   Following the poor law of 1836 it was enlarged to hold three hundred people, but was superseded by the building at Chell intended to accommodate the poor of both Burslem and Wolstanton. The early building was used as a barracks by the military during the Chartist's disturbances, and later converted to a pottery, which became known as the Barracks Pottery.

The demands of industry attracted families to Burslem. The first streets were built, and a transformation started which continued at an ever increasing rate. It was not long before the population doubled, with little or no attention being given to any cultural activity. The church seemed moribund at this time and evangelism was in its infancy. Books were scarce and then mostly confined to a bible and a prayer book. It is not surprising therefore that the public house became the centre of social life, particularly since the incoming families no longer had a village green on their doorstep, but were confined by urban constrictions, repetitious work, and fixed hours. Once the novelty of the changed conditions had worn off, life became irksome for many and resulted in brutal sports, heavy drinking and gambling.

Drink and its consequences were the constant curse and were regularly attacked with threats and exhortations from church, state, municipal authorities and manufacturers, both verbally and with printed proclamations which preceded the publication of newspapers. Drunkards in Burslem were often punished by being committed to the stocks. Mr Wilcox Edge in one of the lectures he gave in Burslem, said: *"He had in mind that the stocks were removed much earlier than in fact they were, but he met a friend of similar age to himself, who had seen his brother in the stocks, and another who had put bricks under the feet of a prisoner to relieve the strain"*. Ultimately, he found that they had been removed as late as 1851, the event being described in the *Staffordshire Advertiser* as *"the removal of the last barbarism"*.

The plague had brought a dramatic halt to the growth in the Country's population, but a rapid increase in births followed, and by the beginning of the 18th century it had doubled. This brought an increasing demand for food, and in turn a pressing need for change in farming methods. Large enclosed areas and better drainage were imperative for intensive production, and the existing mass of common land and smallholdings were a severe restriction on farming methods. The large estate owners, mainly titled gentry, dominated parliament, and in 1730 began to issue 'Enclosure Orders' on a massive scale. This allowed the Commissioners, whose findings were final, to dictate where a peasant could farm or to order him to fence his holding at his own expense, or to leave the land with only nominal cash compensation. Thousands of smallholders had no hope of meeting this cost and had no option but to leave their holdings, which then reverted to the landlord. Many took compensation payment which was quickly dissipated. The ultimate result, it is said, was that some lordships finally owned almost a whole county. Of those displaced, some became landless farmworkers, but large numbers moved in search of work to the growing industrial centres like Burslem. This rapidly increasing population required not only food and work but housing and furnishings, which included pottery products, consequently there was every incentive for the Burslem potters, with their knowledge and skills, to become adventurous and build for the future.

Of the first factories built in Burslem it is not surprising that a house for the owner was integral or built in close proximity, no doubt influenced by the former customary compact arrangement of farmhouse, outbuildings and kiln. The layout of the new factories usually comprised a frontage of two or three storeys and an arched entrance in the centre leading to a square, which was either open, or in which the owner may have built his house. An example is still to be seen at the Spode Factory in Stoke, where Josiah Spode's house is still in the centre of the original works. On two sides of the square were more buildings, and access to any upper floors in these, usually by outside steps from the square. The fourth side would normally be occupied by the kilns, or ovens, both of which names were commonly used.

This pattern of building was subsequently followed in the surrounding Potteries towns as the industry grew, and a number of frontages still retain original features, particularly the entrance, even if the remaining areas have been transformed. These early buildings had to rely on natural lighting, or when darkness fell, the use of candles. Heating was by fireplace or stove pot and the coal for these and the kilns was delivered by horse and cart, or in the very early days in panniers strung on horses. Rainwater had to be conserved, but in addition, water would be brought to the factory in mobile tankers, or obtained by sinking a well and a standpipe as with the old village pump. There would be few, if any, trees, as these would already have been sacrificed to the voracious appetite of the early kilns; doubtless the site of the future Burslem was by now treeless. Some of the factories were even built without sanitary arrangements, or they were primitive and used by both sexes.

Up to the 19th century hiring of workmen was on a yearly basis from varying dates in the year. From the 19th century it was from Martinmas (November 11th). Included in the contract was a payment known as an 'Earnest' which comprised an initial cash payment, together with a payment in kind. An example from an early agreement read:

"Hired....... for three years. He is to have 10/6 Earnest each year, and be paid 7/-per week and the gift of old clothes to the value of 5/-".

Although in many trades there had been and still were guilds where apprenticeship was enforced and indentures signed, this practice seems to have largely died out during the industrial revolution, and certainly so, with few exceptions, in the pottery industry.

A wide variation has been given for daywork wages, but the following are examples of payments made in the second half of the 18th century, the difference presumably reflecting the degree of skill, or competitive demand for labour:

Throwers	8/- to 17/- per week
Handlers	7/6 to 15/- " "
Ovenmen	5/6 to 12/- " "

A consistent and major problem confronting the factory owners was that of maintaining production levels, since, in the radical change in lifestyle from agriculture to factory conditions, the newcomers experienced the constraint of indoor work and its repetitive nature, which together with long daily hours, resulted in the widespread practice of irregular attendance and excessive drinking. This was further influenced by increasing affluence resulting from the provision of year round paid work, not only for himself, but for the whole family. To satisfy the drinker was no problem since early in the 18th century, out of less than one hundred and fifty buildings in Burslem, twenty two were ale houses!

The manufacturers' response to absenteeism was to introduce 'payment by results' in the form of a contract similar to the Butty system in the mines. For example, a contract price would be agreed for a given output from a journeyman presser, who would in turn employ and pay his mould runners - immature children, in some cases his own. A journeyman printer would be paid a lump sum from which he would employ and pay his cutters and transferrers, usually young females. At the close of the week the manufacturer would give the contracting journeyman a promissory note from which he had to pay his

The Brickhouse, adjacent to the Brickhouse works

(Fig. 74.)   THE BRICK HOUSE.

Brickhouse Pottery built by John Adams about 1650. It was leased to Josiah Wedgwood 1759-1760 and became known as the Bell Pottery

Fig 9   BRICK-HOUSE WORKS OTHERWISE THE BELL WORKS

The Ivy house works, the first house and pottery rented by Josiah Wedgwood when he returned to Burslem and started his climb to fame. The house was owned by Thomas and John Wedgwood, who also built the Big House

team, who would follow him to the ale house, since the publican was the only means of providing change. He of course would demand his commission in the sale of ale.

In theory the introduction of contract work was expected to diminish the owner's problem of maintaining output, but in practice failed to achieve regular hours of work or less drinking, and brought additional misery to the child labourers since journeymen constantly failed to turn out for work on Mondays, or even on Tuesdays, after a weekend of solid drinking, with the result that earnings for the week had to be achieved in the remaining days. The effort demanded of the poor boy mould runners was horrific and inhuman. They had arrived at dawn and prepared for work on one or possibly two days to no purpose, and for the remainder of the week it would be a frantic effort, with constant bullying, even physical assault, to satisfy the adult potter's increasing demands as the remaining days were extended to make up for lost earnings. Infant mortality was high, for some probably a happy release, but it was not until 1833 that the first parliamentary attempt was made to control conditions for children in factories and to appoint inspectors to enforce the regulations, and change was slow to be implemented until sufficient inspectors had been appointed.

There were no banks in Burslem until the 19th century, the nearest being in Newcastle. Josiah Wedgwood, realising the damage that the enforced resort to the publicans for the payment of wages was causing, ordered £100 lots of loose change from Matthew Boulton's Soho mint in Birmingham for delivery in barrels by canal.

It was 1842 before a factory inspector visited the district and made an exhaustive survey, embracing both owners and employees. His findings were published and give a vivid picture of conditions in the factories at that time. One employer interviewed gave these comments to the inspector:

"With the children we have nothing to do, as they are employed by the plate makers, printers and others who employ them. Drunkenness is a common vice and I have no doubt arises from the practice of paying the older hands of large amounts for several who work in the same department, but it cannot be helped because small change can only be obtained in small amounts. It is expected by the ale house keepers, of whom there maybe four hundred in the district, that a certain amount shall be expended for the privilege of changing. Many of them being young boys and children of both sexes. For example, I have twentyfour printers, each employing two women and a girl, these I pay in three bills of twenty-four pounds each, consequently, twenty-one persons follow each printer to the ale house and allow a percentage, which they drink or leave. If the legislation contemplates restricting the working hours of children, I think it would be an advantage to them as they are often worked fifteen hours a day, occasioned by the irregular hours of the working men who neglect the beginning of the week. They know what amount of wages they can get by the amount of work they can accomplish in a given number of hours, so that after they are paid on Saturday, they drink hard until morning, renew it the next day, and begin, as they express it, to soften up on Monday, which they complete perhaps on Tuesday. I think the people would consider it a hardship at first, but I do not think they would suffer by it, as seventy two hours a week is as much work as masters would require, and the child, being paid by the day, would get the same wages as before."

A youngster, who worked at Davenports in Longport, in answer to the inspector's questioning, had this to say:

"I am eleven years old and run moulds for John Moss. I ought to be at work at half past six, I am allowed half an hour for breakfast, but only take ten minutes as John takes his quick, and gets to work pretty quick. I leave work on Mondays at six, and half past eight other days. When I get home my legs ache, I'm too tired to play, and get my supper and go to bed. Sometimes my father tells me a chapter; He prays to us every night, I can read pretty well; I don't write, but I shall try soon. My father is a dipper at Mr Alcocks, my mother has been dead a year. I get three shillings a week and carry it home to father. We should not have been what we are if he had not been teetotal. I have signed for four years. Father used to be a great drunkard; he is now a good father and steady; he is in a Rechabite club".

The testimony of a workman, employed at the factory now occupied by Doultons, perhaps gives a graphic illustration of what this leg work was like for the young mould runner:

"I have been in the pottery trade for twenty years, first at Don Pottery in Yorkshire, then at Southwick in

Durham, later at the Herculean Pottery in Liverpool before coming to Burslem. I'm a jigger-turner and complete twenty to twenty five dozens of saucers a day. The dozens are counted as thirty-six. Say 70 dozen or 840 in twelve hours, or 1125 for fifteen hours. The mould runner has to run too and fro from the jigger to the drying stove, with generally two saucers at a time, and this twice over. I have always considered mould running very laborious and the excessive heat and the constant steam from the work very injurious; although it doesn't produce deformation of the body, it stunts growth and produces physical debility, such as to produce Asthma or Consumption; very few live beyond the age of forty five. I should say that the poor little mould runners are the lowest and most degraded in the whole business of pottery. The treatment of children in some rooms is rough and sometimes brutal, I have known many cases where children are obliged to fetch liquor for the men and drink a portion themselves; they are prompted to steal and commonly told to lie. Morals of children and adults, manufacturers and foremen treat with contumely. Those who have improved, or seem to have a desire to improve themselves, their efforts are looked upon as affectation. A great evil is getting change at ale houses. If a person does not follow the party carrying the charge bill, he or she forfeit three pence. If they drink their quota all well and good."

To those not familiar with the pottery industry the above figures must be conflicting, but locally they are an example of 'potters' arithmetic'. It is very old and established practice and is based on relative values. If, simply as an example, a 10 inch diameter plate size was the 'norm' for all flat ware - plates, saucers and the like - then, with an agreed price for making 10 inch diameter pieces, instead of having a variety of making prices for similar articles of greater or less diameter, the potter would make an agreed greater or less number of pieces for the one price. As a jigger-turner, the man who made these observations to the inspector would have a limited number of plaster moulds for the article which he was currently making. On each mould he would place a piece of clay, transfer it to a potter's wheel and as the wheel turned the clay would be formed by a profile into shape. The mould, still carrying the clay piece, would now be carried by the boy and placed in an extremely hot stove, to be brought back when both were dry and the mould ready for use again. When it is seen how many pieces were produced in twelve or fifteen hours, it seems hardly feasible that a boy could last the day, or that parents or employer would have tolerated such abuse.

In questioning one young boy, the pathetic response was *"I can't read, I can't write, I went once to the church school, but I don't go now cause I got no trousers. I come to work at six o'clock and remain till five. I stay up in the oven sometimes till four o'clock in the morning, I've done it twice; I help Thomas Asprey the oven man to bait the oven".* This term 'bait' - another pottery expression - was used to describe the feeding of the coal to the mouths of the old bottle type oven. The mouths were spaced at intervals round the circumference, and the coal fed to each using a wheelbarrow and shovel, and the work was continuous and heavy.

In the Inspector's general survey of working conditions, there were, as might be expected, good and bad. The working areas of potters received the severest criticism. He spoke of children being employed in hovels of every description, and in unswept rooms in which there were stoves at almost every degree of heat. He commented on the mould runners having to get the stoves lighted and woe betide the wretch who had not got it well heated before the potter arrived, although no kindling was supplied and the youngster had to steal hot coals from the ovens. They were expected to arrive at 5.30am and, due to the irregularity of their taskmaster, in numberless instances work until 8, 9 or even 10 o'clock at night.

The inspector seems to have been very impressed with the decorating sections, where girls were employed, and remarked on the masters and mistresses who superintend their work, as selected for good moral conduct and long service. *"They allow the girls the indulgence of singing hymns, and I have visited their rooms and been charmed by the melody of their voices. To see them working in groups is literally like viewing a school of art".* He cited earnings as being the best of any staple trade. Skilled men, such as Throwers or Printers, earning from £1.10s. to £2.00. Women from 9/- to 10/-. Boys and girls aged eight to thirteen, average 2/- - and since it is a process in which a whole family can be involved, global earnings with two three or more children, were between £3.00 and £4.00. He went on to say that *"the proceed of*

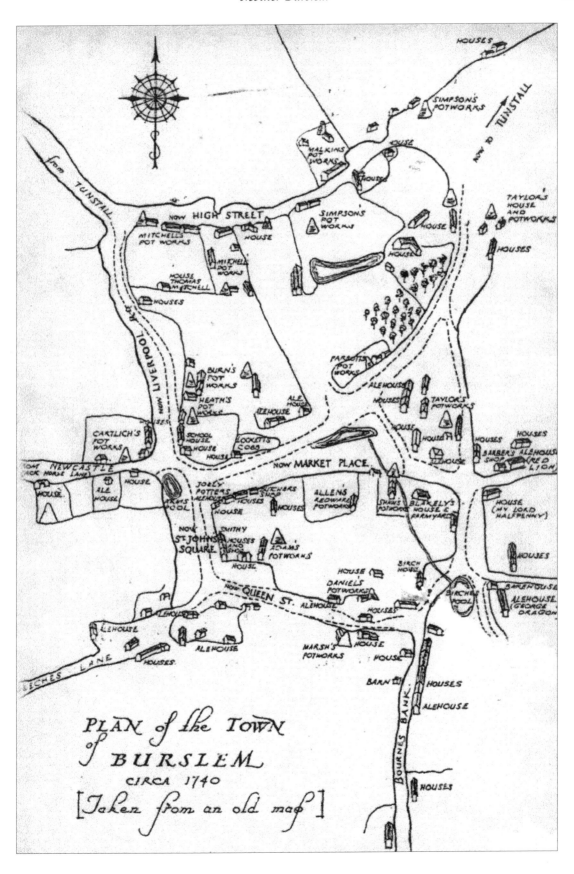

PLAN of the TOWN of BURSLEM CIRCA 1740 [Taken from an old map]

their labour is spent on gaudy dress, or at the skittle ground and ale house, so that when taken by illness or other casualty, and thrown out of work for a few days, they would resort to their masters for a loan, or to the parish workhouse for relief. Their habitations are respectable, cleanly and well furnished. Before the strike of 1836/7, many were tenanted by their owners, but that unfortunate and mistaken attempt to co-erse the masters - provoked by some few itinerant demagogues that visited the neighbourhood, under the pretence of improving the conditions of the occupants - occasioned most of them to change hands, and reduce those in a state of prosperity and happiness - to one of dependence, humiliation, and poverty from which they have not recovered."

The inhuman treatment of children in this period of social and industrial revolution, by both parent and industrialist, is hard to understand and was by no means confined to the potteries. Conditions in the cities, in the mines, and in the weaving industries, were equally brutal. Large numbers of abandoned or orphaned children from the Poor Houses were apprenticed in the weaving mills and died prematurely. Some mills even had their own graveyard. It savours of hypocrisy that, while allowing such indefensible treatment of the young, there was at the same time, a vociferous clamour for the abolition of slavery, and although slavery had been abolished by act of parliament in 1807, this report on the pottery industry by a factory inspector, was not published until 1842.

The growth of the pottery industry in Burslem, and the other towns around, although vast, was not accompanied by a continuous advance in output, since there was periodic curtailment from upheavals caused by wars with France, Spain and the American colonies in the late 18th and early 19th centuries. Nevertheless, despite these disruptions, Britain had, through forced emigration, appropriation, colonisation, and treaty, created world markets of which the potters took advantage, and which, apart from war periods, seemed to provide an insatiable demand for pottery.

Mother Burslem was seriously affected by the wars; with America and other export markets closed, she found it difficult to compete with five growing sons, all themselves anxious for trade, while America having declared her independence, was rapidly establishing her own industrial base.

As conditions improved again the demand for labour in the industry increased, but at the same time serious attempts were being made to persuade skilled operatives to emigrate to France and America, both of whom were experiencing industrial advance. The problem was obviously not confined to this area alone. Parliament was concerned and an act was passed in the reign of George III to protect against foreigners gaining information regarding trade or trade practices. The act further prohibited the export of certain tools and implements, and in 1786 was extended to include the pottery industry. Any attempt to persuade skilled operatives to work abroad was also subject to a penalty of a fine and imprisonment; for a second offence, a £500 fine and imprisonment for two years. Evidently the problem was acute; when Josiah Wedgwood was recruiting labour for his Etruria works, with demand for his product growing, he issued leaflets which warned against accepting work abroad. The Rhead brothers said these were published in 1783. One was entitled, *An address to the workmen in the pottery trade on the subject of entering into the service of foreign manufacturers By Josiah Wedgwood F.R.S. Potter to His Majesty:*

Englishmen in arts and manufactures, as well as in arms, can only be conquered by Englishmen; the enemy must gain over some traders and renegades from among ourselves before he can obtain any decisive advantage. Is there a man amongst you then who will stand forth and acknowledge himself to be that traitor to his country and fellow workman? Who will openly avow, that for the sake of a paltry addition to his own wages for a few years he would betray their interests, and wantonly throw away into the hands of foreigners, perhaps of enemies, the superiority we have thus laboured for and obtained.

Other psychological appeals from Josiah followed:

About 17 years ago Mr. Bartlem, a master potter, who had been unsucessful here, went to South Carolina, and by offers made from thence, very advantageous in appearance, prevailed upon some of our workmen to leave the country and to come to him. They took shipping at Bristol, and after more than a quarter of a year in storms and tempests upon the sea, with narrow escapes from shipwreck, they arrived at last safe, and began work near

Charlestown. The fine wages, puffed up by the Governor of the province, turned out a delusion and a snare, and the unfortunate workmen were all attacked by a disorder of mind peculiar to Staffordshire people, which took them off so fast that recruits could not be found to fill the place of the dead men. Mr. Goodwin, who was one of them, said in his own words, they fell sick as they came and all died quickly, his son among them.

He went on to relate the fate of Mr Lymer's family; Lymer being a brother in law of Bartlem. "

Lymer was heir to a pretty estate, but he left with his wife and two children. Storms and tempests were encountered with, on this occasion, actual shipwreck near an unnamed island. Most of the sailors were drowned, and survivors in a comfortless situation, which was intensified by Mrs. Lymer giving birth to another child. Young Lymer shipped himself into another vessel, too impatient for Mrs. Lymer's recovery, and was never heard of again. Bartlem, deprived of his whole colony of workers, returned to England to raise fresh supplies. One workman who returned, William Ellis, said that wages were good enough, one guinea a week with board, but they never got half of it.

Describing an equally fruitless and horrific journey to Pennsylvania, and the subsequent experience of another group of immigrants, Josiah said that,

....not only did the new employers not honour their undertaking, but silenced the just complaints of the poor injured workmen, by clapping one of them in prison. The rest never got half their wages, and were reduced to begging in the streets.

He proceeded with a lecture on *"the grasping and discontented nature of those who do not content themselves with the good things of this land, a land flowing with milk and honey",* and exhorted them to beware of falling into like errors, if they would wish to escape the fatal consequences. He further drew attention to the same perils to be experienced in France, including:

.....low wages, which would afford miserable subsistence to Englishmen, brought up in their infancy to better and more substantial fare than frogs and hedgehogs and the wild herbs of the field. Your indignation, I make no doubt will rise at the idea of such wages and such fare, and say NO, at the worst we can but leave them and their country when they attempt to reduce our wages, but do not deceive yourselves, you may not have it in your power to leave them, for, under arbitrary government, your master has ways and means enough of keeping those they do not chose to part with, such as inducing them to run in debt and arresting them, but, if this or any lesser plot should fail, they have another which must always succeed. They can insinuate to the governors that you had come among them under false pretence, that you have learned some of their valuable arts and manufactures and are preparing to leave the country and carry those aquisitions to your own. This would be sufficient to have you detained, and perhaps kept prisoner during life.

Still referring to France, he mentions a George Shaw, who had been in France for ten years and then returned to Britain, and was canvassing others to return with him to France, promising wages which, Wedgwood said, were impossible to afford, or if given, would only be for a short period and then be reduced. *"You might be ready to ask me why does Shaw leave his native country again to that scene of misery? The question is very much to the purpose, but there is a clear and satisfactory answer to be given to it. He is a deserter from the army (from the 20th regiment of foot) and as such his life is forfeited to the laws of this country, so that his continuing here is impracticable".*

In the review of early Burslem potters reference is made to a Ralph Shaw, who persistently sued his fellow potters in Burslem for infringement of patents in connection with the production of slipware, and, having lost an action in court, he moved to France with his family and commenced manufacturing there. I assume that Josiah's refers to his son who was still serving in the British army when they went. The pamphlet concludes:

That no motive may be wanting for the performance of your duty in concurring with your masters in every endeavour to secure you and your children the full enjoyment of your birthright in the manufacture you are brought up to, they offer you fifty guineas reward, besides what you are entitled to by Act of Parliament, for every person apprehended by you who shall be convicted of endeavouring to entice, or hire, any of our potters into foreign service.

Top left: A Tyg, love cup or fosset.   Above: Elers pottery

Left: Whieldon cauliflower ware

Below: Three Tobys. Far left, Ralph Wood,
the other two, Whieldon

CHAPTER THREE : Prominent potters

Observations on the industry. Influential potters 17th & 18th century.
Increasing demand at home and abroad. Increasing number and size of factories.

In a work of this nature, it would be impossible to cover in full the life and achievement of every one of the early Burslem potters, and indeed many, as will be seen, fell by the wayside. Of others, their product was utilitarian and inconspicuous, while a few were outstanding for both utility and artistic products, such as Josiah Wedgwood, a point which Gladstone emphasised in his speech at the laying of the foundation stone of the Wedgwood Institute.

Over the years there has been styles in pottery, as in other materials, such as fabrics or wallpaper, where a successful innovation by one firm or individual has been widely copied. Some of these, and the potters involved, will be reviewed as we follow the growth of the industry. From an examination of an early map of Burslem, and using today's road names, it would appear that the early potters were mainly located in an area bounded by 'Westport Road' to the west, 'Greenhead Street' running east, then south to 'Wedgwood Street', turning west below 'Bournes Bank', then north to 'Fountain Square' - presumably building their factories in or near the site of their previous rude establishments.

Among the earliest Burslem potters were the Wedgwood families, two of whom, John and Thomas, were among the original builders. They were sons of Aaron Wedgwood, and were the builders of the Big House works. Built in 1751 it was the first pottery in Burslem to have a tiled roof; previously the roof of a building was of clods and thatch and this new development astonished the natives who were critical of the need to incur such expense. The brothers were obviously intent on ensuring a sound construction and appear to have been their own clerk of works. Mr. Emery of Newcastle was the contractor, and the brothers are reputed to have themselves dipped every facing brick in water and handed each to the bricklayers.   Thomas, a descendant of Gilbert Wedgwood, built the Overhouse Works, and a son of this Thomas, Thomas jnr., the Churchyard Works. Thomas jnr died in his early forties but not before siring 13 children, the last of whom was Josiah Wedgwood.

Families who also built around this period were those of Cartlich, Daniel, Malkin, Simpson, Wood, Locket, Stevenson, Marsh, Adams, Shrigley and Marshall. Apart from the local potters, in the year 1690, two brothers named Elers from Holland built a single oven pottery at Brownhills, on a bed of beautiful red clay. From this they produced attractive ware of such a high standard that it created a deal of attention from the local potters. The brothers were very protective of their practices, but, like the Chinese before them, they were craftily robbed of the secret of their work, and it was widely adopted by fellow manufactures, resulting in a rapid improvement in the quality of Burslem pottery. The Elers were the first to use a lathe to turn the clay to enhance the appearance and produce a more uniform product, and Josiah Wedgwood himself acknowledged his indebtedness to them. The pottery produced at Elers appears to have been sent to London where one brother dealt with sales, production in Burslem being the responsibility of the other who lived at Bradwell Hall. It was rumoured that there was a means of communication between the hall and the factory to warn the latter when strangers were arriving. Nothing was found when the factory was demolished, but when the hall was taken down, parts of a primitive type of speaking tube were found in the cellars and these are preserved in the Potteries Museum. The factory was in operation for only a few years, after which the Elers left the district; it appears to the London area.

Of these early potters, John Mitchell was the biggest in his day. He was a religious man, illiterate, and unfortunate, since he died in much reduced circumstances. He is said to have been the first to use clays from outside the district, and apparently his illiteracy did not deter his intent to expand his trade; but like many who followed him he lacked business ability and had too profound a faith in human nature. Ward describes his sales practice with a beautiful indirect inference to this apparent virtue:

'Mitchell had four travellers, Mr Dale of Mole Cob (since of Exeter) Mr Dickens (since of Plymouth) Mr Bowers (since of Falmouth) and Mr Dean (since of Bridgwater). It was customary for the travellers to take out pottery without invoices and, on returning, they would empty their pockets to be paid their wages, five or six shillings per week, their expenses having been paid out of their takings. Each traveller would endeavour to save sufficient to avail himself of any opportunity to become a dealer."

The use of variety in clays to create contrasting decoration or slipware, as it is termed, was a feature of the late 17th and early 18th centuries, and pieces from this period are much valued by collectors. Most however are now in museums, and the Potteries Museum has one of the finest displays. Probably the largest number of slipware dishes which have survived are from the Toft factory of Shelton, but Burslem potters, especially the Simpsons and the Malkins, are well represented. This was a rich period in the history of Staffordshire pottery, both in the art of potting and the virtuosity of decoration. Early dishes were thrown on the wheel before the introduction of plaster of Paris, some measuring from seventeen to twenty two inches in diameter, which implies a rare skill in making and a remarkable achievement in firing in the primitive kilns of the day. Loss in this, the final stage in the production, would be a heart-breaking sacrifice of much skilled labour.

Popular decorations included heraldic arms, animals, birds and biblical subjects; the latter leading to the suggestion that such dishes could have been used for church offerings; and

Early slipware by Toft

one Burslem maker, Malkin, was a member of Parish Vestry and a one time Parish Clerk. An interesting late find was of sixteen of these dishes in Chirk Castle. They were fixed to the whitewashed walls in the dairy and passages, and a number have been attributed to Simpson. In the British Museum there is a slipware dish with an inner circle depicting a clock face, on which is written in contrasting clay, "Samuel Malkin the maker in Burslem 17" and with the fingers pointing to 12 o'clock, it is assumed that 1712 was the date of manufacture. Another design depicts lions interspersed with fleur de lis round the rim and in the centre a pair of lady's gauntlet gloves. This appears to illustrate the Elizabethan practice of presenting ladies with gloves on ceremonial occasions. Apart from dishes, this art was applied to all manner of ornaments by a number of potters with varying degrees of success. The Rhead brothers, writing at the beginning of the 20th century, said that many tombstones were made in local clay, with the lettering in contrasting clay - some of these have found their way into museums.

It was a period that could be called *The Expressionists in Clay*. One individual who took a proprietary view of slipware was a Burslem potter named Shaw, who took out a patent for his use of it on domestic ware. He used a white engobe on the inside of vessels and white bands on the outside to contrast with the colour of the local clay body. Shaw evidently considered his patent entitled him to a monopoly in applied slips, and he threatened injunctions against so many of his fellow potters that they were forced to take to court in self defence. Shaw's patent was declared void, which made him so incensed that he took his family to France and started manufacturing there.

Many pottery lovers have deplored the end of this period which was to be replaced by one where foreign wares, particularly Japanese and Chinese, were slavishly copied and the previous spontaneity declined, resulting in critical observations like *"perfection of workmanship displaced the old native picturesqueness"*, *"vigour sacrificed to finish"*, *"originality to elegance"*. On the other hand, from those who loved the later product *"it was a period of apprenticeship."*

Among popular items made in large quantities during the early era, were 'tygs'. These were a communal drinking vessel with multiple handles, some having as many as ten. Each handle was personal to an individual, and in effect reserved that person's space on the rim for them to sup. Some of the vessels had small pegs, spaced at intervals down the inside, either to ensure equality of consumption, or sometimes to wager who could imbibe the most liqueur with a single draught, from which, legend has it, the saying 'taken down a peg' originated. The common domestic pottery of this period was known as 'Crouch ware'. It is not certain where the name originated, but one conjecture is that it came from a contemporary factory near Matlock, producing ware from a Derbyshire clay called Crouch. The composition of the Crouch Ware made in Burslem consisted of local clays mixed with sand from Mow Cop, or Mole Cob as it was then known. It would appear that the sandstone was mined and children used to break it down to a fine state using wooden mallets, the use of wood mallets minimising the chance of metal chippings mixing with the sand, oxidising during firing, and discoloring the final product.

Salt was used for the glazing of the product towards the end of the 17th century, replacing powdered lead, which already had a reputation for its devastating effect on health, but the change was not without its discomforts. Ware was fired once weekly, usually commencing on Thursday and reaching its maximum temperature on Saturday on which day the firemen, swathed in wet cloths, would climb a scaffold which surrounded the kiln, and shovel quantities of salt through holes in the top. The salt volatilized and combined with the silica in the sand to form a glaze. At the same time, clouds of vapour poured out of the kilns and formed a dense cloud over a wide area, causing people, it is said, to collide, or lose their sense of direction. Not only could it last for up to five hours, it could also be seen for miles around Burslem.

Changes were taking place at such speed at this time that it is impossible to confine them

1348. William the Pottere gives 6*d*. for licence to make earthern pots (*facere ollas terreas*).
1353. Thomas the Throgher is amerced for a default at Chatterley.
1363. John Pottere is presented for an affray in Borewaslym (Burslem).
1369. Robert le Potter gives 12*d*. for licence to get earth for making pots until the following Michaelmas.
1372. Thomas le Thrower takes up land in Thursfield.
1405. Robert Potter is recently dead in Burslem.

Tunstall Court Rolls from showing, above, references to early potters in Burslem and on the right inhabitants of Burslem in 1671. from *Staffordshire Pottery and its History* by Josiah C. Wedgwood c.1920

John Muchell	Wm. Simson	Sam. Cartlech
Thos. Flecher	Joseph Simson	Thos. Marsh
John Royle	Raphe Simson	John Marsh
Raphe Bech	Thos. Cartlech	Thos. Copland
Ric. Edge	Arthur Monsfield	Thos. Armstrong
John Hord	John Roden	Ric. Stonner
Wm. Hord	Wm. Monsfield	Rob. Wood
Moses Wedgwood	Thos. Denyell	Rob. Wood
Moses Wedgwood	Wm. Denyell	Wm. Twomlow
Thos. Lounes	John Clowes	Rob. Simson
Samuel Leigh	Sam. Clowes	Ric. Hand
Fras. Foster	John Denyell	Thos. Cartlech
Wm. Marsh	Joseph Malken	Thos. Addames
John Barlow	Wm. Wedgwood	Raphe Borne
Wm. Hord	John Jones	Jas. Rushen
Jossua Leigh	John Ward	John Shaw
Izac Ball	John Cartlech	John Sickes
Izac Monsfield	John Lockett	John Tonstall
Raphe Flecher	Jas. Standley	Thos. Gratbache
John Flecher	John Rowley	Ric. Twomlow
Ric. Flecher	Raph Shaw	Wm. Browne
Wm. Steele	Hen. Bourne	Wm. Edge
Wm. Steele	Wm. Harrison	Fras. Rogers
Raphe Steele	Rob. Denell	Ric. Borne
John Simson	Wm. Marsh	John Denyell

Above: the works of Ralph Wood in the early 19th century

Two Turner teapots

to specific periods. The use of lead was gradually superseded by salt as salt was by the use of liquid glaze. Similarly a radical change followed the use of plaster for moulds, the use of flint in the body of the ware, also clays from Cornwall and Dorset, while twice firing which accompanied the increasing use of mineral colourings became commonplace. What was known as Egyptian ware, very popular for a period, accompanied the introduction of a black body using local clays mixed with 'Car' or 'Can', a strange name for a material recovered from water from coalmines by evaporation, and sold to the potters at one guinea per cart load. Josiah Wedgwood is said to have used this for his Basalt ware. Also widely used was zaffre, or cobalt, to stain both bodies and glazes, also manganese and copper oxides, all used singly or in combination to give some rich variety of colour and effects.

It is difficult to assess the number of potteries in Burslem from the beginning to the end of the 18th century, since it was only later that some, but not all, began to stamp their ware. Furthermore it was common for popular lines to be copied by more than one manufacturer - origin and dates could increasingly be obscure, although illustrations in directories published late in the century were helpful. Llewellyn Jewitt in his *Ceramic Art of Great Britain*, which is extremely exhaustive, cites only thirty to thirty-five potteries from the beginning to the middle of the 18th century, and during the period a number of the original names vanished and were replaced with new.

From Wood's map of 1750, one would assume more than double Jewitt's figure. Certainly the map shows a far larger number of buildings but these would not necessarily all be potters, or if so, maybe of negligible size. The frequent change of ownership is so striking that one would assume that despair, illness, or death, were constant companions. Scarratt, a local writer, said in 1906. *"We have seen the descendants of old houses so absorbed in the art for art's sake, that they have gradually become impecunious, yet so devoted have they been in their zeal and love of this fascinating art that they have gone from disaster to disaster".* In 200 years, covering the 18th and 19th centuries, it would seem that no more than 50% of the factories were owned or occupied by the same individual or family for more than ten years!

A Wedgwood style vase produced by a number of Burslem potters including the Adams and Wood families, Alcocks, and Brownfields

Outstanding among the influential potters of the 18th century were the Wood family. From the Cheddleton area, with important ancestry from the Elizabethan era, Ralph Wood, a miller at Cheddleton and Shelton, was father of two sons both born in Burslem; Ralph, in 1715 and Aaron, in 1717. Since most millers by this time were involved in grinding materials for the pottery trade, it is perhaps not surprising that his sons should become involved in the industry. Ralph married the heiress of Thomas and John Wedgwood and appears to have founded the Hill Top Pottery, or Hill Pottery as it was commonly known. The factory was situated in what is now Westport Road. He created a flourishing business with a prosperous American connection and made a wide variety of products, domestic ware, jasper ware, ornamental ware, figures, etc. The firm's quality of product was such that Josiah Wedgwood placed orders with them when he was pressed to meet his customers needs. Ralph's two sons, John, born 1742 and Ralph, born 1748, joined their father in the business. John, the elder son left the partnership after some ten years and built his own factory and dwelling at Brownhills. Ralph, the father died in 1772. Ralph, the younger son, carried on the Hill Top business, but died six years after his father, and the factory passed into other hands. Probably the first potter to take over the Hill Pottery following the death of Ralph Wood would be Ralph Wedgwood whose artistic work is much prized. He came from the Thomas Wedgwood

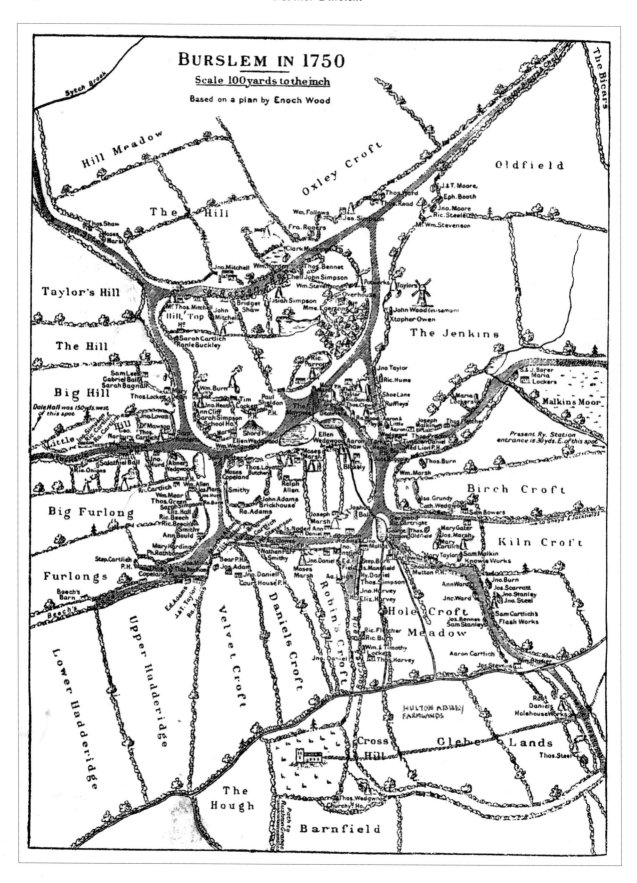

clan and was a cousin of Josiah Wedgwood and at one time a working partner. Evidently influenced by Josiah, he experimented technically but had none of Josiah's controlled application or business acumen. Initially he was said to have a thriving business and was apparently prepared to share the profit to be obtained from his technical skills with his competitors as evident from the following address to them:

"HILL POTTERY: After a series of fourteen years laborious and expensive experiment, I have the pleasure to inform you that I have so far accomplished some of the important ends to which they have been directed as to encourage a hope that a diffusion of the results of these experiments, which have the improvement of the manufacture of earthenware for their object, will tend to the reciprocal benefit of the manufacturers of it and myself. If I am not finally persuaded that the advantages which I have to propose are of the first magnitude, both in the point of profit to the manufacturer, credit to the manufacture, and benefit to the public, I should certainly not presume in calling your attention to this matter which I now do, by requesting your company at the White Lion, Lane End, on Friday at 11.o'clock in the morning at which specimems will be produced. In the interim I have the pleasure to subscribe myself a friend of the Staffordshire Potteries, and as such your most obedient servant. Ralph Wedgwood."

Alas, his forecasts must have been presumptious since in 1796 he was declared bankrupt and his assets sold at the Legs of Man on the 31st of March 1796, along with other lots. They make interesting reading:

"Lot 1. All that dwelling house pleasantly situated in Burslem aforesaid, with or without a valuable Croft of Piece of Land lying at the back of same, containing one acre or thereabouts, and also all that set of Potworks adjoining the Dwelling House wherein the said Mr. Ralph Wedgwood's manufacturing has been carried on for several years, and which was well adapted to an extensive trade. The utensils and fixtures thereto belonging may be procured at fair valuation and if desirable immediate possession to the House and Manufacturery, a part of the Warehouse only excepted for a short time. The remaining part of the Household Furniture, Stock in Trade, Utensils and Fixtures of the said Ralph Wedgwood, consisting among other things of excellent Feather Beds and Bedsteads, and articles of Kitchen Furniture, A Gold Watch. A One Horse Chaise, built upon a new construction with Harness complete. A Weighing Machine, and a quantity of Shelves and Drawers. A Press for copying letters. Two Lathes complete. A quantity of Ware laid out in lots of about two crates each."

There were other interesting lots at the sale but it is uncertain whether they were all associated with Ralph Wedgwood's estate:

"Lot V. All that Sliphouse and Yard with an excellent spring of water and good pump with Dwelling House for the Slipmaker, also a Stone House for clay, situated at the Sytch. Also several complete and valuable Engravings and various working Utensils. A Stove Pot, Boards, Tubs, Mills Etc."

Other lots at the sale give an interesting indication of some of the remaining rural development areas adjacent to the town at that time:

"Lot 11. A valuable piece of Meadow Land lying below Burslem Church, capable of irrigation without expense being laid out now for development. Lot 1V. A Butt of Land called Butty Furlong lying near the town of Burslem. Lot 111. A plot of Land very eligable for building on adjoining Burslem Church where a new street is forming called Commercial Street".

In 1798 Ralph went to Yorkshire as a partner at Knottingly Pottery, Ferrybridge. The partnership was based apparently on a claim that he could bring secrets that were worth £200 per year over and above his share of the profits. He persuaded his Yorkshire partners to provide him with a laboratory and equipment, but it seems significant that in 1801 he was paid £1025 to leave and he returned to Burslem.

Whether he patented his improvement which was to bring great blessings to people and profits is not recorded, but pottery manufacturers of the time were prone to fly to the patent office, and in many cases their claims were tenuous. The following are early examples:

"PATENT POTTERS OVEN: Valentine Close and James Keeling have obtained His Majesty's Royal Letters Patent for the sole use of their new invented Ovens or Kilns for the firing of Porcelain and Earthenware for the term of fourteen years from the date of the said letters patent, aquaint those concerned in the said manufacturers that by the use of their invention their goods will be fired with much more regularity, and certainly the injuries

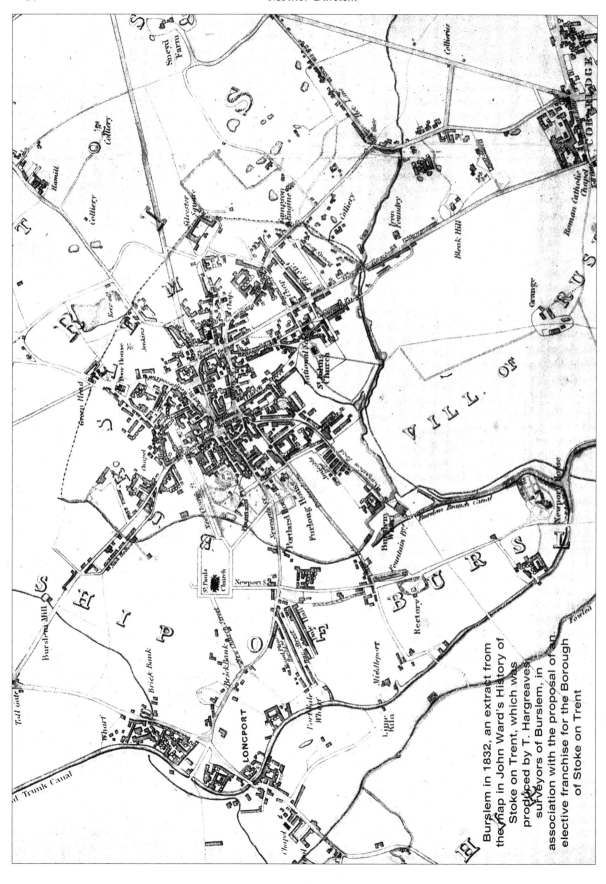

Burslem in 1832, an extract from the map in John Ward's History of Stoke on Trent, which was produced by T. Hargreaves surveyors of Burslem, in association with the proposal of an elective franchise for the Borough of Stoke on Trent heretofore usually sustained by the Wares will be entirely prevented. the process of firing rendered more simple, convenient, and easy to the workman, and nearly half of the coal or fuel usually consumed saved".

15th July 1796.

BY THE KING'S PATENT: The manufacturers of Earthenware &c. in the Staffordshire Potteries are informed that Keelings substitute for White and Red Lead for making Glazes for Cream Coloured, White and China glazed Earthenware, Porcelain &c. was intended to have been brought forward for use sometime since as proposed, but has been prevented by neglect in the carriage of materials. The patentee however has no doubt he will be enabled in the course of next week to get a sufficient quantity prepared to supply any demand for the same. Without entering into minute detail of the advantages that may arise to the country from the use of this invention, the patentee briefly observes that his substitute is to be made use of in preparing Glazes &c. in the same as White and Red Lead are usually used. That a greater quantity of Composition may be added to the substitute than has usually been done with White or Red Lead will be cheaper by one half in the price of these articles and will be found to be harmless to the workman to be employed in the dipping or use of same. Orders for the Substitute will be attended to by being left at the office of Mr. Heath at Newcastle when the terms on which the Manufacturers will be supplied may be seen".

Many physical changes and ownerships followed at the Hill Top pottery in the 19th century. There appears to have been a number of short occupations, but in the 1830s it was purchased by Alcock and Keeling, later Alcock & Co. This title is interesting since it appears to indicate that this was probably one of the earliest transitions in Burslem from individual ownership to a modern company. In 1839 Hill Top was largely rebuilt, at the same time incorporating adjoining factories. The frontage was far more ornate than anything previously built in Burslem and was much admired - but it has unfortunately failed to be preserved. Alcocks were a progressive firm and produced a variety of ornamental and domestic wares for the American market. Samuel Alcock was an experienced potter and for twenty years he produced much beautiful pottery, including, like Josiah Wedgwood, pieces based on historical and mythical subjects, including the copy of a vase which was said to be equally as famous as the Portland Vase.

Samuel Alcock died in 1848 and the pottery was taken over by Barker & Son in 1851, but by 1860 they were insolvent and the factory and its contents were sold to Sir James Duke, an MP for the City of London. The firm traded under the title of Sir James Duke and Nephews, but in 1865 they appear to have had second thoughts, probably having bought it as a family investment but found that the manufacture of pottery was far from being a profitable hobby. The factory was again up for sale. The firm was purchased by Thomas Ford who, in 1865 employed one Richard Daniel to manage it. This Daniel is most probably the one who was previously in financial trouble, if so, his troubles continued to follow him, since the Hill Pottery was bankrupt again in 1867.

In 1870 it was split into two units, earthenware being made in one and and china in the other. The china works was operated by Bodleys who were also owners of the Crown Pottery in Newcastle Street, where the firm made finger plates for doors, knobs for various trades, lamp bases, artists palettes, many of the articles in coloured and marbled effect. The Rhead Brothers described their products as clever and good. The earthenware side was occupied by Burgess and Leigh, who left after building a new factory at Longport, where it still operates under the same name, but at this time were famous for the form and beauty of their toilet sets, with patterns sold under such names as 'Imperial Albany', 'Melborne', 'Rococo' and 'New Venetian'. Until gracious living was introduced for the many by the introduction of the bathroom, the sale of ewers and basins must have been enormous.

The history of the Hill Pottery is somewhat confusing from then on, but it is recorded that in 1893 J and G Vernon, sons of James Vernon, took over Hill Pottery from their father, employing 250 operatives making domestic earthenware. The firm had a large export trade, South Africa being one of their main markets and this probably influenced the renaming of the building as African Pottery. Despite the new name and an impressive new frontage this once proud building declined and in 1906 Scarratt said it was in the occupation of Howletts - who I recollect myself as kiln builders. In other words, it had become a builder's yard - and he says it was in a sorry state. Humbled, it survived until 1969 when it took the

The Descent from the Cross
modelled by Enoch Wood.

demolition route of many of its contempories, but the memory of the original building will survive from the association it is believed to have with the Sytch Pottery of Arnold Bennett's novels.

Reverting to the Wood family; Aaron, the second son of the miller was apprenticed to Thomas Wedgwood and ultimately became a distinguished self-employed modeller and die cutter. His work is prized and examples are to be found in the Victoria and Albert Museum, and a dish, previously in his son Enoch's possession, is now in Hanley Museum. Among those potters for whom Aaron worked were his brother Ralph, Whieldon, and Mitchell.

An interesting reference to Aaron Wood concerns the introduction of the use of of plaster in Burslem. It appears that a member of an old established family of Burslem potters named Daniel, came back from a visit to Paris with samples of gypsum rock from which he had been told the French were making moulds. It was evidently assumed that the rock was to be die cut to produce the mould and Aaron Wood appears to have attempted this with disbelief, and presumably without success. However, Daniel went to Paris a second time, and from this visit learnt of the necessary calcining process which created from the gypsum the powder material 'plaster of Paris', which created a

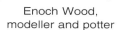

Enoch Wood,
modeller and potter

revolutionary change in the pottery industry. Despite his outstanding skill Aaron Wood does not appear to have accumulated great wealth. He died a widower, survived by seven of his eight children. His will, after bequests, stipulated that the sale of his bed, his bedroom furniture and his club money, would pay for his funeral.

Enoch Wood, Aaron's youngest son, was the star of the family. Born in 1759 he inherited his father's skill in modelling. At the age of eleven he is said to have modelled a copy of the Wood family's heraldic arms from a rough drawing on a wall in Cheddleton Church. At this same age he was sent to Liverpool to learn the art of drawing and anatomy with his uncle William Caddick, a portrait painter of some repute. His stay in Liverpool could not have been long, since on his return he went to a private school run by Richard Bentley and Aaron Wedgwood. Following this he was apprenticed to William Palmer of Hanley, a modeller and pottery manufacturer whose products were considered by Josiah Wedgwood to be very competitive with his own. At the age of eighteen Enoch produced an intricate and striking model of the Crucifixion. This was said to have been inspired by two itinerants who came to Burslem with a model of the

The entrance and packing house at Enoch Wood's Fountain Pottery. The parish church of St John is seen in the background

The bust of Wesley modelled by Enoch Wood and a painting showing John Wesley sitting for Enoch.

Crucifixion in coloured wax in a box lined with velvet and having a glass top draped with silk. The two men took it in turn to carry the box on their back and evidently it created a deal of interest and prompted generous donations, so much so, that Enoch had in mind to model something similar and to take to the road himself. Had he have done so it would have been a great loss for Burslem.

Fortunately, at twenty four years of age, he decided to become a master potter, renting the Brick House Works recently released from renting by Josiah Wedgwood. Such was his progress that he decided to build Fountain Pottery, facing Fountain Square, and was ultimately said to have operated four factories in the adjoining area and also Knowle Works in the Hamil. He earned the title "Prince of Potters", and for his civic work "Father of Burslem". Like Josiah Wedgwood, he produced figures from classical mythology and also contemporary figures. Many of these were his own modelling. It has been suggested that it was seeing items from this production that influenced Josiah Wedgwood to produce cameos.

One notable example of his work was a bust of John Wesley, modelled from life when Wesley visited Burslem. and said to be an admirable likeness which proved to be very popular, so much so that it was modified as Wesley aged to reflect his increasing years since, using a modern term, it was such a 'bestseller'. Ward in his history recounts an anecdote concerning this bust of Wesley. At a Conference in Leeds in 1781 copies of the bust were on display and in keen demand. Some time later Enoch Wood was approached by a cleric and asked if he was the one who had produced the bust. Confirming that he was, the reverend thereupon entered into a lengthy illustration of the comparison between Enoch manipulating the clay and God's work in moulding man through trials and afflictions to an image of himself.

Knowledge of the bust must have been widespread. About 1880, it was decided to create a life size model of Wesley in marble, and the sculptor Samuel Manning was commissioned to do the work. Apparently he failed to get a likeness until, having been informed of Enoch Wood's bust, one was loaned him and provided a satisfactory solution. In 1790 Enoch Wood was joined in the business by James Caldwell, a local man of influence who probably provided capital but had little involvement in the running of the business. The partnership lasted until 1818 when it was dissolved and Enoch's sons were incorporated under the title Enoch Wood & Sons. About this date the firm was considered to be the largest exporter of pottery to the United States. The business was taken over by one of his sons following his death, but like many other family businesses in Burslem it failed to survive a second generation.

The Fountain Pottery which Enoch built had its main entrance facing Fountain Square, but the bulk of the buildings were sited in Liverpool Road, divided on the ground by Packhorse Lane. When the pottery ceased to be in the ownership of the Wood family, it followed the pattern of the Hill Pottery and was divided. In the second half of the 19th century Goodwin & Davison were occupying part. They had some 90 employees; a considerable difference to the 1000 employed there in Enoch Wood's day. However it was said by Scarratt that the bell was still there and functioning, if somewhat hoarse with age, but although a bell housing still stands silhouetted against the sky today, it is not the handsome one shown in early drawings, nor is it in the same position, while the historical bell itself, like Wedgwood's horn, is missing, and what buildings are left have a more humble use.

The Knowle Works on the Hamil, another of Enoch Wood's when his trade was at its peak, was also said by Scarratt to be vacant in 1843. It ultimately came into the hands of one of the Adams family and was finally demolished.

Enoch Wood was an avid collector of anything appertaining to the pottery industry and amassed a large collection of pottery dating from the reign of King Charles. His collection included butter pots of a very early age. He was kept informed of any excavations in Burslem from which he might find additional items for his collection, which unfortunately never seems to have been catalogued. Among the items he acquired were knives and forks embellished with pottery handles previously belonging to Dr Johnson - thousands of these ceramic mounts were made in Burslem to supply to the cutlery manufacturers. In 1835 Enoch presented 182 pieces from his collection to the King of Saxony through the king's ambassador. As a reciprocal gesture, Enoch received in return a selection of Chinese and Saxon pottery.

Unfortunately on his death in 1840 his whole collection was sold and dispersed. Some went to the Mayer collection, which later went to Liverpool Museum. Arnold Mountford, the late Curator of the City Museum, was personally asked if any pieces had been bought for the City and his reply was that he thought they had a few, but he was unaware of how they were acquired. Of the substantial number of pieces which went to Saxony, and were on exhibition in Dresden, fortunately many, but not all, survived the War.

Besides Enoch's acquisitiveness, he also had a habit of secreting objects in new buildings even from youth. An early example of this was at a time when he was friendly with Thomas Wedgwood, who was living in the Big House and having a wall built at the rear. The two friends decided to conceal items during the construction, and evidently in the passage of time knowledge of this was lost, since it came as a surprise when this wall was demolished in 1879 and the following article appeared in the press:-

"CURIOUS DISCOVERY OF POTTERY AT BURSLEM

On Monday March 3rd 1879 a number of workmen employed in pulling down an old sandstone wall at the back of the old Conservative Club, formally known as the "Big House", Burslem, found a quantity of old pottery ware of various kinds which had evidently been secreted seventy or eighty years ago. Some of the stones composing the wall are very large, and, from the centre of one of them, a square tile fitting into a suitable space suddenly became detached, revealing below a roughly hewn cavity fitted with such articles as have been mentioned. Four cavities were subsequently discovered, all similarly replete with curiosities. Of all the articles which have been found here, the most interesting is a small glazed porcelain box, about four inches by three inches by half inch deep, which, when deciphered, bore on its underside some clue to the secret of the original depositor. The glaze has broken off in many places, owing to the action of frost, and a few of the key bits are missing, but enough has remained to enable the following to be easily made out *"This wall was built by Thomas Wedgwood, son of John Wedgwood of the Big House. Near this will be found specimems of various articles of the manufacture of the neighbourhood, which may in future time give pleasure to the possessor. June 20th 1810".* Inside is written in white on a faded gilt ground *"Enoch Wood fecit".* It is well known that Enoch Wood was a potter living in

The Big House built by John and Thomas Wedgwood. It is still standing and in use, although the wall has gone

Burslem about this time, and in his intimacy with Thomas Wedgwood, used most probably to spend many happy hours at the house of the latter."

Fairly recently a quantity of ware was found in the stonework of Burslem Church whilst the restoration was in progress, which had been placed there by Enoch Wood. It is equally well known that the Wedgwood family were tinged with the eccentricity. The articles found in the wall of the Big House consisted of jasper jugs, cameos, seals, teapots, figures and other specimens of the potters' art, besides a few dozen copper tokens which bear the arms and mottoes of the various boroughs and companies that issued them. Among them was a Birmingham halfpenny with the motto "Industry has its sure reward" together with coins issued by Coventry, Liverpool, Anglesea Mines Company, Associated Irish Mines and others. An amusing item in the list is a couple of old clay pipes, one of them bearing in lead upon the bowl "Thomas Wedgwood" and the other "Wood's Pipe", which would give the impression that the hiding of all that has been found was part of a joke conceived by the two men. The reporter said that *"the ware which*

To face p. 267.

WEST VIEW OF THE HOUSE & MANUFACTORY OF ENOCH WOOD, ESQ.

EAST FRONT OF THE MANUFACTORY OF ENOCH WOOD & SONS, BURSLEM.

An engraving of Moses Wood's sons in the paintress's section of the pottery

An advert showing the versatility of product at one of Moses Wood's Potteries

has been discovered is not that known by the name of Wedgwood, as it was certainly not the work of the great father of pottery, though closely resembling it in most respects".

Enoch Wood's valuable public work is covered later in the book. He died in 1840 and, as seemed so often to happen in Burslem, when the original dynamic character departed, the heart of his business soon followed and in about 1846, as with his private collection, the works and its contents were sold.

Enoch Wood had an older brother Moses Wood who was also a pottery manufacturer in Burslem, but although the two brothers were contemporary they operated independently. Unlike Enoch, Moses seemed to have no active interest in civic affairs, and was not mentioned in the minutes of the Board of Health, it being left to his grandson to become mayor of the town in 1895/6. Moses' heirs carried on the business and over three generations the family were ultimately operating three factories, one in Furlong Lane, one in Navigation Road and a third in Newport Lane. This latter factory has been rebuilt and still bears the name of Wood & Sons, making domestic and ornamental pottery of repute, but, like the Wedgwood factories, no longer in family ownership. The other two factories once owned by the Woods are among the many which have been demolished in Burslem.

Josiah Wedgwood's name is synonymous with pottery and it is appropriate that he should have been born in Burslem. There are many detailed studies of his life and works, and while he had a tremendous influence on the growth and fame of the pottery industry as a whole, he moved to Etruria when Burslem was in the process of becoming prosperous and the town only partially developed.

Josiah Wedgwood was not a practising artist himself, in the manner of the Wood family, but his appreciation of art was profound and his thirst for perfection had an immense influence on the work of his contempories in Burslem. His father, as we previously remarked, died young leaving a large family. Josiah, the youngest, was apprenticed along with another brother to learn the art of throwing from their eldest brother, who had taken over the business on the father's premature death. Josiah was indentured and the terms of his indentures were stern, restricting him from visiting ale houses, embezzlement, playing cards or marrying. Shaw recounts meeting a man named Fletcher who was employed to make clay balls for the two brothers. He was paid fourpence a week for the first year, and being about the same size as Josiah, claimed he had some of his old clothes.

Reflecting Josiah's competence and growing maturity, when the eldest brother refused Josiah a partnership, he left Burslem with a princely patrimony of twenty pounds and jointly with a Mr Harrison of Newcastle commenced potting in a factory in Stoke. This partnership was short lived and he left to join Thomas Whieldon at his works in Fenton where he was able to experiment and perfect his work, until he made the decision to return to Burslem to commence producing on his own in the year 1759/60.   He leased the Ivy House Works, a two oven factory with a small thatched dwelling adjoining, and here he produced a variety of articles in imitation onyx, marble, etc, and products with a beautiful green glaze which he had developed. His output extended to items for medical use, sick feeders, inhalers, spitting pots and chamber pots; also ewers and basins, mortars and pestles, and even bathroom tiles.

Simultaneously he was perfecting his 'Cream Ware' which was to be an instant success with its delicate appearance and favourable comparison with imported porcelain, but far greater mechanical strength. The seal of approval for this new product was an order from Queen Charlotte, who granted him the title 'Potter to the Queen'. Wedgwood in turn renamed it 'Queens Ware'. The demand for perfection, which continued throughout his life, was evident in every detail of Queens Ware, every part was in complete accord; plates nested, lids fitted, spouts poured and handles suited. Its introduction influenced all subsequent English pottery production - and it even influenced the naming of Queen Street in Burslem.

Business increased rapidly and he rented a further factory opposite the Ivy House Works, and in 1764 a third, the Bell Pottery, a five oven unit. In addition ware was made for him by a cousin at the Overhouse Pottery. In 1771 he moved to the factory he built at Etruria, while still maintaining some production at Burslem. An observation by one who studied his life and work was that *"Josiah would not claim he was strikingly original, but was no doubt one of those geniuses, who arise from time to time, and who have unique gifts; his gifts included a love of art, a lust to create, and the gift of encouraging talent to further his insatiable ambition, and finally, to crown all, a successful business instinct to bring the whole to fruition".*

Of his attributes, Wedgwood himself made many significant observations; two of which are are the following: *"I made artists out of men", "Competition for cheapness and not for excellence of workmanship is the most frequent and certain cause of rapid decay and entire destruction of arts and manufacture".* His epitaph aptly reads: *"He converted a rude and inconsiderable manufacture into a fine art".*

What was really significant for Burslem, and the expanding Potteries area, was Josiah Wedgwood's realisation that perfecting the art was in itself insufficient; that to prosper the district must connect with the outside world, and he had the vision to initiate the necessary political pressure to ensure this.

The pedigree of the Adams family of potters is extremely ancient, and their pottery is highly regarded. Some members of the family widened their interests compared with their contemporaries. Their products competed with those of Josiah Wedgwood and examples are to be found in most museums. In 1617, in his will, William Adams is described as a master potter; as also is Thomas Adams in 1629. Both appear to have employed others from a very early date. The family is said to have originated in Bagnall and Burslem and had large interests in Burslem, but in time became seriously involved in mining and other interests beyond the mother town. Brickhouse Pottery which was built by John Adams in about 1650 was said to be the first all brick factory in Burslem. Josiah Wedgwood leased it in 1759/60, and added a bell tower to replace the previous use of a horn to call the workers, and following this innovation it was usually known as the Bell Pottery. Pottery production by the Adams family at this pottery appears to have paused in 1757 due to deaths in the family and the young age of the male heir. There followed a series of leases, and periods of disuse, or divided use. One part was eventually demolished to form the site of an Independent chapel, and in 1876 a further part was purchased to make way for a covered vegetable market. The remainder was purchased by George Beardmore of Rode Heath, by whom it was demolished.

William Adams, living at Fenton Hall, purchased Wolfe's factory in Stoke. This was a large factory extending the length of the current High Street. William died in 1829 and his sons Thomas and Edward continued the business. They had a large export trade, and an office in Liverpool to which Thomas went, leaving Edward to run the factory. Edward went to live at The Mount in Penkhull, a stately home built by Josiah Spode. The Wolfe factory has long disappeared without trace, The Mount survives but part of the estate grounds were purchased for the Royal Infirmary, to the building of which Burslem citizens made their financial contribution. (see Ch 8) Edward's son, who joined the firm, unwisely speculated, with the result that it was subsequently forced to close. Lewis Adams, a bachelor brother of Thomas and Edward, was Chief Bailiff of Stoke and Master of the Hunt. The Adams family crest was adopted for the arms of Stoke on Trent and as part of the arms of the federated towns.

John Adams, who built Cobridge Hall, is said to have eventually owned five factories, but retired from the manufacture of pottery in 1820 to concentrate on his mining interests. He gave an acre of land on which to build St. Paul's church, and a further acre to build a vicarage. He died in 1831 leaving among his possessions 250 bottles of thirty year old port!

William Adams, who became hereditary owner of the Brickhouse Pottery, married Mary Bourne, daughter of a Newcastle shoe manufacturer. William was a very wealthy landowner whose wife presented him with eight daughters, none of whom ever married. It was said that whenever the parents left the house, the daughters were locked in until their return.

The Ivy House Pottery, belonging to Thomas and John Wedgwood, was situated at the corner of Shoe Lane and Shore Street. These two streets were parallel, running in a northerly direction from the top of Waterloo Road. Shore Street is said to have been only wide enough to take one vehicle, and eventually the present broad Wedgwood Street was developed and both Shoe Lane and Shore Street disappeared within it. Llewellyn Jowitt in 1883 said *"The visitor to Burslem who wishes to know the exact site of the Ivy House should stand at the corner of the modern built "Shambles", or Butchers as it is commonly called, and face down Swan Square. He can rest assured that he is standing on the little enclosed garden in front of*

The churchyard pottery and house. Josiah Wedgwood was born and educated here. St John's church is seen in the background

(Fig. 52.)   CHURCHYARD, HOUSE, AND WORKS.

A pottery figure showing a typical pedlar with a pottery crate on his back

(Fig. 49.)   OVERHOUSE, BURSLEM.

The Overhouse, built by Thomas Wedgwood. The house no longer exists, but the pottery of the same name built on the site is still there

Wedgwood's house. The front faced an open space called "Green Bank" and adjoining was a low half timbered building called the Turks Head". This is the factory and dwelling to which Josiah Wedgwood came when he returned to Burslem to commence manufacturing on his own - only a short distance from where he was born. Obviously when Llewellyn Jowett wrote in 1888 both house and factory had gone, but if the visitor now, following his advice, looked for the Shambles, he would fail to find that as well.

The Churchyard Pottery, where Josiah Wedgwood was born, was bought in 1780 by Josiah himself, but sold in 1787 to his brother John, who himself sold it in 1795. In its roughly two hundred year life it changed hands at least ten times. It was enlarged in 1858 and split into several holdings but eventually demolished in 1906. It is perhaps sad that, with such close association with Josiah, this pottery, and more particularly the Etruria Pottery, did not come into the hands of the National Trust, since there was the potential of developing a history of pottery on the scale of the fascinating display of the history of cotton at Styal in Cheshire. What a difference it would make to Burslem now!

The Washington Pottery in Waterloo Road, said to date from about 1838, was host to some interesting personalities. William Sadler Kennedy occupied it in 1847, from previously being in partnership with William Maddock in King Street making pottery palettes for artists. At the Washington Pottery he produced door plates, umbrella handles, artists palettes, etc. In 1852 Kennedy took into partnership his brother in law, James MacIntyre, who came to Burslem as a clerk with Alexander Bell & Co, Canal Carriers, but whose family appear to have been very influential since they formed The Anderton Canal Carrying Company whose barges were everywhere when canals were in their prime. Kennedy moved to London in 1854 leaving MacIntyre to run the business. MacIntyre then took into partnership Thomas Hulme who was originally a clerk with a Tunstall pottery. MacIntyre's son in law, William Woodall, who had come to Burslem in 1857 to manage Burslem Gas Works - and to whom we shall later give prominence for his public work - also became a partner. MacIntyre's now diversified their production and prospered from the introduction of a ware in a rich cream body which they called 'Ivory China'. By 1868 both McIntyre and Kennedy had died and Thomas Hulme and William Woodall had become the sole owners. Besides domestic tableware they produced a distinctive ornamental ware with what they termed slip trailing and underglaze colours, using the skills of Thomas Moorcroft. Following the death of William Woodall in 1901, differences arose over policy and it was decided to withdraw from decorative ware and concentrate on more profitable electrical porcelain.

Thomas Hulme, like Enoch Wood, was an art lover and a keen collector. He left his collection to the town of Burslem where it was originally housed in the Wedgwood Institute. It later moved to the Potteries Museum. He contributed both time and money to his beloved Burslem, in particular through his generosity to the Burslem School of Art and his public work both as Chief Bailiff and later as Mayor.

Another Thomas of the Wedgwood clan built the Overhouse Pottery, which is situated at the northern end of Swan Square and still in use. The factory was prosperous and in 1818 he retired and sold it to Edward Challinor who had another pottery in Tunstall. Thomas died in 1826. Challinor dabbled in many projects and may have operated the pottery, but he certainly let it to a number of different potters before, in 1869, he rebuilt or at least extensively renovated it, and installed machinery. A plaque over the entrance, reads *"Edward Challinor commenced business here in AD 1819 and rebuilt the premises AD 1869"*. After the renovation it was occupied by Ralph Hammersley, previously of Church Bank Pottery, Tunstall, and at one time a clerk in Challinor's employ. In 1883 it carried the name Ralph Hammersley & Sons and the firm are said to have had a very healthy trade with America, Canada, and Sweden. In 1906 Scarratt, who obviously had a deep concern for Burslem, said *"If Challinor was here to see his empty and neglected factory he would regret the capital he has spent."* Fortunately the factory has been brought back from this unhappy state and thrives under the name of Barratts of Staffordshire, Royal Overhouse Pottery. Besides the interests already mentioned, Challinor partnered John Wedgwood in the Woodlands Pottery, and also had a close association with a publican from Nile Street named Bowers, running in partnership the Brownhills Pottery which they rented from Samuel Marsh of Marsh & Haywood, who had previously occupied it. Bowers died in 1867 and his son took over, but the all too common failure came in 1871. Challinor was a contemporary of Ward's in Burslem, and they would more than likely have moved in the same circles, but surprisingly Ward never mentions him.

The Waterloo Pottery had an association with a number of influential families and appears to have been older than the name would imply. One family which appears to have been associated with it at an early date was that of the Daniels. There were Daniels in the district in the early 18th century since one, as previously recounted, brought to Burslem details of the use of plaster on the Continent. Another Daniel of Hanley, who was described as potter & enameller, had a very unusual arrangement of renting an area of the Spode factory in Stoke, in which he employed two hundred enamellers. He is said to have bought pottery in the plain state from Spode and sold it back to them in its decorated form. At a later date a Richard Daniel was at the Waterloo Pottery. He seemed to have previously had an unsuccessful life as a potter in Stoke and Fenton, and at one time served a turn in prison for debt. In 1809 the Waterloo Pottery was taken over by a progressive couple, Josiah Machin and Jacob Bagguley who made both china and earthenware. They were the first to introduce roller printing and obtained a patent which covered *"Printing on Biscuit in various colours and an application of the same principle to the ornamenting of paper and japanned Tea-trays, Oilcloths, Table Covers, and articles of prepared Canvas, Leather etc. surpassing every former attempt at transferring pictorial design to each kind of goods"*.

In 1850 the factory came into the hands of Richard and Thomas Boote, who were also innovative and took out many patents covering their products. They made jugs, tableau, etc, in a manner of encaustic tiles. This was an innovative variation since instead of applying embossed work to the article, in the manner of Wedgwood Jasper Ware, the embossing was in the mould and into this area they pressed a different coloured clay to that used for the main body of the piece, Ultimately they discontinued this class of product and produced tiles and domestic ware.

The Cobridge Pottery is a pottery with interesting associations, but another which is no longer in existence. It appears to have been built in 1808 and occupied by Bucknall and Stevenson, but following the all too familiar pattern, in 1819 the firm was bankrupt. From this date there is conflict of opinion as to who were the occupiers - not surprising considering the frequency of change. Llewellynn Jewett says it was taken by James Clowes until 1829 when it again closed. Ward says it was purchased by J and G Alcock who founded the Burslem Commercial Bank, while Shaw states that in 1828 Alcock and Stevenson were producing at this factory *"a series of busts of a most eminent character of the time, many of them in gold"*. In 1836 it became Robinson, Wood and Brownfield. Robinson died in this same year, Wood retired in 1850, but Brownfield continued to operate an increasingly thriving business, employing six hundred or more operatives. Arthur Brownfield was himself an exceedingly good potter, and the firm produced many beautifully modelled pieces which are much prized by collectors and museums. According to the Rhead brothers, *"Brownfield lacked staying power"* but nevertheless solved many ceramic problems and was innovative. One of his innovations which he called 'Adventurine Effect' was created by using multiple particles of metal suspended in the glaze, but it proved too costly to produce on a commercial scale.

The firm employed many talented men, among them Mr L. John as Art Director. He was a clever artist, particularly as a figure painter. In 1888 a commission which gave the firm prominence was the production of the Gladstone Testimonial Vase. They employed many sculptors, among them a Monsieur Carrier Belleuse, who had originally come to Mintons, but later was self employed and did work for Brownfields including a Globe Vase eleven feet high. It appears that Monsieur Carrier Belleuse was known for his love of big sculptures. This particular Globe Vase was produced for the Crystal Palace Exhibition in London in 1879 and depicted the Globe and the Four Seasons. Eleven feet high and six feet in diameter, in porcelain, it took nine months to produce the exhibition model. The globe was made in two parts, and there were many failures in firing, but to produce it at all with the limited control they had over the coal fired kilns of the day, was a remarkable achievement. The finished masterpiece comprised some fifty pieces in all and was on show locally for three days, during which time 30,000 people came to see it. Following its display in London, it was sent to Paris for exhibition, but was broken on the journey. The pieces were returned to Cobridge, where it was apparently cleverly repaired only to be finally lost in a fire at Brownfield's works.

Brownfield was joined by his sons in 1871. The firm produced a considerable variety of elaborate pieces in Majolica and Parian ware in addition to domestic ware in China and Earthenware. The Rhead brothers said that, due to speculation, the Brownfields withdrew from the firm in 1890 and it became a co-operative with a cumbersome committee, many of the operatives owning shares; the result they claim was grotesque, and the firm was wound up in 1898. The premises were subsequently demolished and the land sold for building purposes.

It cannot be said with certainty that Bleak Hill pottery at Cobridge was the one occupied by the Warburton family who were known as potters in the Cobridge area in the 17th century. Certainly John and Ann Warburton were producing domestic ware in the 18th century, but in 1761 John died and Ann, who must have been a talented woman, continued to successfully run the business. She introduced a number of improvements, including a process to facilitate 'on glaze enamelling' and according to Shaw, was the first to print effectively in gold. She took her son into partnership as Warburton and Son, and along with her brother Ralph developed a flourishing export trade with Holland and Russia. She had a close relationship with Josiah Wedgwood, and decorated some of his ware. She is also said to have persuaded potters

The 15 foot high ceramic piece made at Brownfileds for the Great Victorian Exhibition, Crystal Palace 1851

from Delph to bring their skills to England, although it was Ralph Daniel who employed them surreptitiously in Bagnall, possibly to hide them from other Burslem manufacturers.

There was said to be an Abbey Works at Cobridge which existed from 1703 and had various occupants. It was occupied in the last decade of the 19th century, after which it was evidently demolished.

By the end of the 19th century the transformation in quality, design, variety and volume compared with the period of the Sun Kiln Potteries was incredible; all achieved without a technical research centre, and mainly by trial and error. The industry had grown from using malleable clay prepared by hand on a beating board, to the mechanised pug which delivered clay in ideal condition - the first machine to put a fear for the future in pottery operatives. The introduction of plaster of Paris had brought about slip casting, and the uses of ground flint, substitutes for lead glazes, amongst others, had revolutionised the industry.

Today one naturally thinks of Doulton in relation to Burslem, but despite having a long association with the area, Doulton were not one of the founding potters of industrial Burslem. The firm was by no means new to the production of ceramics when they arrived here. They came from a famous factory in London, to what has now become an equally famous factory in Nile Street, presumably to be among compatable company. The factory Nile Street was, according to the Rhead brothers operated at an earlier date by a family named Riley, who moved to the Hill Top Pottery. Scarratt says that a James Edwards started business in the Nile Street factory. What seems certain is that prior to Doulton's occupation in the early part of the 20th century, they were closely associated with the then occupier, James Carmine Pinder. Carmine Pinder was succeeded by his nephew Thomas Pinder, the business operating under the name of Pinder, Bourne and Company. The firm patented improvements in ovens and printing presses, the latter unfortunately in 1842 at a time when there was so much hostility to the use of machines that, due to threats, they abandoned the project.

Pinder's products won medals at exhibitions in London and Paris in the years 1851, 1855 and 1867. Possibly Doultons collaborated in this success. Following the death of Thomas Pinder, his great nephew, Shadford Pinder, took over in association with Doultons, and when he retired, Doultons became the sole owners. In 1884 they built a china section - from which it could be assumed that little or no china was previously made by Pinders - but vast physical changes in the factory have followed Doultons' ownership, although leaving, one hopes, a few early historical corners. Writing in 1906, the Rhead brothers commented *"while productions at Burslem cannot be said to vie with those of Lambeth, the multifarious types of ware and the exigencies of the market may be pleaded in extension. There is always an attempt to make the ware as artistic as the market will allow."* This was probably a temporary hitch, due to the upheavals of removal, certainly it could not have been lack of local talent, since their products are technically and artistically superb.

Moorcroft, like Doultons, is another Burslem pottery which is familiar to the current generation since, although by no means a modern firm, it has consistently produced collectable decorative ornamental ware of unique colouring and design from the mid-19th century and continues to do so today. The first Moorcroft whose name comes to notice in Burslem is Thomas Moorcroft. Born in the first half of the 19th century, he was trained at Burslem School of Art and appears to have started work at the Hill Pottery, probably then in the occupation of the Alcock family. He worked at Bodleys in Newcastle Street before being employed by McIntyres, presumably until his death in 1885. In 1893 McIntyres decided to extend its range of ornamental pottery, and in 1895 engaged Harry Barnard, who came from London, where he was trained in modelling and sculpture and where he worked at Doulton's Lambeth works. Barnard had a two year contract with McIntyres at the conclusion of which he went to Wedgwoods at Etruria, and was followed at McIntyres by William, a son of Thomas Moorcroft, thus following in his father's footsteps. Like his father, he went to the Burslem School of Art. He finished his training in London and Paris.

Under William the ornamental pottery became an autonomous section within the firm and trade expanded considerably, but apparently not as profitably as McIntyres wished, and in 1911 they gave William notice of their intent to close the department and concentrate on the production of electrical porcelain. Having had sole responsibility for the running of his section, William had developed a personal relationship with customers, particularly with Liberty's of London, owned by the Laseby family. He decided to set up on his own and approached the Lasebys to take a financial interest. Plans were made for the new factory, with an estimate of its cost and expected turnover. The original scheme was eventually modified and the final result is more or less the factory to be seen at its present site in Cobridge.

The Moorcrofts lived at Trentham when the Hall was occupied by the Duke of Sutherland, and many of the early flower designs used on the pottery were from the drawings made by William in the greenhouses at the hall. Many of the operatives in his charge at McIntyre's moved with William to Cobridge and the firm sold him the models and moulds.

Among the early outstanding potters in the Longport area were the Davenport family. Like Doultons, the

Examples of Brownfields' Cobridge Pottery. The firm no longer exists

family had his roots other than in Burslem. John Davenport was a partner with Wolfe in a pottery in Liverpool. This was the Wolfe previously referred to as building a factory which stretched the length of the current High Street in Stoke, and later bought by the Adams family. There were a number of potteries in Liverpool at this time, among them Sadler and Green who were the first potters to use prints from engravings to decorate their own ware, as well as ware of others. Josiah Wedgwood obviously realised its potential and regularly employed a carter in Burslem to take plain ware to Liverpool to be printed, and it was a much later date before engraving and printing became a staple branch of the local pottery industry.

In this same period an important Liverpool pottery, the Herculanium, was attracting families from Burslem, who moved to houses built to accommodate them. It is said that in adopting the name Herculanium, the owners were influenced by Josiah Wedgwood and his Etruria works. However the pottery industry failed to survive at Liverpool, while the shipping industry prospered.

In 1794 Davenport moved into a factory in Longport built in 1777 by John Brindley, brother of James Brindley, the canal engineer. The business expanded rapidly and he purchased two adjoining factories built at an earlier date, one by Edward Bourne and the other by Robert Williamson. He extended these buildings and purchased a further factory at Newport, and was ultimately employing fifteen hundred operatives making not only pottery but glass for domestic and architectural purposes. His architectural glass was used extensively for churches and private mansions. He produced both china and earthenware, highly decorated in the manner of Crown Derby and, needless to say, highly collectable today.

In 1806, the firm was visited by the future George IV when he was Prince of Wales, and he along with his brother the Duke of Clarence toured the works. On his accession to the throne, George ordered a superb service for the coronation banquet and Davenports were given permission to display it to fellow manufacturers and friends before delivery. The service was much admired by foreigners at the banquet and George expressed his satisfaction at the achievement of an English potter.

It is interesting that Davenports received the order since the Prince and his retinue, who were guests of the Marquis of Stafford at Trentham Hall, had also visited the Spode factory in Stoke and conferred on them the honour of *'Maker of Pottery to His Majesty'*. Ward describes the preparations which Spode made for this visit in the following words:

> "Mr Spode had arranged that all persons employed, of both sexes, were in their best attire to manifest the respectful and loyal attachment to the heir apparent and the family on the throne, and, as the royal and noble visitors passed through the different departments, the appearance and demeanour of the working classes drew forth repeated eulogies".

Ward made no mention of similar preparations in Burslem, yet Davenports got the order for the Coronation. One can only assume they were even better dressed and better mannered in Burslem!

John Davenport was at one time Member of Parliament for the Burslem area, but this part of his life, as with that of Enoch Wood's, is left to the chapter on social and political conditions. Ward said of him: *"John Davenport Esq. is well known as one of the most enterprising and successful manufacturers; of his worth as a private individual, the numerous instances of his benevolence is the best testimonial."*

On his retirement from the business, he was succeeded by his eldest son Henry who met an untimely death when his horse failed to clear a stone wall while following his hounds. After this sad accident his hounds were sold into Liverpool and shipped there by canal. Amazingly some are said to have escaped and found their way back.

The youngest son William replaced Henry. He purchased Maer Hall from the Wedgwood family, and was the sole owner of the business from 1848 to 1869 when he died. One of his sons appears to have suceeded to the business, but it was uncompetitive, besides being heavily mortgaged, and like many previous examples, another family owned business went into liquidation.

Scarratt says that at the time of the failure, Belgium cut glass tumblers were selling at 3d each, which was the price Davenports were asking for moulded ones. My own father attended the disposal sale and purchased some pieces of cut glass. The factories were sold between 1876 and 1881 to repay the mortgages. The largest, the Unicorn, was sold to Thomas Hughes, who divided it and worked part, latterly making sanitary ware and tiles, but it was demolished in 1961. William Davenport's beautiful mansion at Trubshaw Cross, which he used in conjunction with Maer Hall, was demolished in 1855 and is now housing.

At Dale Hall, an area between Burslem and Longport, there appears to have been two potteries, both with the name Dale Hall Pottery. One, founded in 1790 by Joseph Stubbs, was later occupied by the Mayer brothers. The Mayers were excellent potters who produced some very beautiful vases. The brothers were said to have once produced a large ceramic table described as a chef d'oeuvre (masterpiece) of pottery art. Voyez, the modeller employed by Josiah Wedgwood, was also said to have worked for them.

When the factory inspector conducted his survey in 1842 their factory was one of those visited, and he interviewed Thomas Mayer who said, *"I employ four to five hundred people, many of them young children, some to serve seven years apprenticeship, painters six years, all with an unstamped agreement; stamped it would be a pound and the parents would not pay"*. This was presumably an attempt to retain labour on the guild principle but without the costs of a legal agreement, although he admitted *"many drifted elsewhere"*.

The brothers are said to have bought many of the celebrated Turner's moulds when the Turner's factory at Fenton failed. The two brothers, John and Joseph (or ?Joshua) had previously been lessees of Cliffe Bank Pottery in Stoke where they are reputed to have employed five hundred operatives. The firm was known as Mayer Brothers but at a later stage it became Mayer Brothers & Elliot, and later still Elliot & Co, then Liddle Elliot & Co, Bates Walker & Co, and finally Bates, Gildea & Walker. This last firm listed their range of products as *"Stoneware, Earthenware, Statuary, Jasper and Commodes for travellers."*

The other Dale Hall Pottery was that of the brothers John and George Rogers. It has been described as the oldest pottery in Dale Hall having been built in the 18th century. George Rogers died without issue and left £1000 in support of the proposed North Staffs Infirmary and £200 to raise the tower of Burslem Parish Church, providing this latter was carried out within two years - a proviso never kept, but there was no time restriction on the £1000 and presumably it is incorporated in the brickwork of the Infirmary.

In 1842 the firm was purchased by James Edwards, formerly a partner at the Kiln Croft Pottery where he was originally in partnership with John Maddock, and later with his brother Thomas. James took his son Richard into partnership and the firm became James Edwards & Son. They were awarded many medals at exhibitions for their products. James died in 1867 and a few days before his death, in expectation that it was imminent, he sent a number of his workers cheques of £20 to £100, dependent on their length of service. The subsequent demise of the firm is another of the numerous instances of a family concern which failed to survive beyond the second generation. In the 1880s, the pottery was operating under the title of Knapper & Blackhurst, and, according to Jewett in 1883 it had ceased production.

Anthony Shaw was a prominent potter in the nearby area of Newport, where he is said to have employed a large number of operatives producing ware for both the North and South American market. He was born in 1827. His product seems to have been mostly domestic pottery, which was described as 'Granite Ware', 'Cream Ware' and 'Lustre Ware', the latter said to have been developed in Derby before being produced in Burslem. It was extremely popular at one period, the effect being created by the addition of metal oxides to the glaze. In 1860 he built the Mersey Pottery in the same area. The last occupier of this pottery in more recent years was A.J. Wilkinson.

In spite of the rapid change in ownership or tenancy, there was never any shortage of individuals anxious to become master potters. New names replaced those of the original founders and many of these were second generation potters, having ancestors among the early Burslem pioneers. Among the earlier of these is John Maddock who founded a factory in Newcastle Street in 1830 which was to flourish with the revival in trade following the Napoleonic and American Wars, and the start of the prosperous Victorian period. A brother of John Maddock emigrated to America and established a thriving pottery there. John's son took over the business in Burslem when his father died. He became the second mayor of the town and was generous in his support of many institutions in Burslem. His mother presented the mayoral chain when Burslem became a borough. Ultimately this firm suffered the fate of so many, and following its closure the buildings were finally demolished.

Other firms listed as being in production in the mid-19th century were:

William Barker & Son. They went into liquidation in 1860 but apparently restarted as Barker Sutton & Till making Lustre Ware, Earthenware and Figures. The Barker and Sutton name later vanished and it became Thos. Till & Sons.

William Beech made ornamental china, china figures and parian ware. William died and his widow ran the business, later taking a partner, the company becoming Beech & Podmore.

Cork & Edge. The Edge in this partnership had previously been a confectioner. The firm made earthenware, lustreware, stoneware, and Egyptian Black, and later became Edge & Malkin, making exclusively tiles. This factory was in Newport and known as the Newport Pottery. It originally belonged to Walter Daniel, a member of the ancient Burslem potting family. He sold it to Davenports, and after they went into liquidation it was purchased by Edge & Malkin. They later moved to the Central Pottery in Burslem town. It is possible that it was then occupied by Anthony Shaw who later sold out to A.J. Wilkinson. Ultimately it came into the hands of Pidduck & Beardmore, Engineering Suppliers.

At the Swan Works in Waterloo Road, there was a Mr. S. Johnson making teapots. At the same time he had a factory in Newport Street under the title of Wellington Works, where he employed 120 operatives. This pottery was previously owned by Keeling and Co. who produced some impressive artistic wares, and Keeling was an old established name in the pottery trade.

There were a number of Godwins, possibly related to an older branch of potters. Around 1850 however there were three separate active Godwin firms; Thomas Godwin, Benjamin Clewlow Godwin and John & Robert Godwin. There were other relatively small manufacturers in Burslem around the time of the Godwins, among them: Henry Bold, George Bowers, Jesse Bridgwood and Timothy Edge, James Edwards, William Emberton, John Furnival, Samuel Hallen, Radulphus Hancock, Harding & Cockson, Joseph Harding, Ephriam Hallam, Hawthorne & Nash, Heath & Rigby, Peter Holdcroft & Co, Jas. Edward Keats & Co, Lythia & Corn, Mellor Venables & Co, Edward Pearson, William Pointon, James Taylor, Thomas Till, James Vernon, Edward Walley.

Peoples' tastes are so varied that it is generally unwise to be dogmatic, particularly in relation to art, but this has never deterred criticism, even of the great and successful such as Josiah Wedgwood. An eminent professor once had the temerity to venture the following: *"At great labour and expense he turned out from his workshops imitations, necessarily unsuccessful, of ancient engraved gems and cameos of jasper basaltes and mottled marble, of gem-like cut glass, such as the Portland Vase, and dull copies, feeble in drawing and hard in texture, of beautifully painted Greek vases. Of the natural methods of decoration suitable for pottery, or the life and freedom of the plastic clay rising in graceful forms under the throwers hand, aided by the rhythmical movement of the wheel, he knew nothing; clearly his pottery is dully scholastic and archaeological in style and therefore on the whole should be regarded as a failure, though a very clever and beautiful failure".*

There are similarly contentious views about what are usually termed 'Pottery Figures and Toys' made in the past in Burslem, under appalling conditions and using the sweated labour of men, women, and boys. The owners of the potteries where these were made, mostly small, but considerable in number, were more or less treated with contempt at the time by those who considered themselves legitimate potters, the product only fit for the fairground. Nevertheless these figures were very popular in their day for the mantelpiece and window ledge, besides being a tempting prize offered by the fairmen. Charles Shaw, who came from Burslem, the author of *When I Was a Child,* gives in his book a heart-rending description of life in the Potteries when vicissitude beset a family in the period of the Industrial Revolution. His father worked in one of the factories which made figures and toys. He describes it as a jumble of broken down cottages with workshops neither square, round, or oblong, and situated in an area with broken pavements and open drains. He said he failed to understand how the churchmen and the methodists could sing about the beauty and the delights of the New Jerusalem and allow such conditions to exist!

Also writing of these and similar products in 1906, Scarratt said, *"These people, buying in the cheapest market, think little of the injury this principle causes to others of nearly the same class. This has caused the production of the cheap and shoddy, glaring and inartistic, glistening in nocturnal sales, to be rudely awakened in time to know that the vision of art on the mantelpiece is but a mockery".*

Today on the other hand many of these Figures and Toys are classed as inspirational and are eagerly sought by collectors and museums, in addition to being the subject of many books. Many of the earlier items are interesting in reflecting the mental attitude of the time, such as the whistles made to place in the chimney to frighten away evil spirits, or miniature cradle fertility symbols. Also produced were many quaint money boxes, some in the shape of animals and birds, lively in both form and colour. Other popular items included historical figures, some factual such as Nelson or Napoleon, some fanciful, such as figures from Gilbert and Sullivan and other popular stage productions. Probably the largest collection of these figures to be seen is one of the fascinating exhibits in the Potteries Museum.

Figures and Toys could well include what are termed Toby Jugs although, from the variety of subjects, Character Jugs would probably be a more appropriate name. The interest in these seems to be ageless. Doultons have in modern times introduced many based on characters from Dickens and other classical authors. These have been mainly aimed at collectors - one of Stanley Matthews was recently auctioned for over £3000 - but the original Toby Jugs were for use as well as being attractive. Although thought of as characteristically English, and widely copied on the Continent, it is from the Continent that the original concept came. The first jug originated from the feud between the Huguenots and the Catholic church, and in particular Robert Bellamine, a Jesuit lecturer in theology, who was a formidable propagandist in the 16th century, and in consequence the vessels became known as Bellamine jugs. The jug was in the form of a grotesque caricature of the Cardinal, the body was bulbous, tapering to the neck and carrying a distorted face. Many were imported from Holland and popular with publicans since, unlike the British jugs, they were produced in various capacities.

Two early outstanding Burslem jugs were made by the Wood family and modelled by John Voyez. Voyez was a Frenchman whose skill, seen while he was working in London, was brought to Josiah Wedgwood's attention by his partner Bentley, and Voyez was persuaded to come to Etruria. He was a brilliant modeller and came on a three year contract, but apparently he was an unpredictable character and fell foul of Josiah, who it was said came upon him modelling his coachman's daughter in a semi-nude state during working hours. He was dismissed - Josiah apparently accused him of stealing models and moulds, and in court at Stafford he was sentenced to seven years transportation, but this was later converted to flogging with a cat-o-nine tails and a reduced confinement. During his term of imprisonment his wife, who had accompanied him to the Potteries, died. On his release from prison, Josiah is said to have offered him thity-six shillings a week for the unexpired period of his contract if he would leave the district, but this he refused to do and went to work for Humphrey Palmer of Hanley, whose artistic products competed directly with Josiah Wedgwood. He also worked as a freelance from his home in Cobridge. Among the items he modelled and personally sold were seals similar to those made at Etruria. He issued a catalogue of his products and described himself as a member of the Royal Society of Arts. He did ultimately leave the district and return to London, and little more is known of him except that he married again, and was employed by a studio to model a statue of General Wolfe for Westminster Abbey.

Of the two jugs he modelled for Woods, probably the one most commonly found in private collections or museums is known the Fair Hebe Jug. It is made in the form of a tree trunk with the standing figure of a fair maid being offered by a suitor a bird's nest containing eggs, the theme obviously intended to be symbolic. The other jug is known as the Toby Jug. This is based on an engraving featuring Toby Fillpot, characterising a well known Yorkshire toper named Harry Elwes who was reputed to have drunk two thousand gallons of beer from a silver tankard without taking any food. The jug was sold accompanied by a printed poem headed METAMORPHOSES OR TOBY REDUC'D:

Dear Tom, this brown jug that now foams with mild ale
In which I will drink to Nan of the Vale
Was one Toby Fillpot, a thrifty old soul
As e'er drank a Bottle or fathom'd a Bowl
I'm boozing about 'twas his praise to excel
And among Jolly Topers, he bore off the Bell

It chanc'd as in Dog-days he sat at his ease
In his flow'd woven Arbour as gay as you please
With a friend and a pipe, puffing sorrows away
And with honest old Stinge, was soaking his clay
His breath doors of life on a sudden were shut
And he died full as big as a Dorchester Butt

His body long in the ground it had been
And time into Clay had resolv'D it again
A potter found out in its coverts so snug
And with part of fat Toby, he formed the brown jug
now secured to friendship and mirth and mild ale
So here'S to my lovely sweet Nan of the Vale

Toby Fillpot

In the early industrial period most Burslem figure makers would model a likeness of military and political figures from an illustrated news sheet, those of theatrical artists from a hand bill or programme, or in many instances from a glamourous portrait printed on a music sheet, the piano being in those days the centre of of family entertainment and music sheets abounded. I personally remember seeing stages on the sands at seaside resorts in the early 20th century, where there would be a pianist and a singer, pumping out popular melodies from stage shows of the day. This was followed by a hard sell of the song sheet which usually had an eye catching illustration of the show principals. Biblical figures were probably a product of the mind or from a fanciful illustration in a sunday school book prize.

Among the many interesting Burslem figure makers was George Hood, who had once been a maker of domestic ware with his own factory, but it failed financially. As a previous "legitimate potter" he probably found it embarrassing to buy Walton's figure and toy factory in Navigation Road, however in the aftermath of the Napoleonic wars he made a considerable number of figures of both Wellington and Napoleon. A large number of parts were required to make one of these figures, but for economy of production, some parts were usable on more than one character. For instance one head would suffice for both Wellington and Napoleon, provided they had a different hat. Similarly, arms and legs were capable of being used for both limbs; who would notice providing that they were bent a bit differently in the clay state? Ill fortune struck Hood again; a warehouse floor collapsed and three women working below were seriously injured; which gives emphasis to the decrepit condition of some of these workshops described in Charles Shaw's *When I Was a Child*.

Obadiah Sherratt, born in 1796, and twice married, was another well known figure maker. He and his second wife were both illiterate but at their factory they produced many interesting animal figures, some static, some in action such as bull baiting, or a tiger at the kill. They also produced domestic parodies, as one might see depicted in Punch. All the figures were very colourful, and today very collectable. The Sherratts were equally as economical as Hood with their moulds. It was rumoured that the teats of cows and the Duke of Wellingtons nose came from the same mould! A particularly elaborate

Wedgwood pottery decorated by Saddler and Green of Liverpool

Wedgwood Creamware

A Wedgwood vase

A vase by Wedgwood and Bentley

Below: The showrooms of Wedgwood and Byerley in London

composition followed a visit to the Burslem area of a circus in 1814 owned by a famous showman named Polito. It featured animals and a multitude of circus characters, all in the brightest colours. It was a very intricate piece and examples are probably rare, but two copies are to be found in local museums, one in the Potteries Museum in Hanley and one in Newcastle under Lyme. When a later circus, Bostock and Wombwells, came to the district, dust was blown off the original Polito moulds, and, following the usual economical practice of manipulating the figures to suit the occasion, the masterpiece was presented afresh.

Bostock and Wombwells circus must have survived for many years, since I have vivid recollections of seeing it round about the period of the First World War. It came to the site of a demolished factory at the junction of Shelton Old Road and Hartshill Road, and I confess that I played truant for the first and only time in my life, along with a fellow student whose parents kept the Noahs Ark in Hartshill. There was no Big Top, just a modest tent in which there was an elevated circus ring. It was standing room only; juniors, including us, were, we thought, privileged to be ushered to the front row with a first class view. There were the usual lions and tigers - I fail to remember if they were introduced as man eating - but I have every reason to remember the grand finale which featured - could I call it "a pride of hyenas"? - all trained to circle at speed round the perimeter, leaping majestically over stools placed at intervals, and encouraged by the long and evil looking whip of the ringmaster who stood menacingly in the centre. Unfortunately there was no pre-warning that the beasts were not house trained and as they reached maximum velocity, one, or maybe more, were taken short, and my friend and I were at the right height and in the right position - the wires of the cage only stopped a limited amount. The deposits of a pig rank high in stench, but I am confident that no one would get a licence to keep a Hyena. How we arrived home in approachable condition, even after sacrificing good handkerchiefs and the use of all the paper and water we could lay our hands on, is difficult to understand.

Obviously there is a moral involved, but it had nothing to do with the Sherratts, and I have digressed from their story. Obadiah died before Sarah, but she continued the business for many years with the assistance of her son Hamlet.

No doubt there are many who recall the woolly poodles or the spotted dalmatians which sat on their haunches staring superciliously from each end of the fireplace, or the 'Flat Backs' made to suit the narrow mantelshelves of the time. Hundreds were made and hundreds have disappeared, broken, probably in child play or the victims of changing fashion. Of the firms who made this type of pottery we have only dealt with a limited number, as also indeed with the many 'legitimate potters'. It is possible that there are still some offspring of old Burslem families who could, from hearsay, add to our knowledge of these early pioneers. It has been said that in the middle of the 19th century there were approximately one hundred and fifty pottery factories in Burslem, employing some seven thousand people.

No doubt the figure also included firms producing building materials, production of which was significant since an abundance of coal and suitable clays were available. An important firm in this capacity was owned by the Haywood Brothers whose business was in the Brownhills area. They made drainage pipes, terracotta figures for architectural embellishment, besides bricks, tiles, chimney pots, etc. The brothers were bachelors and one left money for the poor of Burslem, but following his death there was considerable and protracted litigation in connection with the legacy until finally agreement was reached that the money should be used to build the Haywood Hospital - which is described in a later chapter.

Shaw, in 1829, gives some current prices for the class of materials which Haywood's produced:

> Facing Bricks 30/- per thousand
> Roofing Tiles 34/- per thousand
> Drain Pipes 30inches long x 6 inches diameter. Each eightpence

These prices included a government tax, but who would object to that if one was fortunate enough to find some originally priced old stock in a builder's merchant yard today.

The combined output from all sections of the industry resulted in a demand for labour and the growth of population in Burslem, as the following statistics indicate:

Year	1738	1762	1785	1801	1811	1821	1831	1838
Population	1800	2000	4800	6486	8748	9815	12572	14486

The rapid change of ownership and the number of failures within the industry was so obvious that it influenced Ward to write the following:

"Casting a retrospective glance over the course of events for thirty to forty years, the unwelcome fact is forced upon one's notice that, notwithstanding the great increase in business, and the improvements, and trebled population to which it has given rise, the success of individuals who have embarked on it has been extremely hazardous, and that of their future in more than a majority of instances. We do not hesitate indeed to assert that in the period we refer to, we have witnessed the ruin of a larger number of potters than are now engaged in the trade. On the other hand, we have seen many individuals, who from the condition of operatives have, by their industry, talents, and prudence, acquired deserved respectability, and even opulence, while others, who succeeded to established businesses, have by contrary course gone the downward road."

The experience of one who went the downward road was related by John Wesley in 1784 when visiting Burslem:

"I came to our old steady friends here, but he with whom I used to lodge is no more, he trusted the Americans with all his substance and they cheated him out of all, so he came home and died, leaving an amiable widow and six or seven children."

Ward observed on this particular affair that *"like other branches of English manufacturers, that of Earthenware and China has been sometimes carried to excess, and failure caused by indiscreetly forcing the goods on the market."* Dr. Franklin, who assisted in drafting the American Act of Independence, said in a letter from Philadelphia in 1789 to a bank in Burslem, he would vindicate his countrymen from the imputation of dishonesty, and threw the blame on English merchants who, he said, *"acted imprudently in forcing goods on the Americans which had not been ordered, and were beyond the facilities of their country to consume, and the surplus therefore was sent to the auction houses, where it frequently sold for less than prime cost."* What cannot be denied is that, even if the financial success of the individual pottery manufacturer was all too often in jeopardy, the commercial success of the product as a whole from the Burslem potteries was beyond question. That it had been achieved by suffering, broken health and early death is also beyond doubt, since a good life span of a potter was nearer fifty than sixty years, and would probably include many years of physical inability to work and slowly wasting away.

It was inevitable that Mother Burslem's sons would emulate their parent, and indeed the point was now reached where there was great rivalry between the towns which had grown up around their mother's house, all anxious to prosper in a trade which, apart from the periodic chaos caused by war, seemed at one time to face an insatiable world appetite for its product. But there was a growing world outside, and Parliament in 1910 decided that it was logical for mother and sons to physically unite. Mother Burslem had to concede her matriarchal position and become part of the larger unitary borough of Stoke on Trent. Since then, two world wars have impoverished the country and its towns, including Burslem, which, like many, saw poor growth until late in the 20th century. When she lost her individual identity, the story of Mother Burslem's expansion from hamlet to a self sufficing industrial town was virtually completed.

Scarratt, reminiscing in 1906, said that *"Burslem up to the middle of the last century could boast the finest edifices and expansive manufactures in Staffordshire, Enoch Wood's factory with its front to the East, and its mansion facing the West still has an imposing appearance, but is fast hastening to decay. Alcock's, which was adjacent, and was possibly more imposing, has gone completely, and it is only parts of Enoch Wood's which are left".* He also remarked that *"while artistic excellence is still achieved, it is futile to hold the idea of supplying the whole globe with utilitarian ware, not because they could not, but because of innumerable fixed and other difficulties including competition by distant countries, and even by some of our colonies".*

He might have added that our forefathers left us with a heavy price price to pay for the ruination

The start of the Hamil from Wegwood street. From left to right, the Big House, the Red Lion, and the pottery on the corner

Old Bank, Burslem. An early two kiln pottery

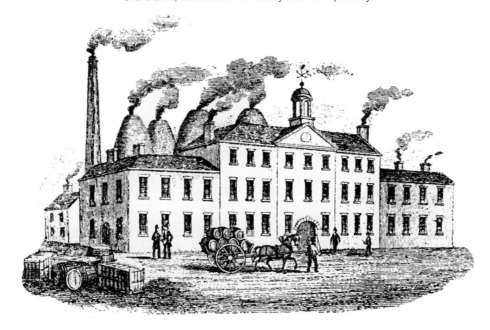

Greengates Pottery

Potters in Burslem in 1787 and 1818

Wm. Adams & Co. Cream-coloured ware and China glaze ware painted.
Wm. Bagley, potter.
John Bourne, China glaze, blue painted, enamelled and cream coloured earthenware.
Bourne & Malkin, China glaze, blue painted, enamelled and cream coloured earthenware.
S. & J. Cartlidge, potters.
Thos. Daniel, potter.
John Daniel, cream colour and red earthenware.
Timothy Daniel, Do.   do.
Walter Daniel, Do.   do.
John Graham jun., white stone, and enamelled white and cream earthenware.
John Green.
Thos. Holland, black and red china ware, and gilder.
Anthony Keeling, Queens ware in general, blue painted, and enamelled, and Egyptian black.
Timothy & John Lockett, white stone potters.
Burnham Malkin.
John Robinson, enameller and printer of cream colour and china glazed ware.
John & George Rogers, china glazed, blue painted, and cream coloured ware.
Ambrose Smith & Co., cream coloured ware, china glazed, blue painted.
John & Joseph Smith.
Chas. Stevenson & sons, cream coloured ware, blue painted.
Thos. Wedgwood, (Big House), cream coloured ware, china glazed, painted with blue etc.
Thos. Wedgwood, (Overhouse), cream coloured ware, china glazed, painted with blue etc.
James Wilson, enameller.
John Wood, potter.
Enoch & Ralph Wood, all kinds of useful and ornamental earthenware, Egyptian black, cane, and various other colours, also black figures, seals and cyphers.
Josiah Wood [*sic*, but should be Wedgwood], fine black, glazed, variegated and cream coloured ware, and blue.

Above: potters in Burslem in 1787 from a survey by William Tunnicliffe

Right: potters in Burslem in 1818 from a survey byParson and Bradshaw

From *Staffordshire Pottery and its History* by Josiah C. Wedgwood c,1920

T. & E. Bathwell, Chapel Bank.
J. & R. Blackwell, Cobridge.
W. Bourne, Bell Works.
Jos. Bradshaw, Booden Brook (Cobridge)
Philip Brooks & Co., Sitch.
Cartledge & Beech, Knowle.
Ralph & J. Clews, Cobridge.
J. & J. Davenport, Newport.
Frank & N. Dillon, Cobridge.
B. & S. Godwin, Cobridge.
T. & B. Godwin, New Basin.
Goodfellow & Bathwell, Upper House Works.
John & Ralph Hall, Sitch & Tunstall.
John Heath, Sitch.
Henshall & Williamson, Longport.
Thos. Heath, Hadderage
Ephraim Hobson, Cobridge.
Holdcroft & Box, Cobridge.
Anne Holland, Hill Top, Burslem.
Ric. Jarvis, Nile Street, Burslem.
Ralph Johnson, Church St., Burslem.
Jonathan Leak, The Row.
Machin & Baggaley, Low St.
Joseph Machin, Waterloo Road.
Sam. Marsh, Brownhills.
Ric. Massey, Castle St.
S. & T. Massey, Nile St.
John Mellor, near the Market Place.
John Moseley, Cobridge.
John Moseley, Churchyard Works.
Wm. Moseley, Queen St., Black Works.
Oliver & Bourne, Cobridge.
J. & R. Riley, Hill Works.
J. & C. Robinson, Hill Top Works.
John Rogers & Sons, Longport.
Spencer Rogers, Dale Hall.
Wm. Stanley, Knowle Works.
Dan. Steel, St. Johns St.
Ralph Stevenson, Cobridge.
Andrew Stevenson, Cobridge.
Ben. Stubbs, Longport.
Sam. Tompkinson, Church Street.
Wm. Walsh, Furlong.
John Walton, Hadderage.
James Warburton, Hot Lane.
John Warburton, Hot Lane.
Wedgwood & Johnson, High Street.
Wood & Caldwell, Fountain Place.
Ephraim Wood, Hole House.

Three pieces by 'toymakers' like Obadiah Sherratt

A pottery model that commemorates a famous lion

Figures by Ralph Wood:
Hercules right
and below left
The Boxer

An example of popular music sheet which
inspired the production of a pottery figure

An example of the many popular satirical
studies in both clay and illustration is this
piece called 'The Vicar and Moses'

Left, a Godwin plate, and right, an Alcock plate

Above: an Adams jug

Right: a Wedgwood teapot.

which early industrialisation created in the surrounding amenities. It is ironic and distinctly contradictory that while producing a product which contributed greatly to the quality and beauty of the life for others, it should lead to the widespread besmirching of our own environment. One can understand the remark of a stranger who, passing through, pondered *"who were the parents, midwife, and undertaker of this vista?"*. Another visitor, on viewing it for the first time remarked that *"Dante had lived before his time"*.

Not all the ills of decline are to be blamed on foreign competition, or on wars. Unbelievable lack of skill in marketing for profit with a product of such beauty, and produced by workers with such artistic skills, is evident in the number of bankruptcies, and the poor quality of the structures in which such works of art were produced. Scarratt spoke of imposing buildings, but these were rare and there is no urge to put a preservation order on those that are left today, yet a significant number of factories built in Lancashire and Yorkshire, let alone the nearby mill towns of Leek and Macclesfield, during the same industrial revolution, are not only still sturdy, but preserved for their imposing appearance. The cotton, wool and silk trade ssuffered equally as the Potteries, but have at least left a look of past financial prosperity in the workplace and civic buildings. A government report in 1986 confirmed the finality of diminished trade:

> "Old concentrations of work, in the great nineteenth century industrial centres of the North and the Midlands seem to be clearly losing their economic vitality. One third of its manufacturing base has been lost since 1970. Britain generally is undergoing post industrial contraction. It is the first industrial nation to experience this, as it was the first to experience an industrial revolution".

Burslem and the other pottery towns may have boasted imposing facades to many of its factories, but to the generations who suffered the vicissitudes of war in the 20th century the conditions within were no longer acceptable, neither was the pollution they discharged. The reaction is symbolised in the book *Potbank*, the author of which was Mervyn Jones, who had resided in the area at one time. Returning on a visit in 1960 he remarked that: *"Dozens of potbanks have closed their gates during the last half century, and rarely has the building been put to other use... A great deal of what seems to be empty land is covered in spoil and waste from two centuries of industry..... You cannot walk anywhere for long without seeing deserted houses, singly, or in rows. Deserted shops, deserted pubs, and of course deserted potbanks.* He further said; *I have heard it rumoured that a smokeless zone is to be decreed in Stoke-on-Trent; I should say this would be the most unrealistic enterprise since American prohibition"*

Of the pottery factories themselves, he said they were *"dark satanic mills, not standing in industrial estates, but along streets with houses leaning on them. Dozens have closed their doors, I went round one, the ash was thick around the cone of the oven, the saggars, a deep burned orange, were carelessly stacked, the machines had been sold off, but the last of the stock abandoned among a litter of mould boards. There is a plan for a proposed civic centre; so far a museum has been built, an adequate but not exactly an exciting building, with a remarkable collection of pottery, but around the building stretches a cinder deposit. The potteries is just entering the motoring age, and for anyone coming from the south, it is astonishing to see how easily the traffic moves through this concentrated urban area. I did not once see a traffic jam when I walked up the main road from Stoke to Hanley at half past five. There is no parking problem, either in working hours, or for Saturday shopping"*.

What an example of how, in a comparatively short time evils can be eradicated, and equally can develop! If Mervyn Jones came back today he would find that the same spirit which made this the centre of the pottery trade in the British Isles has succeeded in converting his areas of cinder deposit into green and pleasant land. On the other hand, people no longer walk as he did from Stoke to Hanley and he would fail now to be astonished at how well the traffic moves!

Brownhills house was built by John Wood (grandson of Ralph Wood) in 1792, together with a manufactory nearby. It was also the home of his son, John Wood, who in 1807 married Mary, daughter of John Baddeley and Mary Wedgwood (daughter of John Wedgwood of the Big House). Brownhills is described as a handsome house with handsome landscaped gardens (after the manufactory was demolished) commanding a fine view of Bradwell Woods, St Pauls and Wolstanton churches.

Shaw describes Watlands House as 'a superb mansion where Spencer Rogers esq. enjoys the sweets of domicillary quiet after the fatigues of commercial activity.' John Rogers and Son were table ware manufacturers in Longport. John Rogers left £1000 for the North Staffordshire Infirmary

19th century Daveport pottery. Highly decorated and nowadays much prized

Longport Hall. Probably the site of John Burslem's earlier Dale Hall, which was extended or
rebuilt by John Williamson and sold by him to John Davenport. When the Davenports left the
Hall to move to Maer Hall it became a school (see Wedgwood Institute, Chapter 24)

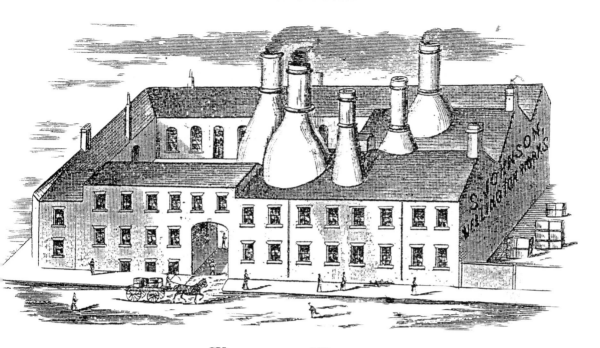

There were two Wellington Works in Burslem, one in Waterloo Road and the other in Newport Street. The latter was for a period occupied by Keelings, an ancient family of Burslem Potters whose work is much sought after now

Samuel Alcock's pottery was on Liverpool Road, now Westport Road, and was later demolished

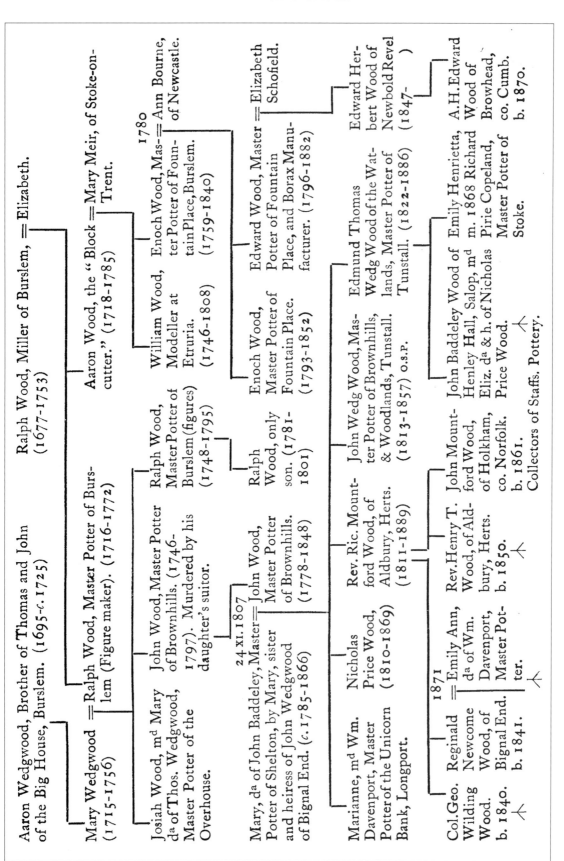

A family history of the Wood family mainly, but showing some of the intermarriage amongst the Burslem potters.
(*Staffordshire Pottery and its History* by Josiah C. Wedgwood c.1920)

The Overhouse pottery, originally owned by Thomas Wedgwood, a cousin of Josiah

Wades' Royal Pottery, on or near the site of the original Hill Pottery at the entrance to the Sytch.

TWO PROMOTIONAL REVIEWS IN A TRADE DIRECTORY C.1870

One of the most important establishments in Burslem is the "Providence Foundry," belonging to the well-known engineer Mr. William Boulton whose fame as the inventor of machinery for tile Potteries and elsewhere has spread over the world. The works were established in 1852. There are extensive moulding shops and wheelmoulding machinery, and one special feature of the department is the famous Helical Toothed Wheels. The pattern shop is sixty feet long. The works cover a large extent of ground, the largest of their kind in the neighbourhood. Mr. Boulton's specialities are the manufacture of Machinery for Potteries and Encaustic Tile Works and Brick Works, Local Engineering work for Collieries, also the manufacture of Heating Apparatus for drying stoves and for warming public buildings, by exhaust or fresh steams, also high or low pressure hot-water system.

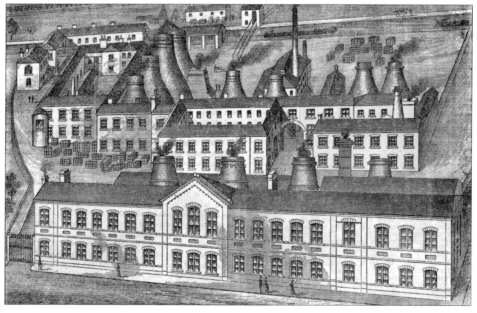

Edge, Malkin,& Co., Manufacturers of Ironstone-China and Earthenware, Burslem is one of the chief centres of the earthenware industry in the Potteries. The founding took place in the year 1817 and ever since it has steadily grown in importance and influence. The works cover altogether about five acres of ground, and are admirably situated as regards railway and water facilities. They comprise finely appointed and commodious offices, spacious warehouses and showrooms, packing warehouses, and workshops and departments for manufacturing. The number of hands is close on three hundred and fifty. Messrs. Edge, Malkin, & Co. manufacture all kinds of printed, painted enamelled, and gilt dinner, tea, and toilet ware, in white, ivory, and other coloured bodies, also gold lustre and black ware. Their productions are remarkable for soundness, durability, thorough efficiency, and high-class finish. A large trade is being done in all parts of the kingdom, the colonies and in foreign countries.

CHAPTER FOUR: Civic growth

Early primitive housing. Wakes, their importance and abuses. The first town hall.

The original Burslem could be called a hill top settlement, and remains today primarily as shown on Enoch Wood's map of 1740, with buildings round the perimeter - but at that time the perimeter was only partially filled with factories, tradesmen's premises, public houses and the odd shop - all facing an open space which was later to become the market place. The whole area, like the roads, was largely unpaved.

With a population of 2000 in 1740 and growing rapidly, house building was spreading from the centre in the direction of Bournes Bank, Nile Street, the Sytch, and Swan Bank. There were no building laws and the original houses were of poor quality, the earliest only having one ground floor room with a staircase off to a communal bedroom. Both rooms had low ceilings. The ground floor fireplace was used for cooking, water heating and for burning rubbish, since there were no refuse bins. Ash was dumped, usually outside the house on to unmade roads devoid of pavements. Lighting was by candle or oil lamp, and everything left or entered the house by the one door. Toilets, or privies as they were commonly called, were for communal use, and were in a separate building away from the houses. The number provided would vary according to the number of houses, but here again there was no legal stipulation. A favoured method was to build the houses in a square block with the toilets in the centre. When later building control was introduced, one inspector found an instance of a single toilet to fourteen houses. Usually the toilets were built as a block and divided into units, each unit having a pit over which was a wooden platform with either one or two holes, the latter one can only assume to cater for either the need for company as with children or the ill or frail. There was no drainage, the pits were manually emptied from time to time by men known as night-soil men, since the operation was carried out at night, the sewage being loaded into horse-drawn carts and dumped on farmland.

The scarcity of shops in Burslem necessitated a weekly walk to Newcastle to obtain food or clothing, other than items which could be bought from itinerants, or, as Enoch Wood observed, the occasional

Burslem workers' terraced cottages built about 1800. There were communal privies to the rear of the houses

Reginald Haggar's painting of early 19th century Burslem housing, built during the period of window tax

carcase brought for sale in the market place. No doubt it is this state of affairs which induced employers to operate the truck system of payment in kind. There was one small charity school, but only one in three children received any education, since it seemed to be an accepted understanding by parents, that children should support the family income as soon as they were capable of understanding the meaning of obedience. The churches were more or less moribund; evangelism was in its infancy and culture was practically non-existent.

It is not surprising that, with long working hours and isolated living, the only attraction for a great many were the ale houses, and the anticipation of the recognised fairs, or wakes, of which there were six per year, 8th of February, 29th of March, 17th of May, 28th of June, 13th of September, and 26th of December. These were occasions of ribald and licentious behaviour, dreaded by the pottery manufacturers for their effect on attendance, but looked forward to with pleasurable anticipation by the workers.

Of these six fairs, the main one was in June and centred on the feast of St John, the patron saint of Burslem parish church. According to Ward, the original practice when the church was a wood and plaster structure, was to decorate it with trees and shrubs, representing St. John in the wilderness, but the garlands which once decorated the church now decorated the entrance to the town to welcome the fair or wake. There were numerous itinerant performers and entertainers, acrobats, wire-walkers, jugglers, dancers, a travelling circus maybe, or a menagerie, the latter usually claiming ownership of rare and extinct specie. Many of the acts would have a prefix of royal, claiming to have performed in the presence of royalty. It was probably at one of these fairs that the young Enoch Wood saw the two men exhibiting their mounted model of the crucifixion.

The infatuation of these fairs for the inhabitants of the town never waned, indeed it increased as the town got bigger and more prosperous. Following the introduction of the steam engine they became even more grand. Excitement mounted when the wagons came within sight, pulled by massive engines belching steam and smoke. There were wire mesh cages mounted on platform trucks with fierce animals and artistes parading in fancy dress beside the trucks, handing out 'flyers' describing the wonders being brought to Burslem. With fantastic speed, the town was covered with amusements, swing boats, helter skelters, hobby horses, and massive ornate organs with figures playing instruments and a cacophony of sound. There were side shows everywhere; bawling showmen describing wonders like the two headed woman or the genuine live mermaid, brought to Burslem at great expense; shooting galleries where

Burslem could literally get its own back, with prizes of dozens of flat-back figures made by Burslem's own potters; roll a penny stalls - and a penny was handsome pocket money in those days. The electric fishing tank was filled with Mediterranean blue water; each contestant with a short fishing rod and as the water was agitated, they attempted to hook the fish with a prize for the one who hooked the most while the water was alive. Coconut stalls; and boxing booths, where a professional pugilist tempted the drunk, or semi drunk, to a friendly bash, offering the successful candidate money, but with the result that he left looking, and feeling, a sadder, possibly wiser, and rarely richer man.

Fighting was evidently in the blood of many, since, at the turn of the century when Burslem had only one constable named Cooper, his constant complaint at fairs was *"what can I do? They're fighting from Enoch Wood's to Billy Barlow's, if there is one man stripped to his buff there is a hundred, and if I charge the peace they won't tak' any notice of may".* He was usually advised by his superiors to *"let them have a go as they generally get tired bye and bye."* On one occasion Mr Cotton, the landlord of the Legs of Man,

A bare-fist fight

who was also a churchwarden, foresaw a fight developing on his premises and appealed to the Chief Bailiff for advice. The Bailiff enquired who were involved and was told it was Burnett and Big Ben; *"Oh well,"* said the Bailiff, *"clear the tables and chairs and see fair play,"* on which advice Mr Cotton went back and is reported to have said, *"you may go at it lads, I've got the permission of the Bailiff"*

As dusk fell, the whole town was a mass of light from the naphthalene lamps on the stalls and the booths, and the strings of lights generated from power supplied by the giant engines which had previously brought the trucks to town, now sending blood curdling shrieks to the heavens like prehistoric monsters. The ale houses were full and crowds seethed around in the night, anxious to absorb it all and knowing that the following day would bring further thrills from established customs. There was cock fighting, still not unknown today although long since banned, but so accepted in those days that many public houses had their own cock pits. The fighting birds were large bodied with short legs and a scarcity of feathers, making them, so it was said, unpleasant to look at. Mains, described in the dictionary as a fight between cocks, were regularly and publicly advertised. One such locally, was advertised:

"The gentlemen of Derbyshire, versus the gentlemen of Staffordshire, to shew and weigh 41 Cocks for the Mains, and 10 Cocks for the Byes, for 4 guineas a Battle, and 50 for the Main".

The sport was of such standing it had developed a language of its own. An eye witness, describing the event, said the birds would be released one at a time, to strut about the pit and be evaluated by the spectators, following which the bookmakers would be busy since betting was heavy. The birds would now be armed with steel or silver spurs attached to the legs and released to fight, rarely giving up before one of them expired. The noise was hardly bearable while the fight was in progress. In *The Folklore of Staffordshire* there is a rhyme which vividly reflects the atmosphere:

At Wedensfield at one village wake
The cockers all did meet
At Billy Lane's the Coalfishes
To have a sporting treat

For Charley Marson's spangled cock
Was matched to fight a red
That came from Wil'n'all o'er the fields
And belonged to Cheeky Ned

Two finer birds in any cockpit
The never yet was seen
Though the Wedensfield man declared
Their cock was sure to win

The cocks fought hard and feathers flew
All round about the pit
While blood from both of 'em did flow
Yet ner'en would submit

At last the spangled Wedensfield bird
Began to show defeat
When on the word Cheeky Ned
Got up and knocked old Charley down

To fight all went like bulldogs
As it is very well known
Till Cheeky Ned seized Billy's thumb
And bit it to the bone

At this the Wedensfield men began
Their comrades part to take
And never was a fiercer fight
Fought at a village wake

They beat the men from Wil'n'all town
Back to their town again
And long they will remember
This Wedensfield wake and main

In Fountain Square there was a bear pit, in which travelling bears were chained and dogs introduced to provide them with company. Bull baiting was another favourite pastime. Collections would be organised for the purchase of bulls, and as many as three or four bulls would be bought for a fair. The bulls, decorated with ribbons, were paraded round the town by a man called the 'Bellat' and subsequently tied by a rope about fifteen feet long, one end attached to its horns, the other end to a ring usually secured in the ground outside a public house. Those with dogs stood around, and individual dogs, or as many as the Bellat ordered, were let loose. Naturally the bull, in playful manner, attempted to toss the dog. If it was successful the dog's neck was usually broken when it fell to the ground. The animal was beaten with clubs, and had cats, dogs, monkeys, and fireworks tied to its tail, all to infuriate it. The bulls did sometimes break loose. One such occasion is recorded where, *"at least twelve people were involved and two or three so seriously injured that their lives were despaired of. One had his thigh lacerated several*

inches deep; a man from Chesterton had two ribs broken and his head cut in a dreadful manner, and a person from Longport so much hurt that recovery was doubtful." The event usually ended with the bull being butchered and roasted in the market place and the inhabitants of Burslem enjoying a feast for a few pence. As with cock fighting, it required the introduction of a law to prohibit this obscene display before it was abandoned.

A curious custom, which took place at Easter, was known as 'heaving' and involved a group of men who on Easter Monday would roam the streets looking for members of the opposite sex on whom they would pounce, and then lift and throw above their heads three times, after which the victim would be expected to kiss each of the men, or pay a silver forfeit. On the next day, Easter Tuesday, the practice would be in reverse, the women would lift or throw the men and demand the same forfeit - which seems to conflict with the appellation "the tender sex". Obviously, differences in stature of the victim must have determined the exuberance with which the practice could be carried out, but, with drink flowing, and the mind confused, it is not surprising that criticism of the custom and demand for its cessation arose, and it is unlikely to be brought back, even as a tourist attraction.

'Goose riding' was another pastime, and involved the use of live geese tied to a horizontal rope by their legs and dangling seven or eight feet from the ground with their necks well greased. The object was for competitors, riding on ponies, to grab the birds by the neck and pull off their heads as they dashed past. Another disgusting practice was 'cock throwing'. A cord about ten feet long was attached to a stake, the other end being fastened to the cock's leg. At a distance of some twenty yards, missiles were thrown at the cock, the object being to hit the cock and grab it before it recovered its balance. If successful, the contestant could claim the bird. A well trained bird was said to be a profitable investment for the owner. Some birds had a remarkable capacity for judging the direction of the missile, showing great agility and surviving for a long time - their great failing was their inability to learn how to throw the missile back!

The noble sport of cricket was not overlooked but the form in which it was played was very different to that of today. There were only two stumps, a foot high, and two feet apart. A third stump lay across the top. The space between the vertical stumps was known as the popping hole. Apparently there was no crease, and the batsman was out if the wicket keeper popped the ball through this space before the batsman had his bat down in line with the stumps. There were occasions when the wicket keeper would howl with pain if his popping hand got in the way of the bat on its journey to earth. The bat was curved, somewhat like a hockey stick, and the bowling was underarm. Should the ball go through the popping hole without disturbing any of the stumps, the batsman was not out. If played seriously the contestants would wear top hats and long coats - presumably sponsors adverts on their shirts had not yet been considered. There were sometimes freak games involving perhaps eleven one armed men versus eleven one legged men and such contestants would not be hard to find in those days among the veterans from the Peninsula and Napoleonic wars. Josiah Wedgwood observed in a letter to Bentley, his partner in London, during a June wake; *"Our men have been at play four days this week, it being Burslem wakes. I have rough'd and Smooth'd them over, and promised them a long Xmas, but I know it is all in vain, for wakes must be observed, though the world was to end with them."*

The old game of cricket

Ward observed in the 1830s when his work was published that *"there was an improvement over the vulgar and demoralising scenes which occurred prior to abolishing the practice of bull baiting"*, but *"the country wakes are at best poor expedients for allaying the cravings of young persons for occasional amusement, and at present observed, they only operate as incentives to excess and licentiousness. The man who should succeed in introducing some wholesome and innocent pastime recreation to gratify the natural passion of youthful liveliness and joy, divested of these gross and immoral results, which wakes and fairs and their concommitant exhibitions produce, would entitle himself to being enrolled amongst the real benefactors of mankind."*

The Reverend H.V. Stuart DD, whose first appointment in the ministry was as curate at St Paul's in Burslem, and who subsequently for twenty years was rector of Stoke, came to the town when the vicar was Lovelace Stamer, who never missed taking advantage of the crowds at the fair. On occasions he invited a Mr Brown, a missionary from London, who he said was 'well respected' by the fair people in the quiet of Sunday morning. On one occasion, the rector and curate decided to hold a meeting on the Sunday night and the whole town centre was filled with a laughing jostling crowd. Very often, one of the bigger shows would offer them a platform outside the show to speak from. On this particular Sunday, the vicar and curate arrived at St John's Square at eight o'clock and Sedgwick's Menagerie promised them the use of a platform. They offered to attract the people by turning on their mechanical organ, although the nearest approach they had to a hymn was the National Anthem. That appears to have been an adequate substitute since it attracted a crowd, so that before long they had two thousand people around, and in the windows of the public houses looking on to the square were many more looking out. Strangely enough for Burslem wakes, Stuart said, it was a lovely warm evening! When it came to his turn to speak he said the lions in the menagerie started to roar loudly - he did not know whether it was a protest against his doctrine, or the proximity of a great crowd, but it was very disconcerting for him, and very amusing for the crowd.

The latter part of the 18th century still saw an increasing demand for domestic pottery in the home market despite the turmoil in Europe. The dramatic reduction in the price of tea brought about a much greater use by families in preference to ale, which had been widely drunk by man woman and child in consequence of the poor quality of the water. Furthermore, the increasingly attractive domestic pottery now available from Burslem and its neighbourhood kept its heat better and was cheaper than pewter from which most domestic utensils had previously been made - the price of which had been strictly maintained by the Pewter Guild. All these factors led to increasing demand and in turn expanding production, the extent of the latter probably reflected in the number of patents applied for in the pottery industry, which in the 25 years after 1760 were more than in the century and a half which preceded it.

As the town prospered, the more enlightened citizens of Burslem were developing civic pride, and in 1760 a group of the more opulent perceived the need for the expansion of education, and proposed that a school should be built in the centre of the blossoming town. A subscription list was opened, and an appeal made to the landowners, Ralph Sneyd and Sir Nigel Gresley, Bart. It was drafted, in Ward's words, *"in a style to which country gentlemen were accustomed"*, and accompanied by the list of subscribers to date. The following copy of this interesting draft makes the proposals of the contributors self explanatory:

"To the Hon, Sir Niegel Greasley, Bart, and Ralph Sneyd, Esq
Lords of the Manner within the Liberty of Burslem.

We whose names are here under subscribed being the Gentlemen and Freeholders within the said Liberty and Manner do humbly petition to your Honours for a small piece of Land lying in Burslem, where the May-pole did formerly stand in order to errect a piece of Building for a Schoole as there is but one Schoole in the Town and for the want of an other two parts of the Children out of three are put to Work without any Learning by reason the other Schoole is not sufficient to instruct them. So we humbly beg your Honours that you will be pleas'd to be aiding and assisting in this and consider that it is a great piece of Charity done by your Honours which will be in memory of you and your posterity for ever and the prayers of the poor will allways be with you so we hope your Honours will be agreeable to this Charitable request, And we your petitioners shall be in duty bound to you for the same. WE whose names are hereunto annexed do firmly promis to advance the sums of money following our names to be applyed in errecting the piece of Building for the use and purpose above mentioned that is to say a schoole for the education of poor children. And that every person who shall subscribe five pounds him is Heirs Execut'rs Administrators and Assignes shall have a voat in the above Schoole. And every person who shall subscribe Ten pounds him his heirs Execut'rs Administrators and Assignes shall have two voats. And every person that shall subscribe more than their Heirs Exxecut'rs Administrators and Asssignes shall have their shares of voats according to their subscription above mentioned. And there shall be chose by a majority a proper Committee to errect and manage the said Building and to take care it be well and strongly built. And that the said Committee shall place a proper Schoole master for the education of the children; provided that the schoole master shall at any time behave himself ill then the said Committee shall dismiss him and place another in is room. And that every person subscrib'd according to the intent above them their Heirs Execut'rs Administrators and Assignes shall have their voats as above mentioned concerning the said Schoole. Dated ye 7th day of Nov'r 1760 and in the reigne of George the 3rd over Great Britain France and Ireland King Defender of the Faith &c".

	£	s	d		£	s	d
R. Sneyd	10	0	0	Wm. Lockett	6	6	
Nigel Greasley	10	10	0	Samuel Lowe	5	0	0
By order of Mr Murhall	10	0	0	James Bould	5	0	0
Tho's Wedgwood	10	0	0	Ralph & Sam Daniel	10	0	0
John Shrigley	10	0	0	Peter Bagnall	10	0	0

Wm. Taylor	10	0	0	Francis Rogers	10	0	0
Burs'em Wedgwood	10	0	0	Ralph Allen	5	0	0
John Taylor	10	0	0	Josiah Marsh	5	0	0
John Brindley	10	0	0	Rob't Bucknall	5	0	0
John Hales	10	0	0	Thos. Cartlich + his mark	5	0	0
Tho's & Isaiah Taylor	10	0	0	Richeard Beech	5	0	0
Taylor Stevenson	10	0	0	John Harrison	5	0	0
Josiah Wedgwood	10	0	0	Ralph Cartlidge + his mark	5	0	0
John Warburton	10	0	0	By order of Tho. Daniel	5	0	0
Tho's & Rd. Daniel	12	0	0	Enoch Booth Jun'r	5	0	0
Jos. Warburton	10	0	0	The quarterly collection	78	17	4
Jacob & Isa. Warburton	10	0	0	Paed from the old club	10	0	0
Stephens & Mare	10	0	0	Jos. Bucknall	10	0	0

Besides the above, there are several smaller sums, subscribed by various Individuals, to the amount of £33, making, in the whole £506 16 6.

Agreement was reached on the lease of the land where the old Maypole stood. The lease was for a period of 500 years at a yearly rental of 6d. to build a market hall, school, or such other public use and purpose as thought necessary. (Our present corporation will be in debt well into the twenty-third century!)

The rapid growth of the town created a wider and increasing demand for civic services since in the end a town hall was built on the site which had an upper storey which was partitioned, one part for a police office and the remaining large area used as a council, or meeting chamber, and magistrates court. The arched basement had a lock-up room for delinquents, but no part of the building appears to have been used as a day school as originally envisaged, but only for Sunday Schools. In 1824, the hall had a face lift, the parapet embellished and a cupola and clock with four faces added, one of the faces illuminated since by that time Burslem had reached the gas age. According to Ward, it subsequently looked a very handsome building, but probably not remaining in this condition for long in the company of coal fired bottle ovens which surrounded it, and it was indeed replaced later in the century despite its beauty. As time progresses it will be seem that Burslem was developing a fondness for building town halls! The building was controlled by a Board of Trustees, and for many years this were headed by Enoch Wood, the patriarch of the town.

One of the earliest functions held there was in 1769, when Josiah Wedgwood entertained his workers to commemorate the opening of his factory at Etruria. It became the first centre for the development of cultural groups. Among the earliest of these was the Burslem Choral Society which later formed the nucleus of the Potteries Choral Society. The hall was also the home of the Burslem Tonic Sol Fa Society, and a centre for musical soirées, at which Enoch Wood usually contributed a song. In 1808 it attracted the attention of a London touring company who distributed hand bills describing their exciting programme:

BY PARTICULAR DESIRE

Snr. Ingleby and his meritorious family from the Royal Circus, London will go through his Mathematical and Philosophical Recreations and Amusement.

He has had the honour of performing at different times before the Royal Family and most of the Nobility in the Kingdom with unbounded applause.

Snr. Ingleby will break any Gentleman's watch into twenty pieces and he will make it whole again at the word of commitment.

He will take two new laid eggs, the whole of the company may examine them, and any person in the room may break them, and a child shall come out of one of them, and a set of porcelain out of the other.

He will allow any Gentleman in the room to take a pack of cards and choose one, then shuffle it into any part of the pack, then lay them on the floor. He will set a foot on them and command the card he drew from under his foot to the top of his head.

He will allow any Gentleman to hold a pack of cards in his hands, and after thinking of any particular card, throw the whole pack of cards at the performer, who will catch the card so thought in his mouth. He can command the cards to do anything but speak.

HIS PIXIDIES METALLURGY An operation never before attempted by mankind and is as follows;-He gives to any person in the company a written paper, together with a box containing a quantity of medals which are of many different metals of different forms and sizes. He then asks them to take out of the box what medals they think proper, which, being done, the paper may be opened, thereon there will be found an exact account of the number of medals taken out, what they are, and the quality of metal each medal is made of. This is looked upon to be the greatest performance in the known world as it incontestably proves that there are possible means of proving knowledge of future events. He will, if required, set the room in such a situation as the Husband cannot know his own Wife, and Wife her Husband, though they sit together.

AN OPERATION IN POPYSOMANCE Snr. Ingleby will discover the real thoughts of any person in the company without asking a single question. He will communicate the thoughts of any person to another without the assistance of speech or writing. Any Gentleman may CUT A COCK'S HEAD OFF, or any other animal under the size of a Calf, and by one word it shall be made whole. Snr. Ingleby will exhibit different evenings with one fowl and one evening there shall be a bullet shot into his inside and any Gentleman may take a knife and cut it out, at the same time he may cut out his heart, legs and wings off, and by Snr. Ingleby blowing his Virtue Breath upon them, he will be made whole and alive as well as ever. Snr. Ingleby has got into such an active art of Gunnery that no man has ever had, or shall have, except himself while he lives. He will allow any Gentleman to fetch his own pistol, which he will perform with much rather than his own. He will allow any of the company make a ball and shoot it out of a piece, which Snr. Ingleby will catch upon any article, though it were as small as a needle. He will also exhibit STICKS OF FANCY which no man can do but himself, with a great variety of other deceptions.

The celebrated Miss Young from the Pireus, allowed by the best judges to be one of the first performers in the Kingdom, will perform in a most outstanding manner on the SLACK WIRE IN FULL SWING. A double Hornpipe by Miss and Master Young, and a capital hornpipe by Miss Ingleby .

Doors open at 7 o'clock, the performance beginning at 8 o'clock and concluding at 10 o'clock.
Admittance Front Seats 2/- Back Seats 1/- Tickets to be had at the Sign of the Leopard.

This was obviously a breath-taking performance, but failed to make Snr. Ingleby, despite his royal connections, a Freeman of the Borough.

The use of the area surrounding the hall as a market place was encouraged; boards and trestles were provided, and a charge made for their use, the proceeds of which contributed to the maintenance costs. Scarratt says that at the inauguration of Enoch Wood as Chief Constable, he said that the first stall erected comprised an old door supported with saggars, but as trade flourished, stalls, or shambles as they were called then, were erected but were of poor quality and many of the boards were pilfered. It is not said how many stalls there were but by 1812 they were boasting an annual rental of £150 and rose to many times this sum in later years, when rents and collection were auctioned off annually to the highest bidder, enabling Burslem to capitalise on their investment.

Whieldon figures believed to have been made by Josiah Wedgwood c 1760

TOWN HALL & MARKET HOUSE OF BURSLEM

On the left, the first Town Hall built 1760-1765 to make way for a larger town hall on the same site. On the right is the Meat Market (The Shambles) built 1835, but which suffered from mining subsidence and was demolished in the 20th century

CHAPTER FIVE: The Coal Industry

If the product of coalmining had as much aesthetic appeal as ceramics, perhaps more would have been written about the industry. There was hardship and disease in a potter's life above ground but for the miner there was hardship, disease, plus the constant danger in claustrophobic conditions. Coal was essential for the potter and North Staffordshire provided both coal and clay in abundance, consequently the communites of potters and miners were closely associated. Indeed in the early days, some families, such as the Wedgwoods, Adams, Coclough and Daniels probably dug themselves for both coal and clay.

The coal seams of the district run roughly north to south, some thrust to the surface by movement of the earth's crust, and here the coal was easily mined. The towns which form the Potteries grew along this geological line, stretching from Tunstall in the north to Longton in the south, a pattern which eventually led to conflict as to which town should become the nucleus when amalgamation was proposed.

Demand for local coal increased not only with the expansion of the pottery industry and iron foundries, but for heating the many new houses. Later as the revolution in transport took place, the local mining industry also became of national importance.

As opposed to most European countries, mineral rights, with the exception of gold, were the property of the landowner, which meant in Britain a comparatively small number together with the Crown. A large area of Burslem was owned by the Sneyd family who acquired it by both inheritance and purchase. The usual practice was for the owner of the land and its mineral rights to employ an agent to organise the extraction, or alternatively to let the right to extract the minerals and exact a royalty on tonnage recovered. Miners in the 18th century had two great problems, gas and water, which imposed a limit on the depth to which a mine could be worked - the deepest in 1815 was 111 yards and there were 32 shallow mines in the short distance between Burslem and Norton. Until the advent of steam engines for moving air and water, the depth and life of a mine was limited and extraction methods were very primitive and entirely reliant on physical labour. The following information from mining accounts dated 1774, gives some indication of the primitive methods in use, and the cost of equipment at that time:

Wicker basket for raising coal		2/4d
51yds. of Pit Rope		17/-
Candles. per lb		7d
Mine rent. per stuck of coal		8d
Royalty to landlord.		One sixth the price of the coal.
Wages. Bankman	per day	1/4d
" Bottomer	" "	10d

These early shallow mines are sometimes referred to as bell mines since a bell on the surface was rung from below to indicate that the basket was full and ready for hauling up. The greater the depth of the shaft and the longer the horizontal workings, the greater the risk from gas accumulating. Gas was often odourless, and poisonous, and it was highly inflammable. Air shafts were in some cases cut above the horizontal workings to the surface and sometimes fires were lit in the bottom of the shaft to induce a flow of air. It is well known that birds in cages were used in the mine as safety warnings, since the bird succumbed to the presence of gas before humans. The site of many of these mines went unrecorded which would create problems in succeeding years, since for the most part they were merely sealed at the top, many inadequately, when abandoned. Alarming collapses have occurred in built up areas, fortunately with only one recorded death. In 1994, on new road works near Longton, unrecorded workings were still coming to light; some have been mistaken for old wells.

Water accumulating in the mine was also a major problem, and some early mines were chosen where the situation allowed for the cutting of a drainage channel to the open from below the level of the coal seam. In 1719, the Earl of Macclesfield drained 150 acres near Burslem parish church, using horse gins. These drew up large casks of water from the drainage area, and the casks were then emptied into gutters.

The Sneyd Colliery & Brickworks Company Limited
Burslem.

It is said that this operation provided some of the water for the town and that the practice extended over sixty years, only being discontinued when steam engines were introduced to operate pumps in the mine. In the early days horses would make two journeys a day from Burslem to the adjacent mines, each carrying on its back a 'draught' of coal weighing approximately two to three hundredweights, costing seven pence at the pit head. There was no precise weight since no coal was weighed.

The first engine to be used in the mine was a beam engine, a type developed for the clay mines in Devon and Cornwall. A few of these machines remain as museum exhibits, but in Burslem they were superseded by horizontal engines which gradually revolutionised the mines. With their introduction it was possible not only to install pumps and fans to deal with gas and water, but men and coal could be conveyed mechanically and shafts could be deeper, opening up further seams; all leading to an increase in the life and size of the mine. The dangers of gas and water still existed, but to a lesser degree with improved ventilation. On the negative side, however, the use of machinery created additional personal risk; furthermore when disaster struck there was far greater loss of life with the increased number now underground, and from these not uncommon tragedies Burslem had its share of communal grief. The mines were now in effect underground factories with the coal faces distant from the shaft to which the coal was conveyed in trucks. Horses and ponies were extensively employed in this work; also women and children. A sad and ironic feature was that,

James Watt and a beam engine at his works
in Birmingham

while the practice of using women and young children underground in mines and for long hours was ignored, national demand for the abolition of slavery in foreign lands was vociferous.

The miners on the whole had a strong community spirit and now attempted to improve their lot. The Reform Bill of 1826 had made it legal to form a trade union and the miners immediately formed their own in this and most other mining areas. In 1831 the local miners demanded a wage increase accompanied with a threat to withdraw their labour. Propaganda began to flow from both master and miner:

"Notice by the North Staffordshire Coal Masters.

At a general meeting of Coal Masters, Proprietors and Agents of collieries on and near the district of the Staffordshire potteries, met this day, and taken into consideration the demands of our respective workmen. We are decidedly of the opinion that no advance of wages can be made under existing circumstances"

Supplemented by a further statement:

"We cannot but feel anxious on this and all occasions, to do full justice to our workmen, but we feel at the same time, that we have a duty to discharge to ourselves and to the country, and that any submission on our part to the demands attempted to be imposed upon us, would in the end, be equally injurious, both to their interest and to ours. We are therefore unanimously determined to resist all and every demand as have been made this day submitted to us by our workmen, by every means in our power, and earnestly request our respective workmen not to listen to the interested and pernicious council of others, and we also agree, not to employ any person who shall be discharged by his employer in consequence of his being in the trade union, or shall have given notice for an increase in wages".

The following advice to miners was published by a 'well wisher'. It ultimately proved good advice:

"Notice to the miners of the Staffordshire District.

Be not rash, pause before you commit yourselves. Your masters are willing to forget your past misconduct and take you into their employ again at the same liberal wages which you have hitherto received, more they cannot give, for they have already informed you [and you know it to be a fact that they cannot raise the price of their coals]. Withdraw from that dangerous union, where so many dangerous oaths have been administered - such oaths are not binding, If you do not work, there are no wages, and how are your families to be provided for; have you seriously thought of this? Funds of the union cannot last long, and what then? why, you will be sorry you rejected the kind offers of your masters, and they will not listen to your requests. It will be too late, your place can and will be supplied by others, who will be thankful to receive the wages you now do, and I know at this moment, many of your masters are preparing to get further men. You and your families will be plunged into greater distress, think not that your parish can, or will, relieve you when your past misconduct is brought to light. Colliers, return to your work immediately, it will be better for both yourselves and your family, if you do not, you will in future regret you have not taken the advice of a...........WELL WISHER."

The formation of miners' unions, and their rise to power, appears to have been more advanced in some counties than in this area. One owner in Lancashire spoke of going to his screening plant and finding two new faces. On enquiry he was told that the previous two had been withdrawn because they owed union dues; two weeks later he found the original two back in their previous job having settled their debt - in neither case with 'by your leave' to the owner. This will no doubt bring to mind similar autocratic practices in the newspaper industry in the 20th century.

The miners obviously realised that the effect of their striking would bring the pottery and other trades to a standstill and issued a public notice with the intention of obtaining sympathy and support:

"COAL MINERS ADDRESS TO THE PUBLIC.

It is well known that coal miners in this neighbourhood have joined themselves in a union, in order to remove the oppression they labour under, but it is a lamentable fact to see, notwithstanding the strong and important ties under which we are united, for observe, in the midst of our affliction, as the chief priests and scribes sought means to destroy Jesus, so our masters and agents are seeking traitors, and to our great misfortune, and their disgrace, they have found Judas's. Shame on you, and behold, the very men who betrayed us sat with us at the table on the 25th of May 1831, but behold, on the 26th these traitors were absent. Behold yes, ye covetous deceivers, beware, the wrath of God is insupportable. But in viewing one of their lives, this is not a solitary instance, for we find him guilty of a crime, too abominable to be named here, which caused him to leave his parents in his youth, and observe here a niceness and scrupulosity of the proprietors, they scruple not to give money to traitors, but they scruple to give their respective workers, so called, a reasonable remuneration for their labour. Observe, we say to you brethren, be peaceable, be firm and united, Judas betrayed his master and his brethren, yet the eleven stood firm and were supported by their lord and came off more than conquerors".

Another exhortation was addressed:

"Manufacturers and operative, We say - do not blame us - the measure has been forced on us although we know that you will feel some inconvenience, yet what man is there among you that would not have adopted the same conduct, had they been placed in the same circumstances. It is a case of every man who is joined to a union, that they are called upon to defend. We ask then, should this attempt on us succeed, how long will it be before users of their trade will be forced to bend beneath their powers of injustice.England expects every man to do his duty."

Mr Kinnersley, who lived at Clough Hall near Kidsgrove, and who had significant local iron and steel interests, took this final exhortation literally and issued the following challenge:

"Any person in the employ of Mr. Kinnersley, whose notice expires before Saturday next, being a member of the union, and who wishes to remain in his service, must sign a declaration, on or before Monday next, that he will immediately leave the union as Mr. Kinnersley will not employ any person who does not sign before that day."

These were strong words to members of a union in its infancy and which had only recently issued a handbook of rules, the first chapter of which included guidance on conduct at union meetings, but could equally apply to a personal meeting with Mr Kinnersley. It stipulated that each meeting should open with a prayer which asked God to assist them in their life's endeavours and all those who laboured under oppression. The rules emphasised the need for courtesy: *"Members should remove their hat on entering a meeting, and sit down in a proper place, none to be covered but the Chairman's"*. However, even if they approached the mineowners with the courtesy the handbook described, neither prayers nor manners availed them. A local mine manager writing at the time on the economy of his mine, said that *"Great Roe" coal had been reduced in price from 8/9d to 6/3d per ton, and "Peacock" from 7/9 to 6/3d without any reduction in wages. The miners have as wages the same as they had in 1820, and his lordship's profits are by no means so large."* He said the charter masters, sometimes called butties, seemed to be making considerable profits.

Charter Masters or Butties were contract workers who operated on a similar principle to that obtaining in the pottery industry where payment of a global sum was made to the individual Master or Butty, who in turn paid the miners in his employ. Since the conclusion of the Napoleonic wars the price of food had fallen considerably, and wages generally had remained static. The question seemed to be was there a reasonable profit for their lordships? - and on that the opinion of the mineowners and miners were diametrically opposed.

The naming of the coals above may seem strange. It was usual to give names to seams from which the coal was mined and which the customer used on ordering, It was of particular interest to the pottery trade since the coal from the various seams had different characteristics and the potters learnt which and when to use particular coals during the course of firing the pottery. There were a great variety of names, but the names for sizes in which coal was sold were fairly universal, viz. cobbles, peas, beans, etc.

There are readers still living, brought up in the coal age, who may think it unnecessary to discuss the sizes and types of coals, but there are already many, and, as time passes, whole generations, who may never see coal, or a coal mine, or a potteries bottle oven in full blast, or live alongside one or more of these as many thousands of families did in the past. I mentioned before that I had an aunt who lived in Cobridge, in Elm Street, which had bottle ovens nearby on four sides, and one of them a stone's throw away at the bottom of Bleak Street which ran parallel to Elm Street. The windows of the house were sash type but could not be opened since they were stuffed with paper in every crevice - even that failed to keep out the fine particles of coal dust.

The miners dispute, from which we have digressed, was a bitter one as evidenced by the notice issued by one employer:

"TWENTY POUNDS REWARD.
Whereas a combination amongst the working colliers lately in my employ at Goldenhill, has obliged me to engage other workers in their place, and now to prevent them from performing their engagement with me, and to deter persons from lodging or harbouring them, menaces have been used, and anonymous letters sent, threatening the persons of men willing to work, and those who lodge, and entertain them with violence. I do hereby offer the above mentioned reward to any person or persons who describe to me the author or authors of such threats or threatening letters, or who shall make known to me the perpetrators of any malicious damage or mischief which may be done to any steam engine, buildings, or works belonging to any of my collieries and, with the aid of the law, to punish all illegal violence, by whoever committed, to prevent my prosecuting my works as I think proper." Robert Williamson. Longport. 28th Jan. 1831."

This same gentleman had already stated his position in the following notice to his employees:

"When I first became possessed of the articles of the union society, I informed you that I should by no means consent to be obliged to rules 13 and 14 which would make the officers of your society judges of my equity. You professed perfect satisfaction with my general behaviour to you, and with your actual wages if I could promise you would not be driven from your work. You have generally earned 24/- and upwards per week, and not the least alteration has taken place from the day of your voluntary profession, and now you have resolved to do me all the injustice in your power by giving me notice to cease work."

Robert Williamson lived at Ramsdale Hall in Cheshire, and he and Kinnersley were brothers in law. The two men no doubt adopted a common policy during the strike. Rule 13, to which Williamson referred, read, *"Four persons appointed by each lodge to look into disputes between master and workman."* Rule 14. *"Any dispute arising from reduction of wages, men must not leave without notice, but report same to committee, who shall examine same."*

As time went by without any sign of agreement, the miners were getting disheartened; this was evidenced by their further public appeal;

"It is well known that the nature of our work is dangerous, and that lives are lost owing to circumstances over which we have no control. Should we escape with life, we are subject to disease incident to the peculiar perilousness of our calling, which very often leaves us incapable of following our employ, often in the prime of life, and many of our members are compelled to beg for the remainder of life. There is want of sympathy that can only be accounted for by the most extreme indifference on the part of those who should at least possess the sympathy of humanity."

The owners canvassed successfully for miners outside the district, and this, combined with the return to work of others and a lack of funds in the union - too recently formed to have accumulated a worthwhile reserve from minimal earnings - brought an end to the strike. The end was ignominious for some, unemployment for others, all no doubt heavily in debt, some even forfeiting their homes as happened with the potters.

The following satirical letter was written by a disillusioned miner towards the end of the dispute. The Tommy Shop to which he referred were shops owned by the employer from which the employee could buy on favourable terms;

"May 1831.   HUZZA   Kidicrew again.
To members of the working class generally. Men who are now not in the union, or men who will leave the union, are particularly wanted. Knoblesticks of all casts, colour and complexion, may have liberal pay and good quarters. They may work their eyes out if they chose, for none will see the wrong they do. Houses will be provided as soon as convenient for themselves and family, also an elegant and commodious, well furnished, Tommy Shop where they may be supplied with candles and tobacco, and all kinds of large and small wares at a respectable Tommy Shop price. Be it known also unto you that none will apply who are in the habit of thinking or saying that men ought to be remunerated for their labour, or who are members of that bug bear the union, or who are either the servants or the slaves of any member of that liberal and benevolent assembly who signed that wise and liberal resolution of the 3rd.instant, which could only have been dictated by a heart which it could only be a complement to call the heart of a demon, unless they bring a written discharge from a brother chip who signed the said resolution of manufacturers and tradesmen of the Staffordshire Potteries. Gentlemen. We hope we shall soon have the union on its beam ends and the flotilla of Kidecrew will be soon at sea again laden with the rich merchandise of "Seven feet" and "Banbury" bound for the ports and then we shall remember those unsightly fellows that signed the aforesaid resolution.   A gent of the pit".

Subsequent to the collapse of the strike an uneasy peace seems to have lasted for ten years until, in 1842, a Longton mine owner gave notice of his intention to reduce wages again which resulted in his operatives taking strike action. After several weeks without any change in attitude on either side, bands of colliers visited other areas successfully seeking the support of the miners and canvassing the towns for relief, until it became both annoying and alarming, since work in the area was coming to a standstill and coal for the pottery industry was becoming unavailable. On Saturday 6th August 1842, three men with a begging bowl were arrested in Burslem and placed in the lock-up in the basement of the town hall. This came to the knowledge of their comrades in Hanley and some 200 assembled around midnight and proceeded to Burslem, broke into the police station, released the prisoners and rampaged through the town, breaking windows, and the dial of the town hall clock, before finally retiring into anonymity before dawn.

The 16th of August was the anniversary of the massacre of workers in Manchester by the military ('Peterloo') and a grand parade was to take place to commemorate it. On the previous day, a meeting in Hanley was addressed by Thomas Cooper, a prominent Chartist from outside the area, and William Ellis

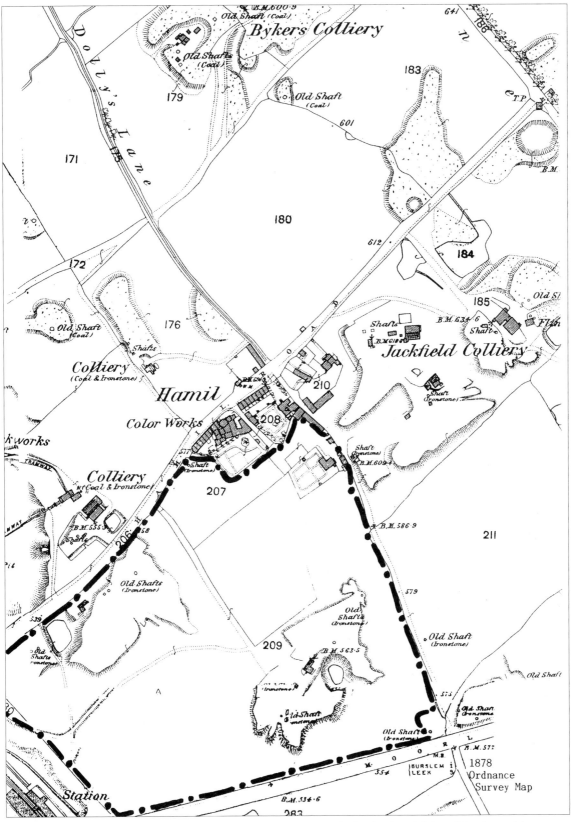

Burslem, 1878 OS map. The map shows the numerous collieries in the vicinity of the town (shown as site 207). Site 180 was replaced by Burslem Park in 1894

from Burslem. Ward, in his history said, *"the weather was beautiful, the fields covered with abundance, and the ringleaders of sedition hence conceived that the time was particularly auspicious for the assemblage of a huge mob, and the achievement of their seditious designs."*

With the miners already in angry mood, the meeting got out of hand and rioting commenced. News and fear soon spread to Burslem where some 200 loyal citizens were enrolled as special constables, to preserve the sanctity of the town. Groups of strikers spread out. In Hanley the police office was raided, also the principal pawnbrokers - never before had so many goods been reclaimed in one day! Albion House at Shelton, the home of Mr William Parker, a magistrate, was set on fire and his fine furniture burnt. Earl Granville's works, "Shelton Bar" as we later knew it, was visited, machinery stopped, and the offices set on fire. Groups gave vent to their feelings by attacking the police station and the rectory in Longton, houses of factory owners in Fenton and Stoke, and a magistrate's house in Penkhull

Havoc extended as far as Apedale, where Mr Heathcote's (of Apedale Hall) ironworks, were the target of the mob. He despatched an urgent letter to Mr Ricardo, the local MP:

"...the disturbances in this neighbourhood have indeed assumed a very serious aspect, and what is to be the end of them I know not. The property in which I am residing was invaded on Wednesday evening. I immediately made with my agent to the point of attack, and for two hours had the pleasure of seeing myself and many thousands of pounds of machinery, and other chattels, at the absolute disposal of as ferocious a set of ruffians as you ever beheld. On no former occasion of outbreaks or stoppages in the Pottery district, has anything of the kind ever occurred here, and I can only account for it now on the supposition that a feeling of discontent amongst the working population, concerned no doubt that reductions in the price of labour, which the continued depreciation of all manufactured articles has rendered absolutely necessary, has spread itself very extensively. You are aware that if the colliers do not go back to work, 20,000 to 30,000 potters must be thrown out of employment, and I am sorry to say that many of them are quite as ill disposed, and as ripe for mischief as their neighbours.

Again and again I urged the magistrates to interfere with all their force to prevent these riotings, but they assure me they have no right to do so, I cannot agree with them. Since the above was written, I have had my house surrounded, and been obliged to return full gallop from Newcastle.

The party that was assembling, came here in my absence and, although they have only alarmed my family, they have done a good deal of mischief at my works. We, here in the country, have nothing for it now but to put ourselves in a state of armed defence, and I have usually twenty or thirty servants within a minutes call, and I dare say I shall be able to protect myself."

A further meeting in Hanley in the evening saw the mob re-group and, inspired by the same speakers they resumed their havoc. Cooper, the same night passing through Burslem, was apprehended by Mr Wilcox Edge, the mayor of Burslem at the time, and taken to the Legs of Man where magistrate Parker was in bed, having fled from his mansion in Shelton, which Cooper's oratory had helped to ignite. Cooper apparently was carrying nothing but a bag at the time, and all it contained were letters from loads of sympathisers, and since nothing else was found on his person, he was allowed to leave.

Fear of further problems led the magistrates to request a military presence, and a small body of Dragoons was sent to the barracks in Newcastle. In the meantime, a contingent of like minded members of the working class from Macclesfield were on their way to the Potteries, intending to meet the local contingent coming from Hanley. They camped overnight in the streets of Leek, and perhaps toasted the morrow in Leek Ale at Leek's expense.

The Hanley battalion, after grouping in the town the following morning, proceeded to Burslem headed by a Longton miner named Cogznelly - a name which might suggest that the union had been infiltrated by 'foreigners'! On arrival in Burslem, without delay they rifled the tills at the George for the second time within a month, and no doubt sampled their ales and spirits before turning to face the Dragoons, newly arrived from Newcastle, and to welcome their Macclesfield comrades who came into the town with banners flying and preceded by a band playing, *"See the conquering heroes come"*. The total strength of the mob was now a formidable 6000.

The Dragoons were drawn up in a line across the road from the Big House to the old Post Office. In the rear of the professionals, and mustered under the chief constable, Mr Samuel Alcock, stood the brave volunteers. The captain of the Dragoons read the Riot Act which provoked a hail of missiles from the mob and they surged forward with all manner of weapons. The military were ordered to fire. Mr Wilcox Edge said the effect was astonishing. *"The whole mob were so shocked that they fell in heaps to the ground. The one man who was killed outright, lay with his brains in his leather apron. He was a shoemaker. Some of the other rioters it is believed died later".* The Dragoons charged and the mob disintegrated and fled, except for some who sought refuge in the George. They finally broke all the windows.

The seriousness of these riotings led to a search for the leading miscreants, particularly Cooper and Ellis whose inflammatory speeches had preceded the devastation. Cooper was apprehended and charged with high treason, and on being found guilty committed to Stafford jail for two years. Ellis had been fleet of foot and was found in Glasgow. He was one of approximately two hundred who were charged, and the ultimate penalties were intended to fit the crimes and act as a deterrent to others.

Imprisoned with hard labour for various terms	146
Imprisoned without hard labour	8
Sentenced to transportation for life	11
Sentenced to transportation for twentyone years	13
" " " " fifteen "	9
" " " " ten "	18
" " " " seven "	3
Acquitted	55

A reward of £20 had been offered for the detention of the individual who broke the face of the town clock, and it would seem that greed took pride of place since one of the rioters named Colclough joined those who were transported for life, accused of this specific offence.

The Justice of the Peace wrote to the Home Secretary describing the events in Burslem. He stated that Constable Ryles said that a pigeon had been sent off by the mob. The pigeon was caught, and a message taken from its neck read; *"We the mob that have assembled in the Potteries this morning 16th August, have been violently assaulted by thirty-six horse soldiers of the Second Dragoons, please send 50,000 men as soon as possible."* It is not surprising that Wellington won battles if those were the odds when facing the British army.

Ellis was one of those sentenced to twenty-one years transportation for burning Hanley Vicarage and assaulting the military in Burslem. This brought not only himself to a sorry state but also his whole family. He wrote a pitiful letter from prison to the Chief Constable of Burslem; *"I respectfully request that the liberality which has always characterised you, will be shown by noticing during my confinement, my poor spirit broken wife, who is now left in the most hopeless state of destitution".*

Thomas Cooper was born in Leicester and edited a Midland's paper at one time. He was a prominent Chartist and an eloquent speaker. He must have been about 37 years of age when he came to the Potteries. He wrote poetry while in Stafford prison which was published on his release, but he also wrote works on politics and christianity and in later years lectured in London. He lived to be 87 years of age, and Mr Wilcox Edge, son of the mayor of the same name, lecturing in Burslem much later, said *"Cooper was in later years a guest of my father, who had taken him before Magistrate Parker during the riots, and it was interesting to hear these two old men speak of those stirring times."* Mr Ward, in his history, had little time for such as Cooper or the mob. He wrote:

"We may be allowed to observe that the political sentiments of the majority of the manufacturers and middle classes here in Burslem, are of a decidedly conservative character than can be predicated of some of the southerly portions of the borough; and, with respect to the operative population, their general demeanour has been orderly and peaceable, even under severe privations; and we venture to hope that few of that class in Burslem have been seduced by those revolutionary doctrines which, under the name of Chartism, are at present so widely and fearfully inculcated by reckless and unprincipled men."

I can bring to mind seeing and hearing miners going to or coming from work, their face and hands black. Their clogs resounded on the pavement until they almost seemed to carry an echo as they moved into the distance. All of them appeared to carry the same type of tin box which held their food - it was a long time before I learned that there are no safe havens in a mine against mice and cockroaches unless the food is in a metal container. Eaten underground as it had to be, coal dust must have taken the place of condiments. As far as the employment of children underground was concerned, it was not not until 1899 that an act was passed preventing boys of under ten years of age from either working in the mines or being paid in public houses. Prior to this legislation some boys of eight or nine years of age were taken by their miner father to work underground, and the practice was ignored by the mineowners.

Coal was vital to Burslem while pottery was fired in the traditional bottle oven. It was said that it took five tons of coal to fire one ton of pottery, and who born before the last War would have visualised that the hundreds of these bulbous monuments to pottery, the reminder above ground of the black gold beneath, would vanish from the Potteries so soon. It is equally difficult to grasp that the 17th century potter fetched his own coal from the mine at 2d per horse load, and five horse loads were one ton. Even at the end of the 19th century, when coal was being delivered, its cost was only 5/-d per ton. How ironical that today coal has little significance, and that after endless hard labour and perseverance and the sacrifice of many hundreds of lives, the miner had to wait until well into the 20th century before ultimately receiving a just reward, only to see, in one short decade in the same century, the whole edifice of his industry crumble, while the pottery trade stumbles on after a "clean" divorce from its one time partner.

So too has the term household coals become almost extinct. When I was young, it was a common sight to see a horse and cart containing probably a ton of coal on its way to a dwelling. The load would be accompanied by a character who hoped on arrival to be employed by the householder to stack it in the coalhouse after it had been tipped in the street or back alley, only often for the poor fellow to suffer, mainly through the economic circumstances of the householder, a reluctant refusal and a long solitary walk home.

> I remember days of national prayer
> Womens tears, A child's despair
> A pick like a cross, A prayer for souls
> The coffined dead, The price of coals

CHAPTER SIX: St John's

The impression may have been given that spiritual life had no place in the growing Burslem and I have perhaps given human excesses prominence, but there were some good-living church-going families in Burslem. Their interests centred on St John's, the parish church, for a long time the only church in an area stretching well beyond Burslem, and with a ministry and congregation who were constrained compared with the fervour of the Non Conformists. The mother church was at Stoke - Burslem only became an independent ministry in 1807, but it had its own minister, appointed by the parent church. It made no payment to Stoke, and the incumbent received an income from parochial resources including tithes.

It is believed that there was a church on the site from the Norman Conquest, for many years a wooden structure with a thatched roof. In 1688 there was a fire, and for a long time after records were sent to Lichfield for safe keeping. Following a second fire the church was rebuilt in brick in 1717. In 1778 it was increased in size and an organ installed. These 1778 alterations and enlargements were paid for by Enoch Wood who was a churchwarden, the cost to be later repaid by the sale of the additional seating. Following Enoch's curious practice, ceramic figures were concealed in the foundations and at the same time he also placed some in the family vault. Of the pieces in the vault, two were original plaques modelled by himself, 'The Crucifixion', and 'The Descent From The Cross'. There were also the originals of the busts of Wesley and of Enoch's son, again examples of his own work.

Some time after Enoch's death there was a near scandal when some of the items from the vault were found in the possession of a well known citizen in the town, but it was explained as arising from the fear of them being lost, and resulted in the whole of the vault's treasures being placed in the vestry of the church, and later in a bank in the town. Later the two plaques were sited in the chancel of the church.

In 1789, there was vandalism by children, who were guilty of daubing the seats in the church, to counter which a warden was appointed at a wage of two shillings per week to be paid out of church rates.

From 1878 to 1880 major interior works were completed and galleries built which enabled the church to seat 850 persons, but as a result of mining subsidence, in 1930 the galleries were found to be unsafe and, with the exception of the west gallery, they were taken down.

The tower is squat and is the oldest part of the church. John Rogers had left £200 for this tower to be raised within two years of his death; the time lapsed without the work being done and it is still as it was originally built, perhaps fortunately, since with mining problems, a taller tower might by now have followed the one at Pisa.

The original bells were installed in 1720. There were four, each inscribed differently;-

"Mr. Timothy Keen. Minister".
"Prosperity to the church of England
"Luke Bennett. Benefactor to church & bells.
"John Marsh. Ralph Adams. Samuel Malkin. Churchwardens.1720".

The original bells ultimately became cracked and dissonant and were recast in 1827/28, but it was decided to replace the four with six and these bore a different inscription:

Numbers 1, 3 and 4 bore the name of the owner of the bell foundry,
"William Dobson, Downham, Norfolk. 1828"
Number two,   "Peace and good neighbourhood"
Number five,   "My song shall be the loving kindness of the Lord",
Number six,   "Revd. Edwd. Whieldon. Rector. Messrs Levi Hanby, Jas. Clews,
                   Thos.Hancock, Thos Weatherby. Churchwardens. 1828".

The bells were tuned and rehung again in 1911 - so they may require attention again in the 21st century. An article by the Rev P.L.C. Smith M.A. in 1971 was critical of the unkempt condition of the

A modern photograph of St John's.

The building at the back of the church, in this early 19th century
engraving, is the church school with its original turret

churchyard at that time. He said it held many interesting graves, vaults and memorials. One, a tall memorial to W. F. Horry Esq. by his Staffordshire friends, was in danger of collapsing. There is an interesting history connected with Horry which Skerrett relates:

Born in 1843, Horry was the son of a successful brewer in Boston, Lincolnshire. In 1867 he was given £800 by his father to buy the George Hotel in Burslem and he later married Jane Wright, a barmaid at the hotel. They had three children, but he developed the conviction that his wife had been unfaithful with several prominent inhabitants of the town. He was often drunk but remained a popular figure in the town. In 1871 the couple separated and Horry sold the hotel. His father gave a home to the wife and children, and Horry applied for a divorce citing five co-respondents. He spent the remainder of the year in dissolute living, but ended up in Boston where, while drinking with friends, he declared a desire for reconciliation with his wife. He persuaded his father to allow him a meeting with her, asserting that he would then leave the Country for good. When he met his wife he shot her.

Petitions were circulated in Burslem and a fund for his defence was widely supported, and in Boston the Mayor headed a similar petition. His murdered wife's brother also appealed for mercy, but Horry was convicted of the murder and was hanged in Lincoln Castle in 1872 at the age of twenty eight. Shopkeepers in Burslem drew their blinds on the day. In a statement before he died Horry thanked his friends for their sympathy and financial assistance and said he felt he had been deeply sinned against, but pardoned all who had so done. On the following Sunday funeral cards were distributed in Burslem depicting him as a christian and a martyr. Hundreds attended a memorial service held in St John's

The funeral service was conducted by the Rev Alfred Watten an Oxford M.A. (who had come to Tunstall as curate, married the daughter of the patron of the living at Burslem, Doctor John Morris, and was at the time of the funeral Rector of St John's). Some of those who attended the service seem to have been disturbed by an apparent emphasis on Horry's martyrdom by the vicar in his sermon; Reverend Watten held strong objections to capital punishment and this influenced the tenor of his address.

The living of St John's later carried a heavy responsibility, since, in addition to having to provide for its own upkeep it also had to give support to St.Paul's at Longport and Christ Church at Cobridge. St John's owned property at Brown Edge, which was originally intended to provide an income, but became a financial liability. These worries, combined probably with personal criticism, culminated in the tragedy of the Rev. Watton taking his own life. An obelisk raised to his memory by his friends bore an apt verse from Thomas Gray's Elegy:

No further seek his merit to disclose, Or draw his frailties from their dread abode,
There they alike in trembling hope repose, The bosom of his father and his God.

Early in the 19h century it had become evident that reform was needed in the established church. Many parsons were very poor, while others, in livings which were the gift of wealthy families, were the reverse. Moreover in some instances the living of a number of churches were bestowed on one individual, a system which left some parishes with the equivalent of an absentee landlord. In a Burslem census of the 18th century, one resident's occupation is given as Vicar of Peel! That there was no self-consciousness in accepting the system is evidenced by the following inscription on a memorial elsewhere:

Here lies all that was mortal of Elizabeth Bate
Relict of the Reverend Richard Bate
A woman of unaffected piety
And exemplary virtue
She was honorably descended
And by means of alliance
To an illustrious family
She had the merit to obtain
For her husband and children
Twelve several employments
In Church and State.

The payment of tithes was unpopular with the farming community. The following lines were sung at harvest time.

> We've cheated the parson
> We'll cheat him again
> For why should the vicar
> Have one in ten

The collection of tithes must have also been a demeaning occupation for a minister. The system was extremely interesting but in many respects mystifying to all who were not involved. Ward gives a comprehensive list of the tithes which appear to have been applicable in Burslem:

CORN.	Eleventh Mole or Shoch if set up. Tenth if thrown out.
WOOL & SHEEP.	A fleece at seven. Two at seventeen. All under seven and all above ten to seventeen. One penny per piece.
LAMBS.	One at seven, Two at seventeen. Under seven and above ten to seventeen must be paid for, half a penny a piece.
PIGS.	One at seven
GEESE.	One at seven. Two at seventeen.
HAY.	All hay in kind except "Board Meadowing" for which a particular modus can be proved if the Minister and Parishioners do not compound.
HEMP.	Threepence for every peck of seed sown.
FLAX.	In kind, if not compounded for.
POTATOES.	After the rate of ten shillings an acre.
COWS & CALVES.	A penny a cow and a halfpenny a calf
COLTS.	Two pence a colt.
EGGS.	Two for a hen, one for a young laying pullet.

This demeaning and archaic practice was operative until the Tithe Commutation Act of 1836, although limited commutations had been agreed between individuals and the church to pay in cash rather than kind, as for example the Burslem Wedgwood's arrangement for *"Board Meadowing"* to be exempt in kind by payment of a modus of two shillings a year, *"Modus for "Bourn Meadow" to be eighteen pence per year, and Modus for the Mill, two shillings a year."* There were various other complicated payment arrangements all of which were ultimately wiped out by the 1836 and later acts. Other income was derived from what were termed Surplice Fees; *Wedding with License, Five shillings. Publication of Bann, Two shillings & six pence, whether man or woman sojourn in the parish or tho' they be married at Stoke. Churching, One shilling. Burying. One shilling. To the Minister for drawing a copy of ye register, Three shillings. Old church books and old Surplice laid aside belong to the Minister.*

Hulton was part of the parish of Burslem and the Abbey owned an Elizabethan type farmhouse together with farm land called the Grange, both being free of tithes and situated in that part of Burslem known as Cobridge Gate, the name being derived from an entrance gate situated in the region of the conjunction of Waterloo Road and Leek Road. It marked the entrance to the path through Sneyd by which the monks came from Hulton. The Monks at the Abbey belonged to a Cistercian order but it was never a very big community. Henry de Audley and his wife were buried in the Abbey. Probably both thought they had a safe and permanent haven, but after the Dissolution of the Monasteries it is thought the two bodies were reburied in Burslem Churchyard where a small stone coffin, thought to be that of Henry's wife, is still to be seen.

With no clear clarification of the responsibility for church dues following the Reformation, Cobridge, situated on what were previously Abbey lands, was always reluctant to contribute to any expense which Burslem or its Protestant church considered a mutual benefit and charge. Cobridge was prepared to argue their immunity, and even to make use of the courts. The house on the Grange has long since gone, but at one period it came into the hands of the Biddulph family and suffered severe damage on two occasions.

View of Rushton Grange.—1800

The Grange (Rushton Grange) at Cobridge, once part of the Hulton Abbey Estate.
The picture shows only part of the farmhouse, left after the damge of the
anti-catholic riots. It finally was in a ruinous state and demolished

Two drawings of the ruins of Biddulph Hall

The Biddulphs were strong catholics and in the reign of James II the house was ransacked by a mob from Burslem and the area around. It suffered a similar fate during the Gordon riots which occurred at the time of the Catholic Emancipation Bill, 1829.

It has already been said that Burslem church records were not all that might be desired; some entries make them rather remarkable. One peculiar feature is the number of names, mainly surnames, which if correct vanish within so short a time that one suspects that the gravedigger rather than the minister made the entries. The following are names entered in the 17th and 18th centuries:

Surnames: Clubb, Owfult, Varm, Finely, Catarem, Whinrow, Whiteale, Duelly, Tibrale, Gervas, Paglar.
Forenames: Males: Richardus, Salathieal, Jodiah, Careless.

A peculiar custom was the entry of a nickname following the entry of the real name, such as:

Mary Jane, (Alias Match Mary), Mary Simpson, (Vulgo Madam), Robert Mitchell (Vulgo Cat Dick), Ralph Hancock, (Alias Cabbage), Thomas Daniel, (Pigein Foot)

In addition it was not uncommon to give the cause of death with entries:

1792.   Sarah, wife of Richard Barker. (Hanged herself)
1792.   Taylor Rainbow. (Hanged himself)
1807.   Sarah, wife of Gregory Hickman. Surgeon. Death occasioned by her
         clothes having catched ye fire.
1807.   John Davenport. Age 20 years. Killed by explosion of Mr Stanway's engine.
1807.   Enoch Ashworth. (Consumption by colour making)

Some entries are short but sufficient to denote a tragedy:

1749.   Died May 30th. Mary, Ann & Martha, daughters of Roger & Dorothy Heath, Mary
         about 6 years, Ann aged 3 years & Martha 9 months.
1791.   Mary Brady. Soldier's child.
1793.   Christening. Joseph George and Pheobe Austin. (six fingers and toes. born blind)
1747.   Thomas and Sarah and one other who died unchristened.

1785 was a tragic year; there were 136 deaths, 65 of them infants, but the infant death rate was high until late in the 19th century. Burslem's death rate of four in ten under the age of five persisted for ages. 1808 was another year when the death rate was very heavy due to an outbreak of Smallpox.

According to the following entries, not all the Wedgwoods were affluent:

Sept. 16th 1786. Mary Wedgwood. Pauper.
March 16th 1801. Ellen Wedgwood. Pauper

An interesting entry is that of July 2nd 1806 when six children of Thomas Wedgwood of the Overhouse were christened together, the dates of their birth were given as:

Thomas	1800
Catharine	1801
John	1803
Josiah	1803
Philip Egerton	1804
Smith	1805

It was also not uncommon to enter the street or area from which the person came, and many of these places are frustrating to locate. Again some may be mis-spellings but most, if they are correct, seem to have vanished without trace: *Snaydales, Kidereive, Cress Hill, Thunder, Peake's Barn, Dog Croft, Snag Daley, Tidmarsh's Row, Rope Walk, Cliff Gate,* and others equally as intriguing.

The Crown was constantly short of money during the period of the French Wars and the American War of Independence, and in 1783 George III imposed a tax on all entries in the church register:

"From and after the first day of October One thousand seven hundred and eighty three, shall be charged, levied and paid into and for the use of His Majesty the following new duty viz;- Upon the entry of any Burial, Marriage, Birth or Christening in the register of any parish, precinct, or place in Great Britain, a duty of three pence; and whoever shall neglect or refuse to pay the same, he she or they shall for every offence forfeit and pay the sum of five pounds".

The income remitted to the Crown from these charges was recorded periodically in the Burslem register. Two such entries are the following;

"Received January 2nd from Rev Henry Babbington, Minister of Burslem, one pound sixteen shillings and twopence three farthings, being the clear income to government for the christening taxes from October 1785-1786"

The following year the sum was *"two pounds two shillings and threepence three farthings"*. It would be interesting to know how the church resolved the discrepancy in the cash when the fee was in round pence, or what action King George's treasurer took.

Another point of interest is how the register illustrates the apparent gradual widening of intercourse between communities, with an increasing number of entries of marriages between couples from widely separated counties:

1795. Benjamon Hands of St. Martin's Birmingham. Widower. & Sally Sale of Burslem. Single woman
1795. John Bottinger of St. James Bristol. Gloucester Merchant. & Suranna Brindley of Burslem.
1797. Alexander Edwin Ewin of Sandbach. Dancing Master. & Francis Fellon of Stoke.

Among the marriages it is surprising how many Burslem girls married Newcastle hat makers.

Enoch Wedgwood was churchwarden and treasurer at the church from 1788 to 1790, and again from 1803 to 1805 and he left some interesting notes of payments from church funds:

Expenses 1789.	Total	£61. 15. 2.
Including new pulpit		36. 12. 4.
Communion table cloth		2. 8. 4.
Summonses for Sabbath breakers		8. 0.
Paid to the apparition		3. 0.
Expenses 1790.		£20. 3. 4.
Including cushions for the pulpit		4. 18. 4.
Summonses for publicans		3. 0.
Court fees		4. 5.

There were over the years a number of endowments to be administered by the church; Catherine Egerton, daughter of John Wedgwood of The Big House, who died in 1756, left a house in the town to be used by the curate. The house was used for several years before the gift was found to have been void, and the property reverted to her heir. However, in her will according to Ward, she left £200 to purchase land to build a rectory, but it was not until 1815 that the first rectory was built, and this was on Glebe land which the church already owned.

Catherine Egerton also presented communion plate for the church which was inscribed with an appropriate recording. In addition she left 50/- yearly to the poor which, with the £5 given by her father, was to be raised on lands and premises at The Overhouse.

Other bequests to the church included one from John Colclough of Burslem of £5 yearly for ever. *"Charge to the paying thereof to be on two pieces of land called Cow Hays and Ryefield in Oldcott in the parish of Wolstanton, and to be dealt with on every Lord's day in twenty penny wheaten loaves. The residue of the money to be given to the poor householders on the second day of February yearly. The bread to be good and substantial, to be brought into church every Lord's day and distributed after the morning service at the discretion of the Minister, Churchwardens, and Overseers of the Poor."*

John Colclough was a descendant of Sir Thomas Colclough, Lord of the Manor of Hanley and a wealthy landowner, who was responsible with others for the rebuilding of Wolstanton Church.

John Wedgwood gave the sum of £5 *"the interest thereon to be laid out in Wheaten bread, and dealt out to the poor upon every Christmas Day at the direction of his executors."*

R. Cartwright of Sneyd bequeathed £20 to the poor, *"the interest to be laid out in bread and distributed quarterly."* The stock from which this sum arose was in the hands of the Trustees of the Workhouse and they used it to rebuild the original workhouse and continued to pay interest to the church.

Thomas Leigh of Jack Fields who died in 1720 bequeathed £40, the interest on which should be distributed annually to the poor.

William Adams who died in 1722 left £10 the interest on which should be distributed annually to the poor of Hulton.

All the poor in Burslem should have a full stomach and money in the bank except that presumably all these munificent bequests have been eliminated by the Mortmain Acts.

Today, the church, historical but not beautiful, stands in an area comparatively treeless and gaunt, causing few to glance as they flash by on a modern ring road. The interior has a quiet beauty with no ornate memorials. The churchyard holds a number of memorials to members of illustrious Burslem families, including Josiah's relatives who are grouped together, but Josiah himself was buried at Stoke.

One grave which is the focal point of a local legend is that of the 'witch' Margaret Leigh, or Molly Leigh as she was usually known, set at right angles to the normal graves.

No doubt in pre Reformation days the monks from Abbey Hulton would on occasions, preach in the parish church and visit the adjoining church house. It is said that the Rev Thomas Astbury took refuge in this house, which has long since been demolished, at the time of the Reformation, hiding in the priest hole. His sister, and heir, married John Shaw, and these two continued living in the house to which Shaw eventually claimed ownership. This was disputed by the church authorities in 1640, but the church failed in their claim. The property eventually passed to Thomas Wedgwood, the father of Josiah, through his family relationship with Shaw. Although the church lost its claim to the property, it won the right to an annual charge - based on the lands on which the house was built having been given to the church authorities by Henry de Eardley in 1450 - to Thomas Crocket and his heirs, the latter paying 20/- a year to the incumbent of the church to pray for ever for Henry's soul, which in the event was a wise precaution since otherwise he could still be buried at the site of the abbey, where monks would normally have provided such service.

An interesting entry in Simms Bibleotheca reads:

"John E. Armstrong, Rector of Burslem and Domestic Chaplain to the Earl of Shrewsbury and Talbot, also Honorary Secretary of the English Church Missions to the Roman Catholics. Author of a sixty two page account of the inquisition practiced by Rome on a free loyal British subject, based on what was known as the Astrop case of kidnapping. He was also awarded a prize for an essay on "The world's wail of misery from Rome's revolting tyranny. (1865)"

During the period when the mother church at Stoke held jurisdiction over St John's, occupants from certain designated properties in Burslem, Sneyd, and Hulton, were named to act as churchwardens, and this was compulsory for them. This was effective until 1789 in both Burslem and Sneyd, but there were claims for exemption from Hulton. However, for a period enforcement from the mother church appears to have lapsed since, in 1803, the Archdeacon of Stoke wrote to the Burslem parish restating the duties of lay officials, the oaths under which they performed, and information which he, Robert Nanes, required from them. He drew attention to the oaths required when taking office. For that of the churchwardens it read, *"I shall swear that I shall truly and faithfully exercise the office of churchwarden within this parish and I will to the best of my skill and knowledge present such things and persons as are presentable by the ecclesiastical laws of the realm. So help me God"*. That of the sidesmen read, *"I swear that I will assist the churchwardens in the execution of their office so far as (by law) I am bound to do. So help me God"*.

The Archdeacon further requested these officials to give him their opinion on the performance of the minister, and to furnish him with the attendance record of the individual members of the parish at holy communion, as he was entitled to do under church laws originating from the reign of Elizabeth.

A Sunday School was formed as early as 1787, the classes probably being held in the old town hall. The rules governing its operation were:

First. For seven shillings per year and upwards a subscriber was entitled to recommend one child, and a further child for each additional seven shillings.

Second. No child shall be admitted but such as work all the weekdays.

Third. No subscriber to withdraw his or her subscription without giving the governors six months notice beforehand.

Fourth. The general meeting of the subscribers to be called by the governors on the Thursday next immediately preceding each quarter day.

Fifth. Two persons to act as governors to receive and account for subscriptions and to visit the school. To admit proper children, and to give directions to the master and to take care that the children behave and apply themselves diligently and constantly, and that the treasurer keeps the books of accounts.

Sixth. To attend to, and see that subscriptions are received half yearly.

Seventh. That the master be allowed two and sixpence per day for attendance and instruction.

Eighth. Every person recommending a child should send a note with the child's name and by whom it was recommended.

Ninth. Persons who are inclined to assist this charity, to enter their names in the subscription book.

Tenth. Any child being absent three weeks together without sufficient cause to be excluded.

It seems strange that throughout the rules there is no mention of a minister being involved.

Following the church's independence from Stoke in 1807 the patronage came into the hands of William Robinson, who in 1809 sold it to William Adams of Cobridge Hall. He in turn left it to his son Thomas who died in 1835 leaving it to his two sisters. They sold it to Charles Herbert who was rector from 1850 to 1858. It then passed to another rector John Armstrong, afterwards reverting to laity; in 1669 John Morris, in 1871 Alfred Watton, and in 1886 Robert Heath. Finally in 1918 it passed to the Church of England Trust.

An Adams family marriage at St John's in the first half of the 19th century

The original Swan bank methodist chapel

A contemporary engraving showing John Wesley visting nearby South Staffordshire-
and getting a poor reception

CHAPTER SEVEN: Dissenters

John Wesley and the growth and division of the dissenting religions

It is questionable whether John Wesley, who was born in 1703 and died in 1791, specifically arranged his first visit to Burslem, or whether as an itinerant preacher it just happened. Equally it is doubtful if Burslem had any prior knowledge of the preacher who had come amongst them and with whom they eventually formed a close and mutually deep respect.

Born at Epworth in Lincolnshire in 1703, he was educated at Lincoln College, Oxford and ordained as a minister of the Church of England in 1725. For the next two years he joined his father as curate, following which he returned to Lincoln College as a tutor for six years. His father was vicar of Epworth and Wroot, an example of a minister with more than one living, but the additional income was a blessing since his wife gave birth to nineteen children in twenty years and they needed temporal as well as spiritual sustenance. While at college John joined a group of undergraduates who ordered their lives strictly on the ordinances of the church and earned themselves the soubriquet of Methodists. Soon after his father's death in 1735, together with his younger brother Charles, he left for America, having expressed a desire to convert the native Indians, but in the event he became instead the resident minister of an immigrant colony.

On the voyage out from England, there was a group of Moravians who had suffered religious persecution and were seeking peace in America. They held services on board the ship which particularly impressed John and Charles Wesley with their emphasis on singing, and the joyful composition of their hymns. The brothers concluded that this was due to their philosophy of Christ being wholly an expression of love and this is thought by some to have influenced the words and music of the immensely popular hymns which they both wrote in later years. John's stay in America was short lived. He returned to England alone and joined a Moravian chapter in Fetters Lane. When his brother Charles returned at a later date, the two combined with Whitefield and others to begin 'Field Preaching' as their mission was termed.

John Wesley's original intention was to create a religious fervour which would encourage people to attend the established church, at the time in an apathetic state, but the established church condemned their approach and banned the group from either preaching in church or giving communion; they even rang church bells to drown their open air preaching, and they were forbidden entry into some towns. Bishop Butler of Bristol, from where the group originally operated, sent this personal letter to John Wesley:

"Sir, The pretending to revelations and gifts of the Holy Ghost is a horrid thing. You have no business here, you are not commissioned to preach in this diocese, I therefore advise you to leave and go hence."

Fellow ministers attacked him in public outbursts. Toplady, a fellow minister and author of the much loved hymn *Rock of Ages* said of Wesley: *"He is the most rancorous hater of the gospel system that ever appeared in the land, a lone puny tadpole in divinity, governed by satanic shamelessness and satanic guilt."* Words which hardly contain the nucleus for another hymn! Another minister described him and his followers as a ragged legion of barbers, cobblers, tinkers, scavengers, draymen and chimney sweeps. Some people, not content with words, stoned him and used enraged bulls and dogs in efforts to break up his meetings, but Wesley was made of stern stuff, and he maintained that his belief was expressed in the prayer:

Oh grant that nothing in my soul, May dwell but thy pure love alone
Oh may thy love possess me whole, My joy, my treasures and my crown
Strange flames, far from my heart remove, My very act, thought and word be love.

Wesley was an ascetic, and his fasts would have had dire effects on some constitutions. Although considered a less powerful preacher than Whitefield he attracted tremendous crowds and his energy and resilience must have been stupendous. On his first arrival in Burslem in 1760 he preached in the market square outside the Leopard. This hostelry was an important meeting place and a coaching inn, situated behind the covered vegetable market. Wesley, referring to this first visit said, *"A multitude assembled at five in the evening, deep attention sat on every face, though as yet accompanied by deep ignorance, but, if the heart be towards God, he will in time enlighten their understanding."*

A subsequent meeting was on the site where the 'Shambles' was eventually built. Ward says that he preached in a warehouse on a site later occupied by Sam and Joseph Alcock, which would presumably be in Liverpool Street, now Westport Street. On later visits he became friendly with and used the house of William Locket, near the parish church and was later registered for the holding of services. His total number of visits to Burslem amounted to about ten, the last being in 1790, the year he died. He had now become reconciled to the animosity of the established church and was prepared with his flock to build alternative places of worship and to ordain ministers himself. He also realised that the movement had reached the stage where it required a constitution which he created in the form of a 'Conference' of both national and local bodies, consisting of lay members and administrators, the latter with the greater power.

Wesley died before the main chapel was built on Chapel Square, Burslem in 1796, lovingly referred to by following generations of Methodists as "Swan Bank" since it faced Swan Bank and was for many years the power centre of Methodism in the Potteries. It was enlarged in 1816 and an imposing Doric portico added in 1836. Of the galleries, which were all round, the front had eight tiers of pews, the side galleries six tiers. There was a handsome organ in a coved recess behind the pulpit, and seating for two thousand people. This was indeed the period of the Chapel's supremacy.

It had further radical internal alterations (a number after the amalgamation of the six towns), but it failed to survive, and like its fellow religious centre St Paul's, has ceased to exist, another sad example of the scourge of mining subsidence in the area. Both places of worship have been replaced by bright clean constructions which are no doubt suited to modern requirements, but the old buildings, begrimed as they were, seem to have taken with them a vibrant atmosphere of those heady revivalist days.

The Wesleyan movement was the first to take a serious interest in the education of children of all denominations in Burslem. The Methodist school was founded in 1787 with managers and teachers under the supervision of the preachers. It soon gained great popularity teaching both religion and general knowledge to a rapidly increasing population of children. It was entirely financed from private subscription and charity sermon, perhaps more commonly known to later generations as Anniversary', proceeds. Seeds of culture were sown, and literary attainments multiplied from both the teaching and the library the school accumulated.

The charity sermon, or anniversary was always a thrilling event when parents, urged by their children, went to great lengths to provide new clothes for the spectacular Sunday procession round the town, accompanied by collectors with their boxes. The chapel, two or even three times on this day, saw the children, seated on a prepared stage in tiered rows, enthusiastically announce to music that they were *"Christ's ray of sunshine."* Notices were circulated advertising the event. The following depicts one which took place in 1806:

BURSLEM 18th OCTOBER 1806 CHARITY SERMON
To be preached on the day at 3 o'clock in the Afternoon.

Christians shall our numerous train
Seek yours doors and plead in vain
Masters like the yielding clay
Ye shall mould us to obey
Are ye friends of human kind
We your liberal care shall find
Love ye England's happy land
Guard from vice her infant hand
Look upon our tender years
Smooth with smiles our little fears
Tell us ere we quit your house
Children at your call we come.

Two views of swan bank at the top of Waterloo Road, probably taken from the steps of the Shambles

The remains of Hill Top, at present in a state of limbo

It is not hard to visualise the tears and money which this appeal would produce.

A schedule of income for the Sunday School for the year 1804 will indicate the financial importance of these anniversary Sundays:

Collections in the Chapel	£ 54	12	11
Mr Child of Edinburgh		10	6
M. Swinnerton, Councillor	1	1	0
Free Masons Lodge		16	6
Friends with do.		5	6
Mrs Smith. Cobridge		10	6
A friend by Mr. S		10	6
Miss Byerley		7	0
Mr S by Mr Hall		7	0
Small donations		12	6
	£ 59	13	11

Relative to its time it was quite an appreciable sum; nevertheless, monetary pressures existed as the 1807 Charity Sermon notice indicated:

"Upwards of a thousand scholars are instructed at this institution. Its pecuniary circumstances are such that it is necessary to inform the kind friends who may wish to be present on the occasion, that everyone will be expected to give silver at the chapel doors at going in, and such as would be accommodated in the gallery will be expected to give liberally. This is not intended to supersede the collection in the chapel, but by keeping out immature persons, to make room for those who wish to promote the excellent plan of training up children to knowledge."

The report of the sunday school in 1808 said *"It is no longer wise to hold the labouring class in darkness, since knowledge is found to improve their manners and better their condition"*.

Burslem, with its predominant Methodist membership, dominated the local Conference in a dictatorial manner. Hanley had a much smaller membership but, encouraged and assisted by Job Ridgway of Shelton, built a chapel in the town and relied on Burslem for a minister to give communion. Burslem it seems dictated rather than co-operated with Hanley with service times, resulting in some acrimony between the two committees. Finally, a deputation came from Burslem to Hanley ostensively to reconcile their differences, but no agreement could be reached, whereupon the Burslem Conference ordered the Hanley members to vacate their chapel which was then locked and the keys taken to Burslem.

Conflict arose in Burslem itself in 1836 in connection with the Sunday School. Attendances had at this time reached between 1700 and 1800 pupils with some 300 teachers attempting to widen the syllabus beyond purely religious teaching. The Wesleyan Conference of 1827 had decided that strict regulations should be introduced in all their schools, although it would appear that the strictness could vary with the interpretation of local ministries, but in 1836 matters came to a head in Burslem. It was decided that the practice of writing on a Sunday should be discouraged, that the time spent on religious study as opposed to general knowledge was insufficient, and that studies should be confined to religious and moral values.

This caused a hostile and protracted dispute with the many devoted voluntary teachers and ended with the Sunday School's doors locked and a feud between the Conference and teachers, parents and friends of the school who had contributed so much to its success. Some might say that God intervened, since on the day of the closure there was a major eclipse of the sun, but even this failed to bring the parties together. Finally, having taken legal action and failed to get possession, the school's supporters erected a temporary wooden building and determined to build a permanent structure as soon as possible. In 1837 a plot of land was purchased at Hill Top and, at great expense, a dual purpose building to serve as school and chapel was built. The schoolrooms occupied the basement and the chapel with galleries was above. The entrance was reached by wide stone steps to a portico supported by twelve feet high doric columns and over these, in large engraved letters "BURSLEM SUNDAY SCHOOL".

This drama took place when Ward was writing his *History of Stoke on Trent*; it is therefore interesting to read the remarks he made at the time:

"These separatists have not coalesced with any other denomination, or assumed any title other than Wesleyan Methodists, by which body they consider themselves governed, though practically excommunicated from the Wesleyan Church. We have recorded their rise, it will remain with the pen of the future historian to describe their progress, but we may be permitted to auger that great good, or an equal amount of evil will undoubtedly be produced by this large and influential school, according as it shall be conducted on sound or unsound principles that, if the pure and self denying doctrines be carefully implanted in the minds of the youthful multitudes, an abundant produce of improved religious and moral conduct may be reasonably expected, but, if the rank weeds, which are indigenous in the human heart be not sedulously eradicated, a plentiful crop of all manner of noxious things will almost certainly spring up."

Any stranger passing the site today cannot fail to be attracted by the massive Corinthian pillars and above them the sign BURSLEM SUNDAY SCHOOL - and think how strange to have built a frontage and not a body. Looking closer they will see that there has once been a body, but its place has been taken by noxious things which Ward feared, for the space which once harboured 2000 young souls is now a resting place for the motor car, now more favoured on Sundays than the building which once towered above!

In many great movements the tendency has been to lose momentum when the founder departs. It has been said that Wesley rose on a combination of apathy in the established church, industrial unrest, squalor, poverty and crime. They could have been liberated by violence or religious zeal; the latter Wesley cultivated and organised into a powerful influence. His original intention of inducing people to return to the established church by preaching in the field failed, but finished with a movement with its own temples of worship. In Burslem, disciples of Wesley, like Bourne and Clowes, thought they should continue with his original pattern of crusade. The National Conference and its local counterpart had other views; they were of the opinion that if such evangelism was allowed it should be conducted by the established ministry, and the local Conference issued the following address, in effect a warning to the deviants:

CAMP MEETING "An address to the Methodists.

The Camp Meeting, held on Sunday May 31st at Mow Cop near Harriseihead, has given rise to various conjectures, and the public in general have been led to draw very wrong conclusions respecting the authors and arrangers of that meeting. We are sorry to learn that the Methodist Connection has been charged as patronising such irregularity and disorder. To vindicate the reputation of the body, they deem it their duty to come forward in this way and inform the public in general, and the Methodist Societies in the vicinity of Burslem circuit in particular, that they highly disprove of these meetings.

The measure has appeared the more necessary as "Observation on Camp Meetings" has just been published, and industriously circulated through the country, in which the writer endeavours to vindicate them, and advertises two other meetings of a similar nature.

At a quarterly meeting held at Burslem on June 29th, the subject of Camp Meetings was brought forward and, after a dispassionate and candid discussion, were declared unwise and irregular, and all the local Preachers (with one exception), the Leader and Steward in conjunction with the travelling Preachers, solemnly engaged to discountenance, and, as far as possible, to prevent any further meetings.

It must be admitted that many serious and pious persons attended the last Camp Meeting, but it was the novelty of the thing that excited their curiosity and, without reflecting either on the propriety or impropriety, the meeting held out the idea of religious exercise and they went with the best of notices, but by a moments reflection they are sensible of the imprudence of such conduct, and indeed, to do justice to some that have been the principal promoters of these meetings, there is reason to believe their design was pure, but in this instance are mistaken in the way of doing good.

We beseech you brethren, and exhort you by the Lord Jesus Christ, that you be careful not to let your good be evil spoken of, and that the name of God, and his doctrine be not blasphemed.

It is your indispensable duty to study that no unnecessary offence be given either to Jew or Gentile, nor the church of God, and take it patently that this is acceptable to God, for hereunto are ye called

Signed on behalf of the Leaders & Stewards   John Riles. Burslem July 8th 1807".

The Hill Top chapel and school built following the dispute

From the report by Samuel Scriven on the employment of children and young persons in the Staffordshire Potteries, 1841

No. 218.—Joseph Wood, aged 53:— I have been the superintendent of this school 24 years. It was first established in theWesleyan Methodist chapel, where it was conducted for a number of years. A dispute took place between the preachers and managers about six years ago relative to the introduction of rules adopted by the conference, which ended in the trustees expelling us from the premises which we previously occupied. This dispute led to the erection of the p resent building for a school to be conducted under the farmer system of management. At that time about 1700 children of both sexes attended it under the tuition of 240 teachers; we have continued our efforts ever since, and now number 539 boys, with 93 teachers; and 728 girls, wilh 107 teachers: there is besides this number a class of adults of 30. The building stood us in between 3000l. and 4000l., out of which we have paid a considerable sum, and stand indebted in the amount of 2093l. 15s:. The only means we have of defraying this is by annual collec-tions and voluntary contributions. Our current expenses are considerable for books, coals, &c., which is also paid by the like means. The system of education pursued is in part upon the Lancasterian and part upon the collective or catechetical principle. The children meet at half-past ten and continue till twelve, meet again at two and continue till four, attending both before and after the religious worship of the chapel; we admit them at five years old, and often before, and continue them as long as they like to remain. We have no day-school at present, when however the debt is paid off we hope to establish one, and support it by the seat-rents of the gallery. The greatest number of these children have no other means of acquiring information but by their Sunday schools, in consequence of their being taken so early to work at the factories. I do not see much difference in the comparative educational condition of the children of the Sunday and day-schools, for this reason, that the time the latter devote to it is limited and during their infancy, and except followed up by the former is of very little use to them. I think the potters' children are above par—I mean those who do attend school; but there is a vast number who are ignorant, grossly ignorant, who attend nowhere; this . results in some instances from the poverty of the parents, in others from their extravagance, in many from their total indifference to religious or secular education.

We have a library attached to the school accessihle to the writing and Bible classes; the books are of history and biography; immoral works are excluded.

(Signed) . Josiah Wood.
I have heard this evidence of Josiah Wood, and being satisfied of its correctness, fully concur in it.
(Signed)   WILLIAM MOLINEUX

This is a magnificent building of three stories, the basement divided into two rooms for boys, the one above being occupied by girls, and the upper forming deep galleries occupied during divine service. It is very spacious, light, well ventilated, and warmed by hot air flues.

The notice failed to have the desired effect on Bourne and Clowes who were both registered members of the Swan Bank, and in 1808 they were barred from preaching in a Methodist chapel.

Hugh Bourne came of farming stock, he was born at Fordhay Farm in 1772 but the family later moved to Bemmersley, north of Burslem. His expulsion did not deter him from his evangelism and he described how, on his way to Cheadle to preach, he was crossing a field when he saw a bright light coming in his direction, finally enveloping him and filling his soul. He gained a great number of like believers and with them he formed a movement under the title of 'Primitive Methodism'. Despite his adherence to open air evangelism the movement ultimately built its own chapels, the first being at Tunstall in 1812.

The first Primitive Methodist chapel in Burslem was a small one in Chapel Lane which, according to Ward, was known as "Salt Box Chapel". From the same source, one was built in Navigation Road. This evidently anticipated increasing membership which failed to materialise since Ward said it was later reduced in size to seat two hundred and fifty.

One contemporary religious commentator's view was that the autocratic attitude of the Wesleyan Conference was due to the control the ruling members exercised over its constitution. This brought about the numerous branches of Methodism - and few places have a greater diversity of religious sects than in the Potteries. Government animosity was akin to the intolerance of catholics and they were likewise banned from standing for Parliament or entering major universities. Attempts were even made to close non-comformist schools that were self-supporting

Nevertheless branches from the same tree continued to grow and further imposing places of worship arose in Burslem. One such was the Independent Chapel in Queen Street, erected in 1837. Scarratt said that this was a handsome structure of brick with very lofty windows. It had an open vestibule in the basement formed by Tuscan columns and pillars of stone, two flights of stairs to the chapel above which seated about four hundred worshippers, a gallery at one end which held an organ, and a basement containing a school room and vestry. It is really amazing that such an apparently imposing structure above and below ground has completely vanished, and nobody appears to know where it was actually sited!

The Bethel Chapel in Waterloo Road was a branch of the Primitives. Ward described it as a handsome brick building with wings rather in advance. The wings formed the school rooms and the preacher's house; the chapel was in the centre and had a gallery similar to the Wesleyan chapel, and the building as a whole seated about a thousand persons. On a tablet at the front of the chapel is the name and the date 1824. Scarratt, writing at a later date, said the front had been renovated and made more imposing and at Queen Victoria's coronation pupils from the Sunday School numbered four hundred. This imposing structure still stands, preserved as a scheduled building, no longer a place of worship but converted internally to form a branch of the native industry.

Ward's history states that a Zoar Chapel is situated in Princes Row, Nile Street. He said it originally belonged to the Primitives, later the Independents, and at the time he wrote, the Christian Society. Built in 1788, it had side galleries and seated 500 worshippers. In 1836 its name was changed from Zoar to Salem, but this failed to save it from the same fate as Sodom, along with other buildings in the same street.

There was a chapel with an adjoining graveyard in High Street which belonged to the Baptists and seated two hundred and fifty people, but the street, the chapel, and the graveyard have since disappeared.

The Woodall Memorial Chapel in Moorland Road was of later construction, built in 1905 by the Congregation movement. It is still active and in prime condition. The building faces the junction of Moorland Road and Hamil Road and can presumably be said to be approximately situated behind Swan Bank chapel. The frontage is interesting in that combined with the brickwork is an embossed head set in a stone ring, and extending beyond this further stone embellishment. Presumably the head is that of Mr Woodall; there is nothing to indicate the artist who modelled it but it is a fittingly deserving tribute to the spiritual worth of a man who gave so much to Mother Burslem both tangibly and by example. The foundation stone of the chapel was laid by C. W. Earlick.

The Congregational school

The new Swan Bank methodist church

CHAPTER EIGHT: Town services

The first Infirmary. The Wood's golden wedding celebration.
Early stage coaches & hackney carriages. The Fire Service.

At the beginning of the 19th century there was a heavy death rate from fever epidemics, especially among the inmates of the Poor Houses. This was thought to have arisen from privation and referred to as relapsing or famine fever similar to that experienced in Ireland during the potato famine. Fear was bred of it being spread by contagion and anxiety expressed at the absence of adequate municipal care. There followed an appeal in the district for the building of a treatment and nursing facility, A circular furthering the project was issued in September 1802, and a meeting was held on neutral ground at the Trentham Institute the same year, chaired by Mr Walter Sneyd. It was decided to open a subscription list, following which land was purchased near the junction of the Cobridge and the Hanley to Newcastle Roads. Support was forthcoming from all branches of the community:

TO THE PUBLIC

"The committee for promoting the establishment of a Medical Dispensary and House of Recovery, make known the following at the request of some well disposed persons who think it may tend to promote the interests of this very useful public undertaking. The workmen in the manufactury at Etruria, have subscribed in the book appointed for the district, twenty pounds towards the building, and also the sum of sixteen guineas to be paid yearly for the support thereof, and this last money they will raise by very small weekly contributions from each person, to be paid into the hands of their employer (Josiah Wedgwood)

How much good can be done with very little money?

Subscribers would be entitled to recommend eighteen persons every year to the House of Recovery, and have besides, eighteen patients on the books of the Dispensary, and supposing those eighteen should be changed once in every month, they will then have it in their power to procure good advice and medication for two hundred and sixteen persons within the year.

Other sums will be entitled to proportional advantages.   *Go ye and do likewise"*

The following is an early account of the extent and cost of treatment at the dispensary:

Patients cured or relieved from the commencement of the institution			
	to Michaelmas	*1805*	*900*
" " " " " " " " " " " " "		*1805/6*	*505*
Vaccinated to		*1805*	*1450*
do		*1805/6*	*545*
Fever patients			*7*
Total treatments to date			*3407*
Receipts for the year		*1805/6*	*£505. 18. 7.*
Disbursements.			*£505. 18. 7.*
Bills outstanding			*£211. 7. 9.*

Like its successor the National Health Service, it had difficulty in remaining solvent.

The authorities' fear of epidemics led to the issue of a circular giving advice on precautions to take, which gives an interesting insight to domestic conditions of that time. These precautions were said to be the rules of Dr Hayworth, late of Chester, now of Bath.

NOTICE REGARDING INFECTIONS -

As safety from infection depends entirely on cleanliness and fresh air.

The chamber door of a patient ill of fever (especially in a dwelling of the poor) should never be shut.
A window in it ought to be open during the day, and frequently at night.

The bed curtains should never be close drawn round the patient, but only on the side next the light, so as to shade the face.

Dirty clothes, utensils etc. should be frequently changed, immediately thrown into cold water and washed clean when taken out.

All discharges from the patient should be instantly removed.

The floor near the bed should be rubbed clean every day, with a mop and cloth with Vinegar and Water.

The air in a sick room has a more infectious quality in some parts than others. Visitors and attendants should avoid the current of the patients breath. The air arising from the body, especially if the bed curtains are, or have been lately closed, and the vapour arising from all evacuations.

Medical attendants, visitors, or nurses, should hold their breath when unfavourably exposed to such dangerous situations.

No person should go into a sick room with an empty stomach, and the mouth should be cleared by spitting or washing with water, and the nose should be blown on quitting it.

The Dispensary was opened in 1804 but was soon seen to be inadequate for the growing needs for medical attention, and the appeal for funds was widened. In 1814 it was decided to build an Infirmary on a site nearby. The cost of the new building was in the region of £5000, and contributions from the affluent and benevolent included £500 from the Prince Regent from revenues of the Duchy of Lancaster; £1000 from Mr John Rogers of The Watlands; receipts from a fancy bazaar at Newcastle £940; and from an Oratorio at Stoke church, £800. Great merit was due, it was said, to Mr John Tomlinson Esq. of Cliffe Bank for his extraordinary zeal and services in promoting the project and establishing a reserve fund which, reaching £20,000, would produce an annual income of £1000 to support the running of the hospital. The foundation stone was laid by Mr John Heathcote who was accompanied by founder members and representatives from supporting societies including the Masons who sang "Hail Masonry Divine", appropriate for such a building.

Following the ceremony the company retired to the Etruria Inn where the success of the project was toasted with the contents of a barrel of ale, provided with the complements of John Heathcote. (This inn would later thrive on custom from the nearby steelworks which ultimately overshadowed both the hospital and Josiah Wedgwood's Etruria works. Apprentices with their pails would trudge up and down Furnace Lane to the Inn fetching the ale considered indispensable for the survival of the men on the furnaces.)

All benefactors of the hospital who contributed twenty guineas and upwards, with annual subscriptions of two guineas, could become governors and be eligible to select an annual committee. Medical and surgical departments were the responsibility of two physicians and the three surgeons whose services were on a honorary (gratuitous) basis. There was also one resident house surgeon. Subscribers were entitled to recommend patients proportionate to their subscription, and workpeople contributing to the hospital were, along with their families, entitled to its benefits. Accommodation was for one hundred in-patients.

The site was an unfortunate choice since the Shelton Iron and Steel Works later became huge and towered above it. For the sick person waking in the depth of the night, with the roar of the rolling mill and the golden glare of molten metal lighting the night sky, it must have confirmed their worst fears. Furthermore, the building began to suffer from the usual malaise of mining subsidence which led to cracks in the fabric of the buildings and in turn unwelcome cockroach infestations. As a consequence a part of the Mount estate at Penkhull, previously the home of the Spode family, was purchased in 1844 as the site for a new district hospital. The new hospital in the parish of Penkhull was to house 167 beds, and the foundation stone was laid in 1844 by Edward VII, then Prince of Wales. On the appointed day he arrived with due pomp and ceremony along with noble company from Trentham Hall, guests of the Duke of Sutherland. A general holiday was declared to enable all to attend the proceedings and bring their individual contributions to the building fund, which were laid on and around the foundation stone in all manner of containers.

The new hospital was maintained by voluntary subscription right up until the advent of a National Health Service in 1948. When I started work I was asked to agree to a deduction of one penny per week from my hard earned wage. Such of the original buildings as are left are now lost among massive new ones, while there is now no trace of the original hospital or dispensary situated in Etruria.

It is interesting to see the treatments which were provided in the original Dispensary and Hospital:

For the mining industry, it was for the treatment of burns from explosions and from Firedamp, also the removal of coal and stones driven into the flesh from shot firing, and the effects from the continual inhalation of dust.

For Shelton Iron and Steel Works and other foundries, it was mostly treatment for burns, damage to the eyes, and heart problems.

For the pottery industry, it was problems caused by Lead poisoning, described as Paralysis, Epilepsy, Anaemia, Cataract and Sterility.

The widespread respiratory problems caused by dust, seem to have been treated as an act of God.

In a preceding chapter, Enoch Wood was acknowledged not only as being a successful potter but as an outstanding contributor to the growth and welfare of the town during his lifetime as its leading citizen. In 1829 he and his wife celebrated the fiftieth year of their marriage and although Mrs Wood does not appear to have played a prominent part in civic affairs, she was much respected. This in any case was a man's world, and although the Suffragette movement was rearing its head, it was not considered worthy of attention by the Burslem Board of Health which was all male. Periodically they received written requests from the movement for the Board's moral support; equally periodically at their meetings the requests were not so much ignored as left on the table. Had Mrs Wood been a member of the Suffragettes it is likely that more respect would have been shown.

The occasion of the Wood's golden wedding was unique since for the first, and probably only time in Burslem's history, the citizens of the town organised such a demonstration of personal appreciation and goodwill. The morning of the anniversary opened with the firing of cannon, the ringing of bells, and music provided by the Longport Band. At three o'clock in the afternoon all the male employees of Enoch's numerous factories were offered ale and the women punch, while the poor of the town received free soup. A family party, with many guests, dined at five o'clock, and among the after dinner presentations to Mr and Mrs Wood was a superb inscribed silver waiter from their children and grandchildren.

The celebrations extended to the town itself in the evening when, in the words of the Staffordshire Advertiser, *"it displayed what must be one of the most disinterested, unsought, and flattering complements that was ever paid to an individual moving in private life"*. A general illumination took place as if by magic. The whole town at seven o'clock presenting one blaze of light in the market place;

"All the lighting in the town hall, and in the windows in the adjoining public squares made a brilliant scene, attracting crowds of observers. A description of the scene having been conveyed to Mr and Mrs Wood, they and their party walked through the town to see for themselves and, on being recognised, received a boisterous reception. At nine o'clock in the evening there was a brilliant firework display in the grounds of the family house, to which all the inhabitants of Burslem were invited," and again, quoting the Staffordshire Advertiser, "we rejoice that the proceedings of the day were unclouded by accident, riot, or disorder, and at eleven o'clock everything was quiet as usual."

Several private parties were given to honour the event, among them, according to the newspaper, one by Thomas Heath Esq. who it was said *"treated the whole of his many employees at his extensive manufactury"*, presumably referring to the local steel and iron foundries which the Heaths' owned.

RECOMMENDATIONS
OF THE
Board of Health,
FOR THE PURPOSE
Of Preventing the progress of Disease
IN THE
PARISH OF BURSLEM.

HOUSE.—To guard against accumulations of refuse matter in drains, cess-pools, dust-bins, and dirt heaps, and to purify such receptacles by solution of chloride of lime, to be procured on application at the Board of Health.

To maintain in a cleanly and wholesome condition all reservoirs, cisterns, and sinks, and to allow impurities, where practicable, to be carried away by running water.

To keep inhabited apartments clean, by frequently washing and very carefully drying the floors, and to ventilate them thoroughly. as well by fires as by a free access of fresh air.

To have the windows, especially of bed-rooms, put in good repair, so that the occupants may not be exposed during sleep to currents of night air.

To change bed-linen and furniture frequently, and to clear out those spaces in inhabited rooms, which are concealed by beds and other furniture, and which are so often made the depositories of filth and rubbish.

Where persons live in crowded apartments, which should be avoided as far as may be practicable, additional vigilance should be used to preserve a free ventilation; and where offensive exhalations arise, they should be destroyed by the solution of chloride of lime.

PERSON.—To maintain personal cleanliness by frequent washing and change of clothing, and, if available, by occasional warm-bathing.

To guard against sudden changes of temperature, by wearing flannel next the skin, more especially round the bowels, and to protect the feet and legs by woollen stockings.

To avoid exposure to cold and wet, particularly at night, and to change damp clothing without delay.

DIET.—To let the diet consist of plain meats, bread, and well-boiled vegetables, rejecting as injurious all indigestible kinds of food, such as salads, raw fruits, nuts, rich pastry and in general such articles as each individual may have found by experience to create acidity, flatulence, and indigestion.

BEVERAGE.—To abstain from undiluted ardent spirits, acid drinks, and stale soups or broths, and to be sparing in the use of sugar, especially if it give rise to a sour fermentation in the stomach.

To maintain regular habits, using moderate exercise keeping early hours, and taking nourishment at limited intervals, so that fatigue or exposure may never be encountered during an exhausted and empty state of the stomach.

N. B. A number of Gentlemen are appointed to visit the different Houses in the Parish, for the purpose of making such observations and giving such directions as may be necessary for the preservation of health. You will therefore be called upon in a few days, and reports will be made to the Board of Health.

Town-Hall, Burslem, Nov. 19th, 1831.

MARY BROUGHAM, PRINTER.

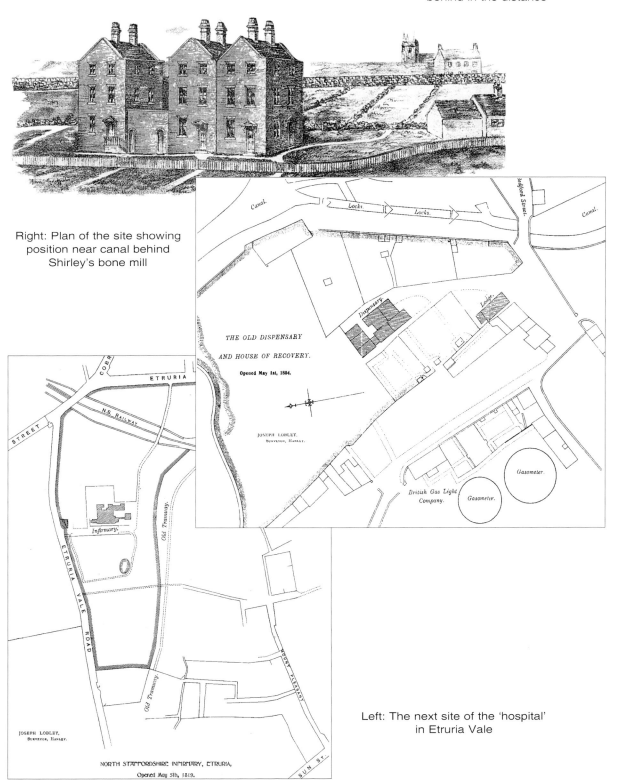

NORTH STAFFORDSHIRE DISPENSARY & HOUSE OF RECOVERY

North Staffordshire Dispensary and House of Recovery - a drawing from memory - opened in 1804 in Etruria. St John's church in Hanley can be seen behind in the distance

Right: Plan of the site showing position near canal behind Shirley's bone mill

THE OLD DISPENSARY AND HOUSE OF RECOVERY.

Opened May 1st, 1804.

JOSEPH LOBLEY.
SURVEYOR, HANLEY.

British Gas Light Company.

Gasometer.

Gasometer.

Left: The next site of the 'hospital' in Etruria Vale

JOSEPH LOBLEY,
SURVEYOR, HANLEY.

NORTH STAFFORDSHIRE INFIRMARY, ETRURIA,
Opened May 5th, 1819.

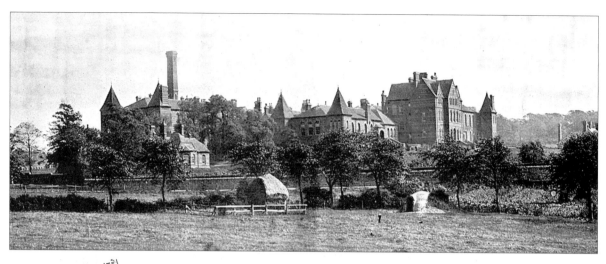

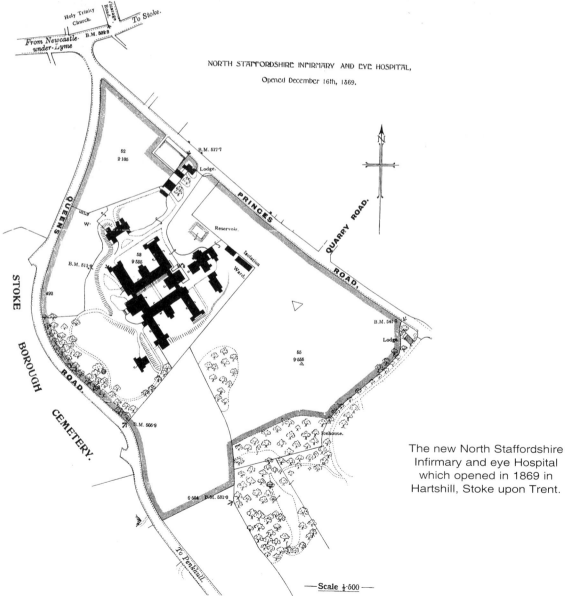

NORTH STAFFORDSHIRE INFIRMARY AND EYE HOSPITAL,

Opened December 16th, 1869.

The new North Staffordshire
Infirmary and eye Hospital
which opened in 1869 in
Hartshill, Stoke upon Trent.

Enoch appears to have been much touched by the demonstrations:

TO THE INHABITANTS OF BURSLEM

""My dear friends, I am quite unable to express the gratitude I feel for the very flattering manner in which you have spontaneously joined my family in celebrating the fiftieth anniversary of my wedding day. I was totally unprepared for the honour, as much as for the manner in which my family have celebrated the day. My feelings are quite overpowered. It always has been my pride and pleasure to witness the prosperity of my native town by birth, station, and inclination. My feelings are identified with the people of Burslem, and it is my heartfelt wish that they may enjoy uninterrupted prosperity when I am no more.

I have the honour to be your obliged and obedient servant.

Enoch Wood. Fountain Place. Burslem. December 17th. 1829.

The occasion of the Wood's golden wedding

Neither before or since has such tribute been paid to a citizen of Burslem in recognition of his personal qualities and his services to the town; services given despite the demands of his extensive business which was far from immune from problems - as in 1810, when his workmen gave him notice of a dispute:

"We have taken into consideration we hare agreable as rest of neibers but we think of being paid for all is dipped so we expect an answer from you wether we are your servants but not one without all but we wish for an anser". (sic)

This ultimation was marked by Enoch as being *"received on Friday evening on the 6th April 1810, being the same day that the plate and dishmakers left the works, and the day following my issuing a large order for plates and dishes"*. The notice from the men is exactly as written here and presumably relates to the practice of payment of *'good from oven'* rather than *'payment from hand'* which was a bone of contention in the pottery industry for generations, and a procedure which is explained in detail in another chapter.

A further incident with which he had to contend occurred in 1827. Someone committed sabotage at the works which led Enoch to issue the following notice:

£20 REWARD "A person in this manufactury is strongly suspected of throwing lime in the glaze for the purpose of injuring the credit of his fellow workers. any person who will give such information as will commit this person, or one of them, if two are concerned, or of one willing to impeach on the other to conviction. The one impeaching shall be forgiven and receive £20 reward.

Burslem December 4th 1827;- the Lime was found in the bottom of the Dip".

An interesting item among Enoch's papers was a plan and correspondence relating to a proposed factory and house by Anthony Keeling, a renowned Tunstall potter, on land he owned adjoining Enoch's principal works. Presumably this was a speculative investment and negotiations by Enoch to rent the premises had apparently got as far as fixing the terms at 7% on the value of the works, and 6% on the house, but a late proviso by Keeling was that Enoch should take Keeling's son into partnership. This Enoch refused to do, and he approached Josiah Wedgwood, as executor for Thomas Wedgwood, to rent the Overhouse Pottery which at this time was apparently unused awaiting an heir to become of age.

Although Enoch Wood appears to have had an amicable relationship with most of his colleagues and friends, his association with John Ward appears to have been brittle. Ward sued him for slander in 1819, the culmination of friction between the two. The disagreement appears to have started in 1817 when Ward had to make a distress for goods for non-payment of rent by Enoch Wood's son in law. This was followed by an incident when a bullet accidentally fired by a tradesman's apprentice went through a window in the counting house of the factory. Enoch Wood was accused of assaulting the perpetrator's father, whom Ward was representing.

A further aggravation arose over some of Enoch Wood's land which was needed for road widening, and also over land which Enoch had engaged John Ward to buy for him. Ward, it was suggested, had told the owner of the land to ask a higher price than Enoch Wood was offering and had offered to buy the land if Enoch refused to accept. This information was passed back to Enoch and perhaps naturally, but unwisely, he expressed to many people his opinion of Ward which did not fit in with the opinion Ward had of himself and he sued Enoch through the court claiming £1000 for slander - a considerable sum in those days - but Ward it seems was only able to justify a tenth of his accusations, since he was awarded £100!

Enoch Wood died in 1840 at the age of eighty one and was buried in St John's churchyard, but his spirit remains in those today who share pride and concern for Mother Burslem and its prosperity.

For the early Burslem potters a journey to London was no doubt an adventure; Uttoxeter would have been well known in view of the trade in butter pots and it was from Uttoxeter that many Burslem worthies must have taken their first coach to the capital, since from the middle of the 18th century there was a service known as 'The Flying Wagon' which carried both passengers and goods. Leaving Uttoxeter on a Tuesday it was scheduled to arrive in London on the following Saturday, which would allow time to ruminate on the aptness of its name. A receiving centre for parcels and passenger booking operated from an office in the centre of Burslem, and as demand increased the service was expanded to twice per week.

However, the state of the roads failed to keep pace with the increase in traffic. Transport had grown from the carriage of goods by a single horse with panniers strapped to its back, followed by wagons similar to the ones depicted in wild west films, to heavy wagons pulled by a team of horses. The congestion which these trains of wagons caused, and the damage they inflicted on the roads, led the government to introduce a law limiting the number of horses which could be used to eight. Congestion and frustration led to claims for the introduction of canals, particularly in reducing breakage in such a fragile product as pottery.

The government failed to introduce a co-ordinated policy for roads but encouraged private enterprise in the making of toll roads. The bulk of the applications seemed to come from wealthy individuals and for comparatively short lengths of highway, each application requiring the time-consuming consent of parliament before construction could take place. 400 such bills were passed between the years 1700 and 1750, and a further 1600 between the years 1751 and 1790. Gradually with more stretches of highway and with lighter coaches with springing, coupled with facilities for changing horses, there was an expansion in frequency and speed of services. By the year 1800 six coaches per day were passing through Newcastle, and by 1830 the number had increased to forty per day and Burslem was now a calling place to and from Manchester, Liverpool and London.

Coaches were invariably given names. The 'Prince Saxe Coburg' left Burslem at seven o'clock in the morning and was billed to arrive in London at three o'clock the following morning; a vast improvement on the mid-18th century. Other familiar names in Burslem were 'Night Post', 'Hero',

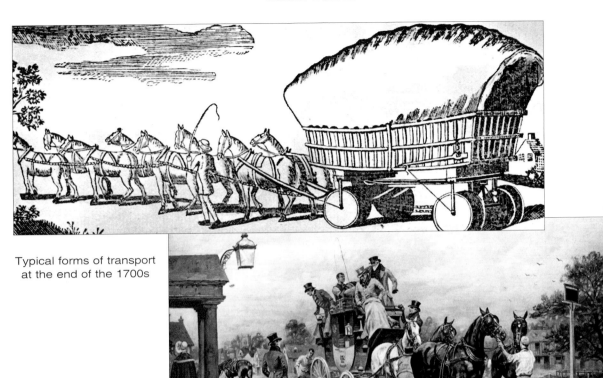

Typical forms of transport
at the end of the 1700s

'Independent Potter' and Sovereign'. The 'Express' and the 'Red Rover' called at St John's Square on their way from London to Liverpool. There was a regular and comprehensive service from London to Leicester. Connecting coaches operated from Leicester to most towns in the Midlands, one coming to the Potteries via Checkley, Tean, Lane End, Stoke, Hanley, Cobridge and Burslem (Market Place).

This volume of coaches would give the impression that a large number of the population was now on the move, but the carrying capacity was usually limited by law to about six inside, consequently the life of the stagecoach quickly ended when the railway age arrived. The service was very labour intensive and required an enormous number of horses. One passenger expressed a forthright view of coach travel through Staffordshire when he said it *"..either dislocated your bones, or buried you in mud"*. The effect on the coaching inns would have been rapid and devastating - the speed with which the rail service developed must have had a catastrophic effect on a large service industry.

In addition to the long distance services, there was a local coach to Leek on three days a week. Starting from Shelton it arrived in Burslem at 8.15am and in Leek at 10.00am. There was also a growth in personally owned carriages, and carriages plying for public hire, both of which were subject to licensing. The cost of licences varied from £1 to £3.10. 0 for private coach, landau, chaise, etc. There was a distinction between those drawn by ponies rather than horses. Vehicles carrying the coat of arms of their owner and the employment of a coachman, carried an additional tax for each. A horse-drawn hackney carriage licence was £1, and when these vehicles were introduced in Burslem they stood outside the town hall displaying a flag when available for hire. As demand grew the number of cabs increased, and gradually further stands were introduced in St John's Square, Swan Square, and when the railway arrived, at the station. Exposed to the elements as cab drivers were, it was not surprising that the cabbies asked for a shelter to be provided, but this appeal was only met for those cabbies who operated outside the town hall. The public complained of lack of uniformity in fares, resulting in a by-law which obliged the owners to display charges, along with the hours the cabs were available - from 8.00am to 8.00pm from May to September and from 9.30am to 6.00pm for the remainder of the year.

> *For the convenient accomodation of Paſſengers from and betwixt the Cities of* London *and* Weſtcheſter, *there is provided ſeveral Stage-Coaches which go from the* George Inn *without Alderſgate upon every Monday, Wedneſday, and Friday to* Coventry, *in Two days for Twenty five ſhillings, to* Stone *in Three Days for Thirty ſhillings, and to* Cheſter *in Four days for Thirty five ſhillings, and from thence do return upon the ſame days; which is performed with much eaſe to the Paſſengers, having freſh Horſes once a day, In Mondays. Intelligence laſt the ſeverall ſums and rates were by the Printer miſtaken.*

An indication of the growth of the town was the need expressed for provision for dealing with fires. A meeting was called to consider the purchase of three fire engines; one for Burslem, one for Tunstall and one for Longport. It was agreed to open a subscription list, the initial result of which, considering the area involved, would give the impression that fires were more rewarding than fire engines.

"We whose names are hereunto subscribed agree to pay the sums respectively affixed to our name, for the purpose of providing three fire engines, one to be stationed in the town of Burslem, one at Tunstall, and the other at Longport, but at all times jointly for the benefit of the subscribers.

£5. 5. 0	£5. 5. 0	£3. 3. 0.	£2. 2. 0
Thomas Wedgwood	Walter Daniel	J & R Riley	Geo. Walker
Wood & Caldwell	Theopholus Smith	Bagshaw Taylor & Co.	Joseph Machin
Jos. Smith	John Sherwin	Cole & Co.	D. Steel
John Robinson	John Gilbert		Richard Wilkinson
Anthony Enoch Keeling	Tim. & John Lockett		Ralph Wedgwood
John Gallimore	John Davenport		Thos. Knight
Robert Williamson	S & T Cartlich		Sam. Oakes
Wm. Clowes	H. Henshall		Wm. Dawes"
Wm. Adams	Marsh & Hall		
John Wood	J & G Rogers		

Extended credit was common in those days - the early potter manufacturers suffered from allowing it - and although this preliminary list totalled less than £150, the purchase of three machines was achieved.

In 1825 fire precautions were reviewed, and it would seem that Tunstall had now made its own provision since the engine now at Cobridge (not provided for initially), must have been the one that had originally gone to Tunstall. The gift was now said to be in a useless condition. A further result of the review was the decision to place the service on a sounder base; the complement of firemen would be ten per engine; each engine would be taken out and worked once a month, and the captain paid three shillings, the remainder of the crew two shillings on each such occasion.

In 1838 tenders were sought for a new machine. Messrs Merryweather's quotation was £162 with an extra charge for springs of £7.10 0. This quotation was accepted and a sixpenny rate levied to cover its purchase. Equipment with the machine included buckets and a leather hose, and there was a stipulation that it should be operated by sixteen to twenty men, but the Burslem Board, appreciating that Burslem men were in a different category, used a maximum of twelve. Once purchased, insurance companies were circularised asking them to pay when the engines attended a fire at an insured property, but the only response it seems, was a gratuitous ten pounds contributed by the Norwich Union; Following a fire at a later date, the Royal Exchange Insurance Company's attention was drawn to the fact that the Tunstall and

Longport brigades had received a payment and that the Burslem brigade had not; the company's response was that the Burslem brigade did not arrive until the fire was out, and were therefore not entitled to payment. A cruel reflection on a crew recently equipped with a new vehicle with extra for springs!

Perhaps bearing this experience in mind, a new arrangement was made with the crews, the first to arrive at the scene of the fire to receive £5, the second £4, and the third £3, but this scheme was withdrawn in 1844, not surprisingly perhaps since it seems to have been devised on the assumption that both machines and crew would be equidistant from every fire.

In 1848, maintenance conditions were revised. Engines were to be examined monthly and exercised at least quarterly; the superintendent to be paid £10 per annum, and the firemen ten shillings per annum, exclusive of clothing allowance. For attendance at fires, payment was one shilling each man for the first hour, and sixpence for each succeeding hour. Charges for the service were made on the following scale for non-ratepayers and insurance offices.

One engine   First hour £2.   Two engines   £3.   Three engines   £4.   After the first hour 10/- per engine.

In 1849 it was agreed to provide uniforms comprising a frock coat, trousers and a belt. Whether these were intended for state occasions, church parade or Mayor's Sunday is speculative, but certainly the uniform hardly seems to fit the needs of firemen in action. A customary polished brass helmet would have ensured immediate recognition, and actually a sample had been obtained but none appear to have been bought, evidently on account of expense, since, when the uniforms were purchased, the suppliers were requested to allow the Board extended credit. No mention was made of ladders until 1854 when there was a proposal to purchase two, both to be kept in the police station and only one to be let out.

Following the formation of the Potteries Water Company, who became Burslem's ultimate supplier, new distribution pipes were installed in the area and hydrants were fitted. Unfortunately these proved to be useless at times since the water company was in the habit of closing down the supply in order to effect repairs or maintenance. This was the position at a fire at Hughes Pottery, and was not uncommon when the water company was in its growth state and a constant worry to both the fire and the sewage services.

A fire occurred in 1844 at the annual Burslem wakes. Among the artistic presentations was the Parish of Preston Guild Theatre, who claimed to have the largest portable theatre in Europe, capable of holding fifteen hundred patrons, and forty artists who provided *"fashionable and moral entertainment"*. In the early hours a fire was observed in one of the theatre company's caravans and the Cobridge brigade was called out, but they were unable to use the machine, and the brigade had to resort to the use of buckets. An investigation into the cause of the fire resulted in the watchman being blamed for negligence by falling asleep while smoking a pipe in a drunken state.

In 1869 it was decided to purchase a new Merryweather, to be emblazoned with the arms of the borough and housed in a new building adjoining the police station. It was capable of raising water to the height of 100 feet, necessary for new buildings such as the town hall. This machine received the title of 'Lord of the Manor' - the inclination in Burslem was for every machine to bear a name; for instance the one at the water pumping station and the ones at the sewage works all had names. The redundant Burslem fire engine ,'Niagara', was moved to Cobridge. The new Merryweather had a double action suitable for operation by up to twelve men on either side and shafts to take either one or two horses. However, whether through gracious living or shortage of suitable volunteers, they could not meet the manning requirement. Fortunately Merryweathers agreed to provide a steam operated machine on replacement terms, although this new monster demanded an engineer and a stoker. Triumph came when in a fire shortly after purchase, steam was raised in twelve minutes. A scale of charges, commensurate with the capability of the new machine. was introduced:

For use of steam fire engine   £5.0.0. for the first hour.
For each further hour   £1,0.0.
If not used   £2.10.0.

Half the above rates to be charged for fires within the district.

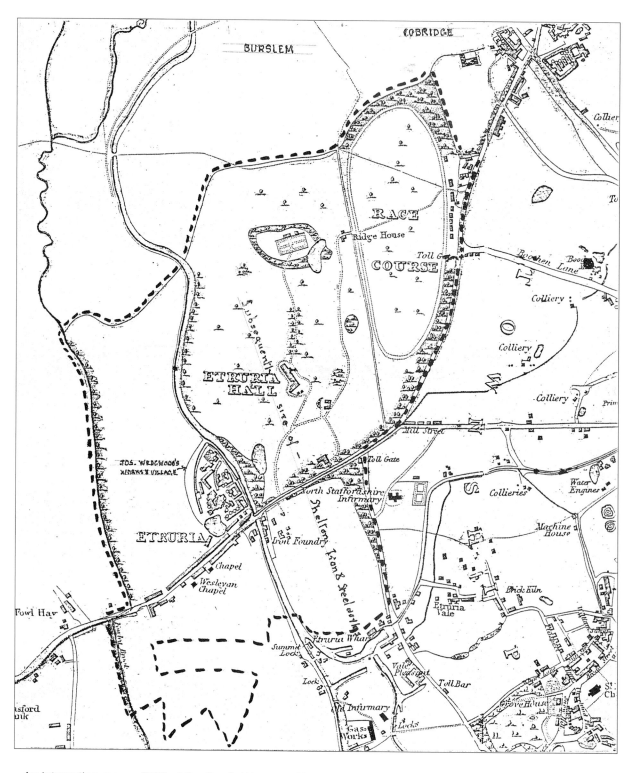

An interesting map c 1850 of the South West outskirts of Burslem showing three toll gates in a small area.
It is easy to see the restriction to the flow of traffic and the cohesive development of roads this would lead to.

CHAPTER NINE: Roads

Growth of shipping & ports.   Inadequacy of roads.   The Lawton and other turnpike roads.

Britain was the first country in Europe to become industrialised and its exports became greater than those of France, Germany, and the Netherlands combined. Success on this scale was due to a number of factors, including her control of the seas. This allowed the movement of armies to create the British Empire, and the supply of administration and immigrants. It allowed the movement of slaves to new possessions and the import to Britain of raw materials to feed our industries. Demand for British industrial products multiplied and led to the growth of an impressive merchant fleet, and the building of huge ports and docks. The East India Company developed an important trade with the Far East, using a large fleet of armed merchant ships to combat the ravages of pirates, and to maintain an extensive trade with India and China.

These advances on the sea were in distinct contrast to the state of the road system in Britain. From the Roman age we had inherited military highways, neglected but capable of taking wheeled traffic. For the remainder, roads were still primarily pack-horse tracks, and this was the state around Burslem well into the 18th century. The two nearest highways to Burslem, both Roman roads, were to the west through Newcastle, and to the east through Leek. Being on a hill, traffic leaving Burslem for the ports faced a decline in both directions; to the west through Newcastle via Packhorse lane and to the east via Nile Street. In wet weather conditions were so bad animals were often unable to retain a foothold with dire consequence for their fragile loads. In many places 'roads' were so narrow that travellers on horseback were advised to start their journey early in the day to avoid being held up by pack-horse trains. Scarratt, in his anecdotes, cites an instance of a poor man from the Nile Street area who died and was being carried in his coffin from the house. Conditions were so bad underfoot the bearers lost control of the coffin, it fell to the ground, burst open and the body finished in the road.

In 1763 it was decided to promote a parliamentary bill to build a turnpike road from Burslem to Lawton in Cheshire. This road was intended to facilitate the transport of goods to and from Liverpool Docks and enable wheeled traffic to be used. Currently packhorse trains were forced to go from Burslem via Packhorse Lane to Newcastle on unmade road and thence on the highway to Lawton. The proposed road would save on time, distance and cost. Furthermore the bill requested that the road be extended south to Stoke. There was intense objection from Newcastle which foresaw the loss of both town trade and income from tolls. Extensive lobbying of Parliament took place by both sides, but the efforts of Josiah Wedgwood, combined with the influence of his London partner Bentley, carried the day, except that permission was only given to carry the road south as far as Burslem.

The main problem that impeded improvement in the road system was the archaic provision for repair and maintenance, governed by the law of 1555 enforcing each parish to nominate two unpaid parishioners to act as road surveyors. Anyone who refused, or failed to find a substitute, could be fined. The duty of the surveyor, without the necessity of being technically qualified, was to order in turn those citizens whose property or land adjoined the road to commit themselves to its upkeep for four days per year. Again this was unpaid labour and in 1563 Elizabeth further increased the obligation from four days to six days. The cost of materials and tools had to be provided from a rate levied by the parish.

The basic principle of turnpikes was that the user in effect paid for the use of the road. and ultimately the initial cost. Legislation for building such roads was available but had been little used, but the parliaments of George III and IV encouraged investment by the private sector and the affluent members of society began to respond, although the Elizabethan law covering liability for maintenance by those living adjacent to the roads was left in force.

Toll roads had gates at each end and usually an adjoining house for the gate-keeper. Those who financed the building of the road often auctioned the collection of tolls to the highest bidder, who then took over the responsibility for the fixing and collecting toll charges, while the auction price became the

An Abstract out of the General Road Act.

MR. *Enoch Wood* — *Church asordin*— ~~Surveyor of the Highways~~, in the Township of *Cobridg* — — and Parish of *Burslem* the same being within your District, YOU are required within seven Days from the Date hereof, to give me in Writing, a true List of all and singular the Inhabitants living within your said District AND ALSO, a true and exact Account of what he, she, or they is, or are chargeable with, for and towards the Repairs of the said Highways, specifying each Person's Rent, (as near as you can) of what Land they occupy in your said District, and likewise of what each Person rents or occupies in any other Township under Fifty Pounds a Year, and each Person that rents, or occupies Land to the Amount of any of the following Sums, is charged in the present Act of Parliament as follows,   *(viz.)*

Any Person occupying Land to the amount of Three Hundred Pounds *per Annum*, is charged with Six Teams and Twelve Men.

£.	T.	Men.	£.	T.	Men.	£.	T.	Men.	Days.
290	5	14	190	3	10	90	1	6	
280	5	13	180	3	9	80	1	5	
270	5	12	170	3	8	70	1	4	
260	5	11	160	3	7	60	1	3	
250	5	10	150	3	6	50	1	2	
240	4	12	140	2	8	40	1		6
230	4	11	130	2	7	30	1		
220	4	10	120	2	6	20	1		
210	4	9	110	2	5	10	1		
200	4	8	100	2	4	5	1		

NOTE. Every Person occupying Land to the Amount of Forty, Thirty, Twenty, Ten, or Five Pounds *per Annum*, and keeps a Team upon such Premises, is required to bring a Team into the Highways; and every Person occupying Land to the Amount of any of the said Sums *(who do not keep a Team)* is chargeable with one able Person, for every Ten Pounds, which he doth Rent or occupy; or, to pay Eight-pence into the Hands of the Surveyor of the said District, for every Ten Pounds, in Lieu of working on such Highway.

DATED this — — — 8 — — — Day of *March* — — 17 40 — from *Jn° Hannersley*. Surveyor of the Turnpike Road, leading from — — *Ash*— *Jo Newenstile*

financial reward of the provider or providers of the capital outlay. How far toll charges varied from county to county it is difficult to say, but the following abridged list will give some idea of customary charges:

> 3d for every coach horse
> 4d for every horse pulling a heavy vehicle
> 10d per score of cattle
> 8d per score of sheep.

Toll charges had to be exhibited on boards, plainly visible at the entrance to each stretch of toll road. Charges varied over the life of the system, from charges related to the weight of the load, number of horses to a wagon, to the width of wheel face. This latter charge however proved to be contentious since it was found that the narrow wheels of the gentlemen's vehicles, while improving the ride, caused more damage to the surface than wagon wheels. The life of a toll keeper was not easy, hours were long, and the innate objection to paying to use the roads when, as one critic remarked, the pavements were free, led to many prosecutions for assault on the toll keeper.

A trust was formed to execute the construction of the Lawton Turnpike in 1763. The trustees, mostly those who had met the costs, were wealthy members of the local community who after completion of the Lawton Road continued a progressive programme of road building; presumably until the local and national authorities took over responsibility in the 19th century. Members of the trust appear to have been chosen on an annual basis, although the original names continued to appear for a long time. Occasionally notices were attached to the toll gates stating, *"The trustees at their next meeting will elect new trustees in room of those who are dead or refuse to act."* Meetings were held regularly in members private houses. Josiah Wedgwood was constantly in attendance and usually the first to sign the minutes.

In 1765 parliamentary approval was obtained for the continuation of the Lawton road down Nile Street and Elder Road to Cobridge, giving access to the Leek road and to Shelton.

In 1776 the trustees promoted a road from Longbridge, through Wolstanton to Newcastle, and placed the contract with a Josepth Jackson for £600, to be paid for in six equal instalments, *"proper bills to be made to subscribers to the said road to answer the said payments."*

Also in 1776, John Brindley, pottery manufacturer of Longbridge, brother of the canal engineer and a highway trustee, agreed to *"build a toll house, for the toll gatherer to live in, on the north side of Longbridge and the south side of Navigation"* the canal), and *"let the same to the trustees for any number of years at a yearly rental of forty shillings"*. A gate was to be erected across the road *"and tolls to be taken thereat at such times as shall be fixed by the trustees. Also a gate to be sited near to Joseph Mountford's house at Longbridge and tolls taken on any part of this road from Longbridge and Burslem, provided the inhabitants of Burslem keep that part of the road in repair."* This latter provision enforcing the Elizabethan law requiring those living adjoining the road to both repair and pay to use the road.

Interesting items from the same minutes were an instruction to the surveyor to purchase 30 tons of Thredswood stone to be brought down to Longport, and that the Tunstall gate be let for one year to Thomas Child for thirty six pounds, to be paid monthly. In 1780 the Longbridge gate was let to a Mr Robert Astm (sic) *"for one whole year for the sum of forty pounds. Mr Astm to sign an agreement and supply securities to the trustees"*. The gentleman could only do so apparently by signing the document with a cross, which would have made it interesting to see how he kept his tollgate records, if any, and to question the surname on his birth certificate. The isolated tollgate at Black Bull on the Lawton road seems to have had a letting problem at times. In 1781, no offer having been received for its letting, the existing keeper was to receive four shillings per week *"until further determination of the trustees"*. In the same year Thomas Brough was employed in *"boating twenty boat loads of gravel from Mayford, to be delivered to Longport and Tunstall Meadows for 10d per ton."* Presumably Cotswold material for the making repairing roads.

In addition to on the spot payment of tolls, other types of payment were arranged. In 1782 it is recorded that *"Captain Child, or any other part of his family, be allowed to pass free upon the Lawton Road for one year with his carriage or horse, not driving any wagon or cart, on paying the trustees one*

TURNPIKE-TOLLS
TO BE LET,
NOTICE is hereby GIVEN,

THAT the TOLLS arifing at the TOLL-GATES, upon the Turnpike Road from *Newcaſtle-under-Lyme*, to *Leek*, in the County of *Stafford*, called by the Names of *Cobridge, Oldfield-lane, Smalthorn-lane, Endon, Endon-fide*, and *Walbridge* Gates, with the Houſes adjoining to each,

will be Let by Auction to the beſt Bidder,

at the Houſe of *James Vernon*, being the Sign of the *Dolphin*, in *Cobridge*, in the faid County, on the Twenty-fifth Day of *September* next, between the Hours of Two and Four in the Afternoon, together or feparately, as fhall be then agreed upon, and in the manner directed by the Act, paffed in the Thirteenth Year of the Reign of his Maiefty King *GEORGE* the Third, " for regulating the Turnpike Roads."

	£.	s.	d.
The Tolls at *Cobridge* and *Oldfield-lane* Gates, were			
Let the laſt Year, at the Sum of	228	0	0
Thoſe at *Smallhorne-lane*, at the Sum of	77	0	0
Thoſe at *Endon*, and *Endon-fide* Gates, at the Sum of	83	0	0
And thoſe at *Walbridge* Gate, at the Sum of	65	0	0

At which reſpective Sums they will be put up.

Whoever happens to be the beſt Bidder, muſt at the ſame Time, give Security, with fufficient Sureties, to the ſatisfaction of the Truftees of the faid Turnpike Road, for payment of the Rent agreed for, and at fuch Times as they fhall direct.

PETER SWIFT,
Clerk to the Truſtees of the faid Turnpike Road.

pound one shilling in lieu thereof." In the same year, *"John Bourne be not confounded with the tolls of the Tunstall gate for carriages not under ten wheels on carriages not carrying goods or other things for hire except coals from his colliery, for one year for the sum of ten guineas to be paid quarterly."*

While private enterprise was progressively used to construct roads, the government was continuing to co-opt individuals who had no professional competence to act as honorary surveyors. In 1814 Enoch Wood and H.H. Williamson were appointed under the act and had either of the gentlemen refused to accept the order they would have been subject to a fine of £5. The act stipulated numerous conditions which it was the surveyors duty to observe and enforce to be observed:

"Every person who keeps a Carriage, Wain, Plough or Tumbrill, to send two men on the days required by the surveyor, and work for eight hours per day or pay for neglect of duty"

"No tree to be planted in any highway, or within fifteen feet of the centre of the highway"

"Hedges on the highway to be cut by those owning the land on which the hedge stands. Cutting to be from the last day in September to the last day in March. Fine for not cutting, £2 for every twenty four feet".

"No alcohol to be kept by tollkeepers on toll bridges".

"If the driver in an empty carriage refuses to give way to any coach, chariot, chaise, or loaded wagon, he is subject to a fine of twenty shillings. If he refuses to give his name, he can be sent to the House of Correction for three months".

Newcastle Street was one of the earliest toll roads to be adopted by the town, despite considerable opposition to it becoming a responsibility of the rates and requiring costly removal of structures which had been allowed to encroach over the building line. When it reopened, Packhorse Lane became redundant and in 1828 the trustees offered the now unused area, part to Enoch Wood specified as *"That part of the said road commencing at the Enoch Wood Archway and the intended road to the new church (St.Paul's) containing 1850 square yards be offered to Enoch Wood, the owner of the property adjoining same, for the sum of one pound"*. The remainder, extending to the present turnpike road at Dale Hall, was offered to Mr William Adams, the owner of the property adjoining, for the sum of one pound. The lane was offered on these terms *"in consideration of the new owners making a road through to the turnpike road at the new church, and to the said lane being useful to any other individual than Enoch Wood and William Adams."* A tollhouse and gate were built in Newport Street at Dale Hall to cover traffic to Port Vale wharf, and in expectation of a continuing use of toll roads, the trustees in 1832 authorised the purchase of 2000 tons of copper slag to be delivered to Burslem, not exceeding 2/4d per ton, the clerk to write to the canal company to allow such material to be carried free. It was either a legal obligation or an accepted custom that materials for roadways were carried free of charge by The Trent and Mersey Company; this particular consignment probably coming from Froghall.

As railways were built, private lines to connect to the arterial system were sometimes laid along roads. Requests for permission to do this became prevalent from mineowners and from Shelton Steel works, and for each of these crossings, the trustees imposed a charge of ten pounds per annum.

The most important road where a crossing was laid was Waterloo Road, a road built immediately following the end of the Napoleonic wars. The act in parliament giving assent was within days of the battle, from which the road derived its name. Two years were taken in the construction and Scarratt said that studs picked up by a traveller on the battlefield were embedded in a stone where the road started in Burslem. A veteran of the battle, who worked on the road, used to display his arm covered in warts to the elbow, which he claimed to have sold to a medical man for half a guinea, to be claimed after his death.

Moorland Road was built in 1820, a time of deep industrial depression. The cost was met partly from a large relief fund subscribed to by the wealthy of the county, and unemployed potters and miners were used in its construction. The present Leek Road from Cobridge was built in 1839, and North Street built from the Hot Lane tollgate to meet it. In 1858 Mr Edward Wood proposed to the trustees that *"in view of the number of able bodied paupers available, they should be used gratis to lower the top of Porthill bank three feet."* (perhaps at the instigation of the tramway company)

There were some twenty five to thirty tollgates in and around the Potteries area. In Burslem there was one at Brownhills, one at Longport, one at Dale Hall, and two at Cobridge, but despite improved highways, there were constant complaints about road conditions generally, and the growth of unmade streets and the lack of compulsory street works.

The usual construction method for roads was to use broken stone for the base and roll in a slurry of smaller material; this would turn to dust in dry weather and in the town constant watering was required. Telford considered the quality of the foundation was most important, but this made the road expensive. McAdam considered that an impervious surface was the best procedure but tarred roads only became a standard in the 20th century. Builders of roads were advised not to have too much camber, otherwise coaches would cause excessive damage by continually using the centre of the road, and although camber facilitated drainage, it was better to raise the level of the road above the adjacent land, using hard stone broken into small pieces, *"an employment suitable for women, children, and those beyond heavy work".*

The growing objections to the principle of tolls generally, led ultimately to their rejection, and civic authorities took over responsibility for maintenance, costs being recovered from taxation. At a public discussion in Burslem in 1875 on the future of toll roads, it was said that Cheshire had dispensed with all tolls. At this time there was considered to be eight miles of toll roads in Burslem and opinions of the inhabitants as to whether tolls should be dispensed with were varied. Farmers said they would have to raise the price of livestock if the charge went on the rates. One person said that *"toll houses were less nuisance than building houses in the middle of the road".* This was obviously aimed at the Burslem Board for the problem they had inherited with haphazard growth, with, in the case of Newcastle Street, building lines ignored. Following adoption by the Burslem Board, buildings which had encroached beyond the original line had to be removed and were the subject of expensive litigation.

Another person attending the discussion said that *"at one of the gates Fish and Ginger Beer carts had been stopped and the drivers told by the keepers that they had forgotten the taste of Fish and Ginger Beer"* inferring that the gate keepers were accepting payment in kind. Another person remarked that it hurt the dignity of some gents on horseback to stop at the gate and pay 3d. Both of these observations may have been interesting and in keeping with interventions usually expected at public meetings but then, as now, hardly likely to influence the outcome.

In the end all toll roads disappeared from the Potteries over the next ten years.

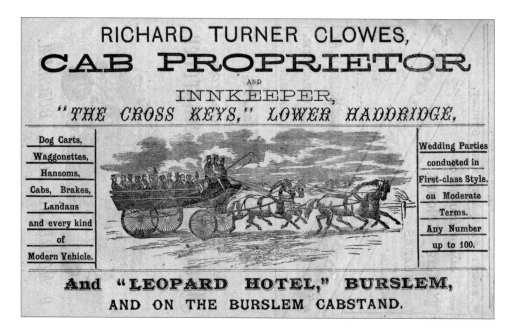

RICHARD TURNER CLOWES,
CAB PROPRIETOR
AND
INNKEEPER,
"THE CROSS KEYS," LOWER HADDRIDGE,

Dog Carts,
Waggonettes,
Hansoms,
Cabs, Brakes,
Landaus
and every kind
of
Modern Vehicle.

Wedding Parties
conducted in
First-class Style,
on Moderate
Terms.
Any Number
up to 100.

And "LEOPARD HOTEL," BURSLEM,
AND ON THE BURSLEM CABSTAND.

CHAPTER TEN: Canals

The Trent and Mersey Canal and the Burslem Branch.

With an ever increasing volume of traffic, and the inadequacy of the roads, the advantages of transport by water, already exploited on the continent, led to the proposal in 1765 to build the Trent and Mersey Canal. Josiah Wedgwood was again to the forefront, creating local enthusiasm and seeking investment and support from influential landowners through whose land the canal would pass, and whose influence in parliament was imperative.

A survey was conducted by James Brindley who ultimately became famous for his achievements in canal construction, of which the Trent and Mersey was one of the earliest. Born in Tunsted, a village in Derbyshire, he is said to have had an indifferent education, and ultimately, at seventeen years of age, his father, now living in Leek, apprenticed him to a millwright named Bennett in Macclesfield. The millwright subsequently retired, unable physically to carry on, and Brindley continued with the business, supporting Bennett's family at the same time. Brindley was exceptionally innovative and hard working, and the reputation he achieved for his work for the silk mills in Macclesfield, brought him to the attention of Sir Nigel Gresley, for whom he developed machinery to remove water from his mines. His reputation similarly attracted the attention of the Duke of Bridgwater for whom he built some spectacular features in the construction of the Duke's canal to carry coal from his mines to Manchester.

Flint windmill built by James Brindley, probably the one shown on Enoch Wood's 1750 map

In Burslem he built a windmill for John Wedgwood in the 'Jenkins' area, the first mill to grind flints in water, and a further windmill for Enoch Wood. The only remains of these is the base of Enoch Wood's on the crown of Packhorse Lane. Active in Burslem from about 1750, as a millwright in premises rented from one of the Wedgwoods, he came into close contact with Josiah Wedgwood, particularly during the survey for the local canal, and more intimately when the canal was being constructed. The Bill presented to Parliament stated:

"...the town of Burslem, and the villages of Stoke, Hanley Green, Lane Delf and Lane End, manufactured and carried at great expense, various kinds of stone and earthenwares to all parts of the kingdom, and exported to our islands and colonies in America. Large quantities of pot ware from Burslem are conveyed on horseback in large crates to Bewdley and Bridgnorth, and then to Bristol for exporting. The ware sent to Hull is now carried by land to Willington, upwards of thirty miles, and that to Liverpool, some twenty miles to Winsford in Cheshire. Uncertainty of floods in Winter, and numerous shallows in Summer, are more than low priced manufactures can bear, and with new established competition in France and America, likely to bring the Potteries to speedy decay and ruin. Great quantities of flints and clays are brought to Liverpool and Hull, and brought at great expense by river and road from these parts to the potteries, an inconvenience that nothing but a canal can remove. Hundreds of packhorse journeys are similarly required to take ware from the Potteries to the ports."

An early c.1850 and later view c 1900 of Wedgwoods factory at Etruria, showing the extent of subsidence

Brindley's famous Irwell aqueduct and left, part of the canal system envisaged by Brindley, shown in an Anderton company advert c.1910

Longport

Middleport

Shirley's Bone Mill at Etruria
Many mills were originally built to
grind grain, but later moved on to
bone, flint and stone for the
pottery industry.

A significant point raised during the negotiations was the reference to competition from America. Demand was already being created for skilled potters in Burslem due to the drain of emigrants to America where factories had started producing domestic pottery for their own market, although this was in conflict with laws that Britain endeavoured to impose to limit competition with British production and which, among a number of restrictive actions, culminated in the Declaration of Independence in 1776.

Following the success in parliament of the Trent and Mersey Bill, construction of a narrow boat canal commenced. On 21st July 1766 Josiah Wedgwood, as a tribute to his foresight and efforts in furtherance of the scheme, cut the first sod at Trubshaw Cross, in company with James Brindley and notables from Burslem and a large crowd of onlookers. In the evening celebrations were held in the town. A whole sheep was roasted in the market square and according to Ward *"other demonstrations of festivity displayed"*. The canal took eleven years to complete and employed 400-600 navvies, mostly Irishmen, who were paid 3d. per yard and earned approximately five shillings per week, plus food and lodgings. The initial estimate of the cost was that it should not exceed £130,000, its length would be 93 miles, with 93 locks, 189 road bridges and 11 foot bridges, the width to be 29ft at the top and 16ft at the bottom, and the depth 4ft 6ins.

The final figures given were that the ultimate cost was £300,000, and the number of locks 75, but even at this enhanced cost, freight rates and breakage losses were drastically reduced, and the canal highly profitable. Toll charges, according to the Bill, were to be 1d per mile compared with the equivalent cost by road of 10d.

The need for improvement in transport facilities is evidenced by the growth in traffic from the Potteries prior to the building of the canal. Between 1739 and 1760 the volume of pottery carried to Liverpool increased six times, most of it for export to the colonies, but some for Ireland, Liverpool itself, and the towns around. Most of the traffic on the River Trent to Hull was for London and the south.

The major, and most spectacular feature in the construction of the canal was Harecastle tunnel, 2880 yards long. It had a height of twelve feet and a width of nine feet, consequently it was so narrow that it could only cater for the width of one boat. There was no tow path in the tunnel and the boat had to be propelled by a man lying on his back, using foot pressure on the roof of the tunnel to move the boat through the water, an operation which took two and a half hours. Meanwhile the horses were led over the hill, the route being known locally as Boat Horse Road. The height in the tunnel was so minimal that boats without payload required ballast otherwise there was insufficient room for the man to propel the boat. Any fires in the boat had to be extinguished throughout the journey due to danger from lack of ventilation. Brindley cut fifteen shafts along the length of the tunnel to the depth of the mines below, which were to have direct access to the canal. He then worked horizontally both ways from the bottom of each shaft, and from each end of the tunnel, and so had thirty two working faces in operation at a time. Such was the interest the project aroused that soon after its completion in 1770, pleasure cruises were operated, and the following is a visitor's impression:

"I visited the tunnel soon after it was finished, when pleasure boats were kept for the purpose of exhibiting this great work. The impression it made on my mind is still fresh. The procession solemn, some enlivened the scene with a band of musick, but we had none. As we entered far, a light of candles was necessary, and about half way the view back upon the mouth was like the glimmering of a star, very beautiful. The various voices of the workmen from the mines were rude and awful, and to be present at their quarrels, which sometimes happen when they meet and battle for a passage, must resemble greatly the ideas we may form of the regions of Pluto."

This comment illustrates that Brindley's secondary objective, of using the canal as a direct connection to the mines for the conveyance of coal was fulfilled.

Brindley was said to have a remarkable memory, with a capacity to complete a project from a mental vision and calculation, and little need for paperwork. It was said that if he had a problem he took to his bed until it was solved and memorised. His fame spread rapidly, and his canal projects extended from London to Scotland. Not only that, he still used his skill to design other projects, but he so engrossed himself in his work and neglected his health, that, as Josiah Wedgwood had feared, he died at the age of fifty six before the canal was completed.

At the time of his death, he was living at Turnhurst Hall, Great Chell, near Burslem, although his father left him an estate at Lowe Hill near Leek. As with so many properties in this area, the hall suffered from mining subsidence and was demolished. He is said to have left a considerable fortune but although there is much tangible evidence of his immense ingenuity still to be seen in the multiplicity of canals which wind through both town and countryside, there is little left to remind us of his personal life other than his gravestone in the cemetery at Newchapel. His brother in law, Hugh Henshall, who assisted Brindley in his survey work, finished the construction of the canal, and ultimately, along with other interests, operated a flourishing canal carrying company. Brindley's widow remarried and became Mrs Williamson. A son of this marriage was the Robert Williamson, the mine owner prominent in the dispute with the miners during the strike referred to in an earlier chapter. Williamson also built a pottery on the banks of the canal at Longport, as did Brindley's brother John, both factories eventually part of the Davenport empire.

The canal prospered from the start with dividends of 25-40%, but its very success led to many grumbles and frustrations, particularly with the congestion at Harecastle, but also in Derbyshire, where boats had to negotiate the Trent against the current and ten to twelve men were needed to haul them. Groups of men who gathered to do this work were a cause of complaint locally on the grounds that they were dissolute and homeless, probably a residue from the navvies employed on the canal construction. The carriers were also accused of favouring large users to the prejudice of individuals; a charge strongly refuted by the companies who claimed that anyone could use the canal at a charge of 1d per mile, with penalties of 10/-d per hour for creating an obstruction, and a fine of 6d for wasting water at locks.

Pressure and frustration, coupled with the evident prosperity, was probably the inducement which brought about a proposal, in 1796, by a new group of influential sponsors, to build a wide canal following a similar route to the existing canal, but suitable for river craft, thus avoiding the existing trans-shipment of goods from canal to river, and so offering in turn a considerable reduction in haulage costs. It was to be called the Commercial Canal, and a comprehensive booklet was issued outlining the project in detail together with the expected advantages and savings, compared with narrow boats. The boats would be 14ft wide, and 75ft long, as compared with 7ft wide, and 70ft long. Each would take 90 crates weighing 18 tons, which was twice the weight carried by a narrow boat. The hauling cost would be approximately 10d per mile compared with 6d for a narrow boat, but there would be no transshipment cost, since the boat was stable and suitable for operating on rivers. Other advantages were that loads on narrow boats were restricted in height to no more than the boat's width otherwise in strong winds it was liable to capsize, and due to repairs to locks and banks, it was estimated that canals could only operate on average forty weeks in a year. The carriage of bigger loads when conditions were favourable, would be a further benefit.

The promoters arranged a series of meetings at various places along its proposed course, each chaired by an eminent citizen or a noble lord. In this area the first of these meetings appears to have been at the Wheatsheaf in Stoke, where it received the first clash of local views. That a wide canal had its merits and local supporters there is no doubt, since there were similar canals already successfully functioning elsewhere in this country. Obviously the proposed canal promised serious competition for the Trent and Mersey into which a lot of local money had been poured. In November 1796 a meeting of pottery manufacturers was held in Hanley, which evidently discussed the project but proposals put to the meeting appear to have been divisive since there were forty three dissenters. Apparently a number of letters followed, either circulated personally or in the press, which upset Josiah and his colleagues, leading them to call a separate meeting of the forty three dissenters. The letter requesting their attendance was addressed to them as follows:

"It appears to us to be indispensably necessary that notice should be taken of the meeting of manufacturers in Hanley on the fourth of November last, The favour of your attendance is requested at Mr Vernon's, "The Sign of the Dolphin" Cobridge, on Monday at 4.o'clock in the afternoon in order to take this business in consideration.

Signed. Jos. Wedgwood. Samuel Spode. Geo. Rogers. John Blackwell Jos. Spode Enoch Wood H. Henshall. Robert Williamson. Theolophulus Smith. J.E. Poole. Thomas Wedgwood. John Davenport. Ralph Baddeley.

Most of these signatories were those of influential potters, the majority from Burslem. All forty three dissenters appear to have attended and as a result, issued the following notice:

19th Dec, 1796.

"In consequence of printed letters which have circulated through the Potteries, signed Wm. Adams, J.Tomlinson, together with the anonymous advertisement inserted in the Sun of 2nd.December, and referred to by such letters, we, whose names are subscribed feel it incumbent upon us to state that the resolution of the general meeting of manufacturers 4th November last, were at the regular half yearly general meeting ordered to be expunged, and although such order was not entered in the books, the leaf containing the obnoxious proceedings was torn out. That the assertions contained in the letter of 7th.December that many of the signatures to the paper agreed by 43 manufacturers expressing their dissent from such proceedings were obtained through artifice and gross misrepresentation is utterly false and unfounded, and it appears to us highly improper, not only sustaining a rash and unjustifiable attack upon private character, but tending to disturb the harmony of the Staffordshire Potteries, and as far as it relates to ourselves, we disavow any authority whatever in the persons whose names appear on such letters to act as delegates on the part of the Potteries in the business to which they relate, nor do we in any shape acknowledge them as such.

This was signed personally by all forty three and headed with Josiah Wedgwood's signature

The disagreement must have related to the proposed canal, of serious concern to Josiah and many of his colleagues who had invested heavily in Brindley's original canal. However, like other canal schemes designed in a vain attempt to compete with rail, it failed to come to fruition, and finally any hope of a world cruise starting from Longport Wharf was denied! Probably as a pre-emptive gesture, the proprietors of the Trent & Mersey did advise the Commercial Canal Company that they currently had a plan under consideration for widening the existing canal, and work had commenced in Cheshire. However, with the rapid expansion of the railways, the use of canals for industrial traffic was slowing down.

Digressing for the moment; one unusual forename which was appended to the call to the meeting at the Sign of the Dolphin, Cobridge, was that of Theophulus. Theophulus Smith was initially a successful potter; he built a mansion, Greenfield Hall, set in forty acres and also built a housing estate nearby. Nevertheless in 1800 he became bankrupt, and at the same time was having marital trouble, accusing his wife of having an affair with John Wainwright, a Liverpool Merchant, a friend, and presumably a customer. In a fit of anger he killed Wainwright and then fled, resulting in the following notice being posted in Burslem:

29th June 1800.

"Theophulus Smith of Smithfield near Tunstall did malevolently cut with a knife and shoot through the body of Mr Wainwright of Liverpool, Merchant, this morning about 3 o'clock at Smithfield aforesaid and has since made his escape. Whoever will apprehend him and give information wherever he is concealed will receive £20 over and above the County Allowance by applying to Joseph Moreton, Constable of Burslem. The above Theophulus Smith is about forty years of age and is a stand well made man (except rather short neck with a little appearance of stooping in the shoulders) brown hair, large full eyes, round face, with muddy complexion and affects gentleman like address."

He was finally arrested in Pall Mall London and confined in Stafford Jail, where his wife and daughter visited him. By some means he had been able to conceal a pistol in his cell, and, having first shot the daughter, shot his wife and himself, only his wife surviving.

Reverting to the Trent and Mersey canal, the company in 1796 applied to build a branch to Froghall, to be known as the Caldon Canal, and to build a reservoir at Rudyard to feed it. A bill was presented to Parliament but failed to get acceptance at the first attempt, the fear being expressed that the water requirement would drain the streams of Cheshire. It was successfully built eventually and was very profitable in its commercial days. Now, both canal and reservoir are very popular recreational features,

The Burslem canal east of Longport.
The Newport Pottery

Below: Westport Lake, produced by
drainage of the wetlands around
Longport

and, despite the fears, the streams still continue to flow in Cheshire - there was constant opposition to the introduction of canals from millowners fearing diminution of the supply to their mill machinery.

In 1823, approximately fifty years after the construction of the canal, Telford, probably the most famous engineer to follow Brindley, was asked to make a critical survey with particular attention to the delays at Harecastle. A second tunnel was built which included a towpath. In his report Telford said he found, adjacent to this great flourishing town of Burslem,

> "a canal little better than a crooked ditch with scarcely the appearance of a hauling path, the horses frequently sliding and staggering in the water, the hauling lines sweeping the gravel into the canal, and the entanglement at the meeting of boats incessant, while at the locks at each end crowds of boatmen were always quarrelling or offering premiums for a preference of passage, and the mine owners hand in their just complaints".

The new tunnel enabled the canal proprietors to increase their efficiency and delay the commercial ascendancy of the railways. Tug boats were later introduced which were capable of hauling a train of up to thirty barges through the tunnel in forty minutes, but, although a great effort was made to impede the growth of railroads, the comparative economy, speed, and facility made the success of rail traffic inevitable. It was delayed by a government who were obviously concerned that with so much capital being involved, and fearing an unhealthy pursuit at the expense of the canals. The government forced the railway companies to become guarantors for a given return on canal capital, which ultimately led to canals being bought out by railway companies.

Originally canal traffic to and from Liverpool went via Preston Brook and the Duke of Bridgwater's canal to Runcorn, but in 1869 via the river Weaver and Anderton, which was the longstanding route for carrying salt to Liverpool. In 1871 the North Staffordshire Carrying Co. was formed to operate this new route to Liverpool, but the company was short lived, collapsing in 1874. Steam was in use to drive the boats in 1880, and in 1882 consideration was given to the construction of a canal for steam vessels between the Potteries and Liverpool, but perhaps not surprisingly in view of the rising supremacy of rail transport, this, along with proposals elsewhere, never got to the promotion stage.

Pilferage a was a constant and serious problem. At a meeting called by Burslem potters, one member described a tool that had been found, formed specifically to facilitate pilferage from crates. He said it was made like a cross bow, the arched end being forced into the crate to part the hazel rods, of which the crate was formed, and create sufficient space to insert an arm. When the tool was withdrawn, the rods, being supple, reverted to normal as did the straw, leaving no visible trace of interference. The manufacturers, together with the carriers and the navigation company, agreed to create a fund to meet the cost of prosecuting pilferers. Each of the these three parties were to contribute 3d per crate and 2d a hogshead, but the scheme ran into problems when the carriers failed to pay their dues, complaining that the dealers, to whom they had passed on the charge, had refused to accept it.

It is likely that many of the current generation will never have seen a pottery crate, other than perhaps by illustration. It was a skilled fabrication, resilient and hard wearing, and capable of many journeys before being discarded. It was a common sight up to the last War to see these crates, loaded high on horse-drawn drays, being moved between the factories and the railway marshalling yards, as no doubt they were in the previous generation between the factories and the canal wharves. The widespread use of crates in the pottery industry led to a large number of crate making establishments in Burslem, each having its own pond in which the timber was soaked to increase its pliability, but as the congestion in housing grew around them, the pools stagnant condition led to many becoming a nuisance, and a common cause of complaint. At one time, there were so many cratemakers in the whole district that they had their own members association, and the operatives their own union. Hazel for the crates was grown in large quantities in the woods in proximity to Burslem. The trees were carefully grown and cut and were a profitable source of income to the growers. The crates made from this timber were made in the form of a box in various sizes, but in skeleton form; pottery packing houses were littered with straw and various sizes of these crates. The straw needed to be long straw which lined the walls of the crate. Modern short varieties caused by mechanisation forced local straw merchants, who purchased from farmers, to gradually canvas an ever wider area to satisfy the demand of the potter.

Walking along the canal from Longport eastwards, it is still possible to form a mental picture of the activity which pervaded the scene 200 years ago. At Longport, the basin which previously housed the boats is filled in and concreted, and on it a host of caravans over winter, emphasising the current supremacy of the road. On the remaining warehouse wall a notice still proudly claims the area to be LONGPORT WHARF.

Wending its way from Longport, the canal passes an area known as Port Vale, adopted by one of the major football clubs that emanated from the vicinity. The canal here is littered with derelict wharf structures once occupied by illustrious canal carriers. We eventually arrive at Newport where there is a wide basin from which a narrow branch canal once went to Middleport. This was the Burslem Canal but it is now blocked at its entrance and dry and overgrown. The wide basin would have been full of boats loaded with flints or clay waiting their turn to enter the Burslem branch. It is also possible to see here the remnants of the railway which came from the mines on the Grange.

At the site of the Burslem canal wharf some of the buildings still stand, a notice on one proclaiming their use before the canal finally closed though both competition from the railways and subsidence. No trace remains of the tramway that once crossed Navigation Road, its horse-drawn trucks hauling heavy loads from the wharf to the Town's potteries, and returning with crates of pots. The track has vanished, as have any horse troughs - and human troughs that lined the road; The Albion, The Three Tuns, The Britannia, The Thistle and Shamrock and The Rose. It is hard to believe that in its heyday 700 vessels passed through Etruria Lock every week, borne on the water from the reservoirs at Bagnall, Knypersley and Stanley.

There was thriving foundry at Stone which made these iron milestones.

CHAPTER ELEVEN: Thrift and traders

Local Banks & Friendly Societies. Retail development

The number of private banks in Britain grew considerably as industry expanded and also because of restrictions placed on joint stock banks because of a monopoly enjoyed by the Bank of England, a reward for financing the wars of the late 18th and early 19th centuries. Private banks, which issued their own notes, were limited to six partners which restricted their resources and favoured the loans of short duration. The first bank in Burslem was founded by Wood and Walker in the first decade of the 19th century. In 1818 it became Wood and Co., subsequently Wood and Holden, and in 1838 was absorbed by the Imperial Bank of England, which, despite its august name, ran into financial difficulties. The Alcocks, potters of Burslem, also formed a private bank which they called Burslem Commercial Bank. But by 1850 joint stock banks were superseding private banks which gradually ceased to exist.

The wars of the early 19th century had a devastating effect in the trade and finances of the Country. It is not surprising that fears were raised about some institutions, including banks, some of which did become insolvent. Doubt arose over the solvency of Woods bank. Moral support came in the form of a public notice issued in July 1818 signed by the leading manufacturers of the district:

PUBLIC NOTICE

Reports having been industriously circulated to the prejudice of the banking concern of Messrs Wood and Walker of Burslem, we hereby express our perfect confidence in their stability and engage to take their notes in payment of any amount.

Among the signatures were those of Josiah Wedgwood and Josiah Spode. The bank survived this period, but doubts arose again in 1825, and to allay these fears public notices were issued by manufacturers and the local authorities:

"We the undersigned being Churchwardens and Overseers of Burslem, declare our utmost confidence in the well known responsibility of the banks of Wood and Holden of this place, and Messrs Kennersley and Sons of Newcastle, and hereby give notice that the collectors have orders to receive the notes of the said firms for the parochial rates".

Churchwardens, Jos. Stubbs. W.D. Hand. Thos. Brindley. Overseers Chas. chadwick. John Bartlam.

A local satirical periodical, *The Public Enquirer*, made the following comment on banks:

Notwithstanding all the lieing audacity of the London journals in endeavouring to vamp up statements to prove the public prosperity, it begins now to assume the state of certainty that the community is menaced with some great commercial convulsion, which must include mischief for many, and consternation to all. The London establishment, which from its connection with the joint stock schemes of 1815 might be aptly designated Bubble Bank, has failed within the present week, and I write confidently, when I predicted that some similar failures are tolerably nigh at hand. Very far indeed will the coming Christmas be from a very merry one in this money owning land. With the vanity of long accustomed opulence, the people of England have wholly forgotten that riches make unto themselves wings and fly away. They have trusted in gold and silver and in representative rags and they will find that no people is so poor as a nation that avouches gold to be their god. From the time of the Old Testament we had had this unheeded and unaltered warning, but the perception of what is opulence must have vastly changed.

But as the century progressed trade began to thrive, and the opportunity of increased business interested merchant banks. Ward said the most striking building in Burslem was the newly erected 1836 Commercial Bank of England, situated on the south side of the market place and built in stone in the Italian style with large Venetian windows on the ground floor, and the upper ones with ornamental balconies. Ward also refers to the Manchester & District Banking Co who were in association with Payne & Smith of London, and the Birmingham & Dudley & District Bank in association with Williams Deacon & Co. Ltd, London. Both were in the market place. Prior to the establishment of banks in Burslem, the town was reliant on Newcastle, particularly the merchant bank of Mr Kinnersley which discounted bills and made loans to a number of the earliest Burslem pottery manufacturers.

The practice of raising money to pay for individual services such as the provision of lighting, and more particularly Poor Rates, which were frequent and unpredictable, must have been a constant worry to both the Board of Health, and the ratepayers, until the introduction of a single rate covering all services.

As early as 1807 means were being examined in Burslem to reduce Poor Rate demands and to give encouragement to the young to start at an early age to make provision for old age, by extolling the virtues of friendly societies. The obvious intent was to alleviate the burden of the poor on Burslem citizens. Today the burden is shared nationally but it is still there, and the same exhortation is being repeated. A number of these friendly societies were formed in Burslem, among the better known the Oddfellows, the Rechabite, the Buffaloes, the Ancient Shepherds, the Order of Druids, the Foresters, and the Masons. All flourished during the 19th century and some had a number of groupings or lodges as they were termed.

The Masons had two lodges, the St Martin's and the Sutherland, the Oddfellows, the Perseverance Lodge and the Hope of Burslem Tent. The Shepherds had the Sir Garnet Wolsley Lodge, and the Loyal Wedgwood, the Foresters boasted three, the Robin Hood, the Foresters Child, and the Royal Pottery Lodge. Sir Garnet Wolsley was a general in the British Army and a member of an old Staffordshire family but the family does not seem to have had any link with Burslem. Most of the lodges held their meetings in inns, but some used schools. The Masons used the town hall. No doubt all encouraged thrift and charity, as did the Church of England, Sons of Temperance and Burslem Temperance Society.

Despite constant monetary problems, Burslem as a town was rapidly taking shape, encouraging an influx of market traders, shopkeepers, and service trades. Some shopkeepers were even opening branches in other towns, as the following advertisement in 1826 indicates:

EXTRAORDINARY BARGAINS
Although through competition I so freely wade,
It was ne'er my ambition to get all the trade
But now I do declare it, that bargains you shall buy,
For still I mean to share it, or find the reason why

T.COX.   BURSLEM & HANLEY

Deeply sensible of the manifest preferences and genuine support he has so universally received from his friends during the time while "Prime Cost and Under" have been the motto of competition, which seems daily increasing from one end of the Potteries to the other. begs to return them his sincere and grateful thanks, and hopes by unremitting assiduity, attention, and perseverance to be enabled to offer his goods at terms not to be surpassed by any in the trade, having been to market and made some cheap purchases, he once more most strongly invites them to his.

LITTLE SHOPS AND LITTLE PRICES
Viz   Two yards of Calico for one penny.

Superfine ditto	One penny per yard.
Extra superfine	One penny halfpenny.
Ell wide ditto	Two pence.
All printed Cottons	Fourpence halfpenny per yard
Flannel at	Threepence.
Pocket Handkerchiefs	One penny
Ladies fancy Silk ditto	One & six pence each
Gents Silk Bandana ditto	Two shillings each.

Variety of Black & Coloured Gross de Naples & other Silks at low prices
Hats and Bonnets of the very best quality at reduced prices
Funeral furnishing on credit of 5 per cent allowed for ready money.

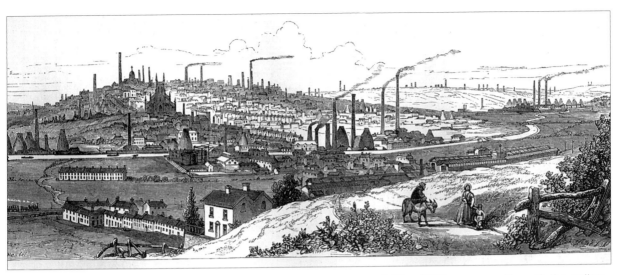

View of Burslem from Bradwell, 1865. St Paul's is seen silhouetted. The A500 now runs through the valley.

Beer shops still outnumbered all others, but the town could now boast bakers, butchers, fishmongers, grocers, greengrocers, drapers, pawnbrokers, secondhand clothes shops, boot makers, hairdressers, even estate agents, and members of the professions and trades. In addition there were a lot of 'house cum shops', particularly in the Waterloo Road, Nile Street, and Newcastle Street areas.

To ensure the amenities in the town kept pace with this expansion, the Board of health was reliant on income from the rates. There were problems with the canal carrying companies who refused to pay local rates on the grounds that the basis of their trade was of a transient character, which in view of the vast profits they were making caused indignation. Cobridge also opposed some charges claiming immunity on the grounds of ancient rights of the abbey lands and further reminding Burslem that great dissatisfaction existed on the part of the inhabitants of Rushton Grange due to the way in which the inhabitants were treated by the Burslem Board under the Lighting and Watching Act. A sort of civil war went on, in the course of which some of the public lamps in Burslem were illegally removed and fixed in Rushton Grange, to compensate they said for the tax which they were paying. The dispute eventually was resolved in court where Burslem lost on the technical grounds of failing to give notice to Cobridge of their intentions, and they suffered heavy legal costs.

In 1843 the government set up a royal commission to examine the condition of large towns but none in Staffordshire were included. Burslem's Board of Health tried to ensure that the growing town was in

Advertisement from the Potters' Examiner 1844

reasonable condition. Pavements and possibly gutters were paved, but open spaces would be hard core with a finer finishing coat compacted with a horse drawn roller. Part of the work was done by the use of direct labour and part by contract. The Board themselves purchased road making material and annual tenders were sought both for labour and materials:

Bricks, Presumably for pavements and gutters.	27/- per thousand
Best Blue Brick	45/- " "
Broken Stone, for road works	8/- to 9/- per ton, delivered by canal to Burslem wharf.
Steel Curbing.	2/- to 2/4 per yard.
Paving Labour	7d per yard.

Presumably the damage caused by the wheels of horse drawn vehicles necessitated the supply of steel kerbing. Iron reinforcement for kerbing was widely used for corners and inclines because horse-drawn vehicles used the kerb as a friction brake. These were prices quoted in the first half of the 19th century, and they remained static year on year. Up to 1883 a horse roller was used, but in that year it was recommended that a steam roller be purchased, after the relative costs and efficiency had been sought from other authorities. An alternative suggestion was to borrow a roller from Hanley. which was rather a reflection on Burslem, the senior town.

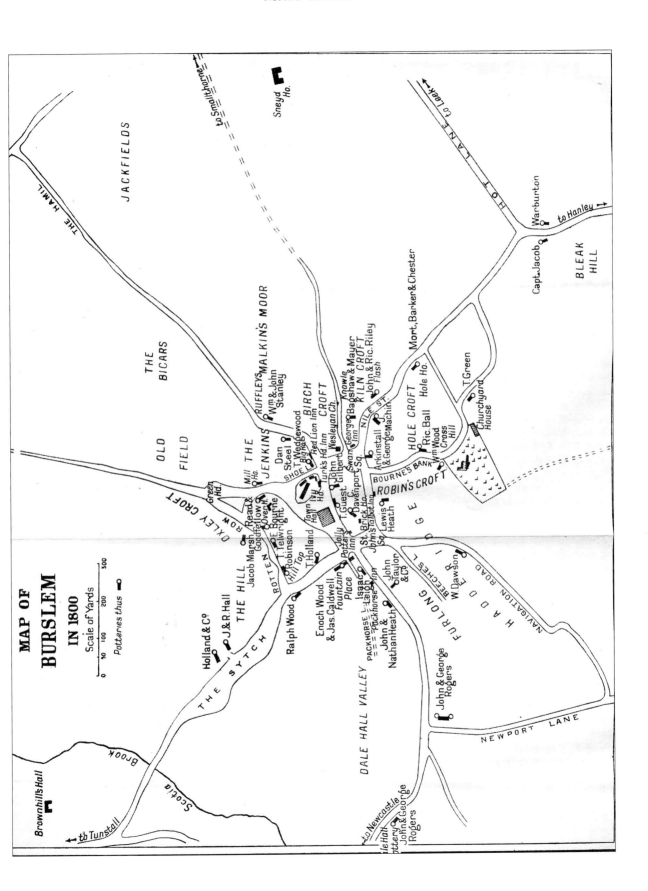

MAP OF
BURSLEM
IN 1800

Scale of Yards

0   50 100   200   300

Potteries thus

Engravings of traders in Burslem
c. 1850

CHAPTER TWELVE: More civic growth

The Shambles Market. Policing and town lighting. First Reform Acts.
New live theatre in Waterloo Road. Concern for the Monarch's life.

The need for a covered market and for legal powers to control this and a number of other civic functions, led in 1812 to an application to the Lord of the Manor, Walter Sneyd Esq. for the lease of further land adjoining the town hall. This was necessary before applying for a parliamentary bill but on the first application the Lord of the Manor refused. The project was kept alive and public support was enlisted. As often occurs with civic propositions, opposition arises if it involves community money which means money from the pockets of the objectors, some of whom tend to say a lot under a cloak of anonymity. This applied to the market project and brought the following public retort.

MARKET HALL
"To the Freeholders and Inhabitants of Burslem.
A Hand-bill having been circulated requesting the freeholders and inhabitants of Burslem to attend a meeting at The Legs of Man Inn on Saturday the 28th inst. to take into consideration certain subjects relative to the Market and Market Place, and such Hand-bill having no signatures, or appearance of having been published by sufficient authority, and being likely to give unnecessary trouble, We, the Churchwardens and undersigned Inhabitants of Burslem, although we should certainly be disposed to pay respect to the wishes of any respectable inhabitants on the above subject, if properly made known, desire at the same time to express our entire disapprobation of the manner of calling any meeting by an anonymous advertisement, and we recommend to the Freeholders and Inhabitants not to attend the meeting which has been advertised as any proceedings which may then take place cannot be expressive of the general wishes of the Inhabitants, and may only tend to disturb the peace of the parish which we wish to avoid."
Thomas Goodwin, William Twigg, J. Williamson Churchwardens. (and others)

Presumably with sufficient support, in 1824 the request to Colonel Sneyd was renewed, this time with success. Further land was obtained at an annual rent of £10 per annum for five hundred years and subject to a 'Fine' of £50 payable every twenty-one years. It was now possible to apply for an Act of Parliament which was comprehensive embracing the functions and services of an expanding town. The Bill was in two parts. The Trustees of the markets were to have powers to create bye laws, to appoint one of their number as Chief Constable, to set market tolls, to keep the markets and town hall in repair, to provide lighting in the centre of the town (since Cobridge and Longport emphatically objected to meeting any cost for lighting in their parishes); to pay Rent and Fines and repay the loan required to build. Any surplus was to be used to defray the cost of policing.

With regard to the policing portion of the bill, discussions had taken place between the local towns to see if they could agree on a communal approach and share the cost of policing. Robert Peel at government level had offered the services of his department in an advisory capacity, but Burslem finally decided not to accept either approach. Before the application was made for legal powers the following notice was displayed:-

REPORT OF COMMITTEE OF POLICE.
"It is proposed to seek a Bill in Parliament for the establishment of Police in the Potteries to be executed by Commissioners. The qualification of Commissioners shall be: Ownership of property to the value of seventyfive pounds per year, or personality of one thousand five hundred pounds or, a tenancy of a bonafide rent of seventyfive pounds per year, or one third of all the preceding qualities, or half of any two.

The Commissioners to appoint a Superintendent Constable at a salary, and such other Constables as are necessary, and to erect a Court House and Prison.

To meet the cost, the Commissioners to levy a general rate not exceeding six pence in the pound on establishments and on all persons inhabiting, using, or occupying any Messuages, Warehouses, Pottery Works,

Pottery workers shown at the
beginning of the 20th century
(*Cup and Saucer Land*
by Malcolm Graham)

Manufactures, Beerhouses, Wharfs, Counting Houses, Gardens and other Tenements. and a specific rate of six pence to cover the cost of lighting in the town. Your committee beg leave to state that although they have not made lighting of the Potteries a part of the foregoing plan of Police, they are not the less sensible that it is an essential and important incident thereto, but they have been induced to leave it out of the plan partly from a desire, very generally expressed, that each town or district should have the management and defray the expense of its own lighting, partly from the great cost of lighting which would render an additional rate necessary."

It was proposed that trustees for the markets would be appointed from the same property owning and opulent residents, and the official application for parliamentary sanction was worded as follows:

"Whereas the town of Burslem in the county of Stafford is large and populous, and a place where great and extensive manufactures of Earthenware are carried on, and the same including the hamlet of Sneyd and the places of Longport, Cobridge and other parts, all in the parish of Burslem aforesaid, contains upwards of ten thousand inhabitants. That markets on Mondays and Saturdays have for many years past been held at Burslem aforesaid, in a place there called the Market-place, for the convenience of, and better supplying with provisions the inhabitants of the said town and its neighbourhood. and a Market House, or Town Hall was many years ago erected and built upon a piece of waste land in the Market-place of the said town. That it would be a great advantage and utility if the said Market-place were enlarged, and the market put on a permanent footing, and if the streets, avenues and places in the town were lighted, and a proper and efficient police and watch were established in the parish."

The act received royal approval in June 1825. Based on meeting the qualifications required, a list of some forty persons were eligible for election to form the trustees and from these a Chief Constable was to be appointed annually. It should be made clear that it had been customary in most towns to annually appoint a Chief Bailiff, who would act as chairman of the Board of Health, the equivalent to today's Council - consequently it is not surprising that the use of this name, as opposed to Chief Constable, continued; and he appointed a Head Constable in charge of the police.

Prior to the parliamentary act, it had for many years been the a practice in Burslem, on the Sunday following the appointment of a new Chief Bailiff, for the Trustees and guests to go as a body in procession to the church. At the conclusion of the service an elaborate breakfast was provided. Enoch Wood said that *"the first elaborate breakfast consisted of Leg of Lamb and Turnips"*, the latter presumably being 'vegetable of the day', but the meal got more elaborate in the following years, when Roast Goose and Giblet Pie was served, and fish, flesh or fowl added to the menu.

The first commitment of the Market Trustees was to promote the building of a covered Meat Market, or Shambles as it was commonly known, but this was delayed on account of old houses and buildings which obtruded on the area required. These were owned by Thomas Wedgwood and were eventually bought along with other property, which, after demolition, cleared an area from the town hall to Wedgwood Place. The ultimate cost of the project, inclusive of the cost of the clearance of the land and the building of the market was £7200, the money to pay for it being raised on mortgage against security of market tolls. The building was of striking appearance, it had a doric portico of six fluted columns supporting a pediment over the principal south entrance, and a double flight of twelve steps. Two rows of spacious vaults extended under the building and the basement at the front housed small shops with arched doors and windows. Incorporated at the rear was the police station. The foundation stone was laid in 1835 with the customary ceremony by Enoch Wood, who was also the first treasurer of the Market Trustees, and a large number of spectators. Under the stone, in a metal case, were buried several pieces of pottery, including one of Enoch Wood's figures, a number of coins and a brass plate inscribed:

"This Foundation laid by the Trustees of Burslem Market,
the first day of December. Anno Domini MDCCCXXV.
Enoch Wood, Treasurer.   John Ward, Clerk to the Trustees.
Samuel Ledward, Architect.   William Smith, Builder.

The trowel used for the occasion was presented to Mr Wood, and on it was inscribed:

"This trowel was presented by the Trustees of Burslem-market to Enoch Wood Esq. their Treasurer, on the occasion of his laying the corner-stone of the covered market, 1st of December 1835, as a token of the high estimation in which they hold his character, and to show their sense for the zeal he has ever manifested for the improvement of his native town."

Charges for stalls in the open market place ranged from 1/6d to 3/1d per day, exclusive of lighting. The annual income from these tolls had by the year 1812 reached £150 and at an early date were auctioned to provide the town with further capital. By 1826 they had reached £552 10 0. Following the erection of the Shambles the practice of auctioning the tolls continued, either annually or sometimes on a three year contract, but it was now on a much bigger scale, and the annual offer peaked at approximately £1500. Then as shops in the town increased in number, it became progressively more difficult to reach the target figure set by the Trustees, and sometimes while waiting for a suitable bid they were forced to employ an individual to collect the tolls.

Like many of the early buildings, alas it is no more, but its function as a building of importance to the community grew less as the number of shops in the town increased and competed with the market for custom. In fact at a later date part of the market was walled off, glazed with white tiles, and provided with a separate entrance for a fish market.

When the demolition took place, a colourful figure of Napoleon was said to have been removed from the site - and it is to be hoped that one day the brass commemoration plate will also come to light. Despite the building's original imposing appearance it became neglected, since it had numerous absentee landlords as a result of the practice of auctioning the tolls. Furthermore, the effect of mining, smoke and dust contributed before the ultimate demolition.

Making the official appointments required under the provisions of the 1825 act, the Trustees elected William Twigg as Chief Constable or Chief Bailiff, and he in turn appointed a Head of Police, sometimes referred to unflatteringly as the Inferior Constable, at a salary of £50 per annum, and two assistant constables at £30 per annum. In addition four watchmen were employed, one each for Burslem, Brownhills, Cobridge, and Longport. All these had to be sworn in by a magistrate in accordance with a legal procedure said to have been inaugurated by Alfred the Great; and since Burslem had no magistrate, the ceremony would most likely have been at a Court Leet held periodically at Tunstall. The watchmen were initially employed for twenty six weeks in the winter at a wage of 12/- per week.

It will be recalled that under the the terms of the act, a maximum rate of 6d was stipulated for these and other specified services, a restriction which became irksome. In 1828 due to increasing disorder including a break in at the prison and the release of prisoners, it was decided to employ the watchmen in summer as well as winter; and after the strike of 1831 such was the fear of the inhabitants, they appealed for the Yeomanry to be stationed in the town. Captain Powys who was in charge, although concerned that there were only 17 policemen to a population of 70,000 inhabitants in the Potteries, was unable to accede to the request, but organised some 450 Burslem volunteers into divisions to take turns in patrolling the town, starting at 9.45 each night, and this continued in operation for some time. As a token of the town's gratitude for the good work of the Queen's Own Royal Regiment during the riots, a voluntary subscription of £630 was raised in a week to defray the cost of the wear and tear of the regiment's equipment.

Ever mindful of the burden of taxation and the difficulty involved in collection, the Board decided to charge the Head of Police with the additional duty of collecting the rates. since defaulting on payment was all too prevalent; presumably they reasoned that fear of the law would improve matters.

But if the collection of rates was one problem for the police, those caused through abuse of drink must have been more time consuming, since in 1834 there were in Burslem 84 beerhouses and 36 inns. Children were seen leaving these premises at one or two o'clock in the morning - but there was little else to satisfy the exuberance of youth. The Reverend Stuart observed that the houses of the operatives were so small and the families so large that it was impossible to invite friends in, and the boisterousness of youth was treated with threats rather than tolerance (nothing changes!), as seen in this public notice from the church authorities:

CAUTION

Whereas a number of young men and boys assemble together in various parts of the town and neighbourhood of Burslem and conduct themselves in a very riotous and disorderly manner, particularly on a Sabbath Day, contrary to the form of statute in such case made and provided. Therefore in order to prevent in future such shameful practices and abuse of the public, We the undersigned Church Wardens in the said parish of Burslem, have given direction to the Constable of the said parish, to apprehend and take all such persons offending before His Majesty's Justice of the Peace, there to be dealt with according to the law. All person bathing in the Navigation on the Sabbath Day will likewise be taken notice of.

Thomas Bathwell
William Rhead
John Prime

The statutes referred to were imposed in the reign of George III. The penalties were:

For using unlawful pastimes on the Lord's Day	3/4d
For not attending church	12d

In 1833 Lord Brougham had introduced a bill for the improvement of parliamentary boroughs. Under this bill the police in each of the six towns which form the Potteries would have been combined, but at a public meeting in Burslem John Ward explained the effects of the terms and this resulted in official opposition from Burslem, perhaps influenced by the constables' extraneous duties, acceptable at Burslem, but not likely to be acceptable by a unified force. John Davenport the then Member of Parliament was requested to oppose the bill, although he apparently disagreed with Burslem's rejection.

Lord Brougham was noted for his clarity of thought and for harmonising conflicting interests in those areas which had common affinity for his proposed measures. It is said these areas ultimately formed the basis for the future counties. It could be assumed therefore that in refusing to accept his proposals, the Potteries may have missed an opportunity of becoming a self contained county in its own right!

The 1832 Reform Act was a belated confirmation that Britain had predominantly become an urban society and that it was no longer possible to tolerate the squalor and health hazards created by the unregulated growth of the industrial revolution in manufacturing areas. The government anticipated that the act would, by widening the voting franchise, stimulate efforts to bring about improvements in and by the Boards of Health. But this was but a start; the 1835 Municipal Reform Act was intended to further reform conditions. The Burslem Board of Health in response appointed a salaried Surveyor, a Nuisance Inspector and a Law Clerk. Nuisances tended to be treated as a costly misfortune rather than due to man's fallibility, but in the early part of the 19th century Poor Law Commissioners had the legal right to abate a nuisance by serving an order on the offender, but this required the signatures of two Justice of the peace and two doctors, and since the nearest magistrate was at Stafford it often resulted in the Burslem Board of Health themselves having to remedy the nuisance.

The Burslem Nuisance Inspector had a short life since, after serving for two years, he was dismissed on economy grounds. Never short of ingenious solutions the Board co-opted thirty five new members in the hope that they could be persuaded to voluntarily share the duties of nuisance inspection in return for the favour bestowed on them, but despite the honour there was no enthusiasm and some even had the temerity to refuse acceptance. The Board then decided that the police could add it as an extraneous duty, but conditions in some areas were so bad that it was said that one constable *"was so overcome by sight and smell on one visit that he took to his bed, and a colleague who took over, himself made one visit and refused to go again"*.

As it happened the government finally decided that the operation of policing was in an unsatisfactory state and lacked uniformity in methods. This led to the act of 1839 which placed the burden for the organization of policing on the County. Even this however failed to go as well as expected, since this act was withdrawn, and replaced by the Parish Council act of 1842, which allowed such areas as Burslem to revert to employing their own police providing the arrangement was acceptable to a head constable paid for out of the county rates. The Burslem Board at this same period decided to institute a night time horse patrol, from which it would seem that Captain Powys' commandos of the night had either lost enthusiasm or been disbanded. Finally, in 1843, another government directive again gave the County control of policing, this time over the whole of the Potteries. Burslem had been forced to increase rates of pay to their constables owing to the more generous terms received by those in Hanley. The cost of the new 1843 directive was to be met by a 5d rate levy imposed by the County. This Burslem calculated would raise £800 for the services of the eight policemen allotted to them by the County whereas the actual payment to the officers would be £373.

The position of clerk to the Burslem Board of Health had from the board's inception been a part-time occupation held by members of a family named Harding, attorneys in the town, and they held it until it was abolished in 1845, again on economy grounds. As a replacement the Board employed a part time book-keeper, or cash-keeper as he was generally known, a Mr Walsh whose main occupation was auctioneer and estate agent, and for his services to the Board, he was paid the princely sum of £15 a year. He died in 1836, and was succeeded by George Powell on £20 a year, but he again only lived until 1838 to enjoy his extravagant salary, and in his place Richard Timmis was appointed at a yearly salary of £15, the Board evidently having regretted their extravagance. Timmis, described in the trade directory as a "Printer and Parian Ear Drop Manufacture" took over the printing business of Tregortha, who printed most of the official town documents - and a character the reader will meet later.

A change of view in 1828 resulted in the employment of a rate collector on a commission basis, receiving 2% of all monies collected, but the appointment was cancelled within months. Why the collector was dismissed is not recorded but, perhaps significantly, his successor, William Walsh was paid 5% commission but had to find a £250 security, which at that time was a not insignificant sum. The position was advertised again in 1842, still on a commission basis, properties with basic rates under £10 - 7%, over £10 - 2%. The terms soon changed to under £40 - 7% over £40 - 2%.

The Board were now clearly reconciled to the fact that rent collection was more than a part time police duty - understandable since the town had grown considerably in size, as had the police work while their only mobile assistance was a horse and a bicycle! 'A policeman's lot was not a happy one' - neither was the rent collector's. In 1833, there were so many householders owing rates, that after a detailed study 188 were written off and 38 issued with a summons, while the law clerk's position was sacrificed in an effort to make ends meet. The Treasurer to the Board was Mr Holden, a partner in the bank of Wood & Holden which dealt with the Town's finances until 1830 when they refused the Burslem Board any further credit. The overdraft was transferred to the bank of John James & George Alcock.

With such money problems it is not surprising that improvements were slow to materialise. The government introduced additional acts in 1848 but none seemed to have much teeth, mainly because shortage of money for public works was endemic in the system. Burslem Board of Health had no option but to keep a tight hold on policies and projects, and for those that were imperative they borrowed monies from individuals and institutions in addition to loans from the Government Loan Board. Monies raised from auctioning the tolls from the markets were also used for capital projects, and offered as security for loans. It might be thought that the Board had so many problems to deal with that delegation would have been noticeable, but no, they still continued to deal personally with all matters related to the town. In 1833, as the annual wakes neared, the Board issued the following warning:-

GAMBLING

"The authorities being fully alive to the pernicious effects of gambling and its demoralising influence to the principles of the young, do hereby resolve that the most effective measures be taken to prevent it at the approaching festival, and that this determination be made as public as possible. Should anyone offend after this notice has been publicly given, the offenders shall be immediately taken into custody and subjected to the punishment the law awards for such offences."

Still adhering to their principles, the Board in 1835 issued a public warning that no theatrical show must be held near the Methodist Chapel, but ignoring this stricture, in 1844 an audacious request was made to build a theatre in sight of the chapel in Swan Square. Fortunately a timely distraction arrived in 1835 with the opening of a theatre in Waterloo Road. It was called The New Theatre and was under the management of a Mr Poynter who *"begged most respectfully to announce to the public of Burslem and its environs that he had engaged the above splendid premises and at the most immense expense has fitted it up for a fashionable place of amusement."* The company he engaged for the opening would, he said, *"consist of performers selected from Metropolitan and Provincial theatres, each of an elegant description, far surpassing anything of the county that has been presented to a Burslem audience, and to give additional splendour the theatre will be brilliantly lit with GAS".* On Tuesday and Wednesday evenings, December the 22nd and 23rd December he would present:

KENATEE LEGENDRY MILE DRAMA

THE BATTLE IMP or the FIEND AND SORCERER

Followed by A COMIC SCENE by Mr. Baker

**Followed by A laughable farce
SMOKED MISOR or BENEFIT OF HANGING**

Good fires constantly made up renders the theatre
warm and comfortable.

PIT. 1/-d GALLERY. 6d.

Doors open at 6.30. Performance starts at 7.0.

In 1840 the Board's patriotism and indignation was fired by the sensational attempt on Queen Victoria's life. It appears that Victoria and Albert were setting out in a carriage when a shot was fired, the horses frightened and brought to a halt. The assailant holding two pistols fired a second shot, which missed both Victoria and Albert; the man was instantly mobbed by an incensed public who urged those close to the man to kill him. A letter was sent by the Board:

We, your loyal and dutiful subjects, beg leave to express to Your Majesty our sincere and lively relief, in common with the rest of your Majesty's people, for the providential deliverance of your sacred person from the late murderous and fractious attempt of an insane or misguided youth to destroy the head of this mighty nation, and inflict on its status an indelible stain, and to plunge the millions which inhabit your wide dominions into the deepest sorrow and dismay, We offer up to the Divine Being, who has on this and a former occasion so signally protected you, our grateful homage of praise and thanksgiving, and we humbly pray that the same manifestations of his almighty care and goodness may still preserve Your Majesty from all dangers, and continue your gentle and beneficent reign for a devoted and loyal people for a very lengthy period.

For the year she was married it was not an auspicious start. The Board also addressed her husband:

To His Royal Highness Albert,
Prince of Saxe Coburgh & Gotha.
Consort of Her Majesty the Queen.

The dutiful address of the Magistary, Clergy, Chief Constable, and Commissioners of the Police, and other inhabitants of Burslem in the county of Stafford.

We, Her Majesty's faithful and loyal subjects desire to tender to Your Royal Highness expressions of our deep sorrow and dismay on account of the late daring and fractious attack directed against the person of Her Majesty, and our devout and heartfelt congratulations upon the happy and providential escape, both to Her Majesty and Your Royal Highness from so wicked and murderous attempt. We take this opportunity of assuring Your Royal Highness of our admiration of your character since you assumed the exalted situation you occupy in the British Empire, and our sincere hope and prayer that Her Majesty and yourself may long continue to exhibit to this nation a bright example of domestic felicity and be favoured by the arm of omnipotence as from the late, so from other future dangers.

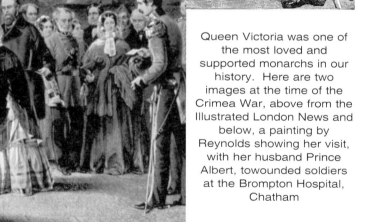

Queen Victoria was one of the most loved and supported monarchs in our history. Here are two images at the time of the Crimea War, above from the Illustrated London News and below, a painting by Reynolds showing her visit, with her husband Prince Albert, towounded soldiers at the Brompton Hospital, Chatham

Back in Burslem, in 1841 the slaughter house at the corner of Fountain Place was officially cautioned for allowing offensive matter to flow into the street; a rag and bone store in Brick House Street was ordered to move all offensive matter out of the building daily, and complaints of the fumes from tallow makers and ironstone burners were also dealt with. A further complaint was of dogs fighting in the town, and the services of the watchmen were brought in to provide the Board with a list of dog owners.

The watchmen were called upon to attend church on Sunday evenings to ensure that the congregations were preserved from annoyance. With their week now extended to the Sabbath, the Board recruited six special constables for two hours, from 8.00pm to 10.00pm, to watch for disorderly conduct.

CHAPTER THIRTEEN: Tregortha

Tregortha; Burslem printer and philosopher.

John Tregortha was prominently associated with the early period of Burslem's growth. He was a printer with premises in St John's Square and seems in his day to have had a near monopoly of public notices in Burslem. According to Scarratt he was also looked upon by the demonic juveniles of Burslem as a symbol of antiquity and a prey for their mischief, even after his death:

> Now old Tregortha's dead and gone
> We ne'er shall see him more
> He us't wear and old grey coat
> All buttoned down before

He was born in Cornwall about 1759 and was trained as a travelling Methodist minister. How he gained his knowledge of printing is uncertain. He was in office in Burslem from 1787 to 1795 and started his printing business in 1796. He had two wives; there is no mention of any children by his first wife, but he made amends for this by having nine by his second.

Apart from his general trade in printing, he published a number of books and pamphlets by others, and some doggerel of his own on topical subjects, which he printed and sold for 'coppers'. He published *"Navigation spiritualised, or A new compass for Seamen," "consisting of forty two points of pleasant observation, profitable application and serious reflection"* by John Flavel in 1807. Another book, which must have been a powerful and disturbing moral work, was *"The French Convert"* in 1808 by an anonymous author, *"Being the true revelation of the happy conversion of a French noble lady from the superstition of Popery to the reformed religion by means of a Protestant gardener servant, where is shown her great and unparalleled sufferings on the account of her said conversion, as also her wonderful deliverance from the two assassins hired by a Papist Priest to murder her, and of her miraculous preservation in a wood for two years, and how she was providentially found by her husband, who, together with her parents, were brought over to embracing of true religion, as were others also"*.

He published a treatise by John Welled MA, *"Primitive Physics as an easy and natural method of curing most diseases."* Among his own works was one titled *"Reflections on the death of His Majesty George III"*. During Wellington's crusades he published, and presumably wrote, patriotic verse which sold *"at a price to suit the humblest pocket"*. The following commemorates the Battle of Vittoria, 21st June 1813, during the Peninsular Wars:

> Come cheer up, cheer up, here's good news from old Spain
> Our soldiers have beat the French robbers again
> On the heights near Vittoria, the conflict began
> Huzza boys the brave British have won
>
> Chorus.-(to follow each verse)   See the enemy flies
>   Follow Wellington cries
>   A Briton in battle
>   He conquers or die
>
> Ten thousand lay wounded or dying or dead
> As many surrendered, the rest of them fled
> We've beat the grand army, we took all their store
> Their baggage and cannon, what could we do more
>
> Sound forth brazen trumpet, and tell George the King
> Let my countrymen know, and all citizens sing
> The Lions of Britain their duty have done
> They have met with her foes, they have fought them and won

CAUTION
TO
PERSONS TIPPLING,
AND TO
PUBLICANS.

THE UNDERSIGNED MANUFACTURERS of Earthen-Ware within the parish of BURSLEM, sustaining the most serious loss and inconvenience, by daily interruptions to their business, in consequence of the habits of idleness and tippling which many of their workmen indulge in, during the regular hours of work, and in which they find encouragement by the very CULPABLE CONDUCT OF MANY PUBLICANS within this parish; Do hereby make known, that from the publication of this Notice, *they are resolved to give every protection and support to such persons as will lay complaints before the Magistrates, against any workmen for the offence of tippling ;* and the undersigned Manufacturers have also resolved,

Individually to notice and to report to the Magistrates

The conduct of all such Publicans as shall from henceforth suffer any workmen to remain tippling in their houses during the regular working hours, or at any other improper time.

THE PUBLICANS ARE HEREBY INFORMED,

That on conviction of the offence of suffering tippling, or unlawful Games in their houses, they are liable to *forfeit their recognizances,* and to have their *licenses suspended* for the space of *three years,* besides being subject to a penalty of ten shillings for every offence by tippling ; and that *the Magistrates acting for this Hundred have come to the resolution of putting these laws strictly in force for the future.*

☞ Any person found tippling in a Public-house is liable to a penalty of three shillings and four-pence, to the use of the Poor, besides the costs of the information.

Burslem, November, 1815.

Wood & Caldwell	*Jno. & Rich. Riley*	*Jno. Rogers*
Henshall & Williamsons	*Tho. & Benj. Godwin*	*Rhead & Goodfellow*
Jno. & Jas. Davenport	*William Stanley*	*Machin & Co.*
Thomas Heath	*John Brettell*	*Wm. Bourne & Co.*
Samuel Tomkinson	*William Moseley*	*James Cartlidge*
Ralph Johnson	*Stevenson and Bucknall*	*J. and R. Blackwell*
Thomas Bathwell	*Wm. Walsh*	*Benj. Godwin and Sons*
Edward Bourne	*John Haywood*	*F. and N. Dillon*
John & Christr. Robinson	*John Wood*	*Ralph Stevenson*
John Hall	*Lindop & Taylor*	*R. and J. Clews*

⁎ Every Publican within this parish will be expected to keep one of these Notices conspicuously posted up in his house, as a proof he is determined to maintain good order therein.

TREGORTHA, PRINTER.

On the twentyfirst day of that hot month of June
We struggled with thousands, and vanquished them soon
Our gallant exploits in that fight, let me tell
But first drop a tear, for my comrades who fell

At the word of command, we did quickly advance
And pointed our guns at the proud sons of France
With eager delight, we our banners unfurled
And midst their deep ranks, Britain's thunderbolts hurl'd

Each infantry regiment, anxious to win
With dreadful effect, frequent volleys poured in
Then straight to the charge, those bold heroes did go
And heaps upon heaps at their feet were laid low

Our valiant dragoons,sword in hand forward dashed
The Life Guards and Blues, thru their lines cut and slashed
Whole blazing battalions in battle array
Before our brave troops, were obliged to give way

In vain did old Jourdon rally his men
We battered their breast works, again and again
Determined to conquer, or die on the field
The savage invader, we forced him to yield.

By popular demand, he also published a mammoth poster of a mythical interview with Napoleon:

PLAIN ANSWERS TO PLAIN QUESTIONS IN A DIALOGUE BETWEEN JOHN BULL AND BONAPARTE MET HALF SEAS OVER BETWEEN DOVER AND CALAIS.

John Bull.	How do you do
Bonaparte.	Pretty well but hope to be better when I am in London.
John Bull.	When do you expect to get there.
Bonaparte.	About the end of September, or October at the latest.
John Bull.	Why would you not remain at peace with us, which you know we are anxious to preserve.
Bonaparte.	Because I had set my heart on the recovery of Egypt, which I had disgracefully quitted, and in recovering Egypt, to pave the way to driving you out of India, to the production of which you own so much wealth.
John Bull.	But what did Malta signify?.
Bonaparte.	I could not clearly get Egypt without it.
John Bull.	Why are you such an enemy of liberty of the press.
Bonaparte.	That's a foolish question John, why! because it exposes all my deep designs, because it makes me odious amongst my own subjects, and in all Europe, by pointing out all the bloodshed, desolation, and rapine by which I have obtained power, and by which I must possess it. For which it recommends love and loyalty and support for a King I mean to dethrone, and to annihilate.
John Bull.	What religion are you Bony?.
Bonaparte.	I was first a Deist, then a Papist in Italy and afterwards a Mohammedan in Egypt, and now I am an Atheist.
John Bull.	Why then did you restore the Catholic religion in France.
Bonaparte.	Because it answered my purpose best.

John Bull.	Why have you suffered your soldiers to burn so many towns, shed so much innocent blood, destroy cottages as well as palaces so indiscriminately murder in cold blood thousands of poor men, ravish thousands of poor women in Italy, Egypt, Syria, and lately in Hanover.
Bonaparte.	Foolish again John. I did not merely suffer, my object has always been to strike terror. I don't mince matters, witntess the massacre of four thousand Turks at Jaffa who were my prisoners and seven hundred of my own soldiers who were of no use to me.
John Bull.	What do you mean to do if you come here?.
Bonaparte.	I won't tell you, it would make your hair stand on end.
John Bull.	Ar'nt you a bit afraid of us?.
Bonaparte.	To tell you the truth I am. But I am not afraid to sacrifice a hundred thousand men in the attempt to invade you.
John Bull.	As an honest man, what do you depend on for success?.
Bonaparte.	On foggy weather, long nights, and want of discipline in your troops, a want of spirit and union in your people.
John Bull.	You had better let it alone Bony, if that is your only grounds for hope, you're a monstrous fool if you attempt it
Bonaparte.	To tell you the truth John, I don't much like some of your late proceedings in parliament, but I am determined on the attempt, so look out.

Tregortha was a contemporary of Enoch Wood, and since Enoch was chairman of the Burslem Board they must have had a close business association, and possibly the friendship induced Tregortha to publish the following verse which describes a day in the working life of Burslem at the beginning of the 19th century. It emphasises the status of Enoch Wood, and reflects a close communal atmosphere. As an introduction to his verse Tregortha made the following observations:

ENOCH'S BELL

"All yields to Enoch's Bell. Should this bagatelle by any accidental circumstance wander out of Staffordshire Potteries, the distant reader would be at a loss to understand the denominator term which is the burden of the ballad, " Enoch's Bell." To such, it may be needful to remark that this bell is erected at the Earthenware factory of Enoch Wood in the town of Burslem to regulate the attendance and dismissal of the workpeople.

Its central situation to the open area on which the factory stands, its altitude and sonorous sound are circumstances which favour it being heard in every part of the town."

"The use of bells is very ancient, as well as extensive. They are found among Jews, Greeks, Romans, Christian and Heathens, variously applied as on the necks of men, beasts, birds, horses, sheep, but chiefly rung in buildings, either religious, as in churches, temples or monasteries, or military, as in camps or frontier towns, or civil as in houses, markets or baths, and in modern times more especially in large manufactures".

"The first instance of this kind in the Potteries was adapted by the late Josiah Wedgwood, about the year 1766, when he occupied the manufactury now carried on by Messrs Bourne and Cromie in Burslem, and which by way of distinction was called the Bell Works.

Before this time, the hour for labour was announced by the sound of an Ox Horn blown here, which was intended as a signal for the three smaller works which Mr. Wedgwood had in the town, but it was found that when the wind was high, the horn sound could not be heard at all the works at once and the erection of a bell was suggested and carried into effect.

The identical horn then used is still preserved by a gentleman resident in Burslem."

ENOCH'S BELL : THE BALLAD

Let high-born pride dissemble all it can
The little things are great to little men
Let facts form'd for lofty verse
Their heroeso praises swell

I sing a theme as dear to me
I sing of Enoch's Bell

Where Burslem's smoking turrets rise
Where glory wares excel
Tis there in balcony secure
Tis there hangs Enoch's Bell

Not e'en the sunbeam on the dial
Can regulate so well
For astronomic art may err
But true is Enoch's Bell

It's potent sound all rev'rence bears
Tis like some magic spell
We sleep and rise and work and eat
And taught by Enoch's Bell

When morning light illumes the world
And night's dark shades dispel
White apron'd potters seek their Banks
When tinkles Enoch's Bell

The thrifty housewife rubs her eyes
And bids her couch farewell
Shutters fly back and chimneys smoke
What power has Enoch's Bell

And Molly who till midnight hour
Hears tom his pashions tell
Renews the scene in slumbers sweet
Till rais'd by Enoch's Bell

E'en Towser from his kennel starts
As instinct powers impel
And shakes his shaggy sides and bays
To the sound of Enoch's Bell

Nor think the cheerful chime alone
Calls forth to labour's spell
For hours of respite and of ease
Are mark'd by Enoch's Bell

At nine the tea and toast invite
All homeward rush pell mell
No sturdy bailiff dare molest
Their passport, Enoch's Bell

So when the smoking Sirloin spreads
It's odiferous smell
At one again in groups they move
At the sound of Enoch's Bell

Then last is heard the merriest peal
That tolls of work the Knell
Tis, six, the whirling lathe stands still
All cease at Enoch's Bell

But when the teeming orders pour
And trade is going well
Then nine the hour of respite marks
For so says Enoch's Bell

Now shops are closed, all bus'ness dropt
No more buy or sell
Night clothes for children we prepar'd
Then bow to Enoch's Bell

Save too the day that ends the week
A day beloved well
Woodhall, at four proclaims release
By ringing Enoch's Bell

Next comes the hour of labour's sweets
That makes each bosom swell
Tis five and wages are paid down
O generous Enoch's Bell

O may thy owner who at first
Gave thee on high to dwell
Have peace as constant, health as good
And sound as Enoch's Bell

Should then some future masters own
A fact one may foretell
Let not ambition change thy name
Be always Enoch's Bell

If from thy presence far I roam
Thro mountain, vale or dell
Still fancy's ear shall catch thy sound
And honour Enoch's Bell

This moral then, my heart impress
To do life's duties well
Prompt to obey the calls of Heaven
Steady as Enoch's Bell

That in life's close, my soul may know
No guilty horrors fell
But quit her days, cheerful as those
Who move to Enoch's Bell

At least what e'er my faults beside
I would of many tell
their number ne'er will be increased
By penning Enoch's Bell.

PRICE 3d.

Around the middle of the 18th century demand for Burslem pottery was such that it was not unusual to work until midnight. By 1790 trade was still brisk and work generally finished at nine in the evening, the extra three hours from six o'clock, the standard finishing time, would count as half a day.

An interesting little booklet printed by Tregortha, presumably for or in association with Enoch Wood, was entitled *Warm Bathing*. Enoch Wood owned Bycars Colliery, presumably to ensure his supply of fuel for his factories. In 1818 he built a bath nearby and offered its facilities to the inhabitants of Burslem, and the booklet starts with a preamble on the value of bathing, followed by a description of the bath:

> Throughout history, water has held humans in its spell for having miraculous properties, although no particular claim seems to have been made for Bycars water, but Dr Plott, who recorded and analysed the properties of many healing waters, mentioned a well in Burslem, but failed to mention where it was to be found, or what cures were claimed for its waters, but he found no medicinal qualities.

The Bycars bath was described as five minutes walk from the town and was fed by a continuous flow of water pumped from the mine at a temperature of 90 to 100 degrees Fahrenheit. The booklet said that:

> Adjoining the main bath, is another reservoir where sufficient water, at a much lower temperature is retained and, by means of a small flood may be let into the bath, so that any temperature may be obtained. Entering the bath there is a dressing room twenty one feet long, which can be made into six rooms by using curtains. The bath is circular, thirty feet in diameter, and surrounded by a wall twenty feet high, open at the top. The wall is painted with panoramic landscapes and seascapes. The inside of the changing room is also decorated with busts and figures in Egyptian Black, Bronze etc. of several of the ancient and modern celebrated characters who have written on the subject of warm baths.

> Terms of admission. One guinea per annum, with privileges to subscribers.
> Under twenty one. Half a guinea per annum.
> Ladies. Gratis, if any one gent in the family subscribes annually.

The booklet expressed *"the appreciation of warm baths for health and medical purposes by eminent men ...... the Greeks took a guest to a warm bath and annointed him with favourite unguents, previous to offering him food which formed an important part of the height of hospitality"*.

Such hospitality in Burslem would have enhanced the prosperity of the George hostelry in walking distance of the baths. Another interesting statement was *".....no people in the world equal the inhabitants of this country in the general cleanliness of their apparel, yet due attention to the strict purity of person is too often neglected."* Had they have had television they would have been inundated with cures.

Other observations were: *Spasmodic cough and other nervous affections are relieved by a warm bath. Bathing of the thighs and legs is the best remedy for those convulsions which sometimes precede Small Pox. One obvious effect of the habitual use of the bath is that it softens and renews the integuments of the body. It is hardly to be doubted that, if not earlier, at least at manhood, cold bathing should begin"*.

It seems that when Tregortha died his premises were taken over by another printer named Timmis, possibly the same Timmis in an earlier chapter appointed as part time clerk to the Board. It was said that some twenty years later the wooden press which Tregortha used was still in his workshop. One of Tregortha's sons must have evidently learnt the trade since he was described in a later trade directory as a printer in premises of his own in Waterloo Road.

Descendants of Tregortha appear to have vanished from Burslem, either from extinction of the male line or by returning to their native county; there are none in the local phone directory today.

CHAPTER FOURTEEN: Public houses

Pubs, hotels & breweries.

It would be unpardonable to describe Burslem without mentioning its numerous inns. In fact the thirsty stranger who arrived in the town in its early days, either up the rise of Newcastle Street or that of Waterloo Road, could not fail to think this was Utopia, not only was the centre well equipped with welcoming inns but, as befitted its situation on top of a hill, the approach roads equally offered hospitality to the toiling pedestrian. The pedestrian has become today's motorist, consequently the numerous inns in Waterloo Road and Newcastle Street have virtually disappeared, and among those that are left some await demolition. One such in Newcastle Street is The Staff of Life to which Mr Scarratt refers to in another chapter and from which the one legged headmaster was brought home inebriated; it still bears its sign but is among those that are derelict and boarded against intruders despite the pumps being dry.

The Duke of Bridgewater, built at the time of the construction of the adjoining canal, and named after the man who was among the first to appreciate Brindley's skills, stands opposite the Packhorse Inn at the Longport end of Newcastle Street. Both are much altered but still a living part of Burslem's heritage, though no longer relying on canal traffic for their income.

Waterloo Road was said to have had at one time fifteen or more inns. Two of these have survived, the America and the Queen's Head; the latter with an attractive sign showing the head of Queen Victoria. Both in their heyday welcomed coach travellers.

The Dog and Partridge is in North Street, with its painted sign in need of restoration and its coloured ceramic mosaic sign built high into a side wall, a prestigious symbol of a once seemingly permanent Parker's Brewery. But it was not to be, ultimately suffering the fate of many brewers who one by one have been swallowed up and then abandoned by the bigger fish. The property is now a scouts' headquarters.

A history of inn signs in Burslem was published in 1944, written by Mr. W.E. Tate, a fellow of The Royal History Society, and headmaster of the Sneyd Church School. It was written at the instigation of the then head of Parker's Brewery which at the time owned some fifty inns in Burslem alone and many more in the surrounding district. Many names of the inns reflect the period of Burslem's industrial growth, and are a useful indication of when they were originally built. Breweries however have an annoying habit of changing the name of an inn or hotel when it changes ownership, as local authorities similarly change the names of streets, and a lot of history is lost by the many who cherish the past.

The Great Britain in Orme Street was named after the first all metal ship which in recent years was rescued from rotting on a far off foreign beach and has now been restored to lie in state in a Bristol dock.

The Great Eastern in Newcastle Street was named after the ship built to carry 6000 tons of cargo and 4000 passengers, which made a record crossing to America in eleven days, compared to the approximately three months taken by those early immigrant potters. The ship was used successfully to lay a cable from the Old to the New World. The project was conceived in 1856, but it took four attempts before a cable capable of meeting the physical conditions was produced.

The Alma in Elder Road commemorated the Crimean battle of that name. The Cobden in Cobridge Road derived its name from the 19th century minister who was at the centre of controversy on the subject of free trade. The Church House Inn in Enoch Street, Tate suggests as the site of a Middle Age inn built as was the custom near a church, in this case St John's. It was similarly customary at these inns for the church wardens to brew ale from malt donated by parishioners, the ale being sold for the benefit of the church - but no doubt palatable and conveniently accessible for the bell ringers after a strenuous toll!

The Bulls Head in St. John's Square is the site of an older house of the same name, derived from the then popular sport of bull baiting. The Legs of Man, situated as it was in the centre of the town, became more or less the civic centre before the town hall was built. The current George Hotel, also built on the site of an earlier inn, of a different name, is certainly part of Burslem's heritage since although much

Two ceramic signs, celebrating the prosperous Parker's brewery, still to be seen in Burslem

rebuilt since Arnold Bennett's day, it holds a prominent place in his novels as the Dragon.

A lot of the inns have vanished because the streets in which they stood have disappeared since Tate's book, and the following inns have either gone or been renamed:

In Waterloo Road, the Eagle and Snake, North Road Hotel, the Blue Bell, the Tramway Inn, the Bull's Head (not to be confused with the one in St John's Square) and the Sea Lion.

In Cobridge there were the Raven Inn and the White Swan, both in Elder Road, the Jug Inn, Sneyd Street; Grove House Inn and the Black Boy in Cobridge Road; Bleak Inn in Bleak Street; the Cobridge Hotel in North Road; the Britannia Inn, Grange Street.

In Newcastle Street., the Foresters Arms and the Volunteer Inn.

In Liverpool Road, [now Westport Road] the Royal Oak and the Liverpool Arms.

Others include the Gladstone Arms, Pleasant Street; the Crewe Arms and the Port Vale Inn, Wharf Street; the Jolly Potters, Blackwell Street; the Grange Inn, Barnfields; the Potters Arms, Ricardo Street; the Goose Inn, Stanfields; the Royal Oak, Newport Lane; the West End Inn, Middleport; the Mitre Inn, Pitt Street West; the Bridge Inn, Brindley Street; the Railway Hotel, Sandbach Road; the Railway Hotel, Moorland Road; the Dolphin Inn, Church Street.

The Foaming Quart, in High Street as it was then known, had a predecessor which had the last thatched roof in Burslem. The Durham Ox in Nile Street was, Tate says, named after an ox which was so enormous that it was exhibited throughout the country and could have visited Burslem. There was a Royal Express Inn on Bournes Bank which was a coaching house named after a mail coach of the same name.

Tate says of the Royal Hotel in Liverpool Road that it was previously the Castle and Flagon with a sign descriptive of its name copied from that of its famous namesake in London.

Of the White Swan at Cobridge he says that the landlords sign not only depicted a white swan, but he had also added doggerel [in Burslem fashion]:

Here is a swan which dips its neck in water
why may not we as well as she, drink plenty of Parker's Porter

There were three White Swans in Burslem at one time, now there is only one in Newport Lane. They were all probably black before the last war, but had they survived they could have now, after a wash, continued living up to their name in the much changed atmosphere.

Tate says an ale house sold only ale. A tavern sold a variety of drink and was sometimes termed a winehouse. A comehouse, a name rarely seen, was similar to a tavern but also provided accommodation. Vaults were the equivalent of a tavern, and stores a beer house.

Arthur Berry, the well known local artist, seems to have been on intimate terms with most of the Burslem inns and spoke of the Star, sometimes called the Star of Bethlehem. He said it was at the corner of the preachers and the tote office, and opposite the Dolphin. Its interior was divided into cubicles called snugs, each with a coal stove, a bucket of coal, and a shovel. These snugs were referred to as pairing pens and were popular with courting couples. Other licensed houses in the town harboured what he termed shilling women, who stood in dark passages holding half a pint; the rest he left to conjecture.

Some of the beer houses brewed their own ales legitimately, and there were others who distilled their own spirits, illegitimately, but commercial brewing was commenced by Mr Parker in Zion Street, formerly Regent Street East. His brewery premises eventually extended over an area from Nile Street to Waterloo Road. In 1889 he took over the Tunstall Brewery and the combined enterprise then owned 110 licenced houses and became a limited company with a commanding trade in Burslem and much further afield.

Parker's beers were popular in the area, and appear to have a 'relaxing' quality attributed to them, since the term "Parkers Purge" was often used. The giant of the industry who swallowed Parker's was Ind Coope - now itself I believe part of a French or Belgian based giant. Of the site of the brewery itself, only the office is left to show it had ever existed.

Not all the inns, it would seem, had modern conveniences, since a bye law of 1851 stipulated that *"every public house, or inn, shall provide a proper urinal with a screen within their premises"*!

The book by W.F.Tate, 1945, with the support of Parker's Brewery. Some of signs are shown here, the Liverpool Arms, Liverpool Road, the American Hotel, Waterloo Road, the George, Swan Bank, the Raven, Elder Road, Cobridge, the Gladstone Arms, Pleasant Street, the Packhorse, Station Street, Longport and the Royal Express Inn, Bourne's Bank, Burslem. In 1828 the Royal Express ran every evening to London via Stone, and every day at 12.30 to Manchester via Lawton and Knutsford.

Above: A dejected looking Staff of LIfe.
It was the resort of the schoolmaster
described by Scarrat. It is now replaced by
a modern building

INNS AND TAVERNS.

Black Lion, Thos. Caton, Queen st
Blue Ball, Joseph Hall, Nile street
Blue Bell, Geo. Mollart, Waterloo rd
Bowling Green, Jas. Payne, Beech ln
Britannia, Rd. Turner, Navigation rd
Bull's Head, (Old,) Samuel Round, Waterloo road
Bull's Head, Jas. Mann, St John's sq
Bull's Head, Walter Pace, Cobridge
Castle and Falcon, John Johnson, Liverpool road
Cock, Edward Nichols, Market place
Crown, Hanh. B. Lea, Liverpool rd
Dog and Partridge, Frederick Eardley, Hot lane
Duke of Bridgwater, James Elsby, Longport
Duke Wm., Js. Lockett, St John's sq
Foaming Tankard, Henry Pointon, High street
Freemasons' Arms, Geo. Jackman Rutherford, St John's square
George Hotel, My. Holland, Swan sq
Highgate Inn, Js. Baylis, Brown hills
Jug, Abigail Moore, Cobridge
King & Queen, Jno. Barlow, Sneyd gn
Legs of Man, John Clarke and Co, Market place
Leopard Hotel, Thos. Lees, (and Inland Revenue office,) Market pl

The Leopard, one of the oldest remaining
taverns in the town. The frontage is
deceptive; it is a large property which
includes residential accommodation which
reflects Burslem's more prosperous past

INNS AND TAVERNS.

land Revenue office,) Market pl
Lord Nelson, Liverpool road
Marquis of Granby, George Eley, Market place
Mitre, Saml. Alcock, Upper Pitt st
New Inn, John Whittle, St John's sq
Pack Horse Inn, Walter Wm. Pace, Longport
Queen's Head, Wm. Cork, Queen st
Red Lion, Jas. Bullock, Moorland rd
Roebuck, Anastasia Worthington, New street
Sneyd's Arms, Thos. Bird, Sneyd gn
Staff of Life, John Creed Mayer Longport
Star, William Wood, Queen street
Swan Inn, William Lander, Swan sq
Waterloo and American Hotel, Thos Green, Waterloo road
White Hart, John Guest, Liverpool rd
White Swan, John Parr, Hot lane

Above and previous page, Burslem trade list in White's 1851 Directory. There were also some 60 beerhouses in the names of individuals. Compare with the 1912 Directory on page 165.

The Millstone Inn

Below: The Roebuck

The Packhorse Inn adjoining Longport Wharf and at the foot of a one time tolled turnpike road

The Saggar Maker's Bottom Maker. To the left is the frontage of what was the first joint stock bank in Burslem

The Duke William and the Fountain in St John's Square

Below: The ancient Lloyds Tavern at the left end. The building in the centre proudly proclaims on its frontage that it is the Liberal Club. Alas since Glasdtone's day it has been deserted by its members.

PUBLICANS—BEERHOUSES.

Antelope Inn, Wellington-st.; proprietor, Wm. Ratcliffe
Albion Inn, Navigation-road; proprietor, H. Yates
Alma Inn, 1, Elder-road; proprietress, Elizabeth Jesshope
Ancient Briton, 14, Hanover-st.; proprietor, John Haughton
Barnfields Inn, 43, Pleasant-st.; proprietor, John Bowers
Beaconsfield Arms, 16, Waterloo-road; proprietor, N. Farr
Blacksmith's Arms, Station-st.; prop., Ed. Bourne
Bleak Inn, 27, Bleak-st., Cobridge, prop., Elijah Whalley
Bricklayers' Arms, Edward-st.; proprietor, John Beard
Bridge Inn, West-street; proprietress, Mary J. Holdam
British Flag, Nile-street; proprietor, Amos Gidman
British Queen, Princes-st.; proprietress, Ciceley Pemberton
Britannia Inn, Grange-st., Cobridge; prop., Jos. Llewellyn
Castle Inn, 19, Wellington-st.; proprietor, George H. Brett
Church House Inn, 289, Waterloo-road, Cobridge; proprietor, Wm. H. Marlow
Church Inn, 1, Enoch-street; proprietor, Corbet Reynolds
Cobridge Hotel, Waterloo-road, Cobridge; prop., G. Freeman
Cratemakers' Arms, 30, Victoria-st.; prop., Wm. Johnson
Crewe Arms Inn, 55, Wharf st.; proprietor, W. Oseland
Cross Keys, 38, Lower Hadderidge; prop., Fredk. Hall
Crosswells Arms, 195, Newcastle-st.; proprietor, E. Kendrick Skitt
Dolphin, 4, Church-street; proprietor, Jas. H. Holdcroft
Dolphin Inn, 55, High-street; proprietor, Thomas Shaw
Duke of York, 17-19, Brownhills; prop., Daniel Dickinson
Durham Ox, 47, Nile-st.; proprietor, Wm. Pack
Eagle and Snake Inn, 38, Waterloo-rd.; prop., T. Clarke
Five Alls, 119, Newport-lane; proprietor, Harry Jones
Foresters' Arms, 70, Newcastle-st.; prop., Matthew Cooper
Grange Inn, Edward-street; proprietor, James Ferns
Granville Inn, Waterloo-road; proprietor, Robert Audley
Great Britain, 277, Newcastle-street; prop., J. Colclough
Great Eastern, 241, Newcastle-street; prop., Jos. Randalls
Greyhound Inn, Furlong-passage; prop., Wm. Burton
Greyhound Inn, 46, Station-st.; proprietor, W. G. Kenyon
Gladstone Arms, 51, Pleasant-street; proprietress, Selena Yates
Globe Inn, 149, Leek New-road, Cobridge; proprietor, Samuel Taylor
Jolly Potters, 32, Blackwell's-row; proprietor, Enos Bailey

King's Head, 61, Church-street; proprietor, George Welsby
Lamb Inn, 15, Furlong-lane; prop., Wm. Copestick
Liverpool Arms, 70, Liverpool-road; prop., Henry Scott
Lord Raglan, 16, North-road; proprietor, Arthur Shaw
Melly's Arms, 2, Edward-st.; proprietor, Thomas Jones
Mersey Tavern, 2-4-6, Pleasant-street; prop., Arthur Meade
Milton's Head, Brook-street; proprietor, A. Willott
Moon and Stars, 118, Newport-lane; prop., J. Pennell
Mceley Stores, 84, Waterloo-rd.; prop., W. E. Hopkinson
Navigation Inn, 61, Navigation-rd.; prop., T. H. Boon
New Crown Inn, 53, New-street; prop., John Caton
New Inn, 168, Elder-road; proprietor, John Brunt
New Inn, 337, Sneyd-st., Cobridge; prop., John Jones
North-road Inn, 122, North-road, Cobridge; prop., Uriah Holdcroft
Oddfellows Inn, 24, Newport-st.; prop., Joseph Riley
Port Vale Inn, 17, Wharf-street; prop., Ralph Nixon
Post Office Vaults, 3, Market-place; proprietress, Elizabeth Ward
Potters' Arms, Newport-lane; prop., George Whitehurst
Prince Albert Inn, 24, Lower Hadderidge; prop., Joseph J. Handley
Railway Inn, 125, Newcastle-st.; prop., Charles Litherland
Railway Inn, Moorland-road; proprietor, John Pascall
Railway Inn, 54, Station-street; prop., John Dukes
Ram's Head Inn, 14, Market-place; prop., Lewis Copestick
Riley Arms, High-lane; proprietor, Joseph Cooper
Ring of Bells, 33, Hanover-st.; proprietress, Mary A. Bennett
Rising Sun, 62, Waterloo-road; proprietor, H. Forrester
Robin Hood, 17, Dale-street; proprietor, Henry Flynn
Robin Hood Inn, 13, Wood-st.; proprietor, Joseph Platt
Rose and Thistle, Brownhills; proprietor, William Sadler (postal address, Tunstall)
Royal Express Inn, 11, Bourne's Bank; proprietress, Annie Bailey
Royal Oak Inn, Newport-lane; proprietor, W. H. Plimbley
Sea Lion Inn, 75, Waterloo-rd.; proprietor, P. Carr
Shamrock, Rose, and Thistle, Bath-street; proprietor, John Rowley
Ship Inn, 128, Hot-lane; proprietor, Wm. Bourne
Spread Eagle, 31, Hanover-st.; prop., Thomas W. Rowley
Sneyd Arms, 82, Albert-st.; proprietor, William H. Wood

Square & Compass, 21, Church-st.; proprietor, Thos. Bettany
Stag Inn, 114, Waterloo-road; proprietor, G. Stanway
The Dolphin, 4, Church-street; prop., James H. Holdcroft
Three Tuns, 40, Navigation-rd.; prop., W. H. Critchlow
Tramway Inn, 100, Waterloo-road; proprietress, Martha Jones
Traveller's Inn, 239, Newcastle-steet; proprietress, Sarah Salmon
Victoria Inn, Bourne's Bank; prop., William Halfpenny
Village Tavern, 10, Lower Hadderidge; prop., George H. Dyke
Vine Inn, Moorland-road; proprietor, G. S. Pierpoint
Volunteer Inn, 142, Newcastle-street; proprietress, Eliza Stonier
Washington Stores, Waterloo-rd.; prop., Frank Stephenson
Waterloo Stores, 30, Waterloo-road; prop., T. Boon
Wedgwood Inn, 262, Waterloo-road, Cobridge. Proprietor, James Hollowood
Wellington Arms, 55, Liverpool-road; prop., Joseph Boulton
West End Inn, 9, Church-sq.; prop., Sydney Henshall
Westport Inn, 15-17, Canal-st., Longport; prop., Fredk. Plant
Wharf Tavern, 8, Slater-street; prop., Sydney Lewis
White Horse Inn, 41-43, Brownhills; prop., George Butler (postal address, Tunstall)
White Horse, Grant-street, Cobridge; prop., Joseph Forrester
White Horse, 31, Liverpool-rd.; proprietor, D. Moreton
White Swan, 107, Newport-lane; proprietress, Mary Holdcroft

PUBLICANS—LICENSED.

American Hotel, 144, Waterloo-road; proprietress, Mary E. Bratt
Black Lion Inn, 41, Queen-st.; prop., John Henry Brookes
Blue Ball, 7, Nile-street; proprietor, Geo. Pickford
Blue Bell, Waterloo-road; proprietor, James W. Myatt
Bowling Green, Bath-street; proprietor, Wm. Wright
Britannia Inn, 69, Navigation-rd.; prop., John W. Whalley
Davenport Arms Inn, 45, Wharf-street; prop., W. A. Johnson
Dog and Partridge, Hot-lane; prop., Fred J. Lander
Duke of Bridgwater Inn, Station-st., Longport. Prop., Geo. W. Clay
Duke William, 1, Newcastle-st.; prop., John Cunningham
Foaming Quart, High-st.; proprietor, William Simcoe
George Hotel, Swan-square; proprietor, Joseph Myatt

PUBLICANS (LICENSED)—continued.

High Gate Inn, Brownhills; prop., Charles Pemberton (postal address, Tunstall)
Jug Inn, 54, Sneyd-street, Cobridge; prop., Richard Gould
Legs of Man, 37, Market-place; proprietor, John Foster
Leopard Hotel, 19—21, Market-place. Prop., Geo. Pople. 'Phone, 420 Central
Marquess of Granby, 31, Market-place; prop., Sydney Plant
Masons' Arms, 21, St. John's-square; proprietor, Wm. H. Rhead
Millstone Inn, Market-place; proprietor, Wm. Smith
Mitre Inn, 1, Pitt-street; proprietor, John Smith
Munros' Vaults, Chapel Bank; prop., Arthur Moore
New Vaults Inn, Market-place; proprietress, C. R. Tennant
New Inn, 50, Market-place; proprietor, Geo. Spedding
Nile Hotel, Nile-street; proprietor, J. T. Kent
Old Bull's Head, 283, Sneyd-st., Cobridge; prop., T. Brindley
Old Bull's Head, 53, Waterloo-rd.; prop., Geo. Ernest Parton
Olde Bull's Head, St. John's-square; prop., T. Curwen
Old King & Queen, 206, Sneyd-st., Cobridge; prop., Arthur Davenport
Pack Horse, Station-street; proprietor, Harry Clement Croxton
Queen's Head Hotel, 5, Queen-street; prop., Wm. Hines
Queen's Hotel, 268, Waterloo-road, Cobridge; prop., W. H. Derbyshire
Railway Hotel, 84, North-road Cobridge; prop., Thos. Cawley
Raven Hotel, Elder-road, Cobridge; prop., Thomas Frith
Roebuck Inn, Wedgwood-place; prop., Wm. Colinshaw
Royal Oak, 61, Liverpool-road; proprietor, Joseph Boulton
Royal Hotel, Liverpool-road; proprietress, Mrs. Hampson
Staff of Life Inn, 255, Newcastle-st.; prop., C. Pemberton
Star Hotel, 49, Queen-street; proprietor, Ar. Bayliss
Swan Hotel, Swan-square; proprietor, J. Lester
Victoria Hotel, Liverpool-road; prop., G. Leese
Wedgwood Arms, Brickhouse-st.; prop., A. Cooper
White Swan, 30, Elder-rd., Cobridge; prop., Chas. Jervis
Ye Old Crown, 10, Liverpool-road; prop., Wm. Bryan

From the Burslem section of the Newcastle and District Directory 1912. Compare with the 1851 White's Directory on pages 161 and 162

The British surrendering to George Washington, above, and below a contemporary cartoon showing the
British 'tars' defeating the French and Spanish at Trafalgar

CHAPTER FIFTEEN: Wars and Chartism

Social disruption from wars on the Continent and in America. Tom Paine. Growth of Chartism.
The influence of John Tomlinson. The waning commercial influence of Burslem.

Towards the end of the 18th and the beginning of the 19th centuries there was widespread unrest, in Burslem and the neighbouring expanding townships as well as other developing industrial towns. Wars on the Continent, together with the dispute with the American colonies and disruption of our foreign trade, curtailed the export of manufactured goods, resulting in unemployment, reduced earnings and a rapid increase in the cost of food, since imports of food from the Continent and elsewhere were seriously affected. Added to this was the workers' lack of voting franchise and fears related to the introduction of machinery and steam power, although these had yet to have the serious effect in pottery trade it had in others. Within the pottery industry there were also a number of long standing disputes.

Robert Owen, an enlightened mill owner and member of parliament who canvased in parliament and outside to draw attention to the problems of the workers, addressed meetings in the district, one at the Bear Inn at Shelton. He urged workers to join the National Union which he sponsored. This failed despite its initial success due to it not creating a fund to support strikes. It is only in this century was Owen's work publicly acknowledged when in 1994 a statue of him was unveiled outside the Co-operative Bank in Manchester to commemorate the 150th year of the Co-operative movement inspired by him.

Ward, in his local history, refers to itinerant orators from a distance, (among whom he would have included Owen) some of whom were later prosecuted for sedition. They demanded reform of the ballot and urged the formation of political clubs, but he said, *"the manufacturers and respectable inhabitants disavowed these associations, although the demagogues denied any intention of creating class discord"*. Ward quoted from what he described as *"the effusion of a malevolent pen"*:

> To all tyrannic employers
> Tyrants short will be your hour
> Soon must end your gloomy power
> Soon shall vengeance hear our call
> And shouting millions hail your fall

Laws of employment in industry were solely in the favour of employers, and the Combination Acts gave employers the right to commit employees to prison for forming trade associations. This was particularly iniquitous in the pottery industry since the operatives had to accept an annual agreement which debarred them from moving elsewhere within the year. Even if they were laid off due to shortage of orders he employer could refuse to allow them to accept employment in factories where work was available.

A incident occurred at Longton when an employer decided to alter the time of the midday break and facing opposition discharged some workmen, threatening to use legal proceedings if they entered the works again. Further to a stoppage, as was his entitlement by law, he had four of his employees committed to Stafford jail. The discharged employees wrote to the Burslem potters appealing for financial support for the families involved.

"April 1791. Appeal for funds to help Longton potter who was sacked by his employer.
"Journeymen potters at The Folly are at this time very ill treated by their said master in refusing to employ them except they will comply to every unreasonable demand he thinks proper to make, four of whom he has by unjust proceedings lately lodged in Stafford jail because they would not submit like slaves to his imperious authority in going to dinner at an hour when neither Mr Turner's men, nor any men in the neighbourhood go, except one work which is of little account near the Toll Gate, and though they have offered their services, desiring to work peaceably observing the same rules with their neighbours, he has been so far from listening to the poor men who have got families that he has absolutely tossed their clothes into the lane and trod them in the dirt, threatening them if they came upon the Bank, neither would he give them their discharge and has kept them from work now

The cartoon above shows one of the attempts on George III's life. His popularity waxed and waned,
and his long reign was later marred by his 'madness'.
George IV was Prince Regent before becoming King. His personal life was extravagant and disastrous.
The Regency period is a reflection of his high tastes as in the Brighton pavilion, below, built in 1820

about a month. We, who are their fellow potters, cannot but take part with them in their distress and have endeavoured since they have been deprived of work to support them by a contribution made among ourselves out of our own wages. We now take the opportunity of requesting your friendly assistance and if it be ever so little we trust when there is occasion we shall not be backward to return the favour and if you will endeavour collect something we will call for it on Monday next and it will be esteemed a particular favour.

We remain with due respect your fellow workmen."

Towards the end of the 18th century Mother Burslem's influence was waning. Growth in what had been surrounding hamlets, was now approaching or had exceeded hers, and with the arrival of the new century Hanley had a greater population. Output from the industry had grown enormously, and when war broke out with France in 1793, the curtailment of exports must have been a considerable shock, and the realisation that competition in a contracted market was likely to seriously affect profits evidently turned the thoughts of the manufacturers to mutual salvation. It was agreed to create minimum price lists, and cover in detail all classes of domestic ware, plain and printed, in the various ceramic bodies, and also to adopt a joint approach to the increasing demands of the workers. The manufacturers used the legal services of John Tomlinson to assist in the preparation of their agreements, which were concluded at a meeting on 5th June 1795, and which would become operative from 25th June. The price lists are interesting, in that they give an insight to values obtaining at that time:

Common Cream Coloured Ware.		
Cups and Saucers [Irish size}	per dozen	1/4d
9" Oval Dishes.	,, ,,	1/3d
10" ,, ,,	,, ,,	1/6d
Teapots	each	3/6d
Tall Candlesticks		1/-
Ewers and Basins		1/9
Printed Ware.		
Plain Teas	per dozen	3/9d
[Irish Size}	,, ,,	4/9d
Ewers and basins	each	7/-
Egyptian Ware		
Fluted Teapots	per dozen	10/-
Oval Pressed Teapots	,, ,,	24/-
,, ,, ,, [with sliding lids]	,, ,,	24/-
Oval Pressed Sugars and Milks	,, ,,	24/-

Agreed 10% for prompt payment
5% for payment in six months

Every manufacturer to name anyone attempting to violate the agreement. Failure to adhere to the agreement would result in a fine of £50 for the first offence, and £100 for succeeding offences.

It would seem that there was a leak which gave the employees the impression that the manufacturers had intentions beyond prices. This led to charge and countercharge. A meeting was called of all pottery workers in the Market Square, Hanley. Then anonymous hand bills appeared refuting imputations made by the workers, who in turn, in an atmosphere of anger and suspicion, called a further meeting which resulted in the following vebose statement:

March 5th 1796.
To the author of an anonymous Hand-Bill addressed to Journeymen Potters and other inhabitants of the Potteries.
Sir.
We cannot do less than offer you our warmest acknowledgment for your zealous proceedings to set us right and reconcile us with Mr T...... but, feeling as all well disposed and sober minded persons must do, that your way of procedure is not at all likely to attain that end, but is rather an additional insult to us and deserves to be treated with contempt, for at the very outset of your proposals, you represent us to be a set of ill disposed and ill minded persons, merely because we do not exactly co-incide with your opinion respecting the proceedings on Monday

the 29th of February, which we believe to be orderly and such that every offender deserves who attempts to rob us of our daily earnings, nor have we any reason to believe that he is the innocent person you represent him ,for think you that the credit of an anonymous writer (and that writer perhaps may be himself) is sufficient proof to attain that end. No such proof, we are convinced, will ever have the desired effect, but come openly and exculpate your friend from the charge wherewith he has been accused, and then we will make him every restitution in our power, till then, we shall believe him to be the author of the Hand-Bill. With respect to the printed letter you speak of, we might be a set of ignorant and illiterate things not capable to comprehend the meaning of that letter without your explanation. We believe ourselves to be candid and reasonable men, and have diligently considered the contents which we entirely disapprove as tending to create a combination of Masters against their Servants, or Servants against their Masters. No good can ensue, for they ought to go hand in hand striving to promote the welfare of both, therefore we would advise the author of that letter, be he whoever it may, if he be a friend to himself and to the Pottery at large, to resist and oppose such combinations and let the trade run in the old course as a rivalship in business creates invention, encourages commerce, and promotes industry, and as you seem so zealous for the reconciliation betwixt us, we assure you we in no ways averse to it, but the more we look over your Hand-Bill, the more reason we have to suppose him to be the author, for certainly no man can have such authority as to vouch for every expression another makes use of that he never did call us "a set of low lived reptiles" you have our authority to declare is a mystery to us, for we believe it to be morally impossible for one man to answer so much for another, therefore on this authority we cannot exculpate him. We grant you that Mr T.... has been of some essential service to the Friendly Society, and likewise exerting himself for the good of the poor, for such we respect him, and hold him high in our favour, and should have continued to have done so had he pursued his former conduct, but he was a Wolf in Sheep's clothing and acting under a cloak of hypocrisy, that as soon as he has got us under his power, he would have sacrificed us to his revenge. It is evident this would have been the case, for if accident had not brought that printed letter to our hands, we should never have known of it, but by it's baneful effects.   The fair and well earned character which we have so long maintained, we will always endeavour to support and maintain. We do not think we ever showed it more than on Monday last. We only assembled to show our resentment to such a miscreant as would have deprived us of our means of subsistence and custom of our calling, but such we will ever support, not in a riotous and tumultuous manner will we ever assemble against the laws and constitution of our land, but use every legal authority to obtain the rights and privileges of our calling. Nor can we ever think that the laws of our country would permit military power to be brought against a set of manufacturers who are only supporting the privilege of their calling. Nor are we ignorant of the consequences which must result in riotously or tumultuously against the laws and liberties of our Glorious Constitution. To the laws we look for protection, and will ever resist such combinations which tend to disturb us in our peaceful employment. So far we think our laws will protect us, you need not have made such an apology that by mentioning military power you did not do it in a menacing way, or to intimidate or overawe us. No Sir, such we were well assured was not in your power as we have not done anything that require civil or military coercion, and hope we shall ever have conduct not to be hurried into such illegal proceedings, though we return you our grateful acknowledgments for your timely warnings. We feel with pleasure the pains our Masters are taking in order to raise the price of their goods, and wish them every success, but at the same time we look with horror at those illicit and illegal combinations to reduce us. This shows that it is entirely for their own advantage, and not for any advantage for the workman, that they are endeavouring to raise the price of their goods, might they not then give their servants better encouragement. They should consider that if some of them are independent, by what means they became so?, and tell us if it is not through their industrious servants, although we do not grudge or envy them their wealth, yet we think they should encourage us that, by our industry and sobriety, we may earn a comfortable livelihood,and to receive the reward we merit is our only wish and aim, for, as good Servants make kind Masters, they should consider that the major part of them cannot subsist without us, than we without them, therefore we should be unanimous in order to promote the welfare of both. We cannot, Sir, take your friendly advice and be sorrowful for what is past, believing as we do, that this friend of Mr T..... is no other than himself, and therefore think him guilty of the offence laid to his charge. But Sir, if you are the friend and advocate of Mr. T...... and a well wisher to us, come boldly forward and openly declare WHO YOU ARE that we may know in whose veracity we have to depend for proof of Mr. T's..... innocence. Till them we must think him guilty.

Journeymen Potters."

Criticism of the manufacturers was not without foundation; some obviously had no concept of their costs. In 1804 one pottery manufacturer issued under a pseudonym a scathing attack in a printed brochure on the manner in which fellow manufacturers undermined their own prosperity by debasing prices. He said they:

> "...were ruining themselves along with others by the devious method of supplying customers with larger sizes in flat ware, bowls, jugs etc, at the price of smaller sizes in the same range to take trade from fellow manufacturers who adhered to the agreed lists. These motives have governed the greater part of the potters who have begun business of late, with the result that many manufactures stand unoccupied. They forget the cost of the greater superfluity of clay at present heavy rates, which the extra size requires, the additional space occupied in saggars, the additional glaze, and coal at double the rate of twenty years ago and the throwing away of profit by such absurd conduct ......there are far too many sizes than are necessary ......if there was standardisation of the trade with a confined range, this evil practice could be controlled .

Today the issue of a uniform trade list would of course be illegal. The Mr T..... who seemed to have raised such bitter recrimination in the dispute, is without doubt Mr .John Tomlinson who although not born in Burslem, came to have considerable influence in the district and is a character worthy of further comment. A lawyer by profession and whose talents were in demand especially in Stoke, his services were called upon by the pottery manufacturers, civic authorities, and for important capital projects. He became wealthy and bought land at Cliffe Bank, one of the last areas in the ownership of the Crown in that district. On this land he built a property which he called Cliff Ville, the mansion which eventually became the nucleus of St. Dominic's School.

John Tomlinson made an exhaustive study of church laws. He found that at Stoke the income from dues for church funds was needlessly reduced by neglect. In addition, on behalf of the Church Commissioners, he created a large capital fund from the astute sale of tithes and tithe lands, which contributed ultimately towards the rebuilding of Stoke parish church and the building of additional local churches. He personally bought the advowson of Stoke Parish from the existing incumbent for £12,000 plus an annual payment of £1800 for the remainder of his lifetime. The ownership of the advowson, besides entitling him to collect church dues, also gave him the privilege of nominating incumbents, and his eldest son later became Rector of Stoke and also inherited the advowson.

Tomlinson set about recouping his outlay by first renewing a long neglected demand for Easter dues of 4d for each household, 2d for each married person, 1d for each single person, applicable to all except those on poor rate. He employed collectors who were apparently far from well received, since he issued the following public warning: *"My collectors have been frequently much abused and ill-treated and I do give notice that if anything of the kind should occur again, the parties will be prosecuted with the utmost rigour of the law. It is my duty to stand by the person I employ, and I will do so firmly"*.

Apparently it was a different matter when he himself was called upon to pay poor rates, since *The Public Enquirer* in 1828 reported that collectors fearing for their lives took him to court, but, according to the paper *"a judicious magistrate refused distraint on a rich man since such men may threaten to go to law with Justice friends, whereas a poor man can only whine in the midst of a howling family"*. Nevertheless, after what was presumably an effort to collect money from Mr Tomlinson, the same paper stated *"the constable walked off with a three legged stool and Mr Tomlinson bestowed 300 loaves on the poor"*, surely proof of a forgiving nature and a sensitive conscience - or maybe relief at the magnitude of the restraint.

Reverting to the differences which had arisen between the manufacturers and their workpeople; whether objectionable remarks had been made by Tomlinson is unclear, but the wording and imputations made by the workers demanded a quick response. Consequently, following a meeting convened for the purpose the manufacturers issued the following:

> "This meeting cannot but view with very great concern the unjustifiable outrage which was offered to Mr Tomlinson in consequence of his official conduct, and thus genuinely regret that men, who have hitherto been

distinguished for their peaceable and orderly deportment, should have suffered themselves to be so much deluded, by false reports and malicious accusations, as to proceed to such violent resentment against an individual, whose exertions have been constantly devoted to their service, and whom they ought rather to have regarded as their benefactor and friend.

An outrage, so flagrant in itself, cannot be sufficiently reprobated, and the committee feel it a duty incumbent on themselves, to stand forward in vindication of Mr. Tomlinson's character, and as justification of his conduct, and which they declare to the world, how totally unmerited the insult was. They avail themselves thus publicly to acknowledge his services."

If the dispute was finally centred on the question of mutual trust, then at least it could not be said that there was a shortage of words either to deny or to support it!

Continental unrest caused increasing strain, hardship and frustration, although not confined to workers in the potteries and the mines. Unemployment and poverty, which had previously been an individual misfortune, now became a national one. The loss of imported grain due to Napoleon's control of Continental ports resulted in dependence on home grown corn and wheat, which increased phenomenally in price. The consequent increase in farmers income resulted in landowners taking advantage of the situation, increasing the rents of the farmers and creating a vicious circle in the price of grain, besides adding to the landowners' already immense wealth. Some of this increasing wealth went into expanding industry, again adding wealth to wealth. Some went in ostentatious living. One duke kept his own private orchestra of twenty seven players. Another was said to have spent £500 for a single suit, which today would be a fabulous sum, while others built additional mansions. Compounding the food problem was the amount of grain which went into the the brewing of ale and the making of spirits. Industrial workers had previously been employed in agriculture and able to provide by their own effort at least some food for their family; now living in urban conditions, they had to purchase all their needs from a wage which was losing its purchasing power.

The use of machinery and of steam, as well as the lack of franchise led to further national unrest and the birth of the Luddite and Chartist movements, causing the government to fear that the masses would emulate the French and force a bloody revolution. There was a panic introduction of hundreds of laws for which the death penalty or banishment abroad could be imposed. Some believe that only the longstanding Poor Law which ensured freedom from complete destitution and which had no equivalent in France, saved Britain from anarchy and revolution.

Burslem reflected most of these troubles along with the the associated problems of dissolution and drink rife in most cities and towns. In 1750 Burslem had a population of 2000, and about twenty ale houses. By the turn of the century the population had increased more than threefold and the ale houses likewise. Ale was a popular drink with all classes since water - in the Burslem at this time sold by the pail from mobile barrels trundled round the streets - was of a dubious quality and scarce. Ale at $1/2$d a quart was affordable and palatable, but its abuse caused problems. Publicans exhibited signs advertising that you could get drunk for a penny, dead drunk for twopence and free straw! - in other words, a drunken sleep on the floor of mine host. Anyone could get a licence to brew and sell beer, and the influx of families had enabled many to earn a regular global family income above that which they earned in agriculture. Furthermore, with a payment system which used the services of the publican to distribute wages, there was a tied clientele, and this no doubt encouraged the growth in innkeepers too. Gin, popular but deadly, had been blamed for a heavy death rate until the increase in duty in 1751 which, together with stricter licensing laws resulted in its decline.

Determined efforts were made by the local minister, churchwardens and the principal inhabitants. They ignored the fact that the principal inhabitants were the same manufacturers who contributed to the problem by their archaic method of payment of employees:

July 1788 NOTICE.

"I. We agree that we will pay our respective workmen and labourers their wages at 4 o'clock on Saturday afternoon.

2. That no shopkeeper, butcher etc be suffered to sell or expose to sale any of these goods on a Sunday.

3. That no barber or hairdresser be permitted to keep their shop open after 12 o'clock.

4. That no public house keepers or victuallers be suffered to fill ale, or sell ale at any time of the Sunday after 10 o'clock of the Saturday night on pain of suffering an attempt to have their licence drawn, and that every person found tippling in a public house, or drunk in the open street on the Sabbath day, shall be punished as the law directs.

5. That in order to enforce more effectively these resolutions, twelve persons, principle inhabitants be chosen, at the expiration of every six months from the date hereof, as assistants to the churchwardens, consignable etc.to inspect into any offences against these articles and agreements.

Written our hands 8th day of July 1788.
Henry Boddington. Minister.
Enoch Wood. Samuel Worthington. Churchwardens".

Exhortations were of little use without effective police support and a stipendary magistrate's court. A similar notice was issued in 1815 with the threat of a magistrate (see page 152 ch. 13 'Tregortha'). It would have been interesting to see the manufacturers operating as vigilantes.

Ward was scathing of drink and deplored the notice *"Licenced to be drunk on the premises"* as a legislative invitation to the *"free indulgence by the people of their darling propensity, and makes the victim totally unfit for the sacred duties of the Sabbath."*

One national body of reformers who had "a vision" was the Society for the Reformation of Manners who encouraged the reporting of individuals using profane language or objectionable behaviour. Thousands of tracts were issued against Sunday trading, drunkenness, public indecency and swearing. The response was amazing; thousands of prosecutions followed leaving both the transgressors and the courts so overwhelmed and unhappy with "the vision" that the Country experienced near riots. Burslem, now experiencing the vigour of Mr Wesley, continued to need to issue exhortations and threats:

TO THE INHABITANTS OF THE PARISH OF BURSLEM
"The Ministers and Churchwardens of the parish of Burslem having repeatedly witnessed with deep regret the open and wilful profanity of the Sabbath which prevails in the parish by the hawking of goods, opening of shops, and by individuals following their worldly calling on the Lord's Day.
Also by the assemblage of groups of disorderly characters in the streets, and by the disgraceful practice of gambling which is carried out in the more retired parts of the town to the great annoyance of the people and the manifest injury of the public morals.

Ministers.	Churchwardens
John Cooper	Robert Williamson
Thomas Nunns	George Baker
	Thomas Brindley
	Edward Withenshaw

We are determined to stop you".

The threat of fines, with the rigor of the law, for those using bad language was issued by designated Constables Joseph Moreton and Thomas Hulme, listing the penalties as follows:

Labourers, Common Soldiers, Common Seamen.	- One Shilling
Every person under the degree of Gentleman.	- Five shillings for the first offence.
	- Second offence. Double the amount
	- Third offence .Treble the amount.
	- Those unable to pay to be put in the Stocks.

Another movement was the Democratic Movement. An ardent supporter of this was Thomas Paine who preached Deism. Paine had no room for monarchy or religious bodies. Religion he said was a national institution based on fables and purely man-made. His written works, mostly politically based, had an immense impact not only in England but throughout Europe in the turbulent time of the French Revolution and the Napoleonic wars, and also in America during the War of Independence.

The pottery manufacturers, including Josiah Wedgwood, must have been aware at this time that Paine's influence was considered to be contributing to the cause of riots in Birmingham and Manchester, and similarly aware of the contemporary notice that was issued by the Staffordshire County authorities, the substance of which will be seen later. Among Enoch Wood's papers was a printed notice of Paine's alleged arrest, his trial for treason and alleged hanging, together with his apparent lengthy admission of remorse for the error of his ways, which concluded with a warning in the following verse:

> Britain take warning of my fate
> Revere your King, protect the state
> In hopes of sharing others Pelf
> E'eer lead you from your country's cause
> Or book you to deplore the laws
> The laws of England just and fair
> Safety and peace to all ensure
> And whilst the honest they defend
> they bring the villain to his end
> Then by my fate instruction gain
> And shun the schemes of Thomas Paine

Tom Paine was born in Thetford in Norfolk, the son of a Quaker father and a Presbyterian mother. His father was a self employed boned corset maker, and he was apprenticed to him. His education was at the local village school and since the trade was a dying one, Tom moved to London where the company he consorted with and his use of the libraries, along with the appalling conditions he witnessed, gave substance to his philosophies. He obtained work with the Customs and Excise and became embroiled in union work. He now wrote *The Rights of Man* which brought him fame and money.

Paine realised that the cost of the book was beyond the reach of the bulk of the workers, so he ploughed its earning back into a cheap edition and flooded industrial areas with copies, many no doubt reaching Burslem. This coincided with the period of the French Revolution; when the British Government were in a panic lest it should spread to Britain, and despite an already formidable list of offences which carried the death penalty or deportation, they continued to add more. But the fame of Paine's work and the admiration he was receiving from the working class was such they feared to charge him with treason, lest it might fuel the turmoil; instead they adopted a subtle response by employing a constant watch on his movements, obvious enough to give him the impression that it was only a matter of time before something would happen to him. In addition they paid for the widespread issue of pamphlets supposedly detailing his trial and hanging, hoping that constant harassment, physical and mental would cause him to leave the country. This tactic appears to have been successful since he ultimately fled to France.

Arriving in France, Paine was welcomed as a fellow revolutionary and employed by the French government in propaganda work to bring about the fall of British imperialism and the success of American independence. He left France for America and continued his work with the independence movement there.

Perturbed by the surrounding disorder, magistrates at Stafford issued to all parishes the following warning of the dire result of riotous behaviour:

NOTICE

The following is humbly submitted to the good sense of the inhabitants of the County of Stafford. warning them of the dire consequence of misbehaviour and outlining offence and penalty.
If three or more assemble with intent to mutually assist anyone who oppose them in unlawful assembly, or
If they move forward towards execution, it is a Rout. or
If executed, it is a Riot.
All three are subject to fine or imprisonment.
If Rioters number twelve or more and continue for space of one hour, having been called in the King's name to disperse, it is a Felony and the penalty is death. If Rioters pull down a Church, Chapel, or any building for Religious Worship, or any Dwelling House, Barn Stable, or any wind water or other Mill. The penalty is death.
Any person encouraging Riots by exciting Mobs. death.

With still no sign of peace on the Continent and food shortages, a cargo of grain arrived at Etruria canal wharf, but the skipper of the boat was told to proceed with his consignment to Manchester. This came to the knowledge of locals who intercepted the boat at Longport, returned it by force to Etruria and distributed the grain, along with that of a further cargo which arrived in the meantime. The recipients of the grain were charged what was considered a fair price and the accumulated money was handed to the skipper of the boat. The authorities being alerted to what was happening, despatched a group of regular militia from the barracks in Newcastle, headed by Colonel Sneyd of Keele Hall. They descended on the scene and when a lecture from the Colonel failed to resolve the situation, a charge by the militia dispersed the mob. Two of the ringleaders were detained and charged at Stafford, where both were convicted and one was hanged. Ward paid tribute to Colonel Sneyd for "*his humanity, and our good fortune that at the time he happened to be at Keele Hall, whereas normally he would be stationed in attendance on King George III at Windsor, consequently, he received approbation at the time, and was deserving of eulogy even now*"

In this period rumours were rife, and the reaction of the people uncertain. One such rumour led to the issue of the following public notice in September 1800:

"A report having been circulated that there was a large quantity of cheese in my house at Porthill, I do hereby declare that there is no foundation to such a report not having any in my possession either at Porthill or elsewhere. What little I have purchased was not for my own account but to oblige a friend and had I supposed it could have caused any uneasiness in the country it would certainly not have been done. I have sent express to have the cheese brought back which left Longport wharf on Saturday and which shall be sold in the market at prime cost, and I do hereby pledge myself not to purchase any more cheese or other necessaries of life to be sent out of the country."   W. Clowes. Sept. 22nd 1800.

Probably fearing violence, friends hastened to give Mr Clowes their support, maybe even fearing that their names might be associated with the next rumour, and they issued the following statement:

"We the undersigned having been through Mr. Clowes house and buildings at Porthill do declare he has not any cheese on the premises.
John Rogers. George Rogers. Robert Williamson.

All three were much respected business men and their intervention could have saved Mr. Clowes from having to call on the service of Colonel Sneyd.

A printed note circulated to Burslem shopkeepers about the price of grain in 1794 had an ominous tone:
Sir,
"You are requested to buy no more Meal or Flour, unless you can sell the former at 1/6d per peck, and the latter at 2/6per stone; this being the request of at least ten thousand industrious men. If this request is attended to, it will be the means of preventing more disagreeable consequences"

Apparently we were keeping the French at bay and letting the Mafia in! Presumably as a response to this particular incident, the following notice was posted in Burslem:

5th May 1796. TO THE INHABITANTS OF BURSLEM.
"The great scarcity of flour etc. having lately prevailed in this neighbourhood, owing in a great measure to the riotous conduct of some of the inhabitants. A meeting has this day been held, in order to consider some means, calculated to afford an immediate supply".

When the dealers who numerously attended, positively refused to bring in Flour unless they can be assured of protection, and as a continuation of such riotous behaviour must terminate in the most serious consequences, and increase the scarcity of Provisions. I do hereby pledge myself to lend every assistance to protect all Provisions brought to this town, and I doubt not but peaceable conduct will ensure you relief. I have repeatedly told you what would be the consequence of rioting, and I hope you will not render it necessary for Troops, now quartered at Newcastle to be called on. If you consider my conduct upon this occasion in its proper light, you will find I am Your friend and the only person who has born to step forward upon this unpleasant business. I can positively say that, upon my representing the town in a peaceable state to Colonel Sneyd, I prevented offenders being apprehended, and upon publishing this, I have been promised by the Dealers in general, that they will exert themselves to bring in Flour at a price proportional to the sale of Wheat."   Signed.   J.E. POOL

Ward mentions John Ellison Poole as a respected citizen.

The political and economic problems led George III, who was a firm believer in the divine right of kings, to impose his will on parliament. To relieve the financial burden he forced parliament to impose a series of taxes on the American colonies to pay for the resident British military force. These taxes he considered necessary if Britain was to shield America from a potential threat from Indians or the French, but the American Colonies questioned his divine right and instead introduced the Declaration of Independence and the well recorded Boston Tea Party. Taking exception to their attitude, George demanded that the law be amended to enable him to bring the ringleaders back to England to face punishment, in consequence of which a British army was sent to quell the insurrection in what was Burslem's biggest and most friendly market. As a further intended insult the French insolently declared America to be a republic, and a war of independence dragged on until 1783 when we conceded defeat - and Burslem was left with a severely damaged export trade.

It was now the turn of Napoleon to increase the disruption of our trade and that of the rest of Europe, at the same time threatening an invasion of Britain. This threat in 1798 led to the raising in Burslem of a volunteer corp of militia, comprising about seventy infantry and officers under the command of Captain William Sneyd of Bradwell Hall. One brave who joined had, according to Ward, the following engraved on his sword.

> "Leagu'd with my friends, the glitt'ring sword I bear
> To guard from hostile arm my country dear
> Not to oppress, devastate or enslave
> But England's soil from Gallic rage to save
> Not to maintain those "rights of Man" unjust
> Which tend to treason,plunder, blood and lust
> But to preserve our Alters, hearths and laws
> And bleed and conquer in this holy cause".

This no doubt would have terrified the enemy, providing he, or being a French army, he or she, were given sufficient time to read it. This invasion threat however was short lived, as was also the volunteer corps. The corps was disbanded, accompanied by a parade in which some of the warriors it was said wore glass hats produced by Messrs Davenport, no doubt to reflect the glory of their calling. They were ordered to *"deliver up all arms and accoutrements at 10 o'clock prompt, every member to bring any spare Slings or Belts which he may have in his possession or knows of"*. The notice also reminded the members of the forthcoming celebratory dinner and was signed by Richard Rainbow Serg. The total cost of the Dinner was £95.15. 2. according to the account submitted by Enoch Wood and George Rogers, a goodly sum in those days and a handsome feast for seventy men.

Reflecting the severe hardship being experienced by the bulk of the population, a meeting of the townspeople of Burslem was held in November 1800 to discuss the continuing increase in the cost of living. During the discussions one comment was *"that the evil, so much to be lamented, has in part originated from the desolation of small farms, from the acquired capital of farmers, and from speculation of individuals, supported by the enormous increase in paper money which has pervaded the whole country. Two years ago, the price of Corn was 49/2per quarter. To-days price is 109/7per quarter."*

This comment reflects the adverse side of the Enclosure Acts, which although resulting in greater productivity from the land, increased the areas owned by a minority who, when demand exceeded supply, were able to apply monopoly prices, and there was only belated intervention by the state. To add to Burslem's and the Country's problems, there was a failure of home grown crops in the year 1800, and the meeting decided to take steps of their own:

"At a meeting of subscribers for affording relief for industrious poor in Burslem, Longport, Tunstall, and Goldenhill. At this season of wheat scarcity, occasioned by the late unfortunate failure of the crop. It was unanimously resolved that the amount of subscription raised within the several districts before mentioned, be applied for the relief of the poor and indigent within such districts respectively and the same be managed by a committee of subscribers to consist of any two or three. Whole subscriptions shall amount together to the sum of fifteen guineas, and that the money be laid out in purchasing such food and nutritious articles of provision as the respective committees shall, from time to time, judge to be expedient and beneficial, and selling the same at reduced prices, particular regard being to the best and cheapest substitutes for flour and bread. For every indigent person who desires to take benefit of these subscriptions, each shall obtain a ticket signed by a subscriber which shall entitle the holder to relief accordingly, such relief to be proportioned as far as circumstances will admit to the number of the family and other exigencies, but no person shall take the benefit of more than one ticket on the same day. That such gentlemen and persons interested in this part of the potteries as may be willing to contribute towards carrying the above plan into effect, are requested to transmit their subscriptions to The Rev. Richardson of Burslem".

James Caldwell.

As a further sign of the hard times a request was made for the ladies of the town to support the Womens Society organised to help fellow members who through age and infirmity were unable to follow an occupation. This body received the help of most of the manufacturers' wives. The developing 'maturity' of the community was also evidenced by the formation of a Female Provident Society where each member paid a monthly contribution which entitled them to the following benefits:

When very ill	*8/- per week*
When less ill and unable to follow usual occupation.	*4/- per week*
From age 65 to age 70	*2/- per week*
For life after 70	*4/- per week*

The monthly contribution table commenced at: From age 16 to 21 per month 1/1 and rose by 1d or 1¹/2d per month for consecutive years thereafter.

With war continuing, in 1803, there was a renewed call to arms, this time for both the regular militia and the volunteer corps, and notices were posted in the town:

MILITIA

"In consideration of a ballot for the Supplementary Militia, and for filling up the vacancies in the Regular Militia of the country taking place on Wednesday next, the Churchwardens, Overseers and others in the Vestry assembled, hereby inform the inhabitants of this parish that subscriptions of nine shillings each will be received in the Vestry Room in Burslem on Monday next at nine o'clock in the morning, for which sum, they engage to find a substitute for such subscriber who may be balloted to serve either Militia."

Signed J. BOURNE. VESTRY CLERK.

At a subsequent meeting at the Legs of Man it was resolved unanimously that:

"At this important crisis, we feel ourselves indespensively called upon as men and Britons, to stand forward and make the most active exertion for the defence and protection of our King and Country. That the volunteer corp be supplied with Arms and Accoutraments by Government, but that each individual furnish his uniform at his own expense, such uniform to be the same as the undress uniform of the County Militia".

Signed J. CALDWELL.

The desperate poor were the more likely to become the substitute for the full time militia, and those with money to be the ones to stay at home. The Commissioners of the Poor Law were the ultimate losers with responsibility for destitute families left behind. Recruitment for the Supplementary Militia resulted in three companies of infantry known as the Longport Volunteers, each comprising 80 officers and men, under the command of Major Davenport. Their duties were to maintain law and order at home while the regular militia were fighting Napoleon and there was a serious threat of invasion since Napoleon was preparing a fleet of craft for that purpose. The Supplementary Militia were required to perform the combined duties of police and homeguard, a duty which had previously been assumed by a voluntary body with the formidable title of "The Burslem Association for the prosecution of Felons", sufficient one would have thought to deter any miscreant. The association issued this notice in 1805:

PUBLIC NOTICE

At a committee meeting held on the 6th of March 1805 at the Legs of Man, it was unanimously resolved that in order to further encourage any person, whether an accomplice or not, who may have been, or hereafter may be an eye witness to any kind of Robbery, Damage, or Trespass committed against our Houses, Manufactures, Mills, or other buildings. On Gardens, Meadows, Corn and Pasture Lands, the following rewards are being offered in order that offenders be properly and deservedly punished. That the committee are fully determined to prosecute any person who may commit any assault on the members of the association, and also to seek after and find out the receivers of stolen goods and to prosecute them to the utmost rigour of the law. That in addition to the reward hereby offered (which will be paid on application to the Treasurer) this Society will take under their care and protection, any person that will give the necessary information against any Offender or Offenders the following rewards, and all reasonable charges paid by the Treasurer,viz.

Information of stealing Coal from Carts	
On commitment to a Magistrate	£1. 1. 0
On Conviction. An additional sum of	£5. 5. 0
Stealing any Colour from any Mill	£1. 1. 0
On Conviction An additional sum of	£5. 5. 0

Stealing Utensils and Earthenware belonging to Manufacturers, or committing any depredation there on; Implements of Husbandry, Goose, Ducks or Fowls. Breaking or damaging Gates. Stiles. Hedgerows. Any kind of Trespass. Robbing Gardens etc.£3. 3. 0

Highway Robbery. Horse Stealing   £20. 0. 0

In addition to the foregoing Rewards, various Acts of Parliament have declared the informant entitled to other sums on conviction of offenders. In many instances fifty pounds will be obtained thereby.

Despite the warning some individuals were nevertheless audacious:

FIFTY GUINEAS REWARD

Whereas on Saturday Evening last some person or persons have stolen, taken, and carried away from Bycars and Sneyd Collieries, both in the parish of Burslem in the County of Stafford, sundry useful and essential parts of the Engine there used for the purpose of raising and getting Coals, and at the same time have done other mischiefs to the said Engine and Premises. Any person who will give information of the offender or offenders shall, on their conviction, receive a reward of FIFTY GUINEAS. The articles stolen consist of sundry pieces of cast Stops, Safety Valves, together with sundry Wrought Iron Nuts and Screws, Pins etc.some of which are quite new, and had not been in use twentyfour hours

John Hall.   Treasurer of Burslem Association.

Another loss was suffered by John Rogers, an eminent Burslem potter:

ROBBERY JULY 14th 1812.

"Whereas the TOOL COT situated at Wolstanton, belonging to John Rogers of Longport has been broken into by some person or persons who feloniously stole thereout one Broad Spade, one Delving Spade, one new Hoe, one new Pick-Axe and one pair of men's shoes. Therefore whoever will give such information as may lead to the offender or offenders, shall receive a reward of five guineas from Mr. Rogers, and a further reward of five guineas will be paid by Mr. Preston. Solicitor of Burslem, Cobridge, and Longport Association for the prosecution of Felons on Commitment, and ten guineas on conviction of off or off."

Burslem July 14th 1812.

Another problem was suspect coinage. Warning was issued locally in 1795 to shopkeepers, stall holders and others:

"If any person takes a guinea in change or payment and receives a premium with it as a light Guinea; if he does not immediately cut it in two, before the person who tenders it, but puts the whole into his drawer, is liable to prosecution for fraud. For any shopkeeper to receive a half crown coin of the realm, and ask for a premium on the pretence of it being a French half crown. As to half pence. If he refuses to take provincial half pence [that is such as are coined at Birmingham, Macclesfield, Paris Mine etc.] unless the person so offering them will pay them at an under value, and they are detected, having just received them as under valued, again paying them at their original value of one half penny, they are liable, as for guineas and half crowns, to be prosecuted for fraud."

Trade burdens seemed never ending, in 1812 dispute with America broke out again, while in Europe Napoleon followed his conquests by closing Continental ports to shipments to and from Britain including vital shipments of grain. The British government threatened in retaliation an Order in Council to block all shipments to France, but following France's support during the War of Independence, America and France had developed a significant mutual trade, and the American reaction was to issue an ultimatum to the British Government that if they carried out this act, America would in turn prohibit the entrance of British vessels of any description into American ports, in addition to any article or grown produce from the Dominions, Colonies, or Dependencies of Britain, unless the threat was withdrawn.

The extent of our trade in pottery with America at that time may be judged from the following record of shipments:

Crates of ware shipped.

Average for the four years 1803/1806.   Per year 40,125.
Average for the four years 1808/1811.   Per year 45,374

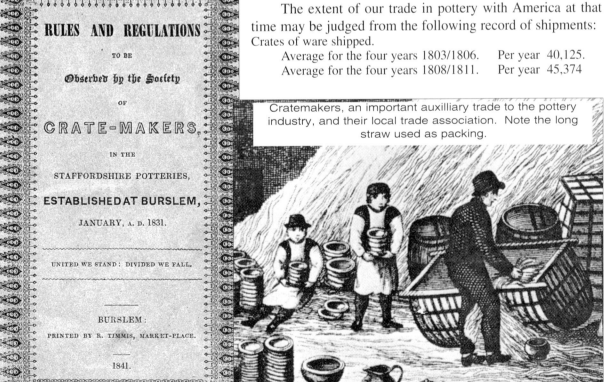

Cratemakers, an important auxilliary trade to the pottery industry, and their local trade association. Note the long straw used as packing.

At the time of this latest threat Burslem had the equivalent of 30,000 crates of ware, equal to the capacity of one hundred 300-ton ships, either ready for shipment or on order.

Since the pottery manufacturers were already feeling the effect of the blockade in Europe, the American threat was devastating. A meeting of manufacturers and others was called under the chairmanship of Josiah Wedgwood, to draft an appeal to Parliament detailing the dire conditions of poverty and bankruptcy which faced the local community, and requiring immediate tangible government assistance. A significant number of the signatories to this document were Burslem pottery manufacturers.

Whether this kindled animosity between mother and sons, not far below the surface at the best of times, but some, mainly eminent Stoke manufacturers, seem to believe that there had been no general agreement on this approach to the government and that Josiah and others had acted unilaterally and precipitately. They sent on their own behalf a further letter which stated that in their view the distress had been exaggerated. Among the signatures on this document were those of Minton and Spode. Following this, to substantiate and pursue their convictions Josiah Wedgwood, Robert Hamilton, and Thomas Lindop addressed the House of Commons in person, emphasising the inevitable dire effects of the Order.

An appeal from the populace was also addressed to His Highness the Duke of Kent as President of the Institute for the relief of Distressed Manufacturers, asking for relief. A worthy institution which would be more than welcome in the present pottery industry!

Fortunately the government climbed down and the threat to America never materialised. That there should have been such conflicting opinions in the Potteries is difficult to understand, since there could be no doubt that any curtailment of American trade would have had a catastrophic effect on pottery production in the whole district. Josiah Wedgwood's influence in parliament had already been effective a few years previously in preventing the East India Co from obtaining a reduction from 59% to 50% import duty on Chinese Porcelain. At the enquiry it was said that China paid their artisans 2d to 6d. a day, while here they receive 3/- to 7/-.

There was great rejoicing in Burslem when pressure led to the withdrawal of the Order in Council and, seemingly by nature, she remembered the old days and resorted to verse:

> Hark hark jolly potters awhile to my tale
> Which to your attention, I'm sure cannot fail
> Come cheer up your spirits, let gloom be demolish'd
> For the Order in Council no longer exists
> Our friends have been zealous and true to our cause
> For work now there is plenty, we are none at a loss
> So we'll drink good success to the Biscuit and Gloss.
>
> Come Throwers away to your wheels now repair
> Let the lad to the wheel turn both steady and fair
> On you much depends, if I must be so frank
> To get full employ for the rest of the bank
> Good Turners away, to your lathes now all hie
> The Handlers are eager the handles to ply
> For work now there is plenty, we are none at a loss
> So drink good success to the Biscuit and Gloss

Temporary relief was succeeded by permanent relief with the ending of hostilities, both on the Continent and in America, and Burslem decided to demonstrate their gratitude. The following notice was displayed in the town on the 7th of June 1815:

The manufacturers and inhabitants of Burslem district of the Potteries , conceiving it proper to celebrate the happy termination of hostilities between Great Britain and the United States of America by some demonstration of joy, propose to dine together at Burslem on Thursday the 19th day of January instant at four o'clock. Tickets at the bar of the Legs of Man. Price one guinea.

After more than twenty years of continuous wars, peace came to Britain - but not for its King; George III was mentally ill and the Prince Regent was acting for him. As ever when joyful, Burslem was poetic, perhaps 'verseful' is a better word, this time to an ancient tune.

THE JOLLY POTTERS

The jolly potters once so gay, have lately all been sad
But here's good news arrived today and every heart is glad
(then follows a chorus which is repeated according to taste.)

Chorus;- Then a throwing we will go

Rejoice all ranks and shout huzza, our glorious cause is won
In social glass boys drink away, and ring dull care begone

Chorus;-Then turning we will go.

We want not title, pension, place, no neighbour we upbraid
We are a peaceful busy race, our hobby horse is trade

Chorus;- Then squeezing we will go

Give us but work and all is right, our wages each week end
Frenchman or devil we will fight, and make the rascals bend

Chorus;- Then firing we will go

We'll trade as usual with great heart, in spite of all our foes,
And as for curs'd old Bonaparte, we'll take him by the nose

Chorus;- Then printing we will go
(Each chorus line to be repeated several times)

Pottery figures of Wellington and Napoleon

Bradford
Leeds
Blackburn
Halifax
Oldham
Bolton
Manchester
Stockport
Sheffield
Macclesfield

Stoke

Wolverhampton
Birmingham

Cheltenham
Merthyr Tydfil
Stroud
Greenwich

Brighton
Portsmouth

The new election franchises
established in the new industrial towns
by the 1832 Reform Act.

Devonport

The Manchester-Liverpool railway c.1830, the epitome of the new railway age

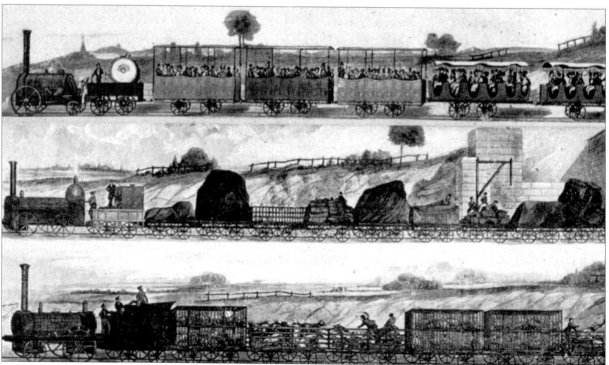

CHAPTER SIXTEEN: Post war unrest

Post Napoleonic era. Peace but not prosperity. Shortage of staple foods. Public disorder.
Large Workhouses. First Parliamentary franchise in industrial areas. Parliament's intransigence and
Royal intervention. First Burslem M.P.s.

The euphoria which followed the peace quickly faded in Burslem and the neighbouring towns. Disruption caused by the wars, and their drain in taxation, produced a depression and eventually drove Burslem and its neighbours to make a direct appeal to the Prince Regent, who was preoccupied, not only with burdens of state, but building a fairy palace at Brighton and annoying matrimonial problems:

DUTIFUL AND LOYAL ADDRESS OF THE GENTRY, CLERGY, MANUFACTURERS & OTHER INHABITANTS OF THE STAFFORDSHIRE POTTERIES.

We your Majesty's loyal subjects the Gentlemen, Clergy, Manufacturers & other inhabitants of the Staffordshir Potteries beg leave to approach your throne with humble offering of our affection of Your Majesty's person and the assurance of our attachment to our admirable constitution. Succeeding as Your Majesty has happily done to the throne of this realm from the House of Brunswick, that illustrious house which at first inspired the confidence, as it has since enjoyed the veneration of the British people, we are encouraged to accompany these dutiful professions with a becoming but honest representation of the present state of our public affairs, and we do this in the well grounded persuasion that Your Majesty will graciously receive the sentiments which we humbly offer as expressive of unshaken loyalty and our genuine patriotism. Amongst our opinions and agitations which surround us, we have endeavoured to draw our attention from public men and public measures , setting before us the stability of Your Majesty's throne and the prosperity of your people.We deem it our first duty to congratulate Your Majesty on restoring to us during your regency, the long desired and inestimable blessing of peace.Happy should we feel ourselves could we equally congratulate Your Majesty of the establishment of commercial treaties with foreign powers; the improvement of our trade and agriculture, the further diminution of our burdens, the lessening of our public expenditure, and a reduction, instead of an increase in our standing army. but we lament to say, so little have the measures of Your Majesty's ministers tended to affectuate these salutary purposes, that the opposite system has in most instances been pursued, Whereby the fears of the loyal have been excited, the confidence of the well disposed shaken, and the feeling of discontent fostered in the great body of Your Majesty's subjects, a feeling which restrictive laws and military power, each unfortunately more calculated to aggravate than to extinguish. It is Your Majesty's felicity to reign over a people impatient of impolitic or coercive measures, but above all others, affectionate to their Prince and zealous for his glory. Your Majesty's people, the pillar of your throne, are become a suffering people. This large manufacturing district is doubly enveloped in this common calamity, yet we have the satisfaction to assure Your Majesty that patience, subordination, and loyalty are the prevailing disposition of all classes of our population. We see round us indisputable proof that the existing laws when impartially and formally administered are perfectly competent of the maintenance of the public peace, the protection of private property, and the punishment of libel and blasphemy. We now further are called upon to implore Your Majesty to adopt such reasonable councils as shall tranquillise the public agitation, conciliate the affection, and ameliorate the condition of your faithful subjects, as shall convince them of the paternal intention of Your Majesty's government, and by redressing these acknowledged evils, which admit of practical remedy, encourage them to endure those difficulties which are at present unavoidable, let Your Majesty not be induced to include us among those vicious and damaging characters, who take occasion from the late proceedings in parliament to lower the dignity and undermine the foundation of the throne. We lament the policy which suggested, and the obstinacy which persisted in the unhappy measure against the Queen, and earnestly entreat Your Majesty to interpose your royal authority that this afflicting and dangerous question may be agitated no more. We devoutly pray that the United Kingdom over which Your Majesty reigns may again be distinguished by the wisdom of its councils, and the prosperity of its people that it may be the admiration of the great, and the protection of the oppressed nations of the earth. That civil liberty, concord and happiness, may dwell in your land, and that Your Majesty may long reign in the hearts of a free and magnanimous people.

The appeal was printed and copies distributed to all the local townships for public signatures to be appended by those who had the ability to sign their own name.

When the cost of living had risen in the wars it might have been expected that the workers would agitate for wages to be increased but the formation of unions was forbidden, and only magistrates had the power to increase wages. But it was thought that if wages were increased to meet rising costs due to a temporary situation, there would be unprecedented unrest if attempts were made to reduce them when peace returned. One solution, was to retain the existing wage rate and supplement it with poor relief in relation to the price of a loaf and the number of members in a family. This scheme was adopted in other counties, but there was no universal practice. The magistrates for Staffordshire adopted the principle that: *A labourer with a wife and three children, earning 12/-d to 15/-d per week was not entitled to relief. If he had a fourth child, he is to be considered an object for relief.*

There were discussions in the House of Commons, and partial recommendations, such as standardising the weight of bread as the staple food. From this discussion and a subsequent Sessions Meeting in Stafford, a circular was issued to the parishes defining weight and price.

Peck Loaf to weigh	17lbs. 6oz.
Half Peck Loaf to weigh	8lbs. 11oz.
Quartern Loaf to weigh	4lbs. 5oz.
Half Quartern Loaf to weigh	2lbs. 2 oz
Quarter Quartern to weigh	1lb. 1 oz.

Wheaten loave to be marked with a large Roman "W" and The Household with a large Roman "H". All other loaves to be sold at prices in proportion to each other. The Household at one fourth less than the Wheaten. None to be sold, other than above sizes, except loaves of white bread at the price of 2d. or under.

A threatening note in Burslem which came into the hands of the authorities, probably illustrated the feeling created by the sufferings of the time:

"Big loaf for a shilling or else damn the King and Gentry
if they don't turn out before we are perished for some of the
master pots will clean us to death so prepare for bulit fare".

Today bread comes in a great variety of shapes and sizes and contains many different flours but legal control is never mentioned, yet reference by law to the weight of bread persisted well into the 20th century and led to regular inspection and prosecution for infringement.

With each local authority responsible for raising its own poor rates, and in the conditions prevailing, more and more demands for poor law money were being made on the ratepayers in Burslem, who at this time only consisted of one in eight of the occupiers of properties in excess of the minimum valuation which made them liable; and unlike the modern method of setting a charge to cover all parish expenses, the poor rates were raised separately as current funds were exhausted; consequently it is not surprising that there was reluctance to pay, particularly to support those families coming from other areas seeking work. This resulted in the commissioners in Burslem issuing the following notice:

To the Manufacturers, Tradesmen, Farmers,and others of the town and parish of Burslem.
"We beg to call your serious attention to the enormous evil which strongly prevails in this parish, namely that of making your servant parishioners [merely for want of having Sundays and Holidays excepted in their hirings] and also that of allowing your workmen to engage assistants [without entering their name and terms of their agreements in the general Hiring Book] such as Lathe Turners, Transferrers, Cutters of paper etc. hundreds of whom have gained settlements in the place through having been engaged by the workmen, which hirings, both by master and workmen. We regret to say [notwithstanding the annual printed customs, and all the exhortations of the Parish Officers, to prevent this rapid progress] are still practiced in the Parish to an alarming extent; but, unless such kind of engagements are immediately discontinued, the property of their Parish will become seriously depreciated in value, through being so heavily burdened with rates. We therefore particularly request that in future you will have an exception of Sundays and Holidays in all the hiring of your workpeople, or else that you will engage them for fiftyone weeks only, instead of a year. This we conceive, will be the only effective remedy preventing future settlements being obtained, and reduce this burden on our resources. "

An examination of the Burslem poor law accounts gives the position 1807-1808:

"Report of the committee for examining and auditing the accounts of The Overseer of the Poor from Easter 1807 to Easter 1808.
The committee having examined the accounts of the late overseer have, according to a plan laid down last year, directed copies of the accounts to be printed and distributed in the parish. The amount of uncollected levies to Easter 1807 from last years accounts was £357. 12. 5 only £88. 11. 1 of which has been collected and the committee are of the opinion that more might have been done. The amount of thirtytwo levies granted for the last year ending Easter 1808 is £3745. 2. 1 of which only £3222. 3. 2 has been collected. Payments for Bastards this year has exceeded the receipts by £73. 0. 6, increasing the balance due to £239. 5. 6, which ought to have been received in the current year. Workhouse charges on the resident poor £385. 12. 2 exceed last year. Out pensions list including bastards and casual relief amounts to £1869. 15. 8 and you will see the hopes of the committee have not been realised. The cost of clothing account £153. 10. 10 has not been kept in a manner the committee wished to find it.

Overseer's salary £100. The committee cannot declare themselves perfectly satisfied and have therefore recommended the additional £30. salary, as ordered by the Easter meeting, to be carried to the Overseer's credit in the accounts".

There was no improvement in sight in following years as statistics show:

Inmates in the Poor House and on Poor Relief.

YEAR 1811.	Men	Women	Children	Total
Persons in the Poor House	17	20	46	83
Persons on the Pension List	42	146	302	490
Persons on the Casual List	39	51	137	227
			Total. 800	
YEAR 1812.				
Persons in the Poor House	18	18	38	74
Persons on the Pension List	63	247	398	708
Persons on the Casual List	21	43	59	123
			Total. 905	
YEAR 1813.				
Persons in the Poor House	81	311	546	938
Persons on the Pension List	42	66	117	225
Persons on the Casual List	35	44	93	172
			Total.1335	

From the figures for 1813 it seems obvious that the Commissioners had considered it more economical to place the needy in the Poor House rather than making individual payments to them. Nationally the position became so critical that in some parishes entrants would only be allowed to stay if they carried an official note from their home parish to say that they would meet any poor law payments received. Stoke in desperation attempted to turn away families, but the notice that allowed them to do this required the signature of two magistrates, and obtaining these signatures was most difficult since the nearest magistrates were in Stafford.

Not only was there this drain on personal incomes for poor relief but money had still to be found to repay debts incurred to prosecute the recent wars. In common with other towns, in June 1805, Wood and Cauldwell, received notice from "The Additional Commissioners":

"Until the sixth day of May next after the notification of a Definitive Treaty of Peace, a contribution of the profits arising from Property Possessions, Trades and Offices, have assessed you the sum of £50, and if you are dissatisfied therewith, you must prefer your appeal to the Commissioners for the general purpose of the act at a time and place to be hereafter named in the parish which will be fixed to the church door within your parish".

This must have been an arbitrary assessment resulting in widespread appeals, since in the following year the government decided to create a national formula for official assessments. The Commissioners informed Enoch Wood and Richard Turner by official letter that they had been selected, apparently without question, to assess:

"By virtue of acts passed in the 43rd, 45th, and 46th, year of his present Majesty's reign, for granting to His Majesty, a contribution on profits arising from, Property, Profession, Trade, and Offices, as the Commissioners for the purpose of the said Acts acting for the Hundred of Pithily North have appointed you Assessors of the Duties granted by the said Acts, and do hereby require you to appear before the Commissioners at a meeting to be held in the Crewe Arms at Madeley on Saturday the eighth of November in order to receive your Warrant and instructions for the execution of the said Acts. Hereof fail not. 18th October 1806".

Apparently it was undignified to mention payment for the work involved, or take into account that Burslem was in Pirehill, not Pithily, Madeley was in Cheshire, and that the Mail Coach did not go that way from Burslem. Enoch and Richard nevertheless undertook the journey, returning with a book of instructions and presumably the Sovereign's blessing.

Earlier laws had obliged every authority to have a Poor House, but its use had been restricted to the aged, the orphaned, and the destitute; now their wider communal use seemed to be a better way of controlling costs and dealing with the increased numbers of unemployed after and due to the war. But most of the existing Poor Houses, whilst adequate for their original use, were now too small, consequently the government was forced to give permission to rebuild, including authority for adjacent authorities to do so for combined use.

In 1794, the parish of Stoke suggested that Burslem and Wolstanton should join with them in building what Stoke termed *"a House of Industry"*. Meetings were called to discuss the proposal. Fortunately for Burslem and Wolstanton they decided to build their own at Chell. Stoke ran into problems at the outset through the hostility of a Mr Wolfe, who was the owner of a factory which dominated the centre of Stoke, and the largest employer in the town.

A notice issued at the time indicates how disagreement had developed:

HOUSE OF INDUSTRY

"Whereas in persistence of an anonymous advertisement circulated within the Parish of Stoke on Trent in connection with the above, unofficial meeting of the inhabitants and parishioners upon business of importance. A numerous and respectable meeting was held in the Vestry Room in Stoke aforesaid on the day and the hour therein stated, when Mr Chatterley was unanimously voted in the chair. After repeatedly demanding without effect from Mr. Thomas Wolfe (who avowed himself the author of the advertisement) the Vestry Book of the said parish, in order to refer to, and inform the meeting of the resolution of the last meeting relative to the intended House of Industry; and who, though in no official capacity, has unjustifiably taken the same from the Vestry Room, and withheld it from the officers and parishioners. After waiting near two hours, and observing that a number of workmen and people, in no wise interested or entitled to vote on the parish affairs had assembled, and were industriously collecting at the place of the meeting. Considering the dangerous tendency Mr. Wolfe's expressions might have upon the minds in representing the intended House of Industry a Bastile or State prison, and considering such epithets were not only dangerous, but unjust when applied to such an institution, which affords the aged and indigent a comfortable asylum which shields them from oppression, and while it administers to their wants and promotes their comfort, tends to relieve the parishioners at large from their present increasing burdens."

Burslem and Wolstanton took fright, and Stoke built their own palace of comfort on the Newcastle Road, where it later became part of the North Staffordshre Royal Infirmary.

I can vividly remember in my youth seeing the vagrants collecting nearby in the late afternoon, anxious no doubt for the doors to open in order that they could enjoy the comforts which the promoters offered. Such was the rural nature of the vicinity at that time, I remember it being said that vagrants hid in the undergrowth such items as would fail to bear the scrutiny of the warden until they left on the following day.

In 1820, such was the severity of the crisis, and lack of uniformity in dealing with the poor, that the government made it compulsory for the local authorities to elect a Board of Guardians to control the Poor House and appoint a Resident Superintendent; so bringing relief to the Commissioners. In order to achieve uniformity, a guide was issued defining rules of conduct, costs etc. The initial sentence in the guide had an ominous ring for those who anticipated a "comfortable asylum." It read:

As soon as a pauper is admitted, he shall be placed in some room to be exclusively for the purpose and termed "The Receiving Ward" and they shall remain until examined by the Medical Officer for the workhouse. Before being removed from the receiving ward, the pauper shall be thoroughly cleansed and shall be clothed in a workhouse dress. To each class shall be assigned that ward or separate building and yard which may be best fitted for the reception of such class, and each class of pauper shall remain therein without communication with those of any other class."

A writer of the early 18th century wrote *"No one would visualise that arbitrary power in Britain would tear asunder husband and wife, parent from children, brother from sister, as it did in the lands of slavery, yet our new poor laws have aimed a deadly blow at this security when some poor family has the occurrence of some chance misfortune."*

Chell workhouse from the illustrated *When I Was a Child* by Charles Shaw. (Illustration by Sue Purdy)

Alas this occurrence befell a family in Burslem, which is vividly described in *When I Was a Child,* written by a man who as a child was forced to move with his destitute parents to the Poor House at Chell. The book was used by Arnold Bennett in his Five Towns novels. In the book, the prescribed schedule for the day in the poor house is given as:

From 25th March to 24th September;
Rise.   quarter of an hour before six.
Work   7am to 12.midday
Dinner   12 to 1.0pm
Work   1.0pm to 6.0pm
Supper   6pm to 7pm
Bed   8 o-clock
For Winter time, rising was an hour later, and work one hour less.
Refusal to work could entail commitment to prison.

A typical menu, Monday to Sunday inclusive:

> Breakfast. Bread. Men. 7oz.   Women 6oz.
> Gruel. Each. 1 pints.
> Dinner.   Cooked Meat. Two days. Men 6oz. Women 5oz. vegetables extra.
> Soup.   Two days. Each I? pints. vegetables extra.
> Suet Pudding Two days. Men. 14oz. Women 12oz.
> The remaining day was each two pints of Soup.
>
> Supper was again a varied diet:
> Bread and Cheese. Two days.
> Bread and thickened Broth. Two days.   [Broth. each 1 pints]
> Men allowed 5oz of Bread and 2oz of Cheese.
> Women 1 oz less.

The author said of the meals "*I have had poor food before but never as offensively poor as this. The concoction of meal and water was most revolting, it might have been boiled in old clothes which had been worn on sweating bodies for three score years and ten*".

If there was any satisfaction to be had by Burslem, it was the knowledge that by deciding to build at Chell rather than join with Stoke they had made a wise financial decision. Not only did Stoke have problems with collecting the Poor Rate but desperate appeals for help were made to the High Commissioner by the inmates of "the comfortable asylum", resulting in a visit from an inspector of the Poor Law Commissioners. The report of the inspector said:

"I was desired to proceed thither in order to investigate its condition and suggest such measures as might remedy the evils under which it is labouring. The inhabitants of Stoke might be conveniently divided into four classes. The first comprising a few manufacturers of immense wealth. The second, consisting of manufacturers less wealthy, but of great intelligence and respectability, giving employment to a vast number of workmen. The third comprised of smaller manufacturers and tradesmen on whom the control of the parish had devolved, and the fourth, made up of working men, or as they style themselves, The Operatives. Of these four classes, the last is best defined, as it is nearly identical with the Trades Union, so far organised as to bring its weight to bear upon the decision of any question affecting its interest. The Unionists of Stoke and Burslem number about 8000. This confederacy, which was on the decline, has recently been gathering strength and advanced to the point of forcing workmen to enrol themselves in its ranks. The two parties, masters and servants may be said to be measuring their strength against each other, and it is a question which of them was to have control over the parochial resources. Every modification of religious opinion has its adherents in the parish of Stoke, so that, in addition to the ordinary causes of mismanagement, political division and sectarian animosity had contributed to embroil its affairs. No party was willing that the reins should be held by the other. The first class I mentioned have long retired from the contest altogether. The second, by secret manoeuvre, forced to relinquish it. The third, from which the last Vestry was selected, had incurred the dislike of all the others, and the fourth class had openly proclaimed their determination to seize power from them, their object being to secure to themselves the disposal of the funds, in case of an open rupture with the employers. In every branch of administration of affairs at Stoke the hand of reformation was wanted, abuses had crept in everywhere, for instance, the Gonvenor of the workhouse had long been contracted for the supplier, and was allowed the earnings of the paupers, the consequences of this arrangement were, first, an unnecessary accumulation of inmates in the house, when the practice was discontinued, the number immediately fell from 2I0 to I36. Second, a great discrepancy in the diet, for, while he did not stint and starve the aged, it was in his interest to allure the stout and able, and maintain them in good working condition. The classification in the house was so imperfect that three unmarried females became pregnant in it last year. The parish accounts were in a state that almost defied investigation. Two officers were convicted of embezzlement during the last eighteen months. The late cashier had absconded, and there had been no entry of receipts for sixteen weeks. The collection of rates was conducted most fraudulently thirty per cent was usually lost and no rate had been regularly balanced for many years. When I went to Stoke, an attempt had just been made to levy a fifth rate for the current year, while only a quarter of the fourth rate had been collected. The four overseers paid the poor in the four principal townships without any uniform system, hence arose great variations in the scale of relief, and it was observable that in one of the townships where the overseer kept a provision shop the rate of allowance was 25% higher than in the others".

It is well known, and seemingly inevitable, that where public money is concerned, its use brings forth many viewpoints, some charitable, some critical. The following is Ward's observation which appears to be half way between both:

"It perhaps answers the design of the legislature to suppress indiscriminate pauperism by throwing the utmost difficulty in the way of applicants for relief, by dealing it out with a niggard hand, and by prison like discipline to which claimants must submit, whose necessities oblige them to avail themselves of the Place of Refuge; we are informed that the palatial structure at Chell will cost not less than £10,000."

Rejoicings which took place at the end of the Napoleonic wars were in stark contrast to the feelings aroused by the subsequent unemployment. In a lecture in Burslem given by Mr J. Wilcox Edge, he said his father witnessed the boisterous exuberance shown by Burslem at the conclusion of the Napoleonic wars. Scaffolding on which was erected a gallows with an effigy of Napoleon, was built round the town hall. The effigy had previously been trundled round the town in Ralph Meir's cart by Charlie Cook, who addressed snide remarks to 'Bony' while on the way. By great misfortune a brick, thrown by a spectator, missed 'Bony' and hit a poor woman who died from the blow!

Without full employment and political franchise, it is amazing what response there was to a widespread appeal for the abolition of slavery with copies placed around the pottery towns for the public to sign. One of these copies has been preserved, and it is pitiable to see the number of crosses of those unable to write. The petition read:

TO HIS MAJESTY'S GOVERNMENT

The petitioners are fully sensible of the blessings which under providence have been conferred upon them by the safe and honourable peace and, rejoicing in the termination of a bloody war, as well as the general realisation of the rights and liberties of Europe, have seen with deepest regret that these blessings have not generally been extended to the poor and defenceless sons of Africa, and that the traffic in human blood, originating and perpetuating wars and oppressions as to be carried on in France for a period of five years to the disgrace of the civilised world.

Your petitioners therefore humbly pray that your honourable house will take such measures as to your wisdom shall seem meet for obtaining an immediate and universal abolition of the trade in slaves, and your petitioners will ever pray etc. etc,

Surely many will have seen it as unacceptable hypocrisy when children and women were still being disgracefully exploited in Britain.

The pressing need was for a speedy recovery in trade and relief from food shortages, while calls for political franchise also became more and more demanding. However a predominantly Tory parliament in 1831 was determined to avoid any political concessions, although the first Reform Bill got as far as the Lords where it was thrown out by the opposition of the bishops. Riots followed, the targets being mainly the bishops and their palaces. The king, fearing that the riots would spread, dissolved parliament, addressing it as follows: "*I dissolve you that I may ascertain the sense of my people in a way in which it can be most constitutionally and authoritative express on the expediency of making such changes in the representation of the people as circumstances may appear to require, and which, founded on the acknowledged principles of the constitution, may tend at once to uphold the just rites and prerogatives of the Crown, and give security to the* liberties of the people." This invoked a stirring printed appeal to all loyal citizens, which confirmed that the dissolved government had been less than popular:

PACKING THE PARLIAMENT

"The King has sent off with just and virtuous indignation the most shamelessly corrupt and selfish parliament ever commissioned to betray the people, but appeals to his faithful and loyal subjects to support him in his glorious office to free both himself and them from the chains of the Borough Gang. The Gang has formed a vile conspiracy to defeat the King's gracious and honest pleas for the country's good. The gang has pulled forth their purses filled with the spoils of the people. This money is to be used by searching out in every direction vile men ready to vote for any scum Borough Monger. Their pockets are filled with money from a stock purse, and bribery is to be the order of the day. It is hoped that a parliamentary then be packed ready to save the Rotten Borough and make the reign of tyranny and corruption eternal. Englishmen, will you suffer this system, shall the King rule you and buy and sell you for ever? Will you bear the appearance among you of their vile tools? Will you endure such individuals? Imitate the good men of Dover who hoisted the black flag when the King's man appeared and forced him to leave the town".

The questionnaire which followed this diatribe is interesting but somewhat ambiguous, and there could even be an element of cynicism:

Englishmen answer these questions.

Do you wish to be taxed by men whom a few Boroughmongers chose for the purpose of raising their pension and salaries?

Do you wish to be governed by your worst enemies?

Do you wish to be left out any longer with the many electors, when in fact others not you choose the parliament?

Do you wish to be ruled all your lives by the tricks of Castlereagh's faction. The men who bragged of corruption, and openly state it is legal?

Do you wish to have a run of public extravagance around till the nation is plunged into misery and bankruptcy?.

Do you wish to have England again taking the part of the holy allies against all freemen; the part of those who defend tyrants the whole world over?

Do you wish to be governed by men like Peel, who have lately avowed their hostility to the press, and grieve for the glorious revolution of July?

Do you wish to be ground by men who are sworn friends of the Polignacs and many other bitter enemies of French, Italian, and Polish Liberties?

If such are your wishes, then reject the Reform Bill of the patriot king and his honest ministers.

(Will future generations blame this for Castlereagh's suicide?")

The attitude taken by the church over the first reform bill was obviously not to Burslem's liking, and in keeping with tradition it demanded a reply in verse:

> I sing a praise of church and state
> Our glorious constitution
> Fat living, Rectors, Bishops pride
> And Tory constitution
>> Chorus
>> And this law I will maintain
>> Unto my dying day sir
>> And whosoever king shall reign
>> I'll still be vicar of Bray sir.
>
> I've done my duty many years
> What they at college taught me
> Drank many a pipe of wine that cheers
> But drunk they never got me
>> Chorus
>
> Lambs of the flock, whatever the weather
> In holiest wedlock, I fasten together
> For joining each pair from the radical mob
> Three shillings and six pence, I charge for the job
>> Chorus
>
> I sprinkle your urchins oh! bring them all in
> For a shilling I free from original sin
> By my absolution they shall be forgiven
> For five shillings more, I send them to heaven
>> Chorus

A bill giving a limited franchise to forty of the new industrial areas became law in 1832 and around the same time there was a radical reorganisation of the church, including an equalization of stipends and discontinuance of multiple livings. In the list of towns specified in the bill the Potteries was initially missing, but following representations one seat was included for the whole area. This was considered unsatisfactory and after further lobbying, when a figure was given of turnover in the pottery trade of £1,245,000 per annum, and weight of the product 10,6828 tons, the allocation was increased to two seats.

The first election in the Potteries took place in 1832. Before that the interests of the pottery district had been ostensibly represented by the county members of parliament, who were mainly from the land-owning class, supported by the votes of the Burgesses of Newcastle, who, according to some took their orders from the Duke at Trentham.

> We are told we are nurtured in Trentham's sweet lap
> And all of us suckled by her golden pap
> From snakes in the grass, now thy ask no more votes
> A tool of their own they would ram down our throats

One of the first candidates to represent the area was Josiah Wedgwood II. Others were John Davenport of Burslem, Richard Heathcote of Longton Hall and George Miles Mason, pottery manufacturer of Fenton. None of the candidates were seen by the workers as a democratic choice, but there was not yet a full franchise. The result was that at the nominations in Hanley there were riots outside the town hall, with missiles being thrown causing the candidates to seek shelter. On polling day, Davenport's committee rooms in the Crown and Anchor in Longton had all its windows broken, and after dark, houses and factories of his friends were vandalised. Nevertheless Wedgwood and Davenport were the two successful candidates.

This parliament of Robert Peel was short lived and dissolved in 1835. Josiah Wedgwood decided against re-election, and in the subsequent contest, the successful candidates were Davenport and Heathcote. Both men were Conservatives and the object of less than genteel criticism. Despite the treatment experienced in the previous election, Davenport entered the hustings expressing himself in democratic style: *"When the day of the people comes, and whenever the signal is hoisted, and the tug of war begins, you shall find me at my post"* However this failed to convince one critic who wrote publicly:

"It would be more satisfactory of Mr Davenport, instead of professing generally to be alive to our interests, had gone on to enumerate the instances in which he has shown himself more alive to our interests than his own. I cannot charge him of carrying on trade by means of what we call 'Truck' his favourite pastime being Barter, or Bastard Truck, by which the manufacturer is tricked instead of the workmen. You will no doubt, many of you remember how much he was alive to your interests, when he supported the Order in Council restricting our American trade, at a time when all of you were petitioning to have the order rescinded. Mr Davenport is convinced of the necessity of reform, if I am not mistaken, this is a new thought, however, it is as well he has hit upon it at last. He seems disposed to make a virtue of necessity and go with the stream, The Vicar of Bray did so before him.

A TEN POUNDER."

Neither was the other successful candidate loved by all:

COMING TO THE SCRATCH

"Does Mr. Heathcote realise from their promises to those persons whose name he has entered in his vote book, but who now regret that they injured the potters and themselves by the promises they have given. Dare Mr Heathcote, (who prosecuted not a month ago a man who caught a fish worth 2d.) vote for the abolition of the Game Laws? Dare Mr Heathcote, whose property consists principally of land, vote for the abolition of the Corn Laws, thereby giving the poor man a cheap loaf? Dare Mr Heathcote (who changes his establishment every full moon) appeal to his own servants for a character as a master and a friend? Does Mr Heathcote appeal to his private character in support of his public profession? Does he appeal to his Coventry constituents for a character now he offers himself as a representative for us? Does he restate to you what he told the citizens of Coventry, viz, that he would attend to his parliamentary dates when it suited his own convenience? QUIZ."

Mr Heathcote, showing admirable tact had this to say in reply:

While I controversially abstain further from doing or saying anything which might have a tendency to revive those hints of bickerings by which the peace of the Potteries is of late so unprofitably disturbed, I shall not fail, when the time comes, to present myself at the hustings. assured that I shall then experience that degree of kindness and confidence with which you have hitherto invariably honoured me, and receive at your hands the highest distinction I can ever covet, namely, that of representing in a reformed House of Commons, the district in which I was born, and with which all my feelings and interests are associated.

The contest took place in January 1835 but in 1836 Mr Heathcote prematurely resigned, and Col. George Anson, brother of the Earl of Lichfield, was elected unadopted.

CHAPTER SEVENTEEN: Potters unions

Rises and falls of Pottery Unions. 1836 futile and impoverishing strike.
Improvement in trade. Operatives fear of mechanization.
1843 revival of Pottery Union. Union Emigration Scheme. Truck payments.

1825 saw the first serious combining of pottery workers to form a single union, and they struck in that year for higher wages and suffered an ignominious defeat.

Probably from lessons learned then, in 1833 they formed a more successful combination, this time with a series of separate lodges where members met weekly and a grand lodge, where representatives from the individual lodges made up the policy body. The new union persuaded a number of influential manufacturers that they themselves were their worst enemy in failing to maintain economic selling prices which would justify a fair wage and an agreement was reached that, in return for the payment of increased but justifiable rates to members of the union, the union would bring pressure to bear on all pottery workers only to accept work in factories which complied with the terms, and thus hopefully bring recalcitrant employers to abide by agreed selling prices.

After an instance of the agreement being broken, followed by an operatives strike, there was a quiet period on both sides, a growing confidence within the union and an apparently more demanding attitude.

The pottery owners now began to feel vulnerable and in 1836 they formed the Pottery Chamber of Commerce and agreed that any member affected by an unjustified demand and resulting in withdrawal of labour, would be recompensed by those who were unaffected. The pottery operatives union increased both in power and numbers, and decided to tackle two outstanding irksome working conditions - the 'Annual Hiring', and 'Good from Oven'. In 1836, before the usual settlement time of Martinmas, and at chosen factories, they requested that the annual hiring should be replaced by one month's notice given by either side, and Good from Oven to be withdrawn. The affected firms refused on the grounds that both conditions were long standing customs which they thought should continue. The immediate reaction was that labour was withdrawn at fourteen factories affecting 3500 employees. The extent of the withdrawal surprised the employers who realised it was impossible to sue individually for broken agreements and so, with practical support from fellow manufacturers, no action was taken, the works ceased to function and the strikers had to exist on payment from the union funds of 5/- or 6/- per week.

When Martinmas came round and no concessions were offered by the employers, sixty-four more factories closed and 20,000 operatives were now idle, with £14,000 per week sacrificed in wages. Appeals were made for financial support from other trades, which resulted in £7,000 in either loans or gifts from as far away as Sheffield, but the strike dragged on, creating destitution also for others like the miners who relied on the pottery trade.

The dispute was conducted with remarkable restraint, but ultimately there was a dribble back to work. As a last gesture of defiance, many of the operatives joined as a body and took their last personal possessions to the pawnbrokers, giving the proceeds to the union funds, but the dribble quickly became a flood, and after 21 weeks it finally ended. For the next seven years there was no fight left, each manufacturer more or less dictating his own terms - which included a further humiliating imposition. It had long been the practice throughout the trade to pay apprentices on a piecework basis, but a deduction was made from their gross earnings which went to the employer, presumably considered by him as payment for training. Usually the deduction was 2d in the shilling. Following the strike some manufacturers adopted the same practice on journeymen earnings, claiming it as their due for injury and loss of trade, and before long it had spread throughout the district, some even increasing the deduction to 3d or 4d in the shilling.

The introduction of machines for production was now drawing nearer. The jolley had been introduced in at least two factories, but due to ominous threats combined with technical problems, their introduction into all the factories was delayed. There were protest marches with songs to emphasise their grievance. One accompanied the introduction of the Jolley:

I will sing you a song of a Jolley machine
Which potters all say is a "rattler"
And exceeds any other, as yet ever seen
I'm sure you'll pronounce it a "spattler"

I am quite in earnest, so pray bend an ear
My song is true,and no folly
As from this machine, you have too much to fear
It's a thief that I call master Jolley

A thief did I call it, aye well you may stare
But prove it I can, and most fully
For it deprives you of making crock ware
Why what will become of your belly

It makes bowls and plates in such mighty big rucks
Believe me I'm no lying sinner
And I am told, by and by, he'll make all our cups
Then what shall we do for a dinner

That Jolley's a robber, deny it who can
And brings on distress the most heavy
And how to avert it, I'll tell every man
Why down with his half crown levy

Some selfish ones tell us that Jolley won't out
I think they are greatly mistaken
It's only to save their half crown, that's a fact
And care not for other men's bacon

If the fate of the weaver you would avert
And ward off destruction so heavy
Why come forward like men that will not be hurt
And pay down your half crown levy

In the manufacture of pottery the introduction of the jolley literally revolutionised the work previously performed by the pottery presser and vastly increased productivity. This was seen as a serious threat to employment but was only the beginning of innovations in the 19th century, often resulting in sporadic stoppages, but only delaying their ultimate introduction.

This doggerel contains some interesting words, rarely seen in modern times; "spatler" is a term given to one who operates a machine, when a strike against its use is in operation; "crocks" was once a common term used when referring to domestic pottery, but rarely used today, although it is a dictionary word; "rucks", also in the dictionary, and possibly derived from the agricultural Rick, is used in this district in the term shord ruck, denoting a mound of broken faulty ware and saggars. The fate of the weavers, presumably refers to the Luddite troubles when the weavers destroyed machinery in Manchester and the military were called out and fired on the rioters in St. Peter's Square; often referred to as the Peterloo Massacre. The "half crown levy" is a long story with a sad ending, and its relevance is left for later explanation in its appropriate context.

Even today protest marches seem to be synonymous with urban living. They are as common in the 20th century as they appear to have been in the 18th, but at that time there seems to have been more originality in putting their grievances to some semblance of verse, rather than in todays boring repetition of "out" "out" "out". Another of the fighting songs is referred to as the "Song of the Staffordshire Men:

There's many a task for the English folk
And a man's a man alway
Who delves in coal and iron ore
And shapes the potter's clay

There are forty shires,that light their fires
And bless the iron strong
And the china bake, the potters make
As they sing the Stafford song

We came of a race of yeomen bold
Whose drink is the best of beer
Our fields feed beasts, for the christian feasts
And you may share our Staffordshire cheer

We shall marshall our rank, on the grey pit bank
And our lads on the football field
If the cause is right, we are game to fight
And were never known to yield.

Chorus...For this is the song of the Staffordshire men
    In forge in kiln in mine
    Our fires shall burn and our mill wheels turn
    And the knot shall be our sign

There was particular fear in the unions of male unemployment and this was addressed by a public warning:

"To Maidens, Mothers and Wives. We say mechanisation is your deadliest enemy. Of all the sufferers by mechanical improvement, you will be the worst. It is a systematised process of.slow murder for you. It will destroy your natural claims to home and domestic duties, and immerse you and your toiling little ones in overheated and dirty shops, there to weep, and toil and pine and die."

The local and national grievances grew ever more vociferous. The workers were convinced that the only democratic way of achieving a workers' charter was by obtaining a universal vote - universal suffrage or franchise. In support of this in 1838 there was a great rally in the Potteries. It started with a fanfare, vividly described in the press:

GREAT MEETING IN THE POTTERIES   17th November 1838.

On Wednesday morning last, the town of Hanley presented a heart warming scene to the lover of liberty. Early in the morning, the drum and fife band were heard, announcing that the day had arrived, when the voice of the Potters, was to join that of their brethren in the demand for freedom. The 'Northern Star' reported that at about 9 o'clock, a procession began to move with flags and music to collect the army of regeneration. They then divided into groups, and went to meet their friends, expected to arrive from the various districts. At half past eleven, the procession moved with hearty cheers and flying banners to the place of meeting, The thousands marched in good order, with flags bearing appropriate mottos, some of which we are enabled to give:

No tax hunting parsons.
May our actions be guided by peace, truth, justice, and love.
These are the weapons we use to gain our rights.
Peace on earth and goodwill towards men. Glory to god in the highest.
No statecraft. No Priestcraft.
United we stand. Divided we fall.
By Union we conquer. Divided we perish.
Reform in Church and State.
We die to live.
No Poor Law. No separation of man and wife.
Support our labour. Tax not our industry.
Plenty of food for eight hours labour.
Splendid silk banner of the pottery union,with the five great principles at full length on one side.
On the reverse; Allegorical representation of the effects of reform, exhibiting Justice. Peace. Equity.
Union, and Prosperity, guarded by the British Lion
Hanley and Shelton Political Union.
Better to die with the sword than to perish with hunger.
Be faithful. Be Watchful. The naked clothed.The hungry fed. May Britain's sons united be free.

The procession started by moving in the direction of Burslem and Tunstall, their train constantly increasing, and returned by way of Longport. On reaching the hustings, we calculated that the numbers amounted to over twenty thousand. Mr George Salt was unanimously called to the chair,and opened the business first with prayer, and then gave out an appropriate hymn, made for the occasion, which was sung by the meeting, after which the worthy chairman said: "Now fellow countrymen, you are assembled today in thousands to demand your rights as freemen, and prove by your conduct, order, and demeanour, that you are entitled to that position which you seek. Give no handle to your enemies, but proceed calmly and deliberately with your own business." He then called on Mr. John Richards to move the first resolution. Mr Richards thereupon said that the great grievance under which they laboured was class legislation. Men representing boroughs were required to have £300 and counties £500 per year and it was obvious that they would represent themselves at the expense of the people. By universal suffrage alone could this great and trying evil be checked.and the great general grievance under which they laboured was class legislation. The power which this system gave them, enabled them to tax all the articles of their produce, and the duty went into the pockets of the idlers. By universal suffrage alone could this great and crying evil be checked".

Mr F O'Connor was introduced to the meeting, and was most rapturously cheered. He said it was the first time he had appeared in the Potteries, yet he had joined with them in their struggle against the masters. He had, he said, intended to address them on subjects connected with the present agitation, but he had just learned from their chairman, that six other victims were sacrificed in Ireland, to the rapacity of the infidel. state church. [hear hear's]. Yes, said he, six more persons have been slaughtered, while our philosophical motto is peace, law, and order (shame shame's) but, with God's blessing, said he, if the law does not right us, we will have an eye for an eye, a tooth for a tooth, man for man, and blood for blood". He was in the act of explaining the tithe slaughter at Rathcormac, when the whole platform gave way with a tremendous crash, and a boy of about thirteen years of age, was severely, but not dangerously injured. When the platform tumbled, Mr. O'Connor, in the words of the press, "sprang with the agility of lightening upon a plank, which was attached edgeways to the uprights. Such, said he, will be the fall of both Whig and Tory governments." Mr O'Connor was then requested by the chairman to proceed to rising ground, where the meeting was continued. Now, he said," I am on God's footstool, upon man's inheritance, which won't give way [cheers].   A thought strikes me that you are poor, and I will tell you the reason why, and why poor laws are necessary. It is because you have about one hundred and thirty master potters who annually share about one million's worth of your labour {cheers & true]. Now, £250,000 would be more than ample for risk and speculation, and the remaining £750,000 would make you independent of the three devil kings at Somerset House.i.e.the three poor law commissioners in London." (more cheers).

Mr. George Salt, in moving the second resolution said that, "the resolution he had to propose embraced many points but only one principle, and that was Universal Suffrage. The others would be good in their way, and would be sure to follow. Therefore, keep to the suffrage, and let nothing divert you from your course". [more cheers]. Mr. Kelsey of Newcastle, in seconding the resolution, said "the five great principles were inherent in the constitution. The Barons had forced Magna Carta from King John, and were they so degenerate that they could not force the People's Charter from the oppressors of the present day.

The O'Connor who addressed the meeting, was Feargus O'Connor, an Irishman, a well known Chartist, and an Irish barrister turned politician. He represented Cork in parliament, but he was unseated for lacking an adequate property qualification. He did later become an MP for Nottingham.

In 1842 there was a huge procession organised in London which marched on the House of Commons. It extended for two miles and carried a petition containing nearly three and a half million signatures on six miles of paper. The petition was carried into the house and strewn on the floor. On the same day, in the House, Macaulay said: "*Universal suffrage would be fatal to all the purposes for which government exists, and for which aristocracies and all other things exist, and it is utterly incompatible with the very existence of civilisation. I conceive that civilisation rests upon the security of property*".

In 1824/25 the government had partially yielded to pressure and reluctantly legalised the formation of trade unions, but this charter was constantly being challenged in the courts, resulting in various judgments and continuing dissatisfaction among the workers and renewed demand for universal franchise.

After the devastating strike in 1836 the union was destroyed and bankrupt. In 1843 William Evans, a Welshman and an idealist came to the area and set about reorganising the union into branches in each of the six towns, and a central co-ordinating committee who would determine policy. The continuing intention was to rid the trade of the loathed annual hiring practice, and to substitute this for a month's notice on either side; also the equally objectional payment by 'good from oven' and to replace it with good from hand.

The first strike had been settled ostensibly by arbitration but in effect by total subjugation of the operatives, but as a gesture from the manufacturers, they temporarily guaranteed the worker sixteen days work every month, which meant that the operative and his family need starve only half the time instead of all the time in lay-offs - still of course without right of employment elsewhere. The 'good from oven' was in theory a penalty for bad workmanship for which the potter could be legitimately penalised, but in practice unscrupulous manufacturers attributed all faults to the potter and in some cases even decided on an arbitrary percentage to apply to his earnings for supposedly faulty work.

Evans set about convincing the operatives that betterment for the workers and those unemployed could only be achieved by a scheme of selective emigration, which would relieve unemployment, and at the same time make the demand for labour more competitive. In 1844 he formed the Potteries Joint Stock Emigration Society with the object of purchasing over a period of ten years 12,000 acres of land in Wisconsin in the United States, the area to be divided into plots of twenty acres on which living accommodation would be built until the whole area was exhausted, when more land would be purchased. The lucky emigrants would be chosen by ballot from those who lost their employment and as the scheme progressed, scarcity of labour at home would enable bargaining pressure to benefit those left behind. It was proposed to raise £5,000 initially in £1 shares - and now we come to the origin of the half crown levy - the share was to be paid for by eight consecutive levies each of half a crown.

Evans also founded a newspaper in which members could air their views and state their grievances. It was called *The Potter's Examiner* and the hope was that it would contribute £100 profit per annum to the emigration fund but alas this proved to be wishful thinking.

New union rules were drafted which incorporated one which commanded interest in the emigration scheme, which would, Evans hoped, ensure the union's ultimate success.

COMMANDMENTS OF THE UNION.
(1) Though shalt not have any scheme but the emigration scheme.
(2) Though shall not propose anyone to become a member who is not a potter
(3) Thou shall not treat the emigration scheme as vain, for the union is determined to carry it out and will not hold them guiltless who refuseth to assist.
(4) Remember that thou attend the duties of the lodge on such lodge nights. In the daytime thou shalt labour and do all that thou hast to do, but on lodge night thy brethren demand thy presence.
(5) Be honourable and punctual in thy union payments, that the days may be long where the brethren of the emigration society intend to send thee.
(6) Thou shalt not murder thyself by doing the work of two men.
(7) Thou shall not work the allowance system for it is a direct robbery of thy labour.
(8) Thou shalt not introduce machinery, nor any invention that will supersede labour, for surely as thou dost evil will come upon thee.
(9) Thou shalt not mistrust, abuse, nor bear false witness against thy brethren.
(10) Thou shalt not covet to toil and sweat fourteen hours per day as heretofore amongst poison and dust, for it is more than thy physical energies can sustain and it is certain to break down thy constitution and bring upon thee old age.

Specific payments were quoted as: Those who make a just and lawful stand for an advance in wages to be paid 10/- per week as long as he is out. 3/- per week for his wife, if married, and if she does not work, For every child under twelve. 2/- per week No man to receive more than 18/-

The Potters' Examiner regularly gave prominence to payment by "truck" which, although the 1831 Truck Act was already in existence, was still rife since there were few inspectors to enforce it. Workers were encouraged to give instances through the paper to draw attention to firms who transgressed, and the following are examples:

MORE TRUCKERY AND TRICKERY

"To the Editor of The Potters' Examiner & Workman's Advocate.

BURSLEM. May 20th 1844.

Sir, Believing that you are glad at any time to show up the bad practices that are being practiced by masters towards their workmen, I take the liberty of informing you of the following, hoping you will make them public, through the medium of that valuable paper The Examiner.

The class of individuals to whom I allude are the china toy manufacturers; a class that have lately become extensive. These masters will sometimes tell their workforce that they have got very large orders, and that they want them to work as hard and as they can.

The men, glad to benefit themselves as well as their employers, make worse than slaves of themselves, and then when pay day comes, the master will often tell them that he shall not pay them the whole of their earnings, for he is expecting a tradesman to call, who deals in cloth,and that he intends to pay them in cloth. I have known cases where men have received only one half of their hard earnings on the pay night, the other half to be left until the cloth man may call.

I believe sir, that you will think with me, that this is a most abominable system that is being practiced by many masters, not only in Burslem, but in Hanley and other parts of the Potteries; and I will tell you of two or three cases where workmen have had their wages stopped to the amount of from five shillings to ten shillings per week,for months, for cloth which they have not seen, and not only does the master take an advantage of them in this way, but, when he has pushed them forward to make slaves of themselves, he turns upon them and tells them that if they can get such wages as that, they can work for less prices, and consequently he lowers their prices.

By showing up these things in your next week's paper, in the best manner you think proper, you will much oblige.

A MANY OF THE SUFFERERS.

P.S. If this exposure should not be sufficient to deter these masters from acting in this manner, I will furnish you with the names of some of them that act in such a manner to their workpeople, together with some facts that you would scarcely credit".

A pamphlet, printed by Brougham of the Market place was issued in 1830 or 1831, whether from personal interest or on behalf of others, but it gave cases of workmen in the potteries who were suffering from this iniquitous practice:

"Jacob Wood of Burslem deposeth that he has worked several months for a truck master and that during that time his wages have not averaged more than twelve shillings per week, and during that time he has not received more than five pounds in money, the rest has been in truck, and further, he has been compelled to pay his rent in truck, not having the ability to pay in money".

"Jos Sherratt of Hot Lane, potter, deposeth that he has worked at the manufactury of Messrs Job and John Jackson of Burslem, who have paid him for his labour for the most part in goods. That for the last six weeks he has not received any money, but has been paid entirely in goods which have been charged at considerably more than the retail prices of the shopkeepers, and that he was obliged frequently to dispose of the goods he received at a very great loss to pay his rent and taxes. Cheese and bacon, thus forced upon him, were often of a quality scarcely eatable. The cheese having been much devoured and damaged by rats. The bacon had to be thrown away. Before he worked for Messrs Jackson, he had been employed by Messrs R and J Clews of Cobridge, who had also paid him in goods. He had there bad beef served out to him at 8d per pound which he could have purchased for 3d in the market. Five and a half pounds of beef was allocated to him which, when separated out, had three and three quarter pounds of bone. Onions forced on the men for payment, for which Jos. received his share, were such a quality that he threw them away as being unfit to eat".

"Thomas Bennett, Druggist of Burslem, deposeth and saith, that men in the employ of truck masters come into his shop for the purpose of obtaining medical relief, and one, not being able to pay for the same in money, was obliged to bring flour to the amount which he stated he had received from his master".

Bankrupt stock of Birmingham jewellery was known to have been used in lieu of coin, even to operatives on short time and hungry. Brooches were valued as half a crown, when they could be bought in Birmingham at one and sixpence a dozen. The practice was carried on long after it had been prohibited by law, so blatantly that some pottery workers wrote to the Head Constable of Burslem and complained, which did result in some manufacturers being taken to court and fined. In some areas, payment before the Truck Act was by what were known as 'Tommy Notes' issued by the employer, stating the employees earnings which entitled him or her to equal value in goods, usually from a specified shop, but the practice does not seem to have been prevalent in the Potteries.

The canal boatmen were evidently the source of some items which were used by unscrupulous employers, resulting in the following satirical verse:

> For Truck's the thing,the only thing
> The order of the day
> If it the boatmen did not bring
> We ne'er could pay our way

> Now thirteen pence I have received
> For many a yard of print
> From women I have deceived

> I gave but ten pence for the same
> As you have often heard
> And that's the way we play the game
> So take it as my word

There was a mass meeting on the racecourse in 1830 when 30,000 workers attended and demanded the practice be made illegal, which it was in 1831. One man at the meeting said he had been paid with a parrot in a cage and a pistol; another had been paid with an old suit.

The initial response to the emigration project was disappointing; only 400 applied for a share and of these a number failed to pay more than one or two of the levies and then lost interest, and with contributions from other sources the sum achieved could only support the purchase of 4,000 acres. The scheme went ahead nevertheless and a Land Steward, a Deputy and a Conductor were chosen to become the pilgrim fathers, and following farewell celebrations which they attended in each of the six towns, these pioneers, along with their families, eleven in all, departed for Liverpool and the Promised Land in February 1846.

It was subsequently thought wise to form an Estate Committee to follow and approve the work of the "Land Officers". One member was to be chosen from each branch, eleven in all, and the cost of this was to be met by a levy of 3d per week from all union members for twelve weeks.

News was received that the Land Officers had arrived after six weeks on the sea. They had seen land they considered suitable, but there were others there who coveted the same land, consequently they were desperate for cash if they were to secure the land of their choice. Appeals were made for half the regular contributions to union funds to be allocated to the Emigration Society, in addition to the separate levies being made. The result was that by now approximately one tenth of the potter's income was being asked for, and the many members who had no interest in pioneering were feeling that genuine union activity was being sacrificed along with their money. However a draft was drawn for £600 and this was sent.

A rift then developed with the Pottery Pressers attacking the scheme promoters, surprisingly not with regard to the principle but with emigration being confined to America, and they broke away to start their own scheme which embraced all British Colonies, and furthermore they thought the scheme should be adopted by a National Union. The chaos this caused led the union to conclude that too much emphasis in the branches was given to the groups representing individual skills. Reorganisation followed allowing anyone connected with the trade to join, and the name was changed to The Potters General Union.

Early in 1847 news came that 1,200 acres of land had been purchased, and Mother Burslem's sons began mentally to visualise a forthcoming harvest from the New World's bounty. Now was the time to activate the Estate Committee and this was reconstituted to comprise all men who were unemployed. Parties similar to those given to the pioneer Land Officers were given throughout the district and along with their families, forty in all, the officers were given a musical send off by canal barge to Liverpool and the great adventure.

The analogy to the biblical story of the promised land in the Old Testament must have provided the seed of another bright idea, since it was now proposed to raise £250 to establish a mutual trading project by the issue of 1,000 5/- shares, and from this project it was expected an annual profit of £1,750 which would benefit the emigration fund; but the fate of the union was sealed before this could come about. The 1847 Martinmas notice from the manufacturers included a demand for a reduction in wages and a continuation of all previous practices; a union which had decimated its resources was in no condition to offer any serious opposition!

News came from America that the Land Officers and the Estate Committee were at loggerheads, and the local traders were denying them credit. This was the end of a dream for the union and the beginning of a long period in the wilderness; death of a potentially remunerative co-operative; the shut down of the printing press; and isolation for those who had gone to prepare the way for others waiting patiently for entry to the promised land. At least they had a dream which could have become a reality, unlike the manufacturers whose constant practice was to reduce wages followed by reduced selling price, followed by bankruptcy, with the sequence rarely becoming an object lesson.

In 1845 a meeting of the Chamber of Trade had been called once more to try to stabilise prices and this came to the knowledge of the union, who despite the ignominy they had suffered from the end of one dream, at least had the wisdom to offer participation in another proposal which might improve their lot, as the following correspondence will indicate:

"We, the Central Committee of the United Branches of Operatives, having heard, with much regret, that in your recent praiseworthy efforts to put an advance on selling prices of the staple manufacture of this district you have been somewhat opposed by one or two of the cheap-labour traffickers of the district, beg to call your attention to the following resolution passed by us, and which we pledge ourselves to carry into practical operation: Resolved, That we the Central Committee, acting by the instructions of and in behalf of the operatives of these districts, pledge ourselves to assist by all legal and moral means the combination of potting manufacturers entitled the Chamber of Commerce, in their present endeavour to put an advance on the selling prices of their ware, believing as we do, that such endeavour is founded on the desire to give a fair and equitable price for the potting industry, and that those who oppose the same are bad in motive and foolishly and mischievously avaricious in practice".

No. 11.   Vol. 2.   SATURDAY, AUGUST 10TH, 1844.   *Price One Penny*

CHAPTER EIGHTEEN: Longport

Growth of Longport. Building of St.Pauls.

Longport, previously known as Longbridge, derived its name from the stepping stones over an extensive marshy area created partly by mining subsidence but mostly by the Fowlea Brook which rises near Harecastle and flows through Longport to Etruria and thence to the Trent at Stoke. The change of name to Longport obviously came about with the arrival of the canal, and the large basin constructed for arriving and departing canal traffic.

The water covered a large area and was used for boating and in recent times has been converted into a man made lake in the centre of parkland. In the 19th century, on Lifeboat Saturday, the Burslem Boat Committee hired it for their Lifeboat Aid Fund effort, charging sixpence for trips on the water, and providing life jackets for the passengers. Near this area and part of Longport is Trubshaw Cross, so called from an ancient cross which stood at the junction of Newcastle Road and what was originally the toll road to Tunstall. The cross, with the exception of the base, disappeared and a handsome lamppost replaced it, but that in turn was made redundant and a twelve foot high stone cross, a replica of an old cross, but looking rather modern, was presented to the borough by Mr Percy Adams F.S.A.

The construction of the canal helped to drain the area and facilitated the building of wharves, which in turn attracted the growth of factories and housing, eventually creating an urban and industrial area large enough to become a separate parish. With the growth of population there was pressure for the parish to have a separate church and Mr William Adams of Cobridge Hall offered land, extending over two or three acres at Dale Hall, midway between Longport and Burslem, as a free gift for the erection of a church. There were many who thought that the new church should be built in Burslem itself, having in mind that Burslem could eventually become the cathedral city of Burslem, the birthplace of an industry that took the world by storm. Many in later generations would visit the place where it all began! One individual's views on the proposal were made public:

"PROPOSED NEW CHURCH AT BURSLEM

The following observations as to the most proper situation for a new church are submitted to the candid consideration of the parishioners.

There is a church in Burslem capable of holding more than one tenth of the population of the town, and the building of another church then for fifteen hundred persons would give accommodation to one third of the mere population of the town and leave all the rest of the inhabitants of the parish, amounting to four or five thousand, just as distant from a church as they now are. The site offered by Mr Adams on the brow of the hill opposite Dale Hall is within a quarter of a mile to the principal part of the town of Burslem, and would likewise accommodate fifteen hundred of the more distant inhabitants of Longport, Brown Hills, &c, who must otherwise have double or treble the distance to come to church as they have now. The church erected at Dale Hall by taking in the population of Longport &c, as well as many townspeople, would vacate a considerable number of pews in the old church and afford means of accommodating the poor with free seating therein. As to any benefit which the situation might give Mr Adams by enhancing the value of his adjoining land, such argument against the site is the very worst in the world, and the offer of two acres of land for a burial ground is a liberal concession by Mr Adams for any adventitious value he may derive. The principle of bringing home church accommodation to people's doors, however specious in theory, is practically impossible to any great extent, as also at variance with the adage (nearer to church &c.&c.) and at any rate does not impugn this serious and incontrovertible truth that; "the clergyman not the church will attract a congregation." 13th May 1824".

This impressive document must have swung opinion in favour of Dale Hall, and with the church commissioners offering the bulk of the money, preparations went ahead to build at a a cost of £14,000, of which the parish contribution was to be £2,000, hopefully by voluntary subscriptions, but unfortunately £500 short at the settlement date. A proposition to impose a rate to raise the shortage was, according to Scarratt, a decidedly unpopular proposal.

The original St Pauls

The current St Pauls

Arrangements were made for the laying of the foundation stone on 24th June 1828 and was organised on the scale of a royal visit. It was propitious that the day dawned with the sun shining on the righteous. The procession started from the Market Square and already at eight o'clock in the morning, a crowd of spectators had gathered to witness the arrival of those taking part in the ceremony. At nine o'clock, the Bishop of Lichfield and Coventry arrived, and the parade started down Newcastle Street.

Heading the procession were two constables followed by the Town Crier; then two men carrying flags, preceding the Longport Band. These were followed by the Parish Clerk, behind him Boys and Girls (students and choristers carrying the flag of the National School), and flanked by two constables. Next came the Band of the Freemasons of the St Martins Lodge; then the Chief Constable, flanked by the Churchwardens, in turn followed by the Lord Bishop with the Rector of St John's, also with a constable on either side. Next came the patron, William Adams, and behind him the Architect and the Contractor, again with constable escort; and towards the rear, *the Church Committee, followed by Subscribers, Another Band, Invited Visitors, and Clergy from other parishes.* The whole procession moved forward in an impressive display of sight and sound, with the first bodies well into Newcastle Street before the rear had left the Market Square. Newcastle Street was lined with spectators, the Staffordshire Advertiser said there were quite 15,000 to witness the ceremony, while the bells of St John's made their debut filling the air with joyful peals, being newly cast and hung.

One of the principal Free Masons offered the silver trowel to the Bishop. The Bishop duly performed his duty as the stone was lowered into position. In its hollow centre he placed a glass case made by Davenport's containing a few coins and other valuables. A brass plate on the stone engraved in Latin recorded the occasion. Translated this read:

The foundation stone of this Parochial Chapel, dedicated to St. Paul,
erected partly by National Grant and partly by Private Contributions, was laid by
The honourable and Right Reverend Henry Ryder D.D.
Lord Bishop of Lichfield & Coventry
In the auspicious reign of George the Fourth
On the twenty fourth day of June In the year of Redemption 1828
The glory be to God, The Honour to our Country

E Whieldon. Rector.	E. Wood. Chief Constable
W. Adams. Patron	Churchwardens
	L. H. Rhead. J. Clews.
	T. Weatherby. T. Hancock

L. Vulliamy. Architect

The press recorded that:

"......after laying the stone His Lordship implored the Divine Blessing on the undertaking in a most devout and impressive manner, and afterwards addressed the persons around, congratulating them on this auspicious beginning and hoping the lively interest now shown was but a happy preface to great future propensity. The 100th psalm was then sung with considerable effect, accompanied by the band. The Reverend Edward Whieldon, the Rector, presented His Lordship with the Silver Trowel as a small mark of Burslem's high regard for his estimable character, and the great zeal and unwearied exertions he had long manifested to get a grant from the Commissioners for the new church. He expressed his happiness at the consummation of their wishes, "for which they were so much indebted to His Lordship, and his hope that His Lordship might live to see the building completed; to hear its walls resound with the Gospel Truth, and to witness numerous congregations taught its divine precepts." The Reverend Gentleman responding, "avowed his hearty wish that thousands of happy souls might, through its influence, be conducted to the Heavenly Jerusalem".

The trowel was engraved with wording recording the occasion, and the Bishop accepting said "he took it as a mark of the regard from his kind flock, who were very welcome to the humble service which he had done on their behalf which had been barely his duty to them, and much less than his duty to his Maker. The satisfaction he now felt by the appearances around him, and the attention shown, were such that few events in his life had given him greater pleasure, or were likely to leave a more lasting impression on his mind." So powerful did the address of the esteemed Rector, and the reply of the worthy Bishop affect the persons around, that they begged His Lordship would give them permission, although perhaps not customary on such an occasion, to give vent to their feelings in three hearty cheers.

At the conclusion of the ceremony the procession reformed to make its way back to the Town Hall, there to partake of a most sumptuous public breakfast, prepared by Mr Pepper of the Leopard Inn. His Lordship sat down to the meal accompanied by thirty clergy from nearby parishes, a number of neighbouring gentry, and most of the respectable inhabitants of the town. So full was the spacious room that upwards of seventy gentlemen were obliged to seek accommodation in the inn. The Revd. Edward Whieldon, on proposing the health of the Bishop, thanked His Lordship for his condescension in acceding to the wishes of the inhabitants of the town. The company all standing raised their glasses and drank. His Lordship in reply, expressed his obligation to them for the honour and the high satisfaction he felt on this occasion, and hoped it would not be the last time he would have the pleasure of coming amongst them, while he would always be anxious for their welfare and prosperity.

After dining the Bishop left, perhaps wisely, but in any case of necessity since he had another appointment in Derby in the afternoon. The celebration at the Town Hall however continued, with F. Twemlow Esq. proposing the health of the Rector and the Clergy of the diocese. This was followed by H.H. Williamson Esq. who proposed the health of the Chief Constable of Burslem. The Revd. W. Wildig, the Rector of Norton, toasted the health of Lewis Vulliamy, the Architect, and then came the turn of others to be recipients of the company's good will: Enoch Wood and family, John Davenport and family, and other most respectable gentlemen followed in sequence up to the retirement of the Rector, due it was said to temporary indisposition. Fortunately the Revd. B. Marsden was on hand and able to be upstanding and officiate in the Rector's absence and, perhaps filled with the spirit of the occasion, this gentleman was said to have "gratified the company with an eloquent address". This was followed by an equally eloquent address from Enoch Wood on the transformation in Burslem in his lifetime. The whole proceedings were said to have lasted an unusual length of time for a breakfast!

The Bishop survived, and accepted an invitation to consecrate the church, but there is no record of a repeat of this sumptuous breakfast, even though two and a half years had elapsed. The consecration took place on 20th January 1831 and the Revd.Thomas Nunn MA was appointed the first minister. According to William Machin, a local resident, the first burial in the churchyard was that of a Mr Pointon, an earthenware manufacturer of Burslem, on 15th June 1831. The church was built in Hollington stone and had an imposing exterior. The tower was 115 feet high with octagonal turrets and ribbed pinnacles, but unlike St John's it only had one bell. Inside it had excellent window light and a smooth stone floor, with under-floor heating. Around the perimeter of the grounds was a stone breast wall with handsome iron railings and four entrances with folding iron gates - all provided with a £1000 gift from market toll income.

Built in a more prosperous time than the parish church of St John, and with more choice of materials available, its memorials and furnishings were on a grander scale. Two memorials of note flanked the communion table. One in black and white marble was to Joseph Stubbs of Longport, who, so his memorial said, *"died on the thirty-first of October 1838 from haemorrhage following an operation"*. The other memorial was to Henry Davenport, a member of the family who were by far the largest employers in Longport, long vanished and hardly remembered today except by discerning collectors of their hand painted wares. The memorial comprised a marble tablet on a stone mount, with the armorial arms of the family at its head. Henry met a tragic death whilst hunting and his horse failed to clear a wall.

There was a beautiful monument on the south wall inscribed *"To the memory of Lieutenant Henry Nelson Poole of the Royal Navy, who died at sea in the Persian Gulf in command of the East India Company's Sloop of War 'The Clive' on the 10th June 1837"*. It bore the inscription *"This monument was erected by his brother officers as a testimonial of their respect of his public worth and private character"*. Henry's father was instrumental in reducing tension in the community during the food shortages of the Napoleonic wars.

The church had an organ which is said to have cost a thousand pounds, and which at a later date was either rebuilt or replaced, since, according to Shaw, in 1835 an upper gallery was removed to make way for an organ built by Bewcher and Fleetwood of Liverpool, which in size and tone was not excelled in the

County. The church also had a beautiful pulpit in alabaster and oak which was installed to commemorate the missions held in the parish by the Rev. W. H. Hay Aitkin in 1885. The Vicar at this time would be the Revd Lovelace Stamer (later the Revd. Sir Lovelace T Stamer, Archdeacon of Stoke). His curate, H.V. Stuart, himself subsequently went to Stoke and later became Dean of Carlisle.

To seek the church today is to seek in vain, since it has long since been demolished. As you approach the site where it stood you will notice the solid stone wall which surrounded the churchyard, but the original handsome metal railings which surmounted them, and the entrance gates, have vanished, crudely removed to be converted to bullets and bombs in the last war; ironically, it is sad to think, some of the bombs may have helped to demolish Dresden cathedral and the centre of that city where Enoch Wood's gift to the King of Saxony rested in the museum. The notice boards at the entrance to the site have been left to serve the modest modern substitute for St. Paul's situated in a corner of the grounds. You may think that the building you are seeking must have been a victim of the wartime blitz; but no it was the result again of Burslem miners below, removing coal for the potters above - and not only Burslem but also the Potteries lost the nucleus of a potential cathedral city.

The rectory was originally Brindley's house which stood in spacious grounds. The house was also demolished, presumably it suffered from the same mining subsidence . A new rectory was built in Newcastle Street, but when the new St Paul's was built with a rectory alongside, the house in Newcastle Street was dispensed with and is now business premises.

The original entrance gate and lamp at the rear of St Paul's

The interior of the now
demolished Holy Trinity church

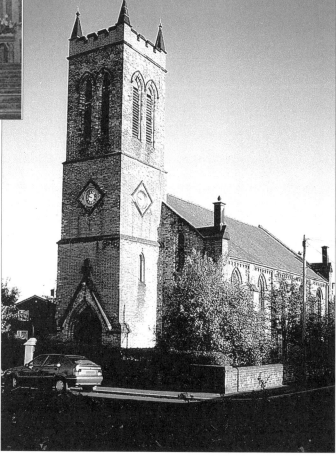

A recent photograph of Christ
Church at Cobridge

CHAPTER NINETEEN: Churches

Holy Trinity Church Sneyd. Christ Church Cobridge. Catholicism in Burslem.
Missionary churches. The Salvation Army.

Twenty years after the dedication of St. Paul's church, the foundation stone was laid for another Presbyterian church in the parish of Sneyd, to the east of Burslem town. This was the church of the Holy Trinity. The construction commenced on 8th July 1851 to the design of the architect who was responsible for the design of the new town hall in the Market Place. The church was not so large as St Paul's. Its cost has been variously given as both £2000 and £5000. It was constructed of stone in Gothic style with a spire and one bell, and was to seat 480 adults and 120 children, all the seats to be free.

The ceremony for the laying of the foundation stone commenced with a breakfast attended by some 150 people at the National School Room, which was adjacent to the parish church. The chairman was the Reverend Charles Herbert, Rector of Burslem and Rural Dean. He was supported by Smith Child Esq. MP, Elizah Hughes Esq, the Chief Bailiff and invited guests. The company was addressed by Smith Child Esq. following which the whole party, accompanied by *"a band of music"* went in procession to the site.

In the now customary tradition the trowel was a work of art. The handle was in parian and the blade in china, the two joined with a silver mount. The blade had a rim of silver and the whole was beautifully ornamented by Alcock's of the Hill Pottery, who made and gave it, and at the conclusion of the ceremony, on behalf of the committee, it was presented to Smith Child Esq. by Elizah Hughes Esq. Below the foundation stone, in a cavity, was placed a vase containing coins of the reign, together with an account of the day on which the stone was laid. A brass plate covering the stone bore the following inscription:

The corner stone of this church, founded for the district of Sneyd, and intended to be dedicated to the Holy Trinity, was laid on the eighth of July 1851 by Smith Child Esq. one of the representatives for the northern district of this county in Parliament.

John Beaumont. Incumbent.
G.T. Robinson. Architect of Wolverhampton.
S & G Holme. Contractors of Liverpool.

"Faveat operi Deus"
In the faith of Jesus Christ and the memory of the Holy Trinity
we place this statue in the name of Jehovah, God the Father.
God the Son, and God The Holy Ghost".

After the concluding prayers the National Anthem was read with the addition of these two verses:

Against Rome's usurping hand
Uphold your favourite land
God save the Queen
From subtle Jesuit's blow
From Romanising foe
God save the Queen

May we protesting stand
With serried shield a band
Around our Queen
Albert will never flinch
Nor Commons bate an inch
God save the Queen

The Incumbent's living in 1882 was listed as £160 and was in the gift of the Bishop, while that of Cobridge church in the same year was £350 and the gift of the Rector of Burslem. The Sneyd parishioners were evidently unswerving in the conduct of their faith, since in 1875 they called a public meeting in response to attempts being made at the time to rewrite the Common Book of Prayer, to which they were averse. They also solicited for membership of the English Church Union, and formed the Holy Trinity Parochial Association to emphasise their adherence to the church's current articles of faith.

An outstanding feature of the church was said to be a beautiful memorial of the Resurrection over the chancel arch, the work of Mr F. Rhead of Stoke in 1891. A Vestry and Lady Chapel were added in 1895, and in 1911-1913 a Mosaic floor was laid.

A bomb fell nearby during the Second World War and some stained glass was broken; nevertheless the church celebrated its centenary in 1952, and continued in use until 1956. It appears then to have suffered a fracture in its foundations from the curse of mining, perhaps accentuated by bombing, and finally suffered the same fate as St Paul's.

One of the stained glass windows from the church is said to be in the Mission Chapel of St. Andrew's built in 1908 in the Hamil to seat 250 worshippers, and this building still stands.

In 1839, under the jurisdiction of St John's, Christ Church was built in the parish of Cobridge as a mission church. Little is recorded of its founding ceremony, perhaps it

An early engraving of Cobridge church

was a simple ceremony for a less pretentious church than Holy Trinity. The Reverend Edward Whieldon was Rector of Burslem at the time and played a major role in the church's conception and fulfilment. The value to the incumbent was £350, which when compared with that of the Holy Trinity, the larger of the two churches, seems anomalous; the Rev Whieldon appears to have either been a man of means, or the finances of the parent church were in a very healthy state - maybe on both counts. It became difficult in later years for less wealthy rectors of St Johns to meet the cost of the Cobridge church.

The original cost of the building according to John Ward was £1500 and it was to seat 550 persons, of which 360 seats were to be free. The structure was in a pale yellow brick and it had a square tower with stone pinnacles. There was no clock in the tower originally, but at a later date following requests from the inhabitants of Cobridge to the Burslem Board for a public clock, one was installed in the tower, presumably at the expense of the town. Funds for the building were donated from St John's; £500 came from the Diocesan Church Building Society and £400 from the Incorporated Society. In 1842 it had to be enlarged, and Cobridge became a separate parish in 1845.

Despite the mining problem, the church still stands in a square, much as it must have done originally, while all around is changing from the grime covered area of the industrial revolution when houses were cheek by jowl with the belching pottery ovens.

There appears to have been a further mission attached to St Johns, since one is mentioned as being in the Sytch in 1894, but this like many other buildings has vanished.

In the early industrial era of Burslem and the adjoining towns, the Catholic fraternity appear to have been very much in a minority, and the church at Cobridge a rarity, There have been several churches on this site, the first about 1223 presumably carrying the name of St Peter. In 1780 work commenced on demolition and replacement of the existing church. This however was a dangerous time; Parliament gave equality in treatment to catholics after decades of repression, then an act renewed the acrimony and culminated in the Gordon riots.

There must have been many anxious moments, since Burslem had previously shown its antipathy to Catholicism against the Biddulphs property on the Grange. But the church survived and prospered, so much so that in 1882 it was enlarged and a new altar supplied by Messrs Harrison & son of Dublin, depicting the Last Supper on the front. Over the altar was a stained glass window, the gift of Mr F. Sutton, a former parishioner and this was said to have cost £400. Another window in the Chapel of The Sacred Heart was a gift from the Bill family. A pulpit was presented by Mr. R. Emery, a manufacturer of colours for the pottery trade in Cobridge and a member of a long standing catholic family. Although apparently much money was lavished on beautifying this church, it was demolished and the present one built in 1936/37 - outside the intended period of this book. No doubt, like most large buildings in Burslem the church suffered from mining subsidence.

It is interesting that on a street map of 1889 there is shown a Roman Catholic Church with a narrow entrance to it off Packhorse Lane, behind where the new church now stands in Hall Street. One side is shown abutting a factory wall and one side in Spens Street. It was probably a mission church administered from Cobridge until a new church was built in Hall Street in 1927. In contrast with the one at Cobridge, the Hall Street church is predominant in its position at the peak of Burslem, and worthy of mention for its strange but attractive architecture, which will be greatly enhanced when its surroundings are improved.

All denominations seemed to have had mission churches. St John's main one was of course at Cobridge until Cobridge became a separate parish. The Wesleyans had missions at Longport, Middleport, Sneyd, Stanfield and Greenhead, and in addition there were the chapels belonging to the breakaway groups. Ward mentions a Baptist chapel in High Street with a graveyard, but this was sold in 1875 to the Ragged School. Both street and building have now gone along with the graveyard. The Baptists also built a tabernacle in Liverpool Road, or Westport Road as it is today, but this also has vanished. The Salvation Army at the end of the 19th century had two citadels, one in Brindley Street and one in Hill Street.

There was an interesting census of capacity and attendance of all the places of worship in 1881, when the population of Burslem had risen to 26,521:

	Accom.	Morn	Aft	Total
Saint John's	800	294	292	586
Saint Paul's	1200	400	450	850
St.Pauls Mission.	180		79	79
Christ Church, Cobridge	250	137	143	280
Holy Trinity Sneyd	550	87	147	234
Wesleyan (Swan Bank)	900	449	518	967
Wesleyan (Sneyd)	74	78	152	230
Wesleyan (Longport)	500	78	103	181
Wesleyan (Middleport)	200	122	168	290
Wesleyan (Stanfield)	80	50	50	100
Wesleyan. (Sneyd Green)	100	38	56	94
Greenhead Mission	60	42	42	84
Methodist (Hill Top)	900	311	467	778
Methodist (Ebenezer)	230	100	194	294
Methodist (Bethel)	700	216	296	512
Methodist (Cobridge)	200	120	137	257
Methodist (Dalehall)	300	60	120	180
Primitive Methodism (Clowes)	750	245	284	529
Primitive Methodism (Hot Lane)	230	127	165	292
Primitive Methodism (Albion Street)	200	118	103	221
Congregational (Queen Street)	350	119	151	270
Congregational (Dalehall)	150		63	63
Roman Catholic Cobridge	600	568	590	1158
Baptists	400	78	95	173
Christian Brothers	50	39	39	78

The last entry it will be noticed is Christian Brothers of whom it would seem no mention is made elsewhere in reference to Burslem.

The River Trent passing the Duke of Sutherland's Trentham Hall, carrying with it an unwelcome effluent from the Potteries towns

NORTH STAFFORDSHIRE RAILWAY.—

TRENTHAM TRAINS.—EXTRA TRAINS, to and from TRENTHAM, will run on STOKE WAKES' THURSDAY, August 8th, from Harecastle, Burslem, Etruria, Newcastle, Stoke, Longton, Stone, and Barlaston, as under, at One Fare for the Double Journey :—

Harecastle, at 12 50 p.m. ; returning from Trentham at 9 0 p.m.

Burslem, at 9 0, 10 10, and 11 0 a.m., 12 0 noon, 1 0, 2 0, and 3 0 p.m

Etruria, at 9 5, 10 15, and 11 5 a.m., 12 5, 1 5, 2 5, and 3 5 p.m.

Stoke, at 9 10, 10 25, and 11 10 a.m, 12 10, 1 15, 2 10, and 3 25 p.m.

Newcastle, at 8 45 and 11 45 a.m., and 3 15 p.m., and also by Ordinary Trains at 9 40, 10 35, and 11 15 a.m., and 12 40 and 2 30 p.m.

Longton, at 9 0 and 11 0 a.m., 12 0 noon, 2 0 and 3 10 p.m., and by Ordinary Trains at 10 5 a.m., and 1 0 p.m.

Stone, at 11 35 a.m., and 1 35 p.m.. and Barlaston at 11 45 a.m.. and 1 45 p.m. : returning at 8 15 and 9 45 p.m.

Trains will leave Trentham, for Stoke, Longton, Newcastle, Etruria, and Burslem every quarter of an hour, commencing from five o'clock up to half-past ten at night.

J. C. FORSYTH.

Stoke, July, 1861.

Trains for Trentham at the time of the Stoke Wakes. A day at Trentham was a great outing for Burslem children

CHAPTER TWENTY: Public services

Sanitation & the Duke at Trentham. Water. Lighting. The post. Purchase of the Gas Company.
Annual wake at Trentham

The lack of sanitation in Burslem was probably little different from that of many other midland towns where growth in population had outpaced services. On the top side of Market Place there was one privy serving six shops, and at least one of these establishments was selling food. In the same year there was a serious outbreak of cholera - the day of its curtailment was declared a day of thanksgiving and all shops and businesses were closed.

In 1851 the Board of Health took the first steps to deal with the problem by appointing a consultant surveyor at a cost of three guineas per day plus travelling expenses. He was to carry out a survey and prepare plans for a comprehensive sewage system.

The Board gave consideration to the type of sanitary fixtures to adopt along with the sewage disposal system. The surveyor said the cost per house for a water closet was £1. 1 0 and rents were usually increased by 2/3d per year for the improvement, but all the council members were not agreed on water closets. One favoured Morrels dry ash system and said one of these had been installed in Villa Road and given satisfaction. The cost would be 55/- and the construction cost £5. Another member of the board said he was opposed to the indiscriminate adoption of water closets since the system was only a theory and was known to have failed. Some of the members preferred duckets. Another said that until it was decided which to adopt they should still install middens and buy another night soil cart. However by 1858 most of the building permits specified water closets, not necessarily with cisterns, many being flushed with a bucket using waste water.

The preliminary estimate for a sewage disposal system was £20,000, but many changes were made during construction and the final sum was in excess of £30,000. The main sewers were built of local blue brick and it was estimated that 19½ miles of pipework were ultimately laid. For many years there were still areas where nightsoil collection was necessary and in the case of houses which had only one door, this could be carried through the premises in buckets. Household refuse and ashes were similarly moved by horse and cart. The amount of ash was considerable due to coal fires, but much waste would be burnt. The use of individual bins came at a much later date. Farmers were anxious to obtain sewage and would sometimes collect it themselves, but when engrossed with the harvest collection was inconsistent, and individuals had on occasions to take emergency measures, which led to the following warning being posted respecting its transport.

PRIVIES WATER CLOSETS & CESSPOOLS
"Every person emptying, or assisting to empty any privy, water closet, or cesspool shall, during the time of emptying the same, depositing, lay down or place the filth or soil thereof on any part of the highway, thoroughfare, street, square, alley, passage, entry or courtyard, or who shall fail to include the use of disinfectants as may be ordered by the local Board of Health, shall for such offence pay a sum not exceeding 10/-"

Farmers expressed their dislike of night work, and their collection of sewage saved expense on the rates, consequently for a period the bye law was relaxed to allow daytime collection, which disturbed a member of the Board of Health and led him to remark *"it is outrageous to the olfactory senses of passengers through the town and a very serious aberration"*. Burslem was fortunately on the upper reaches of the Fowley Brook, and although the major portion of sewage was deposited on farmland, at least 25% went into the Brook and its tributaries, and passed on to Stoke. Stoke in turn added their contribution and the whole finally arrived via the River Trent at Trentham Hall, the residence of the Duke of Sutherland. Stoke took exception to the contribution from Burslem, and the Duke took exception to the contribution from both. There followed threats of legal action, both Stoke and the Duke simultaneously applied to the courts for abatement of the nuisance, but both were turned down since the judge said that no two identical cases could be taken at the same time, much to the relief of Burslem who hoped the work they had in hand would solve their problems. In 1868 the Duke attempted to get a bill through parliament which stipulated penalties against further nuisance of £100 for the first day and £50 for each succeeding day, but the attempt failed.

The manufacturers, who found the brook equally useful for the disposal of industrial waste, claimed it would ruin them, and *"that while there should not be reckless and unnecessary pollution of our rivers, constraint must be given to the declining state of trade, and the manufacturers cannot afford the cost of rendering the rivers clear, and although black as ink, have never been proved to give off emanations injurious to the health of our people. We must deal tenderly with our manufacturers, if we are not to withdraw our capital and emigrate, to America for instance, where water is plentiful, coal in abundance."*

Obviously the Duke's unfortunate circumstances were of less importance than the death sentence on Burslem. The Duke's mistake was to build his mansion on the banks of the river - none of the manufacturers had!

In 1875, the year the Duke left the district for good, he joined a party from Burslem and other towns on a visit to Leeds, to observe what they had done with purifying plant, after which the Duke said, *"I hope you see what Leeds have done in dealing with sewage and purifying water, for a more stinking lot than my friends in North Staffordshire I cannot conceive and I have got an injunction on my friends and I am going to work on you all".* Many members of the older generation who went to Trentham when young, would have seen the gas bubbling up from the river like a witch's cauldron, with a stench beyond description.

In one last gesture before he left Trentham, the Duke proposed that the whole district should have a common efficient system carrying the sewage to Strongford. He introduced a bill in parliament to this effect, but he was ahead of his time, for his proposal has indeed come to pass and clear water now chuckles as it passes through Trentham. Unfortunately the Duke failed to take into account the staying power given by the Staffordshire Oat Cake compared with the Scotch Haggis.

The extent of the pollution seems to have been an ungrateful response to the Duke considering that each year he opened his grounds to the whole local population during the district wakes. While he was in residence, and possibly to his astonishment, thousands travelled to Trentham by foot, train and canal, many of them from Burslem, all apparently undeterred or immune to a pollution to which they had themselves contributed, but which to them was no doubt one still to be preferred to that which they had left! Despite being driven out of his home, on leaving he turned the other cheek and offered the Potteries as a gift the whole estate in a beneficent, but renounced, gesture.

The following notice in The Staffordshire Advertiser of Saturday 3rd August 1861 is typical of many such notices applying to the annual wake:

"STOKE WAKES. Next week will see the return of the great annual holiday of the Staffordshire Potteries, when notwithstanding the scarcity of work and money, all classes will endeavour to forget commercial and domestic anxieties. Trentham Park continues, and we hope for many years, by favour of the noble owner, will continue to be the pre-eminent attraction of the great mass of the people at the wakes, although certain privileges which formerly existed have been withdrawn, solely we are assured, with a view to securing the safety of those whose special benefit the park on "Trentham Day" is thrown open. One of the greatest treats of this day will be a musical one, for if the weather be favourable the Tonic Sol-faists of the district, to the number of five to six hundred, intend to assemble on the face of one of the slopes in front of the hall, and give an alfresco concert of some fifteen of their charming part songs. Late last night we received a telegram to the effect that M. Blondin would perform at Trentham on Thursday."

Trains were advertised in the paper to run from Burslem hourly from 9am to 3 in the afternoon, and return trains every quarter of an hour from five o'clock till 10.30 at night.

Sympathetic consideration for the Duke has diverted us from the saga of the sewers. The main sewers were connected to large settling tanks which in theory divided the solids from the liquid, leaving only the latter to enter the brook, but at this early stage in sewage treatment the method was primitive and constantly failed. Solids continued to flow south until a pumping system was installed to deposit the sewage from the tanks on to farmland at Bradwell. This operation required the use of two pumps, or at least two were actually installed, possibly as a precaution against a breakdown, which would incur the wroth of Stoke and the Duke. Obviously the pumps were highly esteemed, for they were named after the first two mayors of the borough, Hulme and Maddock. The land on which the sewage was deposited was let for farming, but the air was let separately, tenders being requested for shooting rights. It is interesting to note that in 1884 the farm suffered an outbreak of foot and mouth disease, but no instance of mad cow infection was reported.

When properties had been connected to the sewage system there still remained a problem with the water supplies since in the early days the water company would completely halt the flow to perform maintenance work. The satisfactory functioning of the sewage system depended on a regular flow of domestic water in addition to surface water and these intermittent shortages caused a number of bursts due to blockages. The fire service was equally dependent on a constant supply of water particularly during the night. There was one serious incident of failure when a fire occurred at Hughes's Pottery at Longport.

A more remarkable and unexpected incident connected with the sewer system was associated with the borough surveyor, Ralph Hales, who was also a partner in an iron foundry in Waterloo Road. This company were said to have made a connection between the sewer and the foundry boiler which resulted in an explosion and the death of two men. Around this time, John Pidduck, ironmonger of Burslem, had the first water closet in Cobridge fixed in his house, but perhaps to the satisfaction of the critics of the council chamber who had their doubts about them, it failed to work since the drains appeared to be blocked - since his house would be near the foundry, it would not seem impossible to link the two incidents!

In 1908 a new bacteriological system replaced the original and now outdated plant. Sited in the same Longport area it still made use of the Fowlea Brook for its final discharge, but technical advances by now made this a very different fluid. The new works were opened by Sir James Crighton Brown F.R.S. An interesting issue arising from the sewage installation was a threat by Baron Camoy to sue the trustees for loss of benefit. The Baron owned most of the Grange lands, which he let out for farming, and the brook which crossed the Grange and was a tributary of the Fowley Brook which also carried sewage. Periodically it was dammed by the farmer to spread its rich content on his land. With the new sewage system, the rich fluid was no longer available and the farmer, claiming loss of fertility, requested a reduction in his rent, which in turn resulted in his lordship demanding from the Board a resumption of his rights, and compensation for the disruption - but he was unsuccessful.

The name Camoy does not seem to relate to Burslem, and investigation reveals that the gentleman was previously a Mr Thomas Stonor who had claimed the title of Baron Camoy, and his claim had been accepted by Queen Victoria. According to Ward the Camoys dated back to the reign of Henry III and through the female line married into the Biddulph family.

On the whole Camoy seemed to have been a thorn in Burslem's side. At one time he was sent a charge of £32. 15. 6. for the making part of the road adjoining property he owned in Pleasant Street, but this was ignored until he was threatened with court action. He counter claimed that the road had been made two feet higher than it should have been, leaving less headroom under the bridge than had been agreed between himself and the railway company. His interests were also affected when repositioning of the toll house at the bottom of Waterloo Road was requested by the Tramway Company. The Grange was the only open land available adjacent to Waterloo Road and the Board of Health wished to buy an area on which to rebuild the toll house, but he insisted on the agreement being subject to the property becoming his if tolls were abolished.

Despite these disagreements, Burslem has acknowledged the Camoy association with the town by using the name for an interesting terrace of houses off Waterloo Road!

It has previously been said that early manufacturers sank their own wells and also used water from the mines. Other wells in the town, one near St John's Church, and one on Grange Farm, were known to be in existence in the 17th century, but both had a feeble flow. There appears to have been another well at Longport since an outbreak of fever there was attributed to contamination of well water. These wells, together with rainwater and water purchased from carriers with mobile barrels, supplied most of the domestic water, but it was scarce enough for it to be a common practice to use the same washing water on more than one occasion and to use the utmost caution in what water one would drink.

Enoch Wood eventually installed a piped supply from his mines to his Fountain Works adjoining St John's Square, and here, in what became known as Fountain Place, at the site of the entrance to his works, he built a font at a height suitable for the filling of portable vessels, and this constituted the first public supply of piped water. Later a man named John Smith in 1820 established a water works at Ivy House in Hanley with the intention of supplying water to both Hanley and Burslem. He supplied water to Burslem for a time, but his pipelaying seems to have been unacceptable and a constant source of complaint in the town. In 1832, a man named Walsh constructed a reservoir on high ground at Sneyd, from which pipes were laid towards Burslem; however his financial resources were limited, and his death in 1836 ended the project before his pipes could reach the town.

In 1846 the Potteries Water Works Company was formed with the Duke of Sutherland as patron, together with William Davenport, MP for Burslem, and other local influential men. The object of this company was to distribute water from the Duke's lands to all the local towns. Good quality water had been found at Wall Grange and a reservoir and pumping house were built. Water at the Meir was to be similarly conserved and a pumping house built to supply water to the southern towns. The engine to operate the pumps at Wall Grange was a beam type made in Cornwall, and this was sent by sea to Liverpool, but the ship was wrecked in the Mersey and the pump was lost. A replacement arrived and was installed in 1849. With it now apparently being an established custom for Burslem to give all mechanical monsters a name, and with water on hand, it was christened Stafford. A similar engine installed at the Meir was christened Cromarty, from its association with the Sutherlands.

The company supplied water free of charge to the Infirmary but was loathe to supply to rented property since, as with local rates, householders had a natural innate objection to pay for any public service. The water company was prepared for a landlord to have a tap and pay for the water consumed, but in turn, it was his responsibility to obtain payment from his tenants. However the landlord was equally loathe, since when news spread that there was a tap in an area, the number of 'tenants' visibly grew.

With the arrival of this new supplier, the Burslem Board finally decided to cancel the arrangement with John Smith and to pay him compensation. In 1858, in response to a request to the water company for the cost of water for water closets the following price was quoted: *"Houses rated above £6 but not exceeding £10, four shillings per house per annum"*.

The water company presented a number of bills in parliament to extend its influence, some of which Burslem instructed Council to oppose, mainly fearing it would result in monopoly charges, but although the company later became a monopoly, relations with Burslem appear to have remained cordial. Tittesworth reservoir was constructed in 1858 and the pumping stations at Hatton and Mill Meece towards the end of the century. As a tribute to the Duke of Sutherland a subscription list was organised locally for contributions towards the cost of a bust of the Duke which on completion was placed in the pumping house at Wall Grange. The sculptor was a Mr Noble of London and the bust bore the inscription:

> To record the name of George Granville Duke of Sutherland K.G.
> A truly Christian Nobleman, whose great and unobtrusive
> benevolence led him uniformly to promote every judicious design
> for the health, comfort, and well being of his fellow man, the
> promoters of these works commissioned in 1848 and carried out
> under his patronage, have erected this memorial

A tribute to a "Christian Nobleman", as they described him, who gave them clean water in return for their foul!

One of the objects of Burslem's 1825 parliamentary bill was for the provision of public lighting, but this was to be confined to the town since both Cobridge and Longport refused to be included on account of cost. The Bill allowed for a maximum rate of six pence to be imposed to pay for this service. It has been said that there was some lighting in the town before the introduction of gas, but most likely it was reflected light from the shops, who for the most part would use oil lamps in the conduct of their trade after dark. There were still a number of chandlers in Burslem, but as the town became more built up, nuisance created by the fumes from the heating of tallow made candle making increasingly objectionable, besides which gas was also being promoted for domestic use.

An early private gas company had built a gas producing plant at Etruria under the title the British Gas Company and they were approached by the Burslem Board of Health for a quotation for the installation of seventeen lights in the town. In response they were offered a price of £1.10. 0 per annum, per lamp, and this was accepted. This method of tendering seems to have been a general practice and presumably represented a charge for the provision of the lamp and service pipes, the employment of lamplighters and the maintenance of the installation, the cost of the gas itself being charged on metered consumption.

In 1833 complaints about the service coupled with increase charges which the company had imposed, led the Board to consider a change, and a company operating under the title of the Burslem & Tunstall Gas Company were asked to tender. Their tender was for £3.0.0. per lamp and this caused the Board to consider the use of oil lamps. This however was rejected and a contract entered into with the new company for the installation of fifty three lamps, these only to be lit between September and April, and the one at the entrance to St John's church only when services were held. In 1834 a reduced charge of £2.17.0. per lamp was negotiated, and this charge remained almost static up to the time when Burslem bought the company.

Demand for lighting spread when the benefits were realised, but the main difficulty was to balance its cost with the maximum rate of six pence which was allowed to be raised under the act, and regardless of this being stretched, possibly illegally, to one shilling on properties with rateable values above £6. Grumbles were frequent from Cobridge that the lighting in Waterloo Road was inadequate, but at the same time they still failed to ask for lamps to be installed in Cobridge itself until 1840; Longport had asked for twenty lamps in 1838. Criticism was so frequent about the poor quality of light from the lamps that eventually a gas examiner was appointed at a salary of £25 per annum, and equipment bought to enable him to constantly test that the gas was supplied to specification.

By 1850, there were 160 lamps installed and 70 more required. The rapidly expanding service resulted in the creation of a separate Lighting Committee but the committee commenced work with an outstanding debt to the gas company of £511. 4. 4. Further economies were made by leaving lamps unlit for two nights before and two nights after full moon, and, following the making of Newcastle Street, the lamps in Packhorse Lane were removed. In desperation in 1861 it was decided that three faces of the town hall clock should be left unlit, one face only to be illuminated. In 1862 a letter was sent to the Board of Health from the Ratepayers Protection Society, complaining about the poor gas supply.

In 1867 it was decided that lamps should be lit ten months of the year to conform to the practice of the other towns in the Potteries. In 1874 charges by the gas company were increased to £3.0.0. a lamp, except that now technical advances had produced the incandescent mantle and multiple burners known as the Bat Wing burner, and where these latter lamps were installed the gas company charged double the price. The police had before this complained that poor lighting in the town had hindered their detention of criminals.

In this same year, the Board of Health indicated to the gas company that they wished to buy the undertaking and it was offered at £80.000. The Board made an offer of £60,000 but the gas company refused to accept anything less, and said that in any case they were not that anxious to sell. Agreement was eventually reached at the gas company's price. In 1876 the Board successfully promoted a bill in parliament to purchase the company and requested a loan for the sum, expressing at the same time the hope of sufficient profit from the venture to cover the cost of cleansing the Fowlea Brook which was being demanded by the Duke of Sutherland. The Board's hopes were justified since in 1879 the gas works contributed £1700 to the rate fund and periodically made increasing contributions to as much as £3300. There was a great shock in 1887 when the district auditor issued a report on the gas works accounts, which indicated malpractice, causing the then council to call in accountants to investigate - but fortunately all turned out to be above board.

In 1907, Wolstanton, who were supplied with gas from Burslem decided they would have their own works, and dispute arose over recompense for the capital cost of mains etc which had finally to be argued in court, resulting in a settlement in Burslem's favour, and payment of £9357. In 1908 lamplighters asked for an increased wage of £1.2.6. plus five day's holiday. The council in response refused to increase the wage but extended the holiday to seven days, presumably two extra days of leisure without pay.

By this date in any case the days of lamplighters were numbered and citizens who remember seeing, and hearing, them, clip clopping from lamp post to lamppost with their pole in shoulder arms position, will be getting fewer every day. For me as a youngster it was always a puzzle and surprise when the pole was inserted into the lamp cage to see a fork of light like a serpent's tongue result in a sudden glow of light; but the human switch was soon to be replaced by the mechanical switch, and the mechanical switch by the electronic switch, - and ultimately gas lamps themselves to become collectors' items.

The postal service in Britain has been established for many centuries and originated from the enterprise of one man William Dockwra with a scheme for the movement of letters between trading houses in London around 1586. Letters were taken and received by Post Boys, hourly from and to a central sorting office, covering districts throughout the city. The success of this led to its adoption in other cities and towns and eventually to an inter city service. Initially mail was carried by regular coach service along with passengers and goods.

The cost of sending a letter was determined by the sorting office, the price being marked on the document and collected from the recipient. The usual charge for a single letter was:

Not more than 80 miles	2d.
80 to 140 miles	4d.
Over 140 miles	6d
Scotland 8d Ireland	9d.

James I, seeing it as a lucrative source of personal income, made it a royal monopoly and expanded the service using mail coaches in a distinctive red with the royal coat of arms and using armed guards as protection against highwaymen. The first of these services was between London and Bristol, but expanded as toll roads improved and increased in number. This area of Staffordshire was originally reliant on a service operating on the old Roman route to Chester, mail being deposited and collected at Newcastle.

It was not until 1840 that Rowland Hill, the Postmaster General, introduced the principle of prepayment of a standard charges for postage to anywhere in the United Kingdom, using stamps to show the charge involved. From then on demands on the service increased rapidly, in line with the growing commerce of the industrial revolution. Early mail service in Burslem relied on a woman on foot delivering and collecting post from Newcastle, At a later date, as the mail got heavier and bulkier, a man on horseback was used and he would blow a bugle when he arrived in town to indicate that the mail was available for collection at the Legs of Man, where it was customarily deposited and collected.

In 1796 Burslem was pressing Lord Vernon and Mr Curzon for a direct service. The request was passed to the Postmaster General, who in turn passed it to the Surveyor of Roads whose report stated that, *"before a service could be introduced, improvement was required from Ashley to Wooden Box, also at Tean a bridge was required over a brook, and from Tean to Burslem many of the roads were too narrow in places".*

Up to the year 1818 there was still no direct service to Burslem but there were now two deliveries a day from the Legs of Man to Newcastle; every forenoon at a quarter to ten, and every evening at a quarter before eight. Postal charges at that time were still paid by the recipient and depended on the number of sheets in a letter, and the distance it had travelled. The early popular form used for letters was a single sheet, identical in style to the current air mail letter, which folds into the form of an envelope, with provision for an address. At that time it would be sealed with wax, and the amount to be paid usually written on it at the receiving office before despatch. It is not unusual to find letters written one way across the page, the paper then turned 90° and the writing continued at right angles, to save paper.

The changes introduced by Roland Hill revolutionised the service. From then on the public began increasingly to communicate by letter. The same principle was quickly adopted by other countries and both foreign and inland communication became commonplace between families, including many who had been parted through emigration. Post offices with a postmaster were introduced, but it seems to be uncertain when deliveries commenced to individual addresses. Streets were legally required to be named as far back as 1765 and houses to be numbered, but for numbers to be odd one side and even the other was possibly a later facility coinciding with the widespread introduction of house to house deliveries.

Certainly there would be no letter boxes in the doors of early houses. In 1852, the Burslem Board of Health recommended that for street names, cast iron plates with 'Greconite' plates be used (a material which eludes clarification) and iron plates with raised white numbers for house numbering.

In 1852 the Board received a letter from Jabez Wilson, requesting that the town provide a suit for the man who assists in delivering letters, but the Board turned this down on the grounds that there was no available money. From this incident it would appear that there was as yet no clear division of responsibility between town and post.

The first post office in Burslem was in High Street, a street then situated more or less behind the Overhouse pottery. In 1834, the office was moved to Market Place and in 1856 it moved again to the junction of Market Place and Waterloo Road. The first post boxes in Britain were installed in 1812 at the suggestion of Anthony Trollope, the Postmaster and novelist, who had seen them in Paris. The first two boxes in Burslem were installed in 1859, one in Waterloo Road, and one at Dale Hall.

When the railway network arrived and was used for carrying mail the nearest delivery point was at Whitmore, and from there the mail went in sacks in a horse-drawn vehicle to the various Pottery towns, until around 1854, when Burslem mail was delivered from a new office in Stoke.

In 1880, after a short spell in Moorland Road, the Burslem post office was back in the centre of the town in Market Square, but shortly afterwards the Postmaster General said he was prepared to buy land in Wedgwood Place and build a post office, which would be listed as in Burslem, Staffordshire, and the name Stoke-on-Trent would not appear; a belated recognition of the importance of Burslem, and that it was not a parish of Stoke.

The new post office was built in 1904, and coincided with the time when widespread telephone and telegraph services were being introduced. This latter was welcomed by Burslem since it had been forced to use the facilities of Hanley or Stoke. When the 'United Kingdom Telegraph Company' canvassed for permission to install cables, their services were welcomed. The growth in the use of telephones had not been spectacular, by 1890 there appears to have been only some 200 installations in the whole of the Potteries towns, and by 1920 many of the big firms had only one line, among them Wedgwoods at Etruria.

JUNE 25, 1887—THE PENNY ILLUSTRATED PAPER—405

SOUVENIR OF QUEEN VICTORIA'S CORONATION IN WESTMINSTER ABBEY JUNE 28, 1838.

CHAPTER TWENTY ONE: Politics and Railways

Tithe Commutation Act. Victoria's reign. Parliamentary elections in quick succession.
Chartists. The railway era. The Loop Line.

The 1830s saw major changes. In 1836 the Tithe Commutation Act was passed under which all payments in kind were abolished and their value converted into rents on the land. This was a great relief to many, providing landlords did not resort to increasing rents; there had been great ill feeling about tithes, particularly among dissenters whose churches were self supporting - in effect they paid two church tolls.

In 1837, William IV died, parliament was dissolved and the epic reign of Victoria began. New elections took place. Representing the Tories was the retiring member John Davenport, but Colonel Anson, his previous partner, decided against re-election and was replaced by William Taylor Copeland, so both candidates were important pottery manufacturers. There were two Liberal candidates, both strangers to the district, but their proclaimed views more nearly reflected those of the newly enfranchised citizens. One was Mathew Bridges from Bristol, and the other Frank Cynric Sheridan a relative of the famous poet.

It seems strange that having won the franchise, even if not yet a universal one, the result should be another Tory victory, since both Tory candidates were elected. In the customary local interpretation of liberalism, the opposition showered them with missiles, and also wreaked their anger on property in the towns, while the regular police and special constables were powerless to intervene. Several magistrates were drafted in on the following day to demonstrate authority but the disgruntled voters took an instant and active dislike to them also and they were forced to hastily hide until the yeomanry arrived to spirit them away. It must be said for Burslem however that they were the least affected by the wroth of the rioters, which seems to give credence to John Ward's viewpoint of the superior characteristics of those who lived in Burslem, compared with the southern end of the Potteries.

An interesting local figure who was absorbed in politics at this time was Joseph Capper of Tunstall, a blacksmith by trade and much respected both for his work and his integrity. As a keen member of the Chartist movement he addressed meetings in Burslem and other pottery towns. He was the subject of a biography by Mr Frederick Harper, who said that Capper at one of his meetings folded his arms in the form of a knot and requested his audience to do likewise and together demand a people's parliament. Mr Harper goes on to infer that this group gesture was influential in the design and adoption of the Staffordshire Knot, although the design is probably much older than this. At a meeting in Hanley in 1840 Capper urged that a request should be sent to the Queen, to dismiss ministers who were plundering the people by spending £50,000 on a foreigner, and £70,000 a year on the Queen's houses. Obviously racism, particularly royal racism, was not to be tolerated and Capper had to face the consequence in court, where he was convicted and subsequently confined in Stafford jail, from where it is said he returned a broken man.

Only four years elapsed before, in 1841, there was another election and during this parliament Robert Peel, from Staffordshire, became Prime Minister. Following a national failure of the harvest in 1845, he repealed the contentious Corn Laws. Mr Davenport retired, but Mr Copeland fought on, his partner being the Hon. Frederick Dudley Ryder, the younger son of Earl Harrowby. The Liberal Party had a new face in John Lewis Ricardo Esq. a gentleman with no connections or interests within the borough, yet who eventually was to have a long association with Burslem. One observer remarked, *"the wealth of this gent's family connections obtained for him no small favour for the venal portion of the electors"*. On the day leading up to the election, the two conservative candidates were canvassing the towns on horseback along with supporters when they were attacked with missiles and Mr Copeland had this head cut open. Copeland and Ricardo were the two successful candidates.

The customary rioting developed; banners were seized and destroyed, and in Stoke the windows of Copelands works and of houses nearby were broken. At one of the local political meetings Joseph Capper said that all work should cease until the workers' charter was law, and indeed it nearly did in 1842 when the House of Commons was invaded, the floor strewn with paper and the air filled with the song:

Britannia's sons, though slave ye be, God your creator made you free
He life and thought and being gave, But never, never, made a slave.
The verdant earth on which we tread, Was by his hand all carpeted
Enough for all he freely gave, But never, never, made a slave.

Writing in Burslem at this time, Scarratt said that with Chartist troubles still persisting, soldiers and police were patrolling the town, the soldiers dressed in scarlet coats with polished brass buttons fastened to the chin. Their headgear was tall and surmounted with a cricket size ball fixed at the front. The policemen were in blue but cut in military style. In the summer both the military and the police wore white pantaloons. A policeman was sometimes to be seen with a gun, but this was not for fear of the Chartists, but for dealing with dogs, who evidently emulated the rioters as a source of nuisance in the town.

Despite the troubled times Burslem was expanding physically and consolidating its services. Not only were street works going ahead, but some of the early poor building was being removed. Massey Square off Chapel Lane, which had constantly been on the visiting list of the Nuisance Inspector, was demolished and the occupants transferred to new property in Macclesfield Street.

Whether or not such improvements, reflected throughout the Potteries, contributed to an easing in the wroth of the electorate, but when new elections were called in 1847, there was general relief when, with the candidates and winners the same, surprisingly peace prevailed.

In the election of 1852 however, when the two liberals, Ricardo, and another outsider, Gower, topped the poll, the sweet smell of democracy filled the air. There were demonstrations and processions on a scale never surpassed in the Potteries; it is said the Burslem friends of Gower carried in a procession a loaf of bread, the product of thirty three stones of flour baked in a tin in a kiln at a manufactory at Cobridge. The loaf was four feet long, three feet wide, and two feet six high, and symbolised the end of the Corn Laws.

Sir Robert Peel, the Prime Minister from Staffordshire, is remembered for two things: his repeal of the Corn Laws and the police force, from which the old nicknames 'peelers' and 'bobbies' were derived

.   Parliament was now slowly - to some it would appear with endemic reluctantance - extending the laws governing social conditions. In 1842 a law passed prohibiting the use of children as chimney sweeps, a service employing many thousands since heating was almost entirely by coal, and a large number of children were grossly abused in the process. It was a belated law but blatantly ignored for many years.

The steam age was rapidly developing. By 1830 the canal system was ceasing to grow, and canal owners were fiercely opposing the flood of applications to parliament to construct rail systems, which would directly compete with, and kill, what had been a fabulously profitable but short lived canal enterprises. Such was the rapidity and enormity of the change that the government was concerned for the fate of the canal investors. The General Railway Act of 1844 stipulated that companies who provide trains running each way on their lines, must do so every day, except Xmas day and Good Friday, at a rate of twenty miles per hour, stopping at all stations and with a maximum fare of one penny per mile. The speed alone would obviously have dire consequences for the canals where the maximum was four miles per hour, and taking into account the time taken negotiating locks, this average was reduced to two and a half miles per hour. For a journey from London to Birmingham, a fast time on the canal was fifty hours and the cost double that of the rail. Such was the concern of the proprietors of one canal, that they called on all other canal companies, commissioners of turnpikes, proprietors of inns, stage coach companies and parliamentary friends, to oppose railroad bills, which would reduce the value of land, and diminish manual labour. In this district alone it was said that there would be a loss of work for 150 men and 300 horses.

Nothing however could save the commercial traffic on the canals and realising this the government passed a bill in 1846 which required the compulsory takeover of canals by the railway companies, and they were to ensure a continuing dividend to the canal shareholders. In 1846 the North Staffordshire Railway Company, locally known as the "Knotty" because the Staffordshire Knot was its emblem, took over the Trent and Mersey Canal Co.

The North Staffordshire Railway Company was founded in 1845 and the first meeting in 1846, chaired by Mr Ricardo MP, was followed by the ceremony of cutting the first sod at Etruria. The occasion was celebrated by a public holiday throughout the Potteries. A procession a mile long accompanied officials and guests, led by the chief engineer on horseback to where, on a railed off site, a solid mahogany barrow and a silver spade awaited the ceremony. In their exuberance the spectators broke through the boundary fence, and in the turmoil which temporarily followed the engineer is said to have lost his hat, and as there is no mention of it being recovered, we must assume that it became a souvenir, hopefully preserved by some railway enthusiast. The spade was engraved with the arms of Mr Ricardo on one side and those of Viscount Ingestre on the other, but despite this the ground refused it entry and the spade retired humiliated and bent.

The Grand Junction Railway from Birmingham to Warrington, built in 1837, passed through Stafford, Whitmore and Madeley, and long distance travellers from Burslem would, before the advent of the "Knotty", travel to one of these stations by horse coach or horse omnibus, or their own transport. The first station to be built in Burslem to connect with a main system was at Longport, and it was here in 1854 that two boys were killed while crossing the line, which resulted in a foot bridge being built. It was around this time also that the idea was conceived of a separate rail link between Longton, Fenton, Stoke, Etruria, Hanley, Cobridge, Burslem, and Tunstall, known locally when it was built as the Loop Line. In 1846 George Stevenson was asked to survey the district for the preparation of a scheme which would satisfy each of these towns, but by 1854 the line had still to be agreed.

The original site selected for the station to serve Burslem was where the machine house of May's colliery stood, thence the line would run through the valley, past the pool known as "Keep Off", then past Warwick Savage to Mr Bowers manufactury, which would be the site for Tunstall station, then under Mr Haywood's house and on to join the main line to the west. This was too remote for a Burslem station. The town demanded something more central and proposed a line which would cross Earl Granville's branch line at Cobridge, thence over the old racecourse on the Grange, cross the footpath from Burslem to Etruria, cross the path to Middleport, over Navigation Road, Rope Walk Road, Peel Street, Furlong Lane and on an embankment in front of the houses of Mr Ward and the Misses Riley, over Newcastle Street on a thirty five feet arch, lowering Newcastle Street five feet, making it a gradient of one in eleven, thence via Lyndhurst Street to Fountain Place, which would be the station.

The racecourse on the Grange has not been mentioned before. It existed in 1825 but never seems to have achieved the popularity of that of neighbouring Newcastle.

In 1858 meetings were still being held, and indeed in 1863 a fresh scheme was offered which appears to have obtained acceptance, since Burslem and Tunstall were becoming anxious and feeling isolated. In 1865 work commenced, and the line was completed as far as Hanley, but at this point Earl Granville objected to any further extension on the ground that the increased traffic would interfere with his own from Shelton Bar steel works and his collieries, and this despite the fact that Burslem had generously agreed to him crossing Waterloo Road with a rail connection from the 'Deep Pit' to the main railway line which adjoined his Shelton works, a crossing which had a manned gate, installed following an accident, and

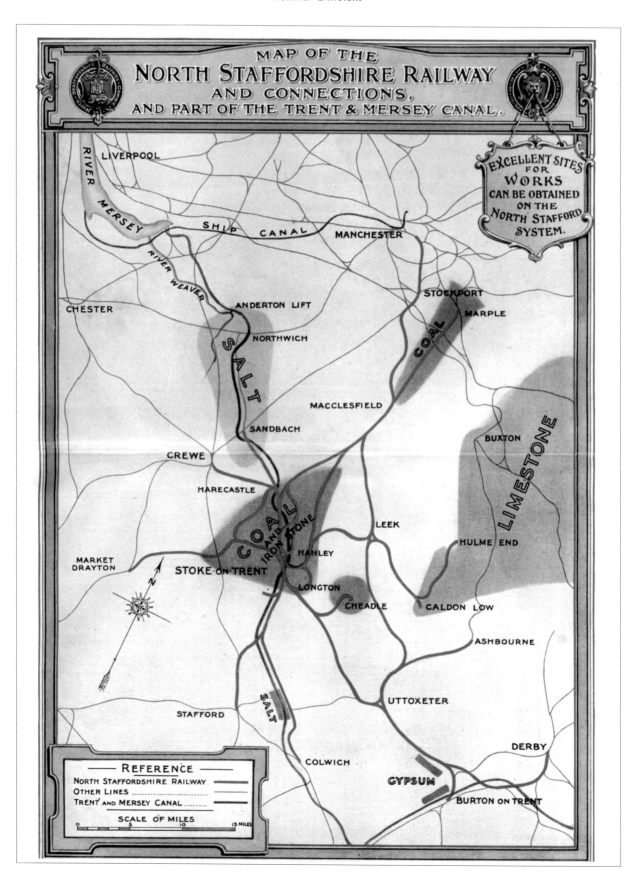

formed an annoying traffic-delaying feature well into the 20th century. Work on the Loop Line had to cease since the government, with no Josiah Wedgwood to fight the decision, found in the Earl's favour, and permission for further development was to be at the discretion of the Duchy of Lancaster.

In 1868, with the stagnant state of trade due to the American civil war, the Railway Company had second thoughts about the scheme and requested parliament to withdraw the Bill on the ground of the proposed line was likely to be uneconomic, and that since the passenger traffic on the horse omnibus between Burslem and Hanley was down to an average of only seventeen persons per journey. the project was likely to be uneconomic. The request was refused by a committee in the Commons, and by 1870 work on the line recommenced and the first sod cut in Moorland Road, where Burslem station was finally to stand. The occasion was celebrated by a function at the Leopard Hotel.

The extension from Hanley went to the first station in Waterloo Road, on the Hanley side of Cobridge, then to a station in Cobridge off Elder Road. Leaving Cobridge there was a short tunnel before arriving in Burslem. Rail connections from the Hanley Deep Pit, Sneyd Colliery and Robert Heath's colliery on the Grange were ultimately integrated with the main line, and for shunting on these secondary lines a number of light engines with fanciful names - Roger, Minnie, Polly, Katie - were used.

There were three classes of carriages on the first passenger trains, each furnished to reflect the importance of the customer. Early third class carriages had wooden seating and no roof; only when roofs were fitted did passenger traffic boom. Initially oil lamps provided the illumination, first and second class had four lamps per carriage, but third class had one lamp fitted above a shoulder high division which was fitted between two adjacent compartments, and it was not until 1893 that they had eight candle power electric lamps, served by a generator fitted under the guard's van. The light from these lamps was adequate when the train was running and the generator operating, but when the train stopped the lights immediately dimmed and the lights were only of token value. When the loop line was at the peak of its use, it is said to have run seventy trains a day, one every fifteen minutes.

According to Scarratt, the Loop Line was opened by the Earl of Dartmouth, since when, he says, *"some nice cottages and new factories have been built adjoining the station ....in the area between Moorland Road and the Hamil was pasture land with cows grazing, plenty of game, and Mr Riley's shooting box"*. The line, for the first ten years, was run on a contract basis by a private company, Messrs Wright & Son of London and Birmingham. There were strict rules applied to ensure safety, viz a hat, cap, arms or any object waved visibly by persons on the line denoted danger; for slow running a red flag was to be waved to and fro by a man facing the engine. Operatives with a minimum of five years service were entitled to a free coffin, whether they died through their own fault or not, which must have been a consolation for the widow. Original passenger fares were usually:

First Class per mile	2d.	
Second Class ,, ,,	$1^1/_2$d.	
Third Class ,, ,,	1d.	
The charges for coal traffic were;	$^3/_4$d. per ton mile in owners wagon	
	1d ,, ,, ,, in Rly. Co. wagon.	

Coal was usually delivered to sidings owned by the Railway Company and collected by the distributors own vehicles. The convenience charge for this service was 1/-per ton, with three day's grace to unload, before a demurrage charge of 2/- per wagon per day was incurred.

The North Staffordshire Railway Co. was capitalised at £6,000,000 which included £1,170,000 cost of buying out the canals. In 1843 there was in all 2000 miles of rail in Britain. By 1848 there were 15000. Surprisingly, there was not the sudden demise of the canals as expected; in fact in 1864 there was a reduction in canal tolls on earthenware from $1^1/_2$d to 1d per mile, and for clay and other pottery raw materials from 1d. to $^3/_4$d. Possibly as a matter of expediency, clays were still coming to the potteries by canal well into the 20th century.

Two photographs showing parts of the loopline in Burslem now a walkway.

Bottom: North Staffordshire Railway company train c.1908
(Manifold collection)

The first staion bult in Burslem to connect to the mainline train system, at that time the North Staffordshire Railway (the Knotty).

Below; the company's emblem

Stockport viaduct in the mid 19th century a typical transport scene of the time

Fountain square was used as a vegetable market. In the background is the Fountain Pottery and Wood's fountain can be seen to the left of the main entrance, set into the wall.

A punch cartoon showing comment on new drinking laws 1870

CHAPTER TWENTY TWO: Legislation

Increasing national & local social legislation.

As a result of government legislation to improve urban areas, Burslem, appointed a full time surveyor in 1825, and following the 1835 Municipal Reform Act, the Board of Health could exercise more control and ensure that planning permissions were obtained and adhered to. No explicit directions existed on sanitary installations but with the sewage system under construction, water closets were obviously to be preferred. However, even by 1852 the Board still had a clause in their bye laws that there could be privies with water closets, provided with a tap to serve two houses. Some recent properties were found to have been constructed with outdated and inadequate sanitary conditions, among the offenders William Pointon was informed that he had failed to provide sufficient privies and ash pits to twelve houses in Holehouse and twelve in High Street.

In 1860 permission was given to build houses in Edward Street, provided they included privies and cesspool. This presumably was an instance of lack of access to the sewage system, since some landlords and individual house owners who already suffered these primitive conditions were now seeking permission to connect to the new sewage system. There was at the same time a threat of litigation against some who had surreptitiously connected theirs without permission.

Progress was made on street works, specifications for buildings were improving with guidance on standards from the government. In 1851 the window tax was withdrawn, which resulted in more light in houses. Houses had been built in Burslem with no windows at their rear - there is a painting by Reginald Haggar in the Wedgwood College, Barlaston, showing a terrace built in this manner. (See Ch. 4)

Some practices had to be curtailed. Among these was the depositing of ashes in the road, and the practice of pottery manufacturers dumping shords in streets. One manufacturer claimed it would ruin him financially if he was forced to desist. Another manufacturer threatened to take the Board of Health to court for prohibiting the firm from storing empty crates in the road outside his factory, a practice for which he claimed he had a right since it had been customary for generations. Freedom of the road had been taken very literally in Burslem - the Board had even had to make a bye law prohibiting the washing and repairing of carriages in the highway, also using it for the killing of any animal, or the sale of cattle. The penalty for any of these offences to be a £5 fine.

The roads which carried the existing traffic had for the most part only impacted surfaces, and both dust and horse droppings were a problem. Constant watering had to be resorted to at times to keep down the dust, which carried with it the smell from the animal droppings. Traffic noise in the centre of the town had also become a nuisance, drowning the words of wisdom emanating from members in the council chamber in the town hall, and causing a member to advocate that paving round the hall should be replaced with wooden blocks, in the manner of some London streets.

The 1848 Municipal Act added to previous provisions, and since it was a period of increasing prosperity, more government inspectors were employed to ensure that these provisions were enforced. Building societies sprang up in Burslem, as they did elsewhere. Originally, these societies were founded on small numbers of thrifty individuals forming a project group, each group to organise and pay for the construction of houses for each member in turn; and as each house was completed lots were drawn, and the fortunate winner moved in to his completed house but continued paying until all the houses were completed and occupied. The result of this method of building can be seen in some of the town streets, where a few of one type of house are built adjoining a number of a dissimilar type, and so on down the length of the street, making it visually very interesting.

Interest was being taken in investing in rented property or in land purchased with a view to development, leading to the introduction of commercial building societies such as the Star Building Society, whose name is still faintly visible on a property in Wedgwood Place. Other societies who were active were the Burslem and Tunstall Freehold Land Society, the Burslem Amicable Building Society and the Town and Country Permanent Benefit & Building Society.

The commerce created by the canal led to Burslem growing rapidly in the Longport direction. In 1838 alone three streets were built, Navigation Street, Bridge Street and Wharf Street. A lot of these early dwellings have vanished, some replaced as in the Pleasant Street area which was once a mixture of houses, shops and at least one pottery, but now a modern housing complex. Fountain Buildings in Newport Lane and Mount Pleasant Buildings in Reid Street, attractive names, have also ceased to exist. Houses were also built by firms for their employees. Earl Granville built 139 houses and a school at Cobridge for his employees and their families. These houses were looked upon at that time as embodying the best in building practices and materials. Apart from private dwellings, applications were made to build lodging houses, one such for 32 persons in Upper Pitt Street in 1855.

It does seem that an unnecessary number of street names which originally formed part of the town's heritage have been changed. Some of the new names may have an association with Burslem, but if only those employed by Arnold Bennett had been used it would have helped to sustain a nostalgic interest. Some examples of original names which have changed:

Elers Street was Freehold Terrace.	Burgess Street was Wharf Street.
Woolrich Street was Foster Street.	Morton Street was Stanley Street.
Brindley Street was Ricardo Street.	Scott Lidgett Road was Alexandra Road.
Brickhouse Street was Croft's Yard.	Furlong Lane was Beeches Lane.
Canal Lane was Old Bag Road.	Westport Road was Liverpool Road.

The 1848 act included legislation covering street works, and these Burslem added to its bye laws subsequently issuing notices ordering owners of premises to *make good the streets and pavements adjoining their properties, in accordance with the surveyors specification; and failing which the local authority would complete the work and apportion the cost to each owner*. More often than not the notice was ignored and it was left for the authority to arrange for the work to be done and then the onerous task of recovering the cost. The highways, for the most part the previous toll roads, were now the responsibility of the local authority to maintain, but there was constant dispute as to whether a road was a highway or a street when it came to who would pay for the road to be surfaced. It was commonly argued by owners of property that if a lamp had been installed it was a highway and therefore the responsibility of the Board.

Illustration from *Tom Browne's Schooldays* c.1860 showing the 'Pats' - Irish navvies - under attack from the young bucks on their way to school. The nature of both road travel and road maintenance at this time are well seen

John Ward refused to pay his assessment and the dispute went on for years; not until 1893 was he put in court and given fourteen days to pay £39. 2.0. which included interest.

The difficulty of settling responsibility through the courts arose from the Board being unable to operate legally without a the signature of a resident magistrate - the nearest being at Stafford - a problem also in relation to confining people to the poor house and common to all the Potteries towns, particularly causing frustration in the control of licenced premises where legal action for infringements required prompt action.

In the end there was mutual agreement in the Potteries towns that it was imperative to have a Stipendary Magistrate for the area. A draft bill was prepared by our friend Mr Tomlinson in 1839, and support requested from the Duke of Sutherland, who in turn succeeded in obtaining additional support from Viscount Sandon, Lord Fetherton, Sir Oswald Moseley, John Davenport Esq., Captain Mannering, N. Walter Hill Coyney Esq, and Richard Clarke Hill Esq. Another generous effort from the Duke. To cover the expense of the appointment a 4d. in the pound rate was to be applied to households and extra rates charged on lock-ups and offices. Mr Thomas Bailey Rose was the first appointment at a salary of £800 per annum. He served the district for twenty five years, retiring in 1864. He was succeeded by Mr John Edward Davis who left in 1870 to go to a similar appointment in Sheffield. This last gentleman's reign though short was very popular - perhaps he was too benign - but on his leaving there was a public subscription for him which raised £306! Mr Davis refused the money, and was instead presented with a piece of silver plate, and his wife with a dessert service, the balance of the money to be invested and the interest offered as prize money to the students of the School of Art; the winning paintings or drawings to be hung in the Infirmary and Longton Cottage Hospital to *"relieve the weary hours of patients, while at the same time encouraging local art"*.

In 1850 there was pressure in the district to increase the magistrate's jurisdiction, increasing his salary to £1000 and employing a magistrate's clerk, but this would have meant an additional levy which Burslem refused to contemplate, and the lack of unanimity prevented its approval in parliament. It was raised again in 1871 and received approval without objection.

Perhaps out of sheer necessity the appointment of a magistrate appears to have been the first cooperative venture where all the Potteries towns agreed to share the cost. Primarily sponsored by Burslem, this first success led to the suggestion that there should be a confederation of the towns but ultimately the cost of policing led to second thoughts and the idea was not pursued.

In 1850 enquiries were made of the Ordnance Survey Office for supply the Burslem Board with a map of the town and its surroundings. The estimated price for the built up area of 500 acres was £400, and for the remaining 1600 acres £200. An order was placed and the bill when it finally arrived was for £623. 15. 7. Another for the plans of the sewage system, received around the same time, was £770. 9. 2.

Whether it was as a result of a recommendation from the newly appointed Gas Committee, town pride or improved income, but in 1851 there was to be an improvement in the appearance of the town, following the the placing of a contract by the Board for the painting of the street lamps. The prices were: Large lamps. 9d. Small lamps. 8d. Large posts. 1/5d. Small posts. 1/4d. Brackets. 1d.

In the same year the position of part time Medical Officer of Health was advertised, the applicant being requested to state his required remuneration. There were three applicants, Samuel Goddard, who requested £25, Joseph Walker who quoted £20, and John Mino Harrison, £10. Harrison was appointed but resigned on account of ill health, and after a ballot by the Board, Samuel Goddard replaced him. Another appointment in this year was that of Inspector of Lodging Houses on the order of the government, because sporadic outbreaks of cholera made them fear an epidemic, and in Burslem there were 51 of these houses!

Despite every effort of the Board to economise, they were increasingly forced to make additional appointments on account of government legislation. Nevertheless 1851 brought the all too customary reward for voluntary service; an accusation from the Burslem Parochial Association that the Board of Health was feasting themselves at the public expense. An anonymous letter also informed them that this same Parochial Society was using its members to fill in voting papers of poor people to the benefit of their own members. Since the Board continued its unilateral control, it naturally followed that they bore the brunt of all complaints. Another was from owners of properties adjoining Swan Square concerning the smell from the pig market and the way it was conducted. It would seem that the pigs were allowed to wander, since the Board agreed to spend £910 for the provision of pig bins.

Emphasising the increasing intent of the government to improve industrial conditions, in 1842 a bill was passed prohibiting the employment of women and children in the mines, and in 1844-1847 the hours of work for women and children were limited to 60 hours per week, a maximum of 10 hours on any one day. This was first introduced in the textile trade but soon embraced other industries. These laws placed a severe restriction on the potter's habit of extended drinking periods, and subsequent long hours of work on the remaining days of the week, a practice which had led to so much abuse of children working for the potters. The act could only bring benefit to most families except those of the publicans. Stricter government laws demanded more local bye-laws, and in consequence increased supervision to enforce them. This led at last to the appointment of sub committees, their reports to be presented to the Board of Health which still retained the controlling voice.

Lodging houses, for which a bye law was introduced in 1851, although requiring a licence, remained a problem for Burslem, mainly because there were so many compared to the number in the other local towns. This was probably a result of Burslem being the first Pottery town to attract labour from outside at the beginning of the industrial age. Some were now found to be unregistered, with chaff and straw beds on the floor, and walls with marks where vermin had been squashed. Charges for residents at these lodgings were of the order of 2/-d per week and demand exceeded supply! The bye law affecting lodging houses included rigorous terms and constraints which were posted in each lodging house:

No person is allowed to keep a lodging house unless it contains beds, bedding, and proper furniture of at least a value of five pounds, and is provided with a constant supply of pure water with soap and towels, and also have a privy or water closet suitable for the accommodation of lodgers.

Every room to be swept daily and washed every Friday before twelve noon.

Every room to be limewashed with Quick Lime six times per year.

Blankets, rugs and covers to be washed at least four times a year.

Tickets will be issued for each approved room to be fixed in a permanent place and showing the number of the room and the allowed number of lodgers.

No mix of sexes, except for married families, and no prostitutes.

Dogs to be kept outside the house and kennels provided.

Windows in every sleeping room to be kept open to their full width from 9.0am to 11.0am. every morning, weather permitting, and from 2.0pm to 4.0pm every afternoon.

The Board received a request from the Head Constable for a van and horse to convey prisoners to courts in the Potteries, since at present they have to be escorted on foot. A problem also arose in connection with alleged misuse of the Shambles, presumably by the purchaser of the rents, who had allowed the market to be used for public entertainment. As a consequence the Board issued the following notice:

There are to be no parillions or plays allowed to be exhibited within the precincts of the market, that is, all theatrical parillions. or shows involving theatrical exhibitions, gambling, or teaching of pugilism".

Care had to be taken in the licensing of anything theatrical in view of the opposition of the religious bodies. A request had been made in 1844 to build a theatre on Swan Bank and this had been refused after religious objections, one observing that there was already a theatre in Hanley and one in Newcastle!

A bye-law was issued in 1851, requiring every public house to provide within the premises a proper urinal with a screen. There was no mention of other toilet requirements, so evidently these establishments were no place for women. Sanitary conditions in other areas were also still wanting - in the mid-19th century the Nuisance Inspector was reporting monthly on the removal of night soil; in December 1853 he gave it as sixty seven tubs.

In 1851, there was a revival of the Chamber of Commerce. The original chamber, founded in 1831 by the pottery manufacturers with the object of creating a closer affinity between firms, was primarily concerned with the maintenance of selling prices for pottery, but hopes of uniformity on this had faded, and with it the chamber. On its revival, it was enlarged by the inclusion of other trades and professions in the community, but in 1854 it broke again, when the iron and coalmasters formed their own body.

In 1854 the Board were granted permission to fix a clock on the house of Mr Slater in St John's Square and approved a contract for the watering of the streets for 6/6d per day.

In 1855, acting under an apparent valid local bye-law, the Board fined a number of people one shilling for not clearing snow from the pavements in front of their property, but some time later it was found that this bye-law was unsound and the fines had to be refunded. Also in this year, the Board applied for legal permission to operate, and received approval for, a third market, on Wednesdays. The existing ones operated on Monday and Saturday. It was also necessary to appoint a new Town Crier, the existing one being considered too old for the duties. An new outfit had to be provided at a cost of £4. 18. 0.

In 1856 the General Rate was set at 2/6d, the highest so far recorded, in addition there was a special rate of 1/10d. Special rates were applied to meet the cost of some capital works, but were also still levied to meet the expense of the poor, and only at a later date was this expense absorbed into the general rate.

For the purpose of applying the general rate, separate costs were kept for each parish since Cobridge or Rushton Grange claimed immunity from some charges. Burslem for the second time decided to test the validity of Cobridge claiming the financial privileges previously enjoyed by of the monks of Hulton, and this time it was settled in Burslem's favour. It is interesting to see the total cost for this period on which the general rate was applied:

Total cost of services	£6916. 10. 8.
Estimate of rate realisation at 2/6d	£7178. 0. 0.
Less for abatements	£897. 0. 0.
Balance	£6281. 0. 0.

GENERAL ANNUAL LICENSING MEETING

of Her Majesty's Justices of the Peace acting for the Leek Division of the County of Stafford, will be held at the TOWN HALL, in LEEK aforesaid, on WEDNESDAY, the TWENTY-SIXTH day of AUGUST, 1896, at the hour of ELEVEN o'clock in the Forenoon, for granting and renewing Licenses and Certificates for the following purposes, namely :

1.—For the sale by retail in Inns of Intoxicating Liquors under the Intoxicating Liquor Licensing Act, 1828, and Acts amending the same ;

2.—For the sale by retail of Beer, Cider, and Wine, under the Wine and Beerhouse Acts, 1869 and 1870, and Acts amending the same ;

3.—For the sale of Spirits, Liqueurs, and Sweets by retail, pursuant to the Licensing Acts, 1872—1874 ;

4.—For granting Billiard Licenses ;

5.—For granting Licenses to keep or use Houses, Rooms, Gardens or places for public dancing, singing, music, or other public entertainment of the like kind, pursuant to Part 4 of the Public Health Acts Amendment Act, 1890 ;

A notice of a meeting of the local JPs at nearby Leek for the granting of licenses in consequence of various acts

The second town hall and the statue of Sir Henry Doulton

CHAPTER TWENTY THREE: Town Halls and Trams

Dismantling the old and constructing the existing Town Hall. The introduction of trams.

In 1852 the lack of space for the administration of the growing borough emphasised the inadequacy of the first town hall. No doubt the old town hall, along with many other buildings, was also suffering from mining subsidence and the universal grime accumulated from sitting in the midst of so many pottery kilns - a visitor at the time remarked that he wondered whether Mother Burslem had married a black man!

A new hall was proposed and the inhabitants of Burslem were asked to submit proposals. Two sites were offered in Newcastle Street and one in Nile Street, but the Board were of the opinion that the hall should remain in the centre of the town, the existing hall to be demolished and a larger one built. John Ward objected and said that in his opinion it would be illegal and contravened the act which covered the building of the first hall, and that he would sustain his objection. Despite this the Board proposed that designs be sought in open competition for a building not to cost more than £5000, with prize money of £50 for the first choice and a consolation prize of £25 for the second.

Several entries were received and these were numbered for display, without bearing the name of the architect in order to avoid any question of favouritism. At a special meeting of the Board the unanimous choice was number twenty nine. The successful architect was revealed as Mr Robinson of Wolverhampton and the runner up Mr Robert W Armstrong. To seal the choice, a dinner was arranged at the Legs of Man and the successful architect invited by the Board to attend. The Board members were told they were each responsible for the cost of their own meal, possibly to avoid the wroth of the Burslem Parochial Reform Association who had already chastised them for wasting ratepayers money on self indulgence.

Materialisation of the project still needed clarification of Mr Ward's claim. It may be unfair to infer that Mr Ward was influenced by personal reasons, but by coincidence at this time he was in dispute with the Board over another matter. The 1825 act which authorised the building of the first hall had stated that the remuneration of the organist at St John's, the parish church would be paid out of market tolls, but now that St Paul's was built there were two presbyterian organists, and payment to both had been made from the tolls until it was pointed out that the new church was not named in the act. The next annual request for payment by the St Paul's organist was not met, and in desperation he put the matter in the hands of John Ward, in his professional capacity as a solicitor. Ward in turn, when he met the Board, seemingly gave the impression that if they would settle with the organist, he would consider withdrawing his objection to the new hall! The Commissioners were apparently unimpressed and proceeded to ask for tenders. Three tenders were submitted:

        No. 1 £7428 -£250 allowed for old town hall
        No. 2 £8432 -£160   "   "
        No. 3 £7725 -£175   "   "

No. 1 submitted by Robert Young of Lincoln was accepted, and in January 1854 Mr Young should have been in Burslem to sign the contract, but he sent a telegram to say that, due to snow, he was unable to get beyond Uttoxeter.

Winter gave way to spring, the old hall was demolished and Mr William Davenport was asked to lay the foundation stone of the new building. The date had to be amended when the special trowel broke on route from Liverpool. Evidently by tradition the trowel had to conform to the high artistic standard of previous occasions, and be more of a museum exhibit than a mundane tool. The date finally fixed for the ceremony allowed for the trowel to be exhibited in Mr Hales window in the town for a week before the event to enable the public to admire it. The ceremony took place but Enoch Wood, who had now been dead for fourteen years, was not able to indulge his favourite pastime of burying treasure under foundation stones, and the practice on this occasion seems to have been overlooked.

The style of the new hall was Italian, and the size 110 feet by 60 feet. The basement had two large windows, and the west end a large porch with an arched entrance, sufficiently wide to admit a carriage and protect the occupants from inclement weather. The upper portion of the entrance was a portico, from which a public speaker could address an audience below, and the building was crowned with a clock tower. The hall comprised three storeys; the lower floor containing police cells, heating apparatus and kitchen. The ground floor comprised an entrance hall leading to a corridor and staircase and on one side of the corridor offices of the clerk and the boardroom. On the opposite side were a dock, a magistrates' bench, a witness box, a reporters bench, apartments for the caretaker, and a stairway to the orchestral balcony. Adjacent to the magistrates' bench were two splendid figures of Justice and Mercy; but Justice and Mercy are no longer to be found in Burslem - they were last seen in a photograph by Ernest Warrilow, lying in an undignified position on a handcart destined it is said for a future as garden ornaments.

The building progressed with only occasional disputes between architect and contractor. One man is said to have been killed during the building. The final sum paid to the contractor was £7178, with a further sum claimed for extras. Externally it is still an imposing structure, and up to the present it has stood the test of conditions both above and below ground.

For most of the interior work there were separate tenders, and many of these were from local contractors which indicates the growth towards self sufficiency in the locality. The interior furnishings were put out to tender, and ultimately one for £1014 was accepted from Robert Chapman of Newcastle under Lyme. Finger plates to the design of Mr Robinson were made at Mayer's factory. Further tenders were accepted for hot water heating for the sum of £150 and for gas fittings £300.

A tender for the construction of a floor in the clock room, and for gilding the clock went to a Mr Young for £81, but it would seem that the original hands on the clock were not in keeping, since there was a charge of £26 from Mr George Slater for supplying and fitting gilt copper hands. To the relief of the lamp lighter, machinery for operating the lighting on the clock was supplied, for a modest £6. The 'crowning purchase', the weather vane, cost £79.

The new hall was connected to the town's new drainage and sewage systems at a cost of £1000. The area surrounding the hall was paved and four gas pillars with multiple butterfly burners erected. The final purchase was two flags, a Royal Standard £7.10.0 and a Union Jack £6.0.0, from Gilbert French of Bolton.

In 1856 the position of keeper and wife between the age of 30 and 45 was advertised at a combined salary of £40 per annum with free housing and heating. A similar advertisement in 1880, except that a salary of £50 was offered, attracted thirty one applicants. Members of the public had, somewhat belatedly it appears, expressed an interest in attending meetings of the Board, but were informed it was impossible to find space at the moment, but ways would be considered, nevertheless some members were averse to any such intrusion, and the 'moment' was extended to five years when, in 1885, it was proposed that a gallery be built which would provide space for citizens. Objection was again raised by Board members on the grounds that there would be dangerous congestion if, in the case of a fire, the gallery and the hall were being evacuated. Perhaps as a result of public frustration, a more radical suggestion was that the Shambles Market, which was now under-used, should incorporate the Vegetable Market, and the Vegetable Market be converted to a magnificent town hall. This proposition was also discarded as being more expensive than building a new town hall, but from the train of thought, and Burslem's apparent growing propensity for town halls, one can anticipate the seed of another and the future birth of the Queens Hall.

The original proposed charges for the letting of the hall for meetings, concerts, bazaars, etc. were: Main Hall £3.3.0. Court Room £1.1.0 with lighting extra after 8 o'clock, 3/- for one light, 6/- for two, and 9/- for three.

The Masonic Lodge, currently using the George Hotel for its meetings, received exceptional terms for the use of the Court Room from October to March on Wednesday evenings for the global sum of £6.6.0. In 1858, the Rector of St Johns requested the use of the Magistrates room at a nominal rent for public prayers, but he was refused any preferential terms. However, in 1860 the charge for the main hall,

Hire cabs outside the town hall, the entrance to the meat market (the Shambles) is seen in the background

Right: The second town hall with the cabbies shelter at the front

Below: The entrance to the town hall from Newcastle Street

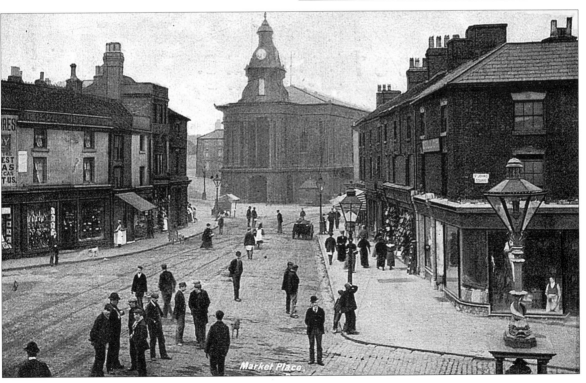

which was capable of seating 630 persons, was reduced to £2.2.0. and for religious use on Sunday 10/-, this latter probably due to the number of religious bodies who had subsequently followed the rector's lead. An advertisement in 1907 seemed to indicate a continued loss of interest in its use, or increasing competition from elsewhere, since the use of the main hall was even further reduced to £1.10. per evening; use of Beckstein Piano 10. 0s. per night, hire of Court Room, if court not removed, 15. 0s.

The official opening of the hall was proposed for 28th January 1857, to be celebrated with a public dinner at a charge of 7/6d per person (excluding wine), this to be followed by a concert in the main hall organised by Mr Powell. To celebrate the inauguration of the new court room, it was proposed that at its first use there would be a civic procession to accompany the visiting magistrate from the George Hotel to the town hall. Regretfully, despite the provision of a court room, the law was lothe to use it, and the Board sent a written request for quarter sessions in turn with Stoke and Hanley.

In 1857 controversy over Palmerston's intervention in China led to the dissolving of parliament and a fresh election. A new candidate presented himself in Burslem, a Mr Samuel Pope, a barrister from Manchester, whose political advocacy was the abolishment of intoxicating drink through legislation, but apparently neither the gentleman's surname, or his proposed legislation appealed to the voters in Burslem and they declined to nominate him. The election was finally fought between old contestants, and resulted in the success of one Tory and one Liberal, the Tory being Copeland, and the Liberal Ricardo, Gower losing his seat. This parliament was short lived and another contest took place in 1859. Undeterred, Mr Pope again put forward his name, and at least succeeded in being nominated, but failed to unseat either of the retiring representatives.

In 1858, the Surveyor's report for the year said that out of 5000 houses, 133 were still without a water supply. In 1859, Mr William Davenport of the firm of Davenport, potters of Longport, had the honour of being appointed High Sheriff of Staffordshire, and the Board called a special meeting to consider whether, considering the reflection on Burslem, he should be escorted to Stafford. It was decided that a representative of the Board should wait on him to discuss the suggestion. Remarkably, the same situation arose the following year when another eminent Burslem citizen, Mr Howard Haywood of the firm of Haywood Brothers received the like honour, and the Board adopted the same procedure.

In 1861, the Potteries Street Railway Company was formed and obtained the right to operate a service from Burslem to Hanley. The company first laid lines between the two towns along the length of Waterloo Road. These original lines were on wooden sleepers, which in turn were laid on the surface of the road, and such was the effect of mining subsidence, that it was not uncommon on occasions to find that the road had sunk and the lines left hanging in places above the road. In 1862 the first horse drawn tram, loaded with important officials from both towns, left Fountain Square in Hanley to the accompaniment of church bells and the cheers of crowds, and arrived at the top of Waterloo Road after a journey which took nine minutes! On arrival in Burslem the privileged passengers retired to Burslem town hall for wine and biscuits, returning later to Hanley for more wine and speeches.

The regular service which followed was half hourly, leaving Burslem on the hour, and Hanley on the half hour. The fare for the whole journey was three pence, and for half way to Cobridge Toll house the charge from either end was two pence. At a later date the rails were extended from the top of Waterloo Road to the market place in the centre of the town. The trams themselves were given names, as fitted the local tradition for important machines.

The threepenny fare later increased to four pence, the tram company claiming it was necessary since toll costs were running at £300 per year, however negotiations were in progress with the Cobridge Turnpike Trust and eventually the company achieved a modified charge which reduced the yearly cost to £100. In 1881, possibly to make way for the rapid changes lying ahead, the name of the company was changed to the North Staffordshire Tramways Company, but not for long since it changed again to the North Staffordshire Steam Tramways, formed to run a steam tramway from Burslem to Longton, a great extension of the service. The introduction of a power unit also enabled the use of articulated trams coupled to the separate propulsion unit which was manned by a driver and a stoker.

The introduction of a tramway proved beneficial not only to the travelling public but also to drivers of horse drawn vehicles, particularly up Waterloo Road, since the drivers found the rails a boon for the horses negotiating the rise up the lengthy road to the town. On the other hand the practice was a constant frustration for the tram driver who, on coming up behind a slower vehicle and using his bell to no effect, had no option but to slow down until finally he was forced to reverse to a lower level to achieve sufficient impetus again! Despite this, the company were optimistic enough to attempt double decker trams, but the Potteries hills proved too formidable.

At full speed, which was eight miles per hour, these steam trams must have been an awesome sight, and the noise pretty horrendous. One councillor said he dared not ride his horse anywhere near one in case it bolted. Another said they were the most dangerous contraptions he had ever seen; and the nuisance inspectors complained of the volume of oily water which leaked from them and the smoke they emitted. In 1882, the tramways company applied to the Board of Trade for permission to work the steam trams for seven years, but Burslem recommended that they should not be worked other than with horse power, and that they should not be allowed beyond Swan Square, which would have kept them clear of the centre of the town. Nevertheless, it seems that the tram company won the day, since in 1879 they requested permission from Burslem to extend the service to Goldenhill. Agreement was presumably reluctantly given, provided the route was via the Market Place, Liverpool Road, Hall Street and Newport Street, but the strength of objections which arose over traction engines in these streets, resulted in second thoughts.

In 1889 the tramway company was bought by the British Electric Traction Company, who were granted a twenty one year contract, with a clause giving the local authority an option to purchase. By 1895 the extension had still to be made and the company were given an ultimatum of six months to extend to Goldenhill, Smallthorne and Longport. The company embarked on a major programme. New heavier lines flush with the road were laid and in 1898, the first run took place from Burslem to Longton; unfortunately on this first day a boy was hit by the tram in Waterloo Road and killed. Electrification obviously had a beneficial effect on the cost of fares since the charge for the journey from Burslem to Longton was two pence, and this badly hit Loop Line railway passenger traffic.

The tram company installed its own generating plant at Stoke, in a building adjoining the Stoke Rectory. The Rector complained that the rectory vibrated to such an extent in the day, and through the night, that he could not sleep, and eventually it affected his health to such a degree that his wife said he was unfit to continue with his vocation. The tramway company wisely purchased the rectory and it was ultimately converted to offices.

Despite the increasing competition from tramways, there was still a frantic urge to invest in new railways, and the Burslem Board constantly received requests to support bills for fresh projects. In 1862, one such was called The Potteries Junction Railway Scheme. The Board generally offered support but nothing seems to have materialised of this particular scheme. The tramways on the other hand were expanding their services, since the local company applied to the Board for a room in Burslem town hall to be used as a parcel receiving office.

The horse drawn tram

Above: The electrical tramway
in Waterloo Road with Hanley
in the distance

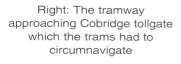

Right: The tramway
approaching Cobridge tollgate
which the trams had to
circumnavigate

THE POTTERIES ELECTRIC TRACTION Co., Ltd.

PARCELS EXPRESS.

LOCAL, INLAND, FOREIGN, and COLONIAL

CARRIERS.

Shipping and Forwarding Agents in conjunction with
all the Leading Carriers and Forwarding Agencies.

HOURLY DELIVERIES.   DAILY DISPATCH
THROUGHOUT THE DISTRICT.   TO ALL PARTS OF THE UNITED KINGDOM.

☞ OFFICES AND AGENCIES THROUGHOUT THE DISTRICT. ☜

Parcels may be handed to the Conductor of any Car, or to the following Offices :—

			LOCAL RATES.
Chief Parcels Office,	PERCY STREET, HANLEY.	Tel. No. 1.	7 lbs. - 2d.
Branch "	MARKET HALL, LONGTON.	Tel. No. 106.	14 lbs. - 3d.
" "	MARKET PLACE, NEWCASTLE:	Tel. No. 0194.	28 lbs. - 4d.
" "	WEDGWOOD PLACE, BURSLEM, Adjoining Post Office.	Tel. No. 01190.	42 lbs. - 5d.
" "	STOKE DEPOT.	Tel. No. 801.	56 lbs. - 6d.
" "	MAY BANK.	Tel. No. 436.	1d. extra for each additional 7 lbs.
" "	HIGH STREET, TUNSTALL.	Tel. No. 18 X 2.	
" "	KING STREET, FENTON.	Tel. No. ——	

W. THOM, *General Manager.*

The second and current town hall with the meat market (the Shambles) to the right .
The latter is now demolished. (*Photo courtesy of the Potteries Museum*)

Steam lorry in burslem at the end of the 19th century

Celebrations for Queen Victoria's Jubillee in front of the Town Hall

CHAPTER TWENTY FOUR: The Wedgwood Institute

Architecturally the Wedgwood Institute is the pride of Burslem. The concept was promoted in 1854 as a School of Art, Museum and Library, but due to stagnation in trade, interest flagged until 1859 when a public meeting was held on 27th January, at which the chair was taken by the Earl of Carlisle, Patron of the Arts. Also present were the Duchess of Sutherland, most of the major pottery manufacturers, civic and church dignitaries, Mr J.A. Hammersley, Principal of the Manchester School of Art, and other interested parties. The resolution was:

> "This meeting, entertaining high respect for the memory of the late Josiah Wedgwood, and the grateful sense of the services rendered by him to the trade and general interest of the Staffordshire Potteries, desire to erect a public monument to his memory in the town of Burslem, his birthplace, and the scene of his early and most successful labours."

The Staffordshire Advertiser reported that Mr Hammersley referred to Josiah Wedgwood as a world wide celebrity; recently, after a day travelling near the Alps, he had been served dessert on a piece of ware of the immortal Wedgwood's and his thoughts were immediately thrown back to the place where he also was born and trained. He said of the project:

> "there has been a good deal said about a School of Design, or School of Art. Burslem has had one of these and they said it failed, although they might properly have used some other term. My experience of that school would lead me to say it had not failed, but that to the extent of its means it had succeeded. Teachers at the school were in every respect adequate, and the productions exhibited to Sir C Eastlake were second to none in the kingdom. The school failed, partly on account of the circumstances in which it was placed, partly from the nation's intention of what a school should do, and partly from its being situated in a villainous room, in a locality where no one having physical decency would go; the manufacturers looked upon the working man as a sort of machine to produce marketable patterns, and conversely, the working man considered that by going to school a number of quarters, he should obtain the power of designing, which would enable him to increase his wages. A school of design had nothing to do with patterns, but was intended to make everybody recognise examples of the great principles which the world had set them, of adding beauty to utility".

Sir Charles Lock Eastlake was at the time Director of the National Gallery and was exerting his influence to improve the Country's schools of art. Immediate arrangements were made for a subscription list, and donations totalling £3000 were promised. Designs were sought on a national scale, with prizes of £20 and £10 offered for the two best. Twenty nine were received, but none enthusiastically, and a second competition was arranged, limited to six of the previous entrants, the one whose design was accepted to be given charge of the construction. Only four designs were submitted and the one by George Benjamin Nichols was accepted. Detailed plans were submitted by him in 1861 but fear of the cost in the prevailing economic conditions delayed the next meeting until 1863.

The meeting in 1863 was delayed by a day for the celebrations that marked the erection of a magnificent bronze statue of Josiah outside Stoke station, the occasion being declared a general holiday throughout the district. The event was the culmination of a belated communal effort of the six towns to acknowledge the district's debt to Josiah and Burslem of its particular debt. The conscience of all may have been pricked that an outsider, Mr Joseph Mayer from Liverpool, had been the one to draw attention to the omission.

The following day the meeting was resumed in Burslem, and the Conservative MP, Mr Alexander Berrisford Hope, attended. At the recent election, this gentleman had successfully replaced the retiring Mr Copeland, and by good fortune, the new member's interest provided the vision and knowledge which this project required. He was a recognised authority on architecture. He suggested that the building should exemplify the structural application of ceramics. This was a radical suggestion which would vastly increase the cost. He disliked Nichols design of the façade which had a preponderance of brickwork due

The inaugural ceremony for the statue of Josiah Wedgwood at Stoke

The original design incorporating medallions in the window arches, ultimately dispensed with for economy reasons, while the statue of Josiah was yet to be designed

to his decision to use roof lighting for the art section. Instead of formal drawings, Mr Hope suggested a further competition to provide coloured sketches of an artistic frontage for the building, and he offered a personal prize of £25. An outstanding design which incorporated ceramic features as part of the structure, submitted by Robert Edgar and John Lockwood Kipling, was accepted.

John Kipling was the father of Rudyard Kipling, who owed his christian name to his parents love of the local Rudyard Lake while in the area. Robert Edgar was an architect and a pupil of Gilbert Scott; Kipling had been involved in architectural terracotta while training at Kensington School of Art and subsequently worked at Pinder Bourne as modeller and later art director, before it became Doultons. He later left for India for the post of architectural sculptor at the Bombay School of Art. Edgar was appointed sole overseer of the construction of the Institute, following the dismissal of Nichols after an acrimonious dispute.

The artist's drawing seen below (from Eliza Meteyard's *Life of Wedgwood*) is probably that which was submitted, chosen and generally followed, except that the majolica plaques shown in the arches over the windows are not in the building today. It is possible they never were, since the committee did attempt to put a ceiling on the cost of embellishments and these may have been sacrificed. Neither is the statue of Josiah to be seen on the drawing but since the building was not completed until 1870, the idea could have been a late conception.

Generally described as Venetian Gothic, the front of the building has ten window bays on the ground floor, five on each side of a magnificent doorway. Above the porch entrance, and completed in medallion style are three bas reliefs representing Flaxman, Bentley and Priestley, and on a pedestal above the doorway stands a beautiful statue of Josiah Wedgwood, flanked by ten huge panels, five on each side, depicting processes of the industry. Above these are twelve panels with signs of the zodiac each representing a month of the year and executed by Salviati in Venetian mosaic on a gold ground. The whole of the frontage in terracotta gives a dazzling insight into the native industry and its production practices, while at the same time demonstrating the possibility of a lucrative expansion in the use of clays for architectural purposes. The modelling was done at the Kensington School of Art by artists trained in the local Pottery towns. The first two to go in 1865 were Rowland James Morris and William Wright, followed in 1866 by James F. Marsh. The school offered artistic help and use of its facilities, in addition to the Controlling Board subsidising the project.

The design of the panels depicting the pottery processes was, with the statue of Josiah, the work of Mathew Eldon, a former pupil of Stoke School of Art and member of Kensington School staff. The modelling of the statue of Josiah was mainly the work of Morris. An example of Morris's later work is the dragon by the fountain in Hanley Park. He is said to have worked in Burslem at Alcocks and for Bernard Moore, and appears to have been the principal modeller of the three who went to Kensington.

Finance was a continuous problem, but an early loan of £1000 from the Public Loan Board, and the product of a 1d rate in Burslem, enabled the organisers to pay 40/- per week to the modellers, and in addition they received a subsidy from the school. All the terracotta work, with the exception of the process panels, was produced in conjunction with Mr Blanchford who at his works at Millwall had, through his collaboration with Minton, experience in the production of encaustic work. The panels depicting the stages in the production of pottery were processed by John Marriott Blashfield at Stamford, in which area he had found a suitable bed of clay and formed the Stamford Terra-Cotta Co. Ltd. (a site which was later found to have housed a medieval pottery).

For the production of the panels it was decided to take an extremely risky course and avoid the usual pottery method of taking clay castings from plaster moulds. Instead, Blashfield provided wood and plaster frames filled with pressed clay, each for the production of an individual panel. These frames were sent to Kensington where, from drawings of each panel, the clay was then cut, and undercut by the modellers, as if cutting a subject in stone or marble. The panels were then returned to Stamford, where each was divided into four or five pieces and fired. The risk in travel, cutting, and firing, and the absence of plaster moulds

OPENING OF THE WEDGWOOD INSTITUTE,

BURSLEM.

COPY OF ADDRESS.

To the Right Honourable the Earl De Grey and Ripon,

Lord President of Her Majesty's Most Honourable Privy Council.

MY LORD,

WE, the undersigned, Chief Bailiff and Members of the Local Board of Health for the District of Burslem, in the County of Stafford; on behalf of the Inhabitants whom we represent, most heartily welcome you in your Personal, as well as in your Official capacity, on your first visit to the Town, and thank your Lordship for having so readily consented to officiate at the Opening of a Building, the Foundation Stone of which was so auspiciously laid by your colleague the present Prime Minister, on the 26th October, 1863.

We are especially glad that your Lordship has given us the opportunity of calling your attention personally to the Educational requirements of the district, which, we believe, to be worthy of your Lordships serious consideration. The population of the Pottery District is in an exceptional degree, composed of the classes which most need the assistance of the Public Funds, the extension of the Factory Acts has to a considerable extent secured the School attendance of a large number of previously neglected Children, the National and Denominational Agencies have provided School Accommodation for them, but we believe experience will shew that the instruction actually imparted to them, might be largely improved and increased.

We regret to inform your Lordship that for Middle Class Education there is in Burslem no provision, and in the Pottery Districts, comparatively little, and we trust that in dealing with the question of Educational Endowments, the wants of so an important a population will not escape the attention of your Lordship and of Parliament.

That "Technical Education" has been much neglected is evidenced by the reply of the Local Chamber of Commerce, to enquiries addressed to it last year, in which the Chamber asserts, that the Manufacturers of the District are only enabled to meet Foreign competition by importing workmen, "who from having received a better education than the workmen of this country, have thus fitted themselves to perform duties which could not be undertaken by our own people;" and one Manufactory in the District is instanced by the Chamber, in which a sum of £2,000 a year is paid to foreign workmen; a state of things which we feel ought not to continue without remedial measures.

We believe a combination of private effort with National Grants, and assistance from Local Rates to be desirable. The Wedgwood Institute has been erected by the employment of these three agencies, and we cheerfully recognize the disposition of Parliament to aid the development of local enterprize by Grants in aid of Buildings, and by Annual Payments for Educational purposes; and on the other hand we refer with satisfaction and pride, to the action taken by the Inhabitants of Burslem, in voluntarily charging themselves with a rate, which will be partly available under local management for the Education in Science and Art, which will be given in the Building, which your Lordship is here to inaugurate.

Allow us my Lord to express our earnest and fervent desire that a gracious Providence may still smile upon our beloved Queen, and that your Lordship, and your Right Honourable Colleagues, may be spared to establish on a firm and lasting basis, the prosperity and contentment of every section of the Empire.

Dated this Twenty-first day of April, 1869,

THOMAS HULME,
           CHIEF BAILIFF.

EDWARD PEARSON.	JOSEPH P. EMERY.
GEORGE WIGLEY.	THOMAS DIGGORY.
JOHN WATKIN.	THOMAS HUGHES.
STEPHEN EDGE.	JOSEPH CORBETT.
WILLIAM WOODALL.	CHARLES B. MAY.
JAMES DEAN.	ROBERT GILMORE.
THOMAS LEICESTER.	

JOSEPH LOWNDES,
           CLERK.

to replace a faulty or broken piece was enormous, and would have entailed the modeller restarting the whole process. The risks fortunately appear to have been avoided and the finished panels give a magnificent three dimensional effect, similar to that which Josiah Wedgwood achieved with his applied figures. A unique feature of the building was the stipulation that the panels were to be part of the structure rather than a facing, which made them tremendously heavy. Edgar himself said that each piece into which they were cut weighed hundredweights. Integral surface drainage has intentionally left the facade free to become an uninterupted masterpiece in stone, but unfortunately left some flooding problems in its wake. Another interesting feature of this frontage is the initials of key persons involved in the project, worked into the scroll work of the piers of the ground floor windows.

Mr Gladstone was asked to lay the foundation stone, but declined, so Mr Grenfell, who had been successful as a local Whig candidate in the 1862 election, was asked to appeal to him. Mr. Gladstone's response was *"I have a very sincere desire to do honour to Wedgwood, as well as to avoid any seeming disregard of the wishes of your constituents, and if they hold the meeting any time no earlier than the middle of October* (1863) *while I am tolerably free from other engagements, I will certainly endeavour to come to Burslem for the purpose of doing honour to a man I regard as a great benefactor of his country"*.

To suit his convenience therefore, it was arranged for the ceremony to take place on 26th October 1863, the occasion to be celebrated with banners across the streets declaring "Welcome to the Right Honourable W.E. Gladstone M.P. D.C.L.", "Peace and Prosperity" and "May honest industry ever prosper". A triumphal arch was to be erected at the top of Newcastle Street to cost no more than £5. Music was to be organised and the ringing of church bells; again the cost specified not to exceed £15. The Rifle Corp Band were to play for two hours before the ceremony and to play the National Anthem at the close.

In accordance with their own request, most of the shops would be closed until 3pm on the day. The stone laying ceremony was to be followed by a lunch, the cost of which would be fifteen shillings for gents and ten shillings for ladies. Reserved seats for the stone laying ceremony were to be five shillings to two and sixpence, according to position. The advertising of the occasion was to be in *The Staffordshire Advertiser, The Sentinel, The Manchester Guardian & Examiner* and *The Birmingham Daily Post.*

A marquee to seat 1200 people was erected on the site and among the assembled guests were Mr Gladstone's wife and daughter, three cabinet ministers, a number of other members of parliament, Earl Granville, the Bishop of Lichfield, Viscount Ingestree, Sir James Duke, members of the Chamber of Commerce, manufacturers, founder members of the insitute and several wealthy collectors including LLewellyn Jewitt F.S.A. (author of The Ceramic Art of Great Britain). Also present were Joseph Mayer, a Liverpool jeweller and goldsmith, a well known collector of Wedgwood ware, who also bought part of Enoch Wood's collection when it was dispersed following his death (now probably in the Liverpool Museum to which Joseph Mayer donated his lifetime collection). Seats for these honoured guests were draped in scarlet baize by Mr Smith of Burslem at a cost of three pence per yard. Senior members of the committee wore rosettes, and others acting as stewards, wore blue and white ties, again supplied by Mr Smith and paid for by the committee. For services rendered on the occasion the Rifle Corp received £3, the Bell Ringers £3, and the Police one shilling per man.

Two addresses were presented to Mr Gladstone, one from the Council on behalf of the town and its inhabitants and one from the working men of Burslem. The civic address was mostly confined to the problems of education, particularly in regard to the needs of industry for technical education in which Britain appeared to be lagging behind the rest of Europe! The address of the working men of Burslem showed no lack of competence in English composition, but cautious in not stepping beyond their station:

"Right Honourable Sir,
We, the Workingmen of Burslem, most respectfully desire to address you, with grateful deference and warm gratification, on this your first visit to our Town; coming, as you do, for the disinterested and generous purpose of rendering us assistance in the accomplishment of an object which will greatly benefit us of the present age, and afford valuable aid for the future education and improvement of our children. Although we are duly sensible, Sir, of the delicacy of our undertaking, still we wish frankly and warmly to express our grateful acknowledgment of the conduct

you have always displayed in reference to the great measures that have been passed during the last twenty years by the British Legislature; measures which have conferred incalculable blessings on the whole community, and particularly on the working classes, by unfettering the trade and commerce of the country; cheapening the essentials of our daily sustenances; placing a large proportion of the luxuries and comforts of life within our reach; and rendering the attainment of knowledge comparatively easy among the great mass of the sons of toil. We know, Sir, that you have had many able and liberal minded coadjutors in the achievements alluded to, and though we are not unmindful of our claims as citizens in common, still we feel it a pleasure and a duty to express our unqualified gratitude for the generous aid they, in connection with yourself, have always given for the general benefit of the class to which we belong. Pardon us, Sir, for alluding to the kindly conduct now so commonly evinced by the wealthier portions of the community, to assist in the physical and moral improvement of the working classes. The wellbeing of the toiling mass is now generally admitted to be an essential to the national weal. This forms a pleasing contrast to the opinions cherished half a century ago. The humbler classes also, are duly mindful of the happy change, and without any abatement of manly independence, fully appreciate the benefits resulting therefrom; contentedly fostering a hopeful expectation of the future. May Heaven favour and promote this happy mutuality! as we feel confident that all such kindly interchange materially contributes to the general good. We may be permitted Sir, on this occasion, to express our gratification that he, to whose memory this Institute is being founded, commenced in life as a working man, and by his genius, providence, and industry, obtained a worldwide and honourable fame, and added his influence to that of a host of other worthies, who have risen from the humbler ranks to assist in uplifting in social estimation the great labouring community. The name of Josiah Wedgwood ought ever to claim the respect and esteem of those who earn their daily bread in the business he so much aided to improve and elevate to one of England's greatest staple manufactures. In conclusion Sir, please allow us most sincerely and earnestly to wish that you may be long blessed with life and healthful vigour, to assist in the councils of our amiable and honoured Sovereign, and to join your exertions with those noble minded and liberal men of the British Parliament, in fully consummating the work you so eloquently sketched in your speech on the New Tariff of 1860, that is, "in striking away the shackles from the arm of industry, giving incentive and new reward to toil, which will win more and more for the throne and the institutions of the country, the gratitude, the confidence, and the love of an united people".

Signed on behalf of the Workingmen of Burslem.
PETER BOWERS., W.H. MAYER., HIRAM COPE.

Prayers were offered by the Bishop of Lichfield and the Stone was then laid. The ceremony continued with a speech from Mr Gladstone:

"It is my practice to decline all invitations to ceremonials of a purely local character, unless such as he had some personal connection, but I consider the present one to be national, because the manufacture of earthenware in its variable and numerous branches is fast becoming, or has indeed become, one of our great and distinguishing British manufactures, and because there are certain principles applicable to manufacture, by the observance or neglect of which its products are rendered good or bad. These principles were applied by Wedgwood with a consistency and tenacity that cannot too closely be observed in industrial production. These principles being his, and being true, were also in no small degree peculiar to his practice, and deserve to be in the permanent annals of art associated with his name. If I, as a learner, appear to be teaching, I submit my opinions with deference, and am anxious, having formed a high estimate of Wedgwood in his relation to the general laws of industrial production, to have that estimate fully and fairly brought to the trial of public judgment.

Again, in the office I hold as a servant of the Crown (Chancellor of the Exchequer) and which places me in incessant contact with the industry of the country in its several branches, I am anxious, from the deep interest I have in its welfare, to bear my testimony to the principles of which Wedgwood was, so to speak, an apostle and moreover, to give to that testimony any little weight which such an office, and such a deep interest and near relation established by it, as maybe likely in the absence of higher personal qualifications, to impart. Thirty years ago, it would probably have been held by many, and it may still be thought of some of the matters of which I have now to speak, are matters which may well be left to regulate themselves. To vindicate for trade in all its branches, the principle and power of self regulation has been for a quarter of a century, a principle of the British Parliament. But the very same stage in our political and social existence which has taught us the true and beneficial of the laws of political economy, has likewise disclosed to us the just limits of the science, and of the field of practical application. The very same age which has seen the State strike off the fetters of industry, has also seen it interpose with boldness for the protection of labour. The same spirit and policy which has taken from the producer the enjoyment of preferences, paralysing to him and most costly to the community at large, has offered him the aids of knowledge and instruction by whatever means, either of precept or example, public authority could command.

Of useful manufactured commodities themselves, production of these should combine convenience with beauty. Beauty in not an accident in things, it pertains to their essence, it pervades the wide range of creation, and wherever it is impaired or banished, we have in this fact the proof of the moral disorder which disturbs the world. Reject therefore the false philosophy of those who will ask, "what does it matter providing the thing be useful whether it be beautiful or not?" and say in reply that we will take our lesson from Almighty God, who in his works has shown us, and in his words, told us, that He hath made everything, not one thing, or another thing, but everything beautiful in His time. Among all the devices in creation, there is not one more wonderful, whether it be the movement of the heavenly bodies, or the successions of the seasons of the years, or the adaptation of the world and its phenomena to the conditions of human life, or the structure of the eye, or the hand, or any part of the human frame, not one of these is more wonderful than the profuseness which the mighty Maker has shed over the works of his hands, an endless and boundless beauty. To the constitution of things outward, and the constitution and mind of man, even though they be deranged, still answer from within, down to the humblest condition of life, down to the lowest and most backward grade of civilization, the nature of man craves, and seems as it were even to cry aloud for something, some sign or token at the least, of what is beautiful in some of the many spheres to the mind or sense. It is that which makes the Spitalfields weaver, amid the murky streets of London, train canaries and bullfinches to sing to him at his work; that fills with flowerpots the windows of the poor; that leads the peasant of Pembrokeshire to paint his cottage in lively colours; that prompts in the humble class of women a desire for some little personal ornament.

This is certainly not without its dangers, for what sort of indulgence can ever be without them? Yet sometimes, perhaps too sternly repressed from the high and luxurious places of society, we trace the operation of this principle yet more conspicuously in a loftier region; in that instinct of natural and Christian piety which taught the early masters of the fine arts to clothe the noblest objects of our faith, and especially the idea of the sacred person of our Lord, in the noblest forms of beauty that their minds could conceive, or their hands could execute, it is, in short, difficult for human beings to harden themselves at all points against the impressions and the charm of beauty. There is a danger of artists neglecting beauty in manufacture as if it was an element of expense, and that their rule should be cheapness, but the cheapest at first was not cheapest in the long run. Mankind was willing to pay a price for beauty, and the neglect of beauty was revenged by the demand for embellishment of some kind; and the manufacturers, unable to supply beautiful embellishment, substituted strength for flavour, quantity for quality, and ended by producing incongruous excrescences, or even hideous malformations of a greater cost than would have sufficed for the nourishment among us of chaste and virgin art.

Wedgwood's most signal characteristic lay, as I have said, in the fineness and fulness of his perception of the true law of what we term industrial art; or in other words, of the application of the higher art to industry; the law which teaches us to aim first at giving to every object the greatest possible degree of fitness and convenience for its purpose, and next, at making it the vehicle of the highest degree of beauty with the compatibility with that fitness and convenience it will bear. This does not substitute the secondary for the primary end, but recognises as part of its business, the study to harmonise the two. To have a strong grasp of this principle, and to work it out to its result in the details of a vast and varied manufacture, is praise enough for any man, at any time, or in any place. It was higher, and more peculiar as I think, in the case of Wedgwood than in any other case it could be, for the truth of art which he saw so clearly, and lies at the root of excellence, was one of which England, his country, has not usually been a perception which corresponded with her other rare endowments. She has long taken the lead among the nations of Europe for the cheapness of her manufactures; not so for their beauty; and if the day shall ever come when she shall be eminent in taste, as she is now in economy of production, my belief is that that result will probably be due to no other single man in so great a degree as Wedgwood. It was no natural unfitness which in former times had given us reputation for ugliness in manufacture, and it has not, I think, been considered what immense disadvantage was brought upon the country as respects the application of fine art to industry by the great revolutionary war; not only was the engrossing character of a deadly struggle unfavourable to all such purposes, but our communion with the civilized world was placed under restraint; and we were in great measure excluded from resort to trade with those cities and countries which are bequeathed with an abundance of excellent examples of art and form.

How could it be expected that with Kings and Governments in a conflict of life or death, and dependant for the means of sustaining it on enormous and constant loans, could spare either thought or money from war and its imperious demands for this ,the most pacific among all the purposes of peace; at any rate I take it to be nearly certain, that the period of war was a period of general depression, and even degradation. in almost every branch of industrial art, that the fabrics of your own manufacturers for instance were, in point of beauty to what they had been at a former time. That the old factories in some cases had died out, in other cases, such as Worcester for instance, had declined, and that, whereas Wedgwood is said to have exported five sixths of what he made, we lost not only such loss as he had gained upon the foreign market. but also the loss, in part at least, to our marked decline in excellence and taste.

Wedgwood had the ability of discerning artistic merit in those he chose to work for him, such as Flaxman, although Wedgwood's own share in designing was, greater than supposed; even the lower works are as much distinguished by the fineness and accuracy of their adaptation to their uses, as his higher ones by their exhibition of the finest art. Take for instance his common plates, of the value of a few pence each; they fit one another as closely as the cards in a pack. At least, I for one, have never seen plates that fit like the plates of Wedgwood, which I apprehend, render them much more safe in carriage. Of the excellence of these plates, we take it for proof that they were largely exported to France, if not elsewhere, and were there printed or painted with buildings or scenes belonging to the country, and then sent out again as national manufactures.

Again, take such a jug as he would manufacture for the wash hand table of a garret, I have seen these made of the commonest material, but instead of being built up, like many jugs of modern manufacture, to such a shape that a Crane could not bend his neck to bend into them, and the water can hardly be poured out without risk of spraining the wrist, Wedgwood's are constructed in a simple capacious form of flowing curves, that a slight and easy movement of the hand discharges the water. A round cheeseholder or dish generally presents, in its upper parts, a flat space surrounded by a rim; but a cheeseholder of Wedgwood will make itself known by being so agreeable in form to the eye, and affording the utmost available space for the cheese. I feel persuaded that a Wiltshire cheese, if it could speak, would declare itself more comfortable in a Wedgwood than any other dish.

Again, there are certain circular inkstands by Wedgwood, on which great care has been bestowed upon the mechanical arrangement, with a view to the preservation of the pen, and the economical use of the ink; the prices are from sixpence to eight shillings. I have one of these, it must have been priced at a shilling or less, it carries a slightly recessed rectilinear ornament, but it has a homely order, and is so tasteful that it would not disgrace a cabinet, and yet so plain that it would suit a counting house.

Similarly, his intermediate productions had restraint and sobriety in colouring to match the classical severity of his forms.

I hope it will not be thought presumptious, to give utterance to the opinion that the forms of Chelsea, and even of Sèvres, in the last century were unsatisfactory, sometimes fantastic, often heavy and ungainly and on the whole neither comfortable to any strict law of art, nor worthy of the material. On comparing the form of these vases with those of Wedgwood, I think it is impossible not to be struck with his superiority, and feeling that his lifetime constitutes in fictile manufacture, nothing less than a new era as to form. It is hard to avoid conjecturing that his eye must have noticed, and must in this respect have condemned the prevailing fashion; and that he must have formed a deliberate resolution to do, what I think he unquestionably did, namely, exhibit to the world in this vital particular, a much higher standard of excellence".

The guests, a number of whom were personally familiar with Gladstone's oratory, were among the many who considered him eloquent, sound and forceful, and there are some today who consider him to be among the greatest parliamentary speakers of the past. A few at the ceremony may have gradually let their thoughts wander over the square to the town hall where the tables were already laid, and from which some enticing odours may have drifted. Disraeli referred to Gladstone as being *"inebriated by the exuberance of his own verbosity",* and this would probably have had Queen Victoria's support, since he was not among her favourites. To the thousands in Burslem who had never previously heard or seen him, his speech no doubt invoked the spirit of Wesley. Gladstone himself may have wished that his address had been made in church rather than a tent, since the church was his earlier inclination, but he was born in an age when a parent's word was law, and his adult future ordained, but his speech on this occasion, though perhaps verbose, is thought provoking, and well worthy of a second if not further readings, since the principles he highlights so eloquently, and attributes to Josiah Wedgwood, are timeless.

In accordance with Burslem's usual practice the instruments used for the laying ceremony were of lavish style. The trowel was mainly the work of Macintyres. The spirit level was elaborately inlaid with subjects in pottery representing Wedgwood for England, Palissy for France, Bottcher for Germany and Giorgie for Italy - all ceramic factories outstanding for their artistic products. The whole of the inlays were produced at the Hill Top Works, at that time in the occupation of Sir James Duke and Nephews. The decorated casket for the tools was by Davenport's and modelled by Marsh, who was the last of the modellers to be sent to Kensington and whose statue of Josiah dominates the frontage of the Institute.

The feast which followed was accompanied by a grand display of pottery from more than thirty potters in the district. Every dining table was decorated with vases, busts and statuettes, and in front of the orchestra was a fine marble bust of Josiah Wedgwood by Fontana, presented by Joseph Mayer, together with reproductions of vases in the Palace of Fontainebleau. A number of these were on loan from Kensington and Liverpool museums, Joseph Mayer procuring the items. Behind the Chairman's seat which was occupied by Earl Granville, were life size busts in Parian of Victoria and Albert, and behind these the Union Jack and the Royal Standard.

Mr Nunn, for the economical sum of £9, provided the musical accompaniment which comprised a group of twelve instruments. His contract, besides the payment for the music stipulated *"no payment to be made for refreshments, or any extra expense."* The principal speaker was Earl Granville, who spoke on current topics when replying to the toast of Her Majesty's Ministers.

A toast was to the Bishop and Clergy of the Diocese and the ministers of other denominations, coupling the Bishop of Lichfield and the Rev. J. Blackwell, a Free Church Minister. The Bishop of Lichfield responding, said he felt proud to be coupled in the toast with the ministers of other denominations, and glad to acknowledge the good which those ministers were doing in places where the Church of England could not reach the people. The Bishop's remarks had a cordial reception from the company and from the Rev. Blackwell. At this stage Mr Woodall made a remarkable interjection. He said that, on behalf of the Rector of Burslem, he had been asked to deliver a written protest against the toast to Dissenters being included in the toast to dignitaries of the Church. In reporting Mr Woodall's intervention the press showed restraint and described it as *"eliciting strong expressions of disapprobation"*, but the company unanimously decided that the communication did not merit the courtesy of being read.

When Mr Gladstone replied to the toast of the Institute he was still overflowing with admiration for Wedgwood, and, unlike the Rector, only found qualities to admire in his fellow man:

"It should be brought to mind by Englishmen, that the memory of Wedgwood was a precious deposit, and the pursuit of his methods and the application of his principles were a sure means to creating wealth; as a means to social improvement; and as a means to advancing civilisation. I call him the Great Wedgwood, that is the proper epithet for him. In my opinion, and I have considered the matter as well as I can, Wedgwood was the greatest in any age, or in any country, to apply himself to the important work of uniting art and industry; he recalled into existence the very spirit of Greek art; before his time, we may say of the earthenware and porcelain manufacture, that it had never risen to the loftiness of the spirit of Greek art, although in all his production you are reminded of Greek art, they are not mere reproductions, but that his style is original. There should be no fear for the future of the Wedgwood Institute, as it is well known that what an Englishman is resolved upon, he rarely failed to do; how much more certain then will that success be, when resolved upon and pursued by a whole community".

The Rector of Burslem, not having attended the function and failing to have his condemnation read, spent the day putting into words his convictions on the matter. These were printed and put into circulation, hoping for the approval of the residents of Burslem who, in Mr Gladstone's own words, were *"the best conducted and the most enlightened men in the country".*

The site on which the institute was built cost £1200. It was estimated that the cost of building including furnishings would be around £4000, towards which it was hoped to obtain a government grant - possibly through Mr Gladstone. In the event however there was a generous gift of words but only a loan of a £1000, and the levy of a penny rate, and consequently it was necessary to raise thousands of pounds from private sources. This was easier said than done; there were temporary halts during construction due to money problems and widespread fund raising efforts, with ppeals to individuals and groups.

SOLEMN PROTEST.

By the Rev. Dr. Armstrong, against the Toast given in the Town Hall of Burslem, on 26th October, 1863.

Rectory, Burslem, 26th October, 1863.

MY DEAR SIR,—I am unwilling to disturb the harmony of the meeting at the Town Hall this day, and if you will kindly read this letter at the meeting I shall absent myself. The toast to be proposed, including the Bishop, Clergy, and Ministers of all denominations, is to me highly objectionable, because it includes in it persons who deny the Divinity of my Lord and Saviour Jesus Christ. It also includes persons who hold and teach the doctrine of the Sacrifice of the Mass, which the 31st Article of the Church of England declares to be a "blasphemous fable and dangerous deceit." My respected Bishop required me to sign the Articles before admitting me to minister here, and therefore I cannot submit to be mixed up with teachers of such false and destructive doctrines; at the same time I protest against being supposed to entertain any hostile feeling against the teachers of such doctrines—I only war with what I consider evil principles.—I remain, &c.,

JOHN E. ARMSTRONG, D.D. L.L.D.,

William Woodall, Esq.   Rector of Burslem.

The foregoing protest was sent to the Secretary of the Wedgwood Institute, (who promised to read it *after* the toast,) but not to animadvert upon it *after* the Bishop's reply, and that without reading it, and thus giving the Meeting no opportunity of approving or condemning it, as they thought fit.

Dr. Armstrong specially wished the protest to be read *before* the reply, and agreed to be absent on that condition and on that condition alone, that his revered Diocesan might have an opportunity of seeing (what he evidently did not see) to what the toast led, viz. to the "recognition" (that was the Wesleyan Minister's word applied approvingly) of Priests Roman, Mormon, Socinian, Arian, Buddhist, and Anything-arian.

Dr. Armstrong gave no authority to any person *even to read* the document *after* the Bishop's speech (as it made him appear opposed to the Bishop) much less to animadvert upon it *without reading it.*

The Meeting could not fairly give an opinion of the protest of the Rector of the Parish without hearing it, because—

"He that answereth a matter before he heareth it, it is as folly and shame to him."—Prov xviii., 13.

The protest is before the Parishioners now, let them approve of or condemn the Rector as they think fit, his consolation is that God will not condemn him for it.

It has been suggested that Wedgwood having been a Unitarian, it would have been *bad taste*, to exclude the ministers of that denomination.

Whether politeness and taste are to be preferred to allegiance to *Immanuel* (God with us,) the Christian Parishioners of Burslem will judge.

If Christians are to be bowed and scraped out of their Christianity, let it be honestly declared such is the policy of Burslem.

ART EXHIBITION AT ALTON TOWERS.

THE RIGHT HONOURABLE the EARL OF SHREWSBURY AND TALBOT having most generously granted to the Wedgwood Institute Committee the use of Alton Towers, for the purpose of an Art Exhibition, to take place there during the latter end of July and the months of August and September next ensuing, the Lords of the Committee of Council on Education have signified their approval of the scheme, and intimated their opinion "that this Exhibition may be made the inauguration of a series of County Exhibi- "tions, to take place annually, at which many valuable Works of Art may be usefully brought to light for the "benefit of Art instruction." Their Lordships have therefore agreed to furnish, free of expense, examples from the South Kensington Museum, in accordance with their minute on Art Schools of the 9th of January, 1865.

The Executive Committee with the view of augmenting and increasing the intrinsic excellence, with attractive character, of the proposed Exhibition, have applied to, and received promises of aid from, Noblemen and Gentlemen whose names are included in the accompanying preliminary list of Patrons; and being desirous of gathering together a collection worthy of the occasion, and of the artistic repute of the Midland Counties, they respectfully invite co-operation in furtherance of the project.

Objects in the following Classes will be received.

1. Paintings and Drawings, of recognized merit, by ancient and modern masters.
2. Framed Engravings, particularly such as are earlier than 1750, and those illustrating the Topography of the Midland Counties.
3. Miniatures and Photographs.
4. Sculpture in Marble, and Works in Terra Cotta.
5. Carvings in Wood and Ivory, and Church objects of a decorative character.
6. Decorative Metal work, Jewellery, Cameos, &c.
7. Mosaics.
8. Pottery, of all countries and periods, especially Wedgwood and other decorative Earthenwares of English origin.
9. Glass and Enamel.
10. Modern examples of ornamental Art in Pottery, Metal, Papier Mâché, &c.; particularly such as have been designed or executed by those who have been or may still be students in the Schools of Art in Staffordshire, and the adjacent Counties.

I.—As the intention is less the formation of a very extensive collection than that of a select and systematic one, it is obvious that the reception of unnecessary or duplicate specimens must be avoided, and that on the other hand the most careful consideration should be exercised, in the selection of the real and acknowledged treasures of art desired on this occasion. These desiderata, however, can only be obtained by the kind co-operation of the possessors of valuable works, in the practical methods devised for carrying the Exhibition into effect.

It is therefore hoped that the possessors of fine works of art, who may be disposed to lend them for the gratification and instruction of the public, will kindly consent to allow such works to be selected from their collections, as may be specially asked for, in accordance with methodic lists, which it is intended to complete if possible before any specimens are actually removed.

II.—All expenses attending the removal of objects so selected and their return at the close of the Exhibition, will be defrayed, and the utmost care will be taken of all works lent.

III.—Photographs of the more important specimens contributed will be taken, and sold in aid of the funds for erecting the Wedgwood Institute, should no stipulations to the contrary be made by the proprietors.

IV.—With a view of affording as much instruction as possible, both in the catalogues and the labels attached to the objects, lenders are requested to supply the Committee with the fullest description of the objects, together with facts of historical interest.

BY ORDER OF THE EXECUTIVE COMMITTEE,

WILLIAM WOODALL, LONGPORT, STAFFORDSHIRE, } HON. SECS.
PHILIP C. OWEN, SOUTH KENSINGTON MUSEUM, }

March, 1865.

In 1865 a major Art Exhibition and Bazaar were held at Alton Towers by permission of Lord Shrewsbury, and this raised a magnificent sum of £1850. A more modest money raising concert in Burslem contributed at least another example of Burslem verse, inspired no doubt by Mr Gladstone's eloquent address, and Mr Woodall's pragmatism.

> How oft here we'd hope, and his wealth of fine talk
> 'bout art and the branches of science
> And once we had hope of his plenty of cash
> On this hope we have now no reliance
>
> Still let us like men, put our shoulder to the wheel
> And prove by our action we are good all
> For the crowning Success of the Institute's worth
> Like -- why! - - like our good friend Mr. Woodall
>
> On pottery supreme therefore, great Woodall was set
> But now it is said that our situation
> Is not so advanced as the German or French
> Where potters have Art education
>
> Shall England be beat? in the race lag behind
> Forbid it ye Staffordshire workmen
> In Wedgwood's own temple, aquire Wedgwood's own power
> And ne'er from your duties shirk men
>
> In beauty tis standing, a temple of Art
> Its object to honour and nourish
> The name of our Wedgwood, the art he adored
> May then it be useful and Flourish
>
> Add fame to the list of Staffordshire men
> Whose names are pride of the nation
> And foster the taste for its beautiful art
> By its science and art education

Groups and factories were canvassed and subscription books to enter donations were distributed. One factory pledged itself to raise a material portion of the outstanding debt in their desire, so they said, *"of intimating their cheerful means of evidencing their appreciation of the flattering compliment paid to them by Mr Gladstone, in repeating in Parliament the language of their address as indicating the sentiment of the best conducted, and most enlightened men in the country".*

The first building on the site, in 1862, a caretaker's house, cost £216. 4. 11. In 1864 tenders were received for the first stage in the construction of the Institute. The lowest was for £3360. This was submitted by Mr T. B. Harley of Burslem. The highest was £4293.

It was early 1865 before the modellers were established in London under the scrutiny of the Committee of the Council of Education at Kensington School of Art who agreed to contribute to each £2 per week, one pound of which would be guaranteed, the remaining pound subject to satisfactory performance. In March 1866 a considerable amount of modelling must have been completed since a quotation from Mr. Blanchard was received for £553 for Terracotta Plinths, Entrance Columns, Sculptured Tiles etc. The Committee also received a letter from Morris requesting an increase of ten shillings per week since he was evidently finding living expensive in the city and his remuneration inadequate. However it came at an inopportune moment, in the middle of a protracted strike in the building trade and consequent curtailment of progress on the Institute.

In October 1866 new quotations were received based on revised plans of Mr Edgar which covered a final stage of the building. The lowest of these quotations, the one accepted, was tendered by Mr Barlow of Stoke for the sum of £3500. The highest was £4143.

A further letter was received from Morris repeating his request for an increase of ten shillings per week but on this occasion offering to work extended hours. Eventually a compromise was reached and the money paid. In February 1867 a tender price of £681 was received from Mr Blanchard for the balance of the terracotta work assigned to him. A price of £6 each was also received from Mr Blashfield for his work on the Process Panels, also his agreement to provide new clay panels free should any fail in the firing process. Work seems to have progressed smoothly throughout 1868 and the fabric was completed in 1869. In the September of 1869 Mr Woodall presented to the committee the account of Mr Barlow, certified by Mr Edgar, which amounted to £4040.18. 10. which included providing a floor and an iron roof, also unpacking, storing and fixing terracotta work, and for an additional school room for fifty students, extra to contract. There was a bill from Minton Tiles for £55. 13. 0.

In October 1869 the Government Loan Board agreed to pay the promised loan of £1000, satisfied that Burslem had complied with the terms of the Public Libraries Act. This act came into operation during construction of the Institute and is described in a later chapter, but its location in the Institute had been agreed. Repayment of the loan was stipulated to be in twenty equal instalments of £50; in addition to other urgent outstanding debts for which the Committee at this stage agreed personally to be responsible.

To commemorate the official opening of the Institute by Earl de Grey and Ripon in April 1869 it was decided to install a plaque. At the same time tribute was paid to William Woodall who had been the life and soul of the undertaking, and it was doubted if there would have been such a building had it not been for his efforts. Mr Woodall was actually a native of Shrewsbury, and educated in Liverpool. He joined The Liverpool Gas Co. and came to Burslem to manage the local Gas Company. He married MacIntyre's daughter and became a fellow director of MacIntyres along with Hulme, and eventually part owner. He was a member of the Burslem Board of Health, Chief Bailiff 1871/72 and a councillor following Burslem becoming a borough. He was also a magistrate and in 1880 Member of Parliament for Burslem going on to hold a cabinet position.

Encouraged no doubt by the success of the exhibition at Alton Towers, the Institute Committee decided to organise a similar event in the Institute to coincide with the official opening. Kensington School of Art loaned a valuable collection of works which formed the nucleus of the display which, from its impressive quality, it was hoped, would stimulate the local industry to emulate Josiah Wedgwood's productions. Art works of all classes were sought from public and private collections, and among items on display were pictures by two local eminent artists, George Mason and James Holland. Professor Colvin of Cambridge University who opened the exhibition, said of George Mason, who had recently died, that he became poor at 30 and left the country for Italy. Returning in 1848 he lived in poverty in the Potteries district and went frequently to Wetley Common to paint. Holland, he said, began life as a designer in a Burslem pottery but soon gravitated to London where he excelled in flower painting. He died in 1870. His work was popular and besides flowers, he painted landscapes, some in the Dane and Dove valleys.

George Hemming Mason, to give him his full title, was actually born in Fenton in 1818 and went to school in Newcastle; his grandfather was Miles Mason who founded Masons Pottery. He began to train as a surgeon in Birmingham but his interest was in painting and in 1843 he and his brother left England, on foot it is said, for Rome. Certainly he did not arrive in Rome until 1845 and then his artistic work had to be subservient to his medical experience, which was called upon for tending the wounded in Garibaldi's army, at that time in the throes of war. He lived in Rome on what commissions he could attract and here he met and became friendly with Lord Leighton. On his return to England, he lived with his wife and parents at Wetley Abbey, and became well known for his idyllic studies, presumably using the Common for his atmospheric background. He ultimately went to London, renewing his friendship with Lord Leighton, President of the Royal Academy where later Mason himself was an exhibitor. He died in 1872 and left a wife and five children. Some of his work is in the Tate Gallery including Harvest Moon. Whether he experienced the degree of poverty which Professor Colven inferred is perhaps open to doubt.

James Holland was born in 1799 in Burslem where his grandfather owned and worked the Hill Top pottery along with his wife, Tomason, a prominent flower painter on pottery. He was illegitimate although his mother later married Timothy Edge who took over and ran the pottery. James learnt flower painting from his mother and grandmother, and after completing a seven year apprenticeship was an accomplished painter and left for London at the age of 20 to make his fortune. By 24 his paintings were hung in the Royal Academy and he went on to be one of the most celebrated and prolific painters of his time, especiallly renowned for his watercolours, his flower pictures and his views of Venice. There are at least 800 of his works in existence today in private collections and galleries throughout the world, with large collections in the Victoria and Albert Museum, London, and the Potteries Museum in Stoke.

In his address at the opening of the exhibition, the Professor emphasised that he wanted the works of local men recognised in their own town. In his view the pottery towns would not have done their duty until they had trained the eyes and instincts of the people so that they may recall artistically the acceptance of their actual existence. The tall chimneys and the low houses offer so much that is capable of picturesque rendering. Those were very much the thoughts and expressions of Reginald Haggar, a contemporary local painter, many of whose picturesque industrial scenes of the Potteries are in local homes, and also, along with other memorabilia, in the possession of the City Museum. Although possessing a much different style, Reginald Haggar could be called the Lowry of the Potteries.

Appreciable expense was incurred in organising the exhibition, which it was hoped would be recouped, despite the pessimism of many. It never had the popularity and glamour which the Alton exhibition generated. Three thousand catalogues were printed, the bulk of which were sold, and musical concerts were organised in the adjoining Lecture Theatre. Some 12,000 came to view, but the attendance from local schools was disappointing. Nevertheless the project broke even. Such was the value of the exhibits that constant security had to be maintained, and it was a compliment to the organisers that the only loss was an umbrella which a visitor had put to one side on the last day.

William Woodall was made sole trustee and chairman of the Institute in recognition of his work throughout the project. Mr Woodall presented the financial position in April 1870:

Receipts from subscriptions............		3914. 8. 7.
Alton Exhibition and Bazaar...........		1850. 0. 0.
Penny rate for five years...............		934. 9. 3.
Government loan........................		1000. 0. 0.
		7698.17. 10.
Advanced by Bank	391.12. 11.	
Promissory Notes	990. 8. 7.	
		9060.19. 4.
Outstanding liabilities	657. 4. 7.	

It would seem that the Institute in its entirety cost approximately £10,000. Subsequent to the opening a grant was received from the estate of a Mr Alfred Barlow of £800 but this included a stipulation that £344 was to be spent on equipping the science section and £454 on the art section. It would be interesting to know if this was the man who built the building.

Among the many efforts to raise money in 1870, there was a performance arranged by Mr Powell and his choir of the Oratorio *Sampson,* and a very profitable bazaar held in February 1870 contributed a welcome £1176. 1. 9.

When the institute opened, both interior and exterior work had still to be completed. On the outside of the building the statue of Josiah was missing, some of the months of the year tiles, some process panels; but these, with the exception of the statue, were received and fixed in 1872. In the meantime Morris wrote a further appeal for money, this time asking for an advance of £10 and indicating that the statue would be finished in six weeks. No immediate decision was reached on this request but Mr Woodall, who was on the point of going to London, suggested that he should personally interview Morris and come to some arrangement. It later transpired that he had found Morris in a depressed state, but that his condition had improved after a short holiday, and he was granted a loan of £10 subject to his repaying it at the rate of

£2.10. 0 per week. Morris apparently finished his work on the statue late in the September of 1872, but there must still have been some hesitancy before it was ultimately fired, not surprising perhaps, since with so much time and money spent to date, failure at this late stage would have been catastrophic.

The Committee received a letter in February 1873 from Mr Blanchard, saying that he was unwilling to undertake his work on the statue, with the risk involved in the firing, for less than £30; however he was instructed to go ahead. Doultons had apparently been asked to quote and given a figure of £45! The actual date of when the statue was ultimately erected is not recorded. However it has been standing proudly above the entrance for 130 years now. One has the impression that Josiah is drawing attention to one of his masterpieces and inviting the viewer to come inside and see more - but they will be disappointed!

When the building was first opened for use, the ground floor became a library and reading room, lecture theatre and two classrooms. The first floor was to be the school of art, comprising an elementary classroom, ladies classroom and painting room, modelling room and masters classroom. The second floor was a chemical classroom.

This arrangement deviates from the first intention when the art section was to be on the second floor and have roof lighting. An approach was made by the Free School Trustees requesting that in return for contributing to the cost of the Institute they should have the sole right in the education section, to the nomination of students and the appointment of the master. This was agreed on condition that they paid the sum of £800.

Minor works were still required within the building to cater for its various uses. A tender was received from a Mr Machin for seating round the Reading Room at one shilling and sixpence a foot, later increased to two shillings to include back rests. The same gentleman quoted £6 6s and £8 for two reading tables, and £8 5s for a reading stand. It seems probable that the tables currently in the library are Mr Machin's work. Mr Birch, bookbinder of Burslem, tendered for binding volumes from the library in half calf and cloth: Volumes 17 x 11 inches, each three shillings and nine pence, volumes 11 x 9, two shillings and sixpence, volumes $7^{1}/_{2}$ x $4^{1}/_{2}$, tenpence.

Among the names of successful students from early prize giving in art were R. Ledwood, who became a modeller of distinction and two painters, David Dewsbury and J.F. Marsh, and numerous students over the years became heads of art in other cities and towns. One pupil W. M. Palin was responsible for portraits of William Woodall, J Wilcox Edge and Thomas Hulme. Another early student who attained worldwide recognition was Arnold Bennett, and from the Science Section one who similarly achieved fame was Sir Oliver Lodge. Eventually educational demands were such that the use of part as a museum had to be postponed since the student numbers soon mounted to 200 for art and 50 for chemistry.

As a perhaps belated tribute to Mr Woodall, a subscription list was opened and and a sum of £400 contributed and presented to him. He, evidently realising that accommodation in the institute would be unlikely to ever allow space for a museum, donated it to an extension for this purpose, and by 1879 this had been built at a cost of £1000 and Mr Woodall himself generously paid for the whole project. The Museum was officially opened in September 1879 by the Venerable Sir Lovelace Stamer, Bart. once parish priest at St Paul's, now knighted and the Rector of Stoke Church. Others attending were Godfrey Wedgwood, Mr S. Wilcox Edge, MP for Newcastle, Sir Sidney Colvin, Slade Professor of Art at Cambridge University; also local burgesses and their wives.

Sidney Colvin had an illustrious career, not only as art critic and tutor, but as a biographer. He was closely associated with both the Fitzwilliam and the British Museums and before coming on this second visit to Burslem had already been knighted. It is perhaps flattering to think that he was so impressed with what he saw on the first occasion, that he retained a keen interest in the progress of the Institute.

In May, prior to the opening, Kensington Museum had promised the Institute to contribute all the articles of pottery and porcelain purchased by the Government at the Paris Exhibition in 1878, together with some specimens of pre-Wedgwood ware. Presumably these were among the art treasures lent for the opening exhibition.

H.R.H. Princess Louise.

Marquess of Lorne, K.

Wedgwood Institute, Burslem,
Showing Jubilee Wing opened by H.R.H. Princess Louise.

Councillor Hulme.

Alderman Lawton,
Mayor of Burslem.

Local coverage of the Royal visit

Thomas Hulme, the first mayor of the borough and an avid collector of paintings and pottery, unlike Enoch Wood, decided to leave his collection to the Institute Museum, and when in 1884 Her Royal Highness Princess Louise visited Burslem, the gift was officially acknowledged. Her Royal Highness, accompanied by the Duke of Argyle came by train to Longport, from where she and the royal party drove in an open landau in fine weather to the Institute, the road being lined with spectators. On arrival the Princess received a deed of gift from Thomas Hulme covering his recent generous presentation, which she received on behalf of the town, and then unveiled the portrait of Hulme which had been painted by Palin and given to the Institute. Following these ceremonies she made a tour of the extension before paying a visit to the Doulton and Washington Potteries, and from thence to Bleak House in Cobridge, where the royal party rested before the Princess travelled on to Scotland.

Gifts of all kinds had arrived long before the building was finished. In 1864 profuse thanks were offered to a Mr Herbert Bach for the gift of a lithograph titled *The Great Fall of Niagara*. This painting, executed in 1857, was by American Artist Frederick Edwin Church (1826-1900). He painted pictures on the grand scale, similar to the Victorian paintings of Stags, which suited the age and commanded high prices. His work is well represented in American Museums. It would be interesting to know if the picture has survived - which applies to so many of the things given to the Institute in its early days!

In January 1869 an offer was graciously accepted of a gift from Mr Felix Miller, Modelling Master at the Kensington School of Art, of four bas reliefs of his own, representing the principal sciences, with the suggestion that they be hung on the Reading Room walls.

In 1882 a complaint was made to the council that persons using the reading room were in a dirty condition. The council said that no matter what they did it was no substitute for personal cleanliness, but the blame was not on the working man, it was on the unemployed.

In 1884 there were complaints of bad smells at the institute, and the matter being referred to the Sanitary Inspector, he said it was the insanitary state of the surrounding area. In fairness it could be said that Burslem was by now changing at such a pace in that area, which was one of the very earliest, that it was soon to become the "Queen" of streets. Pressure on accommodation at the Institute continued to grow and it was agreed that Queen Victoria's Jubilee in 1887 should be celebrated by extensions to the hall in the direction of Brickhouse Street and Baker Street, none of this work however affecting the facade in Queen Street. Again the cost had to be met by the generosity of individuals and groups, and James Maddock and Thomas Hulme each contributed £1000.

Besides money, further gifts of varied interest were periodically donated. In 1882 the Mayor of Stoke presented a collection of Phoenician, Greek and Roman pottery. Details of this collection are not recorded - it can be safely said that neither the Phoenicians or Greeks settled in Stoke. A short time after opening, the museum received a number of native curiosities from Honolulu, a gift of Mr R.W. Podmore.

Members of the Maddock family, successful Burslem potters into the 20th century, were keen supporters of the Institute and financed additions and improvements to the reading room. A daughter, Jane Maddock, left an endowment in her will. Another benefactor who left an endowment was Thomas Leicester, whose family were for many years chemists in Burslem. In 1867 Mr Holland of New York, late of Burslem, sent a dollar Confederate States bill, which was a remarkable foresight if he realised that if it had been held it would in time pay for the museum extension! Mr T. Hughes gave a gift of Paraguay ware. In 1875, Miss Meteyard, who wrote extensively on Wedgwood, gave an autographed copy of *The Wedgwood Handbook*, engravings by Flaxman and some pieces of pottery. A chapter of her work was devoted to the Wedgwood Institute, and five hundred copies of this were allowed by her to be printed and sold at 6d each to augment the income of the building.

In this year Mr Woodall made a gift of seventy-one books, and the Board acknowledged a gift of valuable terracotta specimens from the Watcombe Terracotta Company, but the entry made no mention of form, age or origin of the items. Another entry in 1876 says that Wedgwood & Sons were given permission to take the last of the Fontana busts of Josiah, loaned for the inaugural dinner.

In 1881 a portrait of James Maddock, late mayor of Burslem and a valued patron, was hung in the building, and a bust of William Woodall placed in the museum. In 1882 Mrs Hostage of Winnington, daughter of Enoch Wood, sent a mounted copy of her father's model of *The Descent from the Cross*. In 1876, a valuable oil painting of the Potteries valley was presented by Mrs Furnival. In 1884, a copy of *The Life of Her Highness in The Highlands*, autographed by Queen Victoria, was sent by her secretariat for the Institute. In 1904 Mr Edward Turner left the Institute a legacy of £200, and the previous endowments of Jane Maddock and Thomas Leicester combined were said at the beginning of the century, to be yield a gross income of £204.6.0. In 1875 the salary of the librarian was increased to 12/6d per week.

As a tribute to the many enthusiasts who gave their time, talent and money to making a vision materialise, here is another example of Burslem verse, given at a fund-raising concert after the opening:

> Old Burslem is honor'd in having a son
> Whose name is the pride of the nation
> And though our tribute is tardily won
> Have for him a fond admiration
>
> We stand in the sure light that knowledge is shed
> O'er the broad path of poor human nature
> And progress we've made in science and art
> Shows to us our Wedgwood's true stature
>
> Ten years have passed o'er since the task we began
> Our debt to his memory paying
> Though slowly still surely the movement is spread
> 'Spite obstacles constant delaying
>
> Now all these surmounted the Institute stands
> A tribute to him and the glory
> To us who now live where our Wedgwood was born
> And to all who know his life's story
>
> I said the obstacles were all o'ercome
> But that's true yet my honey
> Though our fine Wedgwood Institute's opened and built
> We have not yet got all the money
>
> If Wedgwood but knew in his nich in the wall
> I truly believe he'd resent it
> Get down from his stand and march out at the door
> And the Burslem you'd repent it

It was fitting that Mother Burslem's treasures should be looked after by a Wedgwood enthusiast and the first curator of the museum section was Isaac Cook in 1906. This gentleman had a record of fifty years continuous service at the Wedgwood works.

The Institute building, unlike so many of Burslem's landmarks, has miraculously avoided the effects of mining subsidence and immediately commands attention, but, like so many national treasures, it has suffered neglect. Fortunately the future looks more promising, the inspiration has long been available, but funding has been elusive. The Institute has in the past had modest sums bequeathed to keep it proud, which, if wisely invested, would perhaps today have become significant, but these gifts appear to have been lost - perhaps in the turmoil which accompanied Mother Burslem's loss of her individuality. Treasures given to her and at one time displayed within the Institute have gone, bequeathed, along with those belonging to other members of the 'Six Towns' family, to what may be termed the land of the favourite son, where an Aladdin's Cave, the Potteries Museum, has been built to house them, and which all who visit the Potteries should live to regret if they failed to make a pilgrimage; it is such an interesting, priceless and unforgettable display!

An engraving showing the ceramic statue of Josiah above the entrance

Laying of the Foundation Stone

OF THE

WEDGWOOD INSTITUTE,

At Burslem, October 26, 1863,

BY THE RIGHT HON. W. E. GLADSTONE, M.P.,

CHANCELLOR OF THE EXCHEQUER.

DÉJEÛNER

Under the Presidency of the Right Hon. the Earl of Lichfield,

Lord Lieutenant of the County of Stafford.

BILL OF FARE.

Lobsters, Lobster Salads.

Roast Lamb, Galantines of Veal, Pheasants, Partridges, Grouse, Rolled Spiced Beef, Chickens, Tongues, Game Pies, Galantines of Fowls, Hams, Larded Guinea-Fowls, Roast Turkeys, Pigeon Pies, Aspecs, Veal Cakes, French Patties, Venison Pasties, &c.

Gelées aux Vins, Charlottes des Russe, Pâtisserie l'Italien, Crème au Citron, Blanc Mange, Gelée de Ponche, Gâteaux des Pommes, Trifles, Crème à la Suisse, Franchonnettes, Gelée d'Orange, Gâteaux demi-ivres, Crème de Vanille, Tartlettes à la Parisienne, Gâteaux Geneve Orné, Custards, Lemon Cheese Cakes, Victoria Sandwiches, &c.

Pines, Grapes, Apples, Pears, Oranges, Nuts, Cakes, and Dried Fruits.

WINES.

Champagne (Duc de Montebello), Sparkling Moselle, Still Hock, Claret, Port, and Sherry.

BOWERING, PRINTER, BURSLEM.

The Months pof the year ceramic plaques
and the front entrance of the Institute

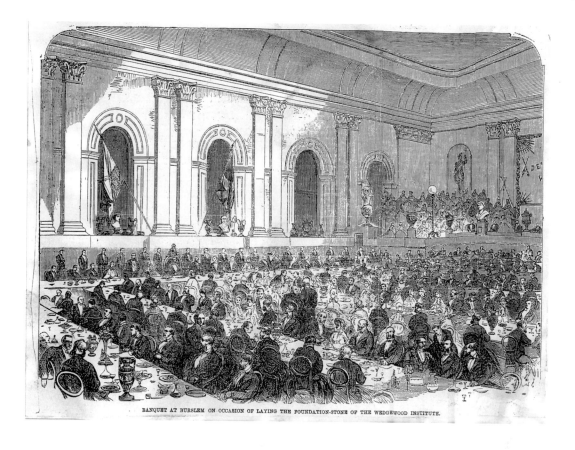

BANQUET AT BURSLEM ON OCCASION OF LAYING THE FOUNDATION-STONE OF THE WEDGWOOD INSTITUTE.

WEDGWOOD MEMORIAL.

DEJEUNER, OCTOBER 26, 1863

CHAIRMAN—The Rt. Hon. the EARL GRANVILLE, K.G.

TOASTS.

	PROPOSED BY	RESPONDED TO BY
1 The Queen.	The Chairman.	
2 The Prince and Princess of Wales, and all the Royal Family.	Do.	
3 The Army, Navy, and Volunteers.	Right Hon. C. B. Adderley, M.P.	Viscount Ingestre, M.P. Captain Buchanan
4 The Bishop and Clergy of the Diocese, and Ministers of all Denominations.	A. J. B. Beresford Hope, Esq.	The Bishop of Lichfield. Rev. J. Blackwell.
5 Her Majesty's Ministers	The Chief Bailiff of Burslem	The Earl Granville, K.G.
6 The High Sheriff.		The High Sheriff.
7 The Lord Lieutenant and Magistrates of the County.	H. R. Grenfell, Esq., M.P.	T. F. Twemlow, Esq.
8 Success to the Wedgwood Institute.	The Right Hon. W. E. Gladstone, M.P.	J. S. Hill, Esq.
9 The House of Peers.	Sir James Duke, Bart., M.P.	The Earl Granville, K.G.
10 The House of Commons.	Smith Child, Esq.	The Right Hon. R. Lowe, M.P.
11 The Chairman.	E. Manningham Buller, Esq.	The Chairman.
12 The Right Hon. W. E. Gladstone, M.P.	The Chairman	Right Hon. W. E. Gladstone, M.P.
13 The Arts, Science, and Commerce.	W. Ewart, Esq., M.P.	Joseph Mayer, Esq., F.S.A. James Bateman, Esq., F.G.S. Colin M. Campbell, Esq.

DEAN, PRINTER, BURSLEM.

Three of the twelve panels depicting the art of the potter

CHAPTER TWENTY FIVE: Growth of Education

The first day school in Burslem was at the top of the town, somewhere near the end of Market Street and the commencement of Westport Road. It opened in 1749 and was for forty pupils, thirty boys and ten girls to be chosen from the poorest families, the children to receive instruction in reading, writing and accounts, and such as were Church of England, were to attend divine worship and learn the Catechism. The school was founded on voluntary subscription, initially the following:

	£
John Bourne. Town Clerk of Newcastle	200
Mrs. Egerton. Relative of the Wedgwoods	60
John Richards of Newcastle	20
John & Thomas Wedgwood of the Big House	50
Richard Cartwright	20
Diverse gifts	165
Total	515

The school was governed by elected trustees who had the power to employ or dismiss the master, and similarly, to approve the pupils or dismiss them for misbehaviour or non-attendance. The buildings comprised a school room and a house next door for the master. Of the funds £250 was invested in a farm at Ipstones, and a small sum in government bonds. The income was expected to be sufficient to maintain the school, neglect over the years however and failure of the trustees to take sufficient interest, resulted in a crisis in 1883; not only in the affairs and condition of the school, but also in the state of the farm, since both had become dilapidated. Instead of the farm being a source of income, it was itself requiring costly renovation, the master was also found to be too old and incompetent and there were no free scholars in the school. The master was discharged and the school temporarily closed for repairs which cost £160.

In 1823 a new master was appointed at a salary of £24 per annum, which was roughly the rent of the farm at that date, however the master was not to receive his full salary immediately, but would be paid £10 per year only until the repair cost had been recovered. He was allowed the house rent free but required to provide his own coal and pay for any broken windows. The free scholars were to pay him five shillings per annum for books, pens, ink and paper; and in addition to the free scholars, the master was allowed to educate thirty paying pupils and his wife twenty. New trustees were elected and sworn in at Burslem court, but friction arose over whether the old or the new body were responsible for the legal costs which had been incurred during the turmoil.

At a later date land was purchased in Moorland Road as the proposed site of a new school. This was built in 1832 and bore on its frontage the words, BURSLEM FREE SCHOOL 1832. Little information survives regarding the school except that it was a single storey building and ceased as a school around the middle 19th century. The old school building in the town was let as a shop with living accommodation, the rent from it to be used to purchase books, paper, quills, ink and coals, besides repairs at the new school.

Cobridge had a voluntary aided school, built in 1766 and paid for by public subscription. It was built of brick and had a cupola with a bell. The building comprised a ground floor constructed as two small cottages, while the whole of the upper area was used as a school. It was situated at the junction of Sneyd Street and Elder Road, but having no endowment from its initial opening it was expected to pay its own way, which resulted in it having a very chequered life. The two important early trustees were William Adams of Cobridge Hall and Captain Jacob Warburton. William Adams was very wealthy but if he contributed to the running cost of the school in his lifetime he does not appear to have left any bequest at his death, but Jacob Warburton at his death left the income from tolls at the Cobridge Gate which he had purchased in his lifetime, to supplement the master's income. When Ward wrote his history in 1838 he said the building was in a very dilapidated condition and frequently out of use. It lost its status as a school and was used as a public building for the use of Cobridge and the Grange youth for the following ten years, but failing interest led to its being let for various service trades, a barber, a cobbler and also branches of the food trade, and around 1850 the Burslem Board of Health requested to take it over. Dispute arose with the Charity Commissioners over the question of ownership. Ultimately, due without doubt to its obtrusive position adjoining roads which were becoming increasingly busy, together with its sad condition, the Burslem Board bought it for £150 and demolished it. The money was paid to the Church Commissioners Endowment Fund, to be specifically used for granting exhibition scholarships to students.

The first National School was erected in 1817 adjoining St John's Church and was primarily intended as a denominational school. The building was built of brick, three storeys high, with a cupola on top but no bell. It still exists, without the cupola, and despite alterations and additions to the main building it is still possible to discern the original structure, which seems to have the characteristics of a Lancashire mill. These voluntary Anglican church schools were all termed National Schools and were built in large numbers around this period in response to the success in education of the dissenting religions. From 1833 these schools received a small government grant, as opposed to those of dissenters which had to be self supporting. The cost of building the school was approximately £2000, towards which the National Society contributed £300, the Diocesan Society and the Dean of Lichfield £50, and, according to Ward, the balance was borrowed on the security of a bond supplied by the trustees, and a life policy on one of their members. The school was built to take 600 pupils, but Ward's comment was that *"it failed in both numbers and usefulness"* a comment on which he failed to enlarge, but at that time the only serious competition would have been that of the dissenters schools. The upkeep of the school was to be met by the receipts from annual sermons, similar to the practice of the dissenters, but in addition parents were expected to meet a small charge imposed for each pupil.

The left side of this building with the pitched roof was the first Anglican chiurch school in Burslem

A school on the same principle was built adjoining St Paul's. This was in Gothic style and cost about £500, towards which there was a treasury grant of £120 and one from the National Society of £60. Presumably the rest was either borrowed or raised by its parent body, St Paul's Church. The school faced Elgreave Street which adjoined the church grounds. A neighbour of mine taught there as her first appointment following her training. She said the playground was so small that it was reserved for the girls and the boys were turned out to play in Elgreave Street. She further commented that the headmaster was a disciplinarian who did not discriminate between teachers and pupils! He insisted that when he entered a classroom, all eyes should be centred and remain on his person until he left. He expected the teachers to instil this requirement into the pupils - pupils that failed would be immediately caned. He never entered a classroom without his implement of correction. Gone now is the building and with it the day when the bottom throbbed while the mind was expected to absorb knowledge.

The Wedgwood Institute which opened in 1869 was soon to become too small to accommodate the number of pupils anxious to use its facilities, consequently partial dispersal became necessary. Boys were moved to Longport Hall. The hall is not mentioned by John Ward but it must refer to a mansion built by Robert Williamson whose main interests were in mining. This mansion with its grounds covered an area of five acres and was later sold to Henry Davenport who much enlarged the building, and probably from then on it was termed Longport Hall. After the sad and sudden demise of Henry while hunting, his brother William Davenport inherited the property but he died in 1869, and with the Davenport business going into liquidation, presumably the hall had no occupant. Arnold Bennett was among the boys who attended here before going to a private school in Newcastle. The hall was demolished between 1890 and 1900.

According to Ward a small school was built by the Catholic community in Cobridge, adjoining the church and presbytery. The present school lies opposite the church in Waterloo Road, but its frontage to the road is obviously of an earlier age than the main buildings which now overwhelm it and is most likely part of the original school. It is said that there was St. Joseph's Catholic School in Spens Street off Hall Street. This could have been on what is now open ground at the rear of the Hall Street Catholic Church. since the area has the appearance of having been developed at one time.

There were two schools belonging to the Dissenters in streets off Moorland Road. One the Cook Memorial School, presumably named after the Reverend Cook (of whom Scarratt spoke so highly), was in Reginald Street. The other, the Woodall Memorial School in Doulton Street was named after William Woodall. Both buildings have gone, but the school built in conjunction with the original Swan Bank Methodist Chapel, and which became the centre of the historical rift, still stands..

It was 1870 before a parliamentary act made primary education compulsory, with costs paid out of local rates. Half of the children up to this time never attended a school and were more or less illiterate. A third of those who did attend left before the age of ten. The act set in motion the belated building of adequate schools and these were known as Board Schools since they functioned under a board of elected governors. In Burslem at least three of these schools were built; Hill Top in 1876, Middleport School in 1878 and Jackfield School in 1903, and all are still active. Schools in Shirley Street and Nile Street, presumably built in the same age but with no date visible, are both now part of commercial premises.

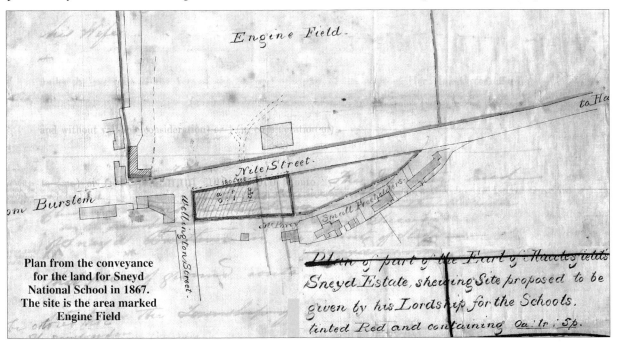

Plan from the conveyance for the land for Sneyd National School in 1867. The site is the area marked Engine Field

The same act doubled the annual government grant from which National Schools had benefited, but now this sum had to be shared with schools operated by Dissenters and Catholics. Local authorities were able to introduce bye-laws implementating the act. Burslem issued a bye-law in 1874:

Parents of every child not less than five years, and not more than thirteen years of age, shall cause such child to attend a public elementary school, except with a reasonable excuse:

1. That a child is receiving instruction in some other manner.
2. That the child is sick.
3. That there is no school for a child under seven years within one mile or if above seven years two miles.
4. That the child is for the time being employed in labour and receiving part time instruction.
5. A parent is allowed to withdraw a child from religious instruction.
6. No child need attend on any day set apart for religious observance by the religious body of the parent.

But the system of using local boards to oversee the standard and content of education was considered too parochial, consequently in 1902 a new act of parliament abolished them and made the local authority responsible, guided by the Government Board of Education through a system of school inspectors. The earliest record in the Burslem Council minutes relating to the rates of pay for teachers was in 1904:

Pupil Teachers.	Male per annum.	£60 plus £5 per annum	to Max. £75
"	Female "	£45 " "	to max. £60
Assistant Teachers.	Male "	£55 " " "	to max. £70
"	Female "	£45 " " "	to max. £60
Certified Assistants	Male " £75 " " "		to max £150
"	Female "	£65 " " "	to max £100

With University Degree add £5 per annum.

In 1906 the cost of education was causing concern to such a degree that the ratepayers called a protest meeting. They asserted that there were too many staff and that there should be a revision of salaries and a curtailment of expenses generally. As a start the budget for the year should be cut by £2000. As a result of this concern the Council resolved that all items of expense over £100 should be referred to the General Purposes Committee. Councillor Gibson, in a generous gesture, requested the Council to act as trustee for a fund of £400 to be called the Gibson Poor Childrens Fund, the income from which was to provide meals for poor children attending council schools.

There were a few private schools in Burslem of a type known as Dame Schools since they were often conducted on a personal basis by a woman in a private house. Warrilow speaks of one somewhere off Waterloo Road between Cobridge and Burslem. Charles Shaw talks in fond terms of his in *When I was a Child,* and Scarratt speaks of one in Dale Hall, conducted by a man and a Dickensian experience. The premises consisted of one room in a house where the master lived. The room was heated by a coal fire, removal of the ashes from which was part of the pupils educational ritual. The man himself was fat and repulsive looking, besides being fond of drink. He had a wooden leg which was screwed on and off each day without decorum by one of the senior pupils in the sight of the class. The master during lessons constantly

Charles Shaw's Dame School from the illustrated
When I Was a Child
(1998 Churnet Valley Books. Illustration by Sue Purdy)

wielded a long rod, similar to a fishing rod, which he played around the pupils heads, since his limited mobility combined with severe congestion in the schoolroom made movement almost impossible. The last straw which led to Scarratt's departure started with the absence of the master for one whole afternoon, at the closing hour of which he was carried home in a drunken state from the Staff of Life.

CHAPTER TWENTY SIX: The Cemetery

In 1872 the Board of Health was faced with a urgent decision. The growth in the population had almost exhausted the space in the churchyards, not only St John's, the parish church, but also the later church of St Paul. At St John's questions had been raised over the sanctity of the graves, since it was alleged that skulls and bones had been seen on the surface, and this, together with the raising of part of the churchyard using household and industrial refuse was causing concern for the health of nearby residents. The church refuted any inference that they had deviated from legal requirements which demanded, *"that no grave be used for other than members of the same family .....in walled graves above ground each coffin be embedded in Charcoal, be watertight, and in all cases a distance of half a yard be left between graves"*. However, on the shortage of space there was no dispute. At the public enquiry which followed the presiding inspector read an anonymous letter:

"Sir, I beg most respectfully to call your attention to an abominable occurrence which is continually going on in St John's churchyard. Graves are continually being opened where the dead have been buried over and over again. Forty years ago I have seen skulls and bones lying about in the churchyard, and this was quite a topic of conversation at that time. You must now submit to the danger to health and be intolerable to this sort of thing. The yard is immediately surrounded with houses, and if you must open your bedroom windows, so essential to health, you are sure to get a plentiful supply of deadly vapour from the churchyard. On behalf of myself and others, I have ventured to address these few lines to you hoping that, in your capacity, you may be able to get the matter complained of eliminated. I am very sorry not to be able to give my name in full for fear of incurring the displeasure of the Rector.

Signed. Sufferer."

Had it been written today it would have been headline news for a Sunday paper and little chance of 'Sufferer' maintaining their anonymity. Mr Wedgwood of the adjoining Churchyard Works said that no noxious fumes had been suffered there. The inspector confirmed that a cemetery was an urgent necessity, and the Board of Health decided to form of a separate Burial Board. As might be expected, there were some who saw the scheme as profligate and saw years of vacant possession in the churchyards. Others saw a financial benefit for the individual family and the town as a whole. Some with evil mind suspected a deal which would personally profit a landowner and the Board!

A rumour circulated that the site of the cemetery would be at Longport. Opposing views soon appeared in print and those in favour of a cemetery issued a forthright appeal:

"Fellow ratepayers. Don't be gulled! how many years have you been compelled to pay high and exorbitant fees at our churchyards. Don't be gulled! save fifty per cent on interment fees, and have the choice of your own minister. Don't be gulled! The "PORT" is not your choice of land for a cemetery. One of the candidates below is prepared to present to the town, free of cost, an eligible piece of land for a cemetery. Don't be gulled! are not the answers to "AN OLD RATEPAYER" strongly in favour of a Burial Board? If you want less rates, and good government, then support: Fred Hulme. Fred Tinnen. George Wigley. Robert Gilmore.

It has already been ascertained that certain persons are illegally filling in voting papers."

The opposition, in the form of "AN OLD RATEPAYER" had this to say:

"Fellow ratepayers, you are being called upon to perform a very important duty to yourselves and fellow ratepayers, as it depends on your present action to what extent you are to be further taxed, as some of the retiring members thought fit to "con" you for powers for the Board of Health to become a Burial Board and still further increase your burden. How far this was necessary, may be seen from the following facts. In the old churchyard, there is at present room for 280 graves; there are also 850 graves in which there is only one body interred, and 180 bricked graves and 50 vaults, all available for burial purposes. Now fellow ratepayers, looking at this, did we need a Burial Board or cemetery, to still crush us down with its expense? I think not, but we are also told the Board has made the choice of a piece of land before they were even constituted a Burial Board, perhaps this belongs to some friend of the old Board who, thinking the ratepayers could pay the best possible price, resolved to ask for power to constitute themselves the

Burial Board, and that without consulting the ratepayers of the facts, then with £400 law suit staring us in the face, brought on by somebody's neglect, it is quite sufficient to justify us in returning some fresh men to the Board and ... Vote for William Boulton. Robert Gilmore. Edward Clarke. James Malkin."

The £400 law suit, mentioned in this appeal, is not connected with the cemetery project. With a majority in favour of the project the Board applied for a loan of £20,000. The usual public enquiry followed which confirmed the need for prompt action and the loan was swiftly approved. Ralf Sneyd had offered the Board thirty acres of leasehold land at £8 per acre per annum but the Board decided to buy not rent, and not at Longport, but 28 acres of land at the opposite end of the town, purchased from the Reverend Walter Sneyd for £7000. Tenders of £1799.10s. for drainage and £745 for walls and piers were accepted - if the existing massive stone walls and piers are those covered by the tender, not only were they a bargain but the Board had a commendable conception of how to contain vandalism.

Areas on the site were allocated to the various religious denominations, and a space was chosen on which to build a chapel. A ceremony of consecration was performed by the Bishop of Lichfield assisted by the Archdeacon of Stoke, Sir Lovelace Stamer, in the presence of a number of local clergy, members of the corporation, and the public. Following the ceremony the Bishop addressed the multitude referring to them as God's people, which was a comforting, but the expected demand for prime sites was slow to materialise -despite a restriction on new graves in the churchyards, burials there showed no sign of abating.

Provision of shelter at the new cemetery was obviously a necessity, a chapel to provide for both spiritual and physical needs. The Surveyor had provided plans for a red brick building with a mini spire, estimated cost £2000. This was well in excess of what the Board intended to spend, and after lengthy discussion it was agreed that £800 would have to suffice. At this stage the Bishop reminded Burslem that if it built on a consecrated site, the building could only be used for members of the church of England, and that non-conformists and Roman Catholics would not be allowed its use. On the other hand, he could not allow his clergy to hold a service on non-consecrated ground.

There was endless correspondence between Church and the Burslem Board; that from the Bishop being conducted through Sir Lovelace Stamer. Enquiries to other authorities were conducted and from these it was found that the same problem had been experienced. A bishop in one diocese had accepted a single chapel for common use; on the other hand Longton had recently opened a new cemetery and built two chapels, one for the established church and one for the rest. Some parishes had even built three chapels, and the Bishop adamantly maintained the legality of his personal contentions, leaving Burslem to resolve the problem. For Burslem to build three chapels for £800 was impossible and it was pointed out that there were chapels at both Stoke and Burslem Poor Houses where burials were regularly conducted by ministers of all denominations. A possible solution was found in a parish where a chapel had been partitioned down the middle. This seemed an economical solution, in fact one member, to minimise the cost still further, had the bright idea of a painted line. Finally, another member thought there must be some civil law relating to the whole problem, and suggested that the Town Clerk obtain Council's opinion. The Town Clerk duly obtained two opinions, both of which suggested the Bishop's ruling was questionable.

But by this time Burslem's problem had become a national one and the government was considering the matter. The Bishop thought that Burslem should await a parliamentary decision but, in desperation they went ahead with a single chapel on unconsecrated ground. A suitable tender was received rom Mr Cook for £850. 8. 9.

It seems inappropriate to describe a cemetery as successful, but it seems so if judged by its memorials and that it is now reaching saturation point. Considerable attention was given to the provision of trees and shrubs, many purchased from Matthews nursery which still survives locally, and which are now mature and scenic. A Registrar-Gardener was appointed in 1879 at a salary of £90 p. a. along with a free house and free water. Later the same year a Lodgekeeper-Gravedigger was appointed at a wage of £1.1.0. a week with similar perks. Distance to the cemetery is now of little consequence and councillors are unlikely to be asked, as they were in the early days, to provide a seat for pilgrims wending their way up Moorland Road. The Surveyor response was that he was paid to move obstructions not to install them - if the Board wished to proceed, they would have to buy land adjacent to the pavement and they could expect similar requests from Waterloo Road and Newcastle Street.

If at the start of the cemetery project, the problems for the Board were religious ones, so also was the final one, brought about by a letter from a clergyman in 1882 to say that, *"in fairness to his Sunday worshippers, he was no longer prepared to neglect them for funerals."* This, members of the Board considered, was an unjust attitude towards the working class, whose only free day was Sunday, but many of the clergy were requesting legal legislation to forbid all Sunday burials. It is also ironical to think that while at that time graves were opened on a Sunday, shops were forced to close, while currently the reverse applies.

Although in the 19th century there was a trade in disinterred bodies, encouraged by medical schools to advance their research and education, in this area 'body snatchers' or 'resurrectioners' were rarely encountered. But in 1831 lights were reported moving after dark in St John's churchyard and a search disturbed a gang, who fled leaving behind recently disinterred bodies, together with tools and boxes. One man was captured, but the remainder got away. He was convicted and jailed at Stafford where he ultimately died of consumption.

The vegetable Market

CHAPTER TWENTY SEVEN: The Vegetable Market

St John's square, at the western entrance to the town, had come to be recognised as the site for market traders in vegetables, but it was considered necessary to have a covered area to compliment the Shambles meat market. The Board decided to buy the old Brickhouse Pottery, or Bell Works as it had become known. In 1878 a government inspector approved the project and the site was purchased for £4200 plus £2036 for additional land. The frontage and entrance was in Queen Street, and built to complement its neighbour the Wedgwood Institute. As early as 1876 it had been proposed to buy the yard of The Legs of Man for £7250 to provide an entrance to the market, giving access from both front and rear. Presumably the coaching days at the inn were drawing to a close.

A price of £13,959 from Messrs Inskip of Longton was accepted for the main building work and one of £1,350 from Messrs Hill & Smith for the roofing, which was presumably a patent steel and glass structure for which this firm was well known. The design of the building was by Mr E. M. Richards, the local Board of Health Engineer and Surveyor. The frontage embodied the main entrance and six shops with rear entrances into the market hall from Market Square. Above the shops were council offices necessitated by growing pressure on space in the town hall. The total length of the building was 125 feet and it was originally topped with a tower. The total height including the tower was 96 feet.

The laying of the foundation stone took place on March 13th 1878 in the traditional manner reflecting the prestige of the borough. The arrangements were for the lady guests to go direct to the site in Queen Street. The gentlemen were to assemble at the town hall at 1.30pm and go in procession at 1.45 pm in the following order: The Rifle Volunteer Band, County Constabulary, The Mayor, Alderman Thomas Hulme and his guests, Members of the Board of Health, and finally the populace of Burslem.

Mr Hulme opened the ceremony. Addressing the company, he said, "*You are standing on the spot where Josiah Wedgwood commenced to manufacture pottery. It was on this site that the first bell for a manufactury was hung*". He concluded by introducing Mr Robert Heath MP to lay the foundation stone. Mr. Heath was handed a trowel, a mallet and a plumb line. The trowel was described as a work of art with a porcelain blade, one face of which had a ground of canary colour, enclosing a panel in which the exact elevation of the building was depicted in colour. On the same side was a copy of the arms of the local Board, the whole enclosed with ornamental foliage in raised chased gold. On the obverse side, the arms of Mr Heath were embossed in a medallion on a pink ground together with the words:

"Presented to Robert Heath Esq. M.P. on the occasion of the laying of the
Memorial Stone of the new Vegetable Market
Burslem. March 13th. 1878.

Round the blade there was a border of silver beautifully chased. The shank was solid silver and the handle made of glass. The whole was a fine specimen of Davenport's work.

It must surely by now be in the mind of readers that there are in diverse ownership a number of these unique trowels, which if brought together would form a spectacular collection, illustrating both Burslem's growth and the inherent artistic attributes of its citizens!

A decorated jar made by Pinder Bourne and Co, containing coins and a parchment with details of the ceremony and the names of the officials of the town, was placed in a cavity under the foundation stone.

Following the ceremony, the guests returned in procession to the town hall for an official luncheon. The hall was decorated with flowers from Biddulph Hall and there was an orchestra and organ recital. The official luncheon was taken as a suitable occasion for the presentation of a full length portrait to Thomas Hulme, the last Bailiff and first Mayor of the borough. The painting was the work of Mr R. Hook of Manchester and was paid for by subscriptions of the town councillors, officials and burgesses, and is presumably the one which was eventually hung in the Wedgwood Institute.

In the speeches which followed Mr Woodall MP spoke of increasing prosperity not only in Burslem but throughout the Country. He said that this was obvious from the following figures; *"the consumption of flour per head had increased annually from 311 lbs to 341 lbs per head since 1835, the consumption of tea, from 1½ lbs to 4½ lbs, and sugar from 19½ lbs to 54lbs, although the latter was frowned upon today".*

Mr Heath spoke of his parliamentary effort to be *"just"* in his voting, *"but prejudiced in any interest which favoured Burslem"*, which should have reassured any lingering doubt of voters; nevertheless *"he did not expect to please all, but it was a pleasant thing that Englishmen should agree to differ."*

Mr Hanbury, another MP, spoke of the common urge of all MPs to further the welfare of the Country, another encouragement for the voters. *"Take on the one hand"*, he said, *"Sir Stafford Northcote and Mr Cross, and on the other hand, the Marquis of Hartington and Mr Gladstone, although they might grumble because the conservatives had as they thought overstrained the strength of the country, the liberals perhaps undervalued its resources, but no more conscientious statesmen ever held the reins of government."* One word about India, he said, *"A cloud is gathering over that country, let them hope it would not grow into a rain cloud; the brave merchants and soldiers who have won a great empire for us deserve our gratitude, but the greatest deed of gratitude is owed by the people of India themselves. If we left them, they would be a prey to anarchy, and to a tyranny even worse than anarchy; it was not for ourselves we desired to retain India, but to give the people a good rule".*

He could not have foreseen a cloud which gathered over Burslem in 1881 and would open and shatter thirty roof lights in the newly-built and still to be paid for Vegetable Market; or that new glass would have to be fitted from the inside, which necessitated major scaffolding and temporary closure. Perhaps it is not surprising to find that the roof is now covered with traditional tiles - sadly the tower has vanished. An unexpected sequel to the opening of the market was when a Mr Middleton opened a Dram Shop adjoining one of the exits and a member of the council suggested that he had deliberately sited his shop to catch shoppers coming out of the market. This it appears was far from Mr Middleton's intention, and a personal insult to which he took strong exception, and many legal threats followed.

It is strange to think that market halls were built to shelter shoppers and traders from the rigours of nature, yet now, in the 20th century, people throng to outdoor markets in the towns, and many traditional shopkeepers think they bring trade, while both face competition from a new phenomenem, the out of town supermarket halls.

Furniture Remover,

BY ROAD OR RAIL.   CAREFULLY PACKED.

COAL MERCHANT.

All Classes of Fuel supplied in Trucks, Loads and Sacks, on the Shortest Notice, and at Colliery Prices.

Office : 340, WATERLOO ROAD, COBRIDGE.

CHAPTER TWENTY EIGHT: Civic maturity

Death of Ricardo MP. Foundation of library. The Haywood Hospital. Incorporation of Burslem
The Maddock's Fountain. The Town's maturity.

In 1862, Mr John Lewis Ricardo the Liberal parliamentary representative for Burslem for twenty years, died and the Board requested that a general closure of all businesses and shops be observed and that muffled bells be rung on the day of the funeral. The Board sent a letter of condolence to the widow, Lady Catherine Ricardo. In a new election, a Mr Grenfell, who was later to become Governor of the Bank of England, was adopted. Another stranger, Mr Alexander Berrisford Hope, was similarly adopted for the Conservatives, since Mr Copeland had decided to retire after twenty five years. Mr Pope again applied for nomination, but failed to achieve it and applied instead for nomination at Bolton. Perhaps after all it was his name that was unfortunate, rather than his policies, since Burslem was a stronghold of dissenters. Another newcomer, a Mr Skee who fought for liberal policies, only secured 32 votes.

While national elections are to the fore for a limited time, domestic problems are constant, and however small, the Burslem Board was continuously called upon to solve them. A request from a resident in Nile Street was for a licence to convert a cowhouse to a residence. Of greater concern was the loss of income from the sale of the market tolls which was decreasing. In 1862 the sale only achieved £1165 but the grant was extended for three years at this figure.

In 1863, a public meeting was called in February to discuss celebrations for the forthcoming wedding of Edward, Prince of Wales, and the preparation of an address to the prince and princess, and the sending of a congratulatory message to Queen Victoria. The address to the royal couple was prepared and printed on china slabs which were on completion exhibited for three days in the court room at the town hall.

This was an important year in the history of education in Burslem. The government, anxious to improve learning and eliminate illiteracy, were offering financial help in the formation of public libraries and local authorities would be allowed to fund continuance of the project by applying a rate not to exceed one penny. A public meeting was called in Burslem to consider the draft proposals,which were also to be publicly exhibited on a prepared broadsheet with space for individuals to sign in support.

The meeting was chaired by Mr J Lowndes, who claimed it was one of the most impressive assemblies ever held in Burslem, and he hoped for his part that it would conclude with seventy five per cent in favour, a figure which he considered to be necessary for its success. He then called for comments. The first comment came from a gentleman in the audience who said that *in his long experience of the work of libraries, his opinion was that next to preaching the Gospel, he knew of no other agency so effectual in harmonising and improving the habits and courtesies of the public of this country, and he hoped that now, since Burslem has taken the lead, the other towns in the Potteries would at once see the desirableness of following so good an example.* Another member of the audience said he could remember the time when a poor girl, applying for a situation as a domestic servant, was asked if she could read or write, and found it was a positive disadvantage if she could, since it was feared she would read her master's letters. Another said that those who wanted to read should pay, and those who did not, should not.

It was emphasised that books would be loaned for reading at home, giving children the opportunity to learn, while it was hoped that the reading room proposed for the library would be a substitute for the public house. The cost of a maximum penny rate, it was said, Burslem would incorporate in the general Board of Health rate. One person suggested they should try it, as they had done in Manchester. A Mr John Grifiths said it was twenty years since he came to Burslem, and with the great advances made he could not see who could oppose the scheme for a penny rate. A Mr Goodfellow said it was not generous to the ratepayers of Burslem to propose adding another rate, even a penny in the pound; there was no knowing where it would stop.

The seven five per cent majority was obtained, and the preparation and distribution of the broadsheets went ahead. At least one of the broadsheets is preserved with a remarkable number of crosses, representing the signatures of the voters who were adult illiterates, which is both sad and yet heart warming in its indication of eagerness to overcome the limitation in the quality of their lives. Probably with the value of this project in mind, a contemporary review of local conditions in the *Staffordshire Sentinel* at the time said that *"smoke, dirt and vulgarity stand foremost in the fancy of a foreigner whenever potters are spoken of, but in the last twelve years much has been done towards improving this impression, regardless of the less prosperous times, but markets and bad debts have still been much the rule"*.

There was an interest in the arts in Burslem and in music. In 1864, the year following the founding of the library project, Mr Davenport offered to provide an organ for the new town hall. This generosity was gratefully accepted, the organ installed, and a Mr Jardine of Manchester contracted to keep the instrument in good condition for a fee of six pounds per annum. Offers were requested for the position of organist, and it was suggested to the successful applicant that he give morning and evening concerts. He would be paid one guinea per performance, out of which he would be expected to pay his own blower. The venture does not appear to have been a continuing success however. Maybe Burslem was not organ minded, since without any sign of public dismay, during renovations to the town hall in the 20th century the organ vanished, either in pieces, or to a new home.

By 1864 growth of the town was adding greatly to the work of administration and the demands on the Board. Expansion had reached a point where the original ordinance survey map was inadequate and required replacing. Enquiries were made but the Board were informed that they would have to bear two thirds of the cost, which would be at least £1000. During this year the board advertised for a full time rate collector at a salary of £80 per annum, and requested two sureties to a total of £300, a princely sum to find as surety for a man of modest station, but no doubt reflecting the growth of rate income and the fact that it would be predominantly paid in cash. It was also decided to change the town's banker. Alcocks Bank, founded by two pottery manufacturer brothers had held the position since 1830, but were replaced by the Hanley branch of the Manchester and Liverpool District Bank

Lord Palmerston died in 1865 and condolences were sent by the Board to his widow. In the period following his death there was a parliamentary election and with it a new face in Burslem, a Mr Melly for the Liberals, but the retiring candidates, Hope and Grenfell held their seats, although margins were getting narrower. Another eminent parliamentarian Richard Cobden also died in 1865 and instruction was given for the town hall flag to be flown at half mast while the Board sent a letter of condolence to his family. The concern shown was in recognition of Cobden's passionate support for free trade on which the Burslem manufactures were so dependent, and which he so successfully advocated in parliament.

In 1866 there were sporadic instances of cholera in Burslem, and fearing the possibility of it developing into an epidemic, precautions were taken by placing quantities of chloride of lime outside the police station and the inhabitants encouraged to whitewash with it. Also in this year, attention of the Board was drawn to the need for a public playground since too many children were playing in the streets. This request indicates a growing volume of traffic in the streets. It was proposed to buy land adjoining Jenkin's Mill, owned by Josiah Wedgwood.

1868 was another election year, but with elections coming round so frequently, the response was poor. Mr Grenfell had decided to follow Mr Pope to Lancashire, and a newcomer, a Mr Campbell, took over the Tory cause and was successful along with Mr Melly. The fire may have been taken out of politics, but smoke abatement was being taken more seriously by all authorities. For this district it was confined largely to plant for steam raising, since little could be done about the traditional bottle ovens, the biggest menace. Thirty seven manufacturers introduced smoke abatement schemes, but it was still a long way from removing the grime deposited seven days each and every week.

1869 saw the first petroleum licences, the first issued to Thomas Deakin in Newcastle Street for the keeping of ten gallons. D. Howarth and J. Ollivant of Market Place were similarly allowed to each keep ten gallons, while Wolstanton Wholesale Stores, Beeches Bridge, were licenced to hold 250 gallons.

Among the building licences issued was one to build a bank at the top of Newcastle Street for the Manchester and District Bank, on land purchased from Enoch Broad. A fund had also been organised for the construction of a fountain to be erected outside the new bank in Fountain Square. The Board considered the proposed design unacceptable, but subsequently approved one submitted by a Mr Garlick. This fountain never seems to have been mentioned again until Mr James Maddock became mayor of the newly incorporated borough in 1880 and offered to build the town a new fountain in St John's Square presumably replacing the old one at the entrance to Fountain Pottery.

Burslem was spontaneously sympathetic to tragedy in 1871 when a fire devastated most of the city of Chicago, which by that time held some two million inhabitants. A public subscription realised £260.

the great fire of Chicago

1872 was not a good year for the Board. There was a fire in Cobridge and Thomas Harris the turncock arrived at the fire station in a drunken state; to make matters worse, when the brigade arrived at the scene of the fire, it was reported that no one including the police knew the position of the hydrants. Then there was the unexpected arrival of a Doctor Ballard, a Government Inspector of Health who came to survey sanitary conditions in Burslem. His report was far from complimentary. He found untrapped drain cesspools, water closets not attended to by the lower classes and the medical officer's duties not sufficiently defined. Cesspools, he said, should be got rid of, and ash pits should be emptied more frequently. Some public roads, especially High Street, were in a disgraceful state, and there had been ninety two deaths in one year due to scarlet fever. In the discussion which followed, it was claimed by one councillor that owners of property in Burslem had been put to enormous cost in providing water closets and the system had proved a failure.

One item of interest in the year's agenda was a request from the Queen's Hotel for permission to build a pigsty. Presumably they wished to ensure the quality of the pork they served, or to find an economic use of their left-overs.

The general rate charge was remarkably consistent in this period, since it was held at 2/6d in the pound for a number of years. In 1874 a memorial was sent to Queen Victoria on the occasion of the marriage of the Duke of Edinborough to Princess Marie of Russia. This same year was memorable for producing the borough's first labour candidate for the parliamentary election, a Mr Walton, but he failed to win a seat.

Other diverse items with which the Board had to contend in 1874, included a report that seventy one loads of night soil had been spread on the Grange, and an objection by local residents, who not surprisingly, complained it was contaminating the local air. Spring this year must have been particularly dry and windy, since it was reported that up to May 632 loads of water had been sprinkled on the roads.

In a salary review, the town hall joint keepers of man and wife had their combined annual salary increased to £75. The Board leased the hall for a Dog, Poultry and Leaping exhibition. The Rate Collector's basic salary was also increased to £105 plus $2^{1}/_{2}$ % of all money he could squeeze from reluctant households for street works executed by the Board.

The long standing dispute with Cobridge over immunity from certain rate charges which the Abbey of Hulton had previously enjoyed, and which had been originally settled in favour of Cobridge, was rescinded in court in 1875. An irate ratepayer referred to the £400 legal costs Burslem had incurred.

Burslem experienced the loss of the Surveyor, Mr Ralph Hales, who died in 1875 after many years service in a period which saw a large amount of new building.

The generosity of the town's people was called upon again in 1875 when the Board together with local church ministers agreed to combine to collect for the relief of famine in India.

To close 1875, agreement was expressed on the need for four public urinals spread over the parishes.

Since the last Haywood brother died in 1874, there had been continuous litigation over the charitable trust set up by the brothers Howard and Richard. The original intention was to build a hospital from the proceeds but the legal interpretation of the trust was in dispute, consequently, pending settlement a house was rented in Waterloo Road by the administrators, and interest from the bequest used to provide meals and nursing for the poor. In 1876 settlement seemed imminent and the trustees considered the purchase of a site for £6000 and spending £14,000 on the building of a hospital, the name to be the Haywood Hospital. A further £5000 it was suggested, would go to the cost of endowing a ward at the new General Hospital in Penkhull, to cater for patients sent from Burslem. The lawyers dealing with the bequest said that using the £5000 in that manner would not comply with the terms of the trust, and in any case the original sum of £30,000 had dwindled, presumably from the long standing controversy and the resultant legal costs! They emphasised that the terms of the will were that the money be used for, *care of the poor in Burslem, their nursing and seaside recuperation*. Further wrangling ensued but ultimately the bequest realised £26,000 and the Haywood Hospital was built and opened in 1877. It had accommodation for twenty four in-patients, further accommodation being added later through the generosity of Mr Maddock

It was proposed in 1876 that on account of its cost, a day nursery which had been open for a number of years should be closed. The nursery had originated from the high death rate in Burslem which, at the time it was opened, was one third of the children under five. It was appreciated that mothers were forced to work to provide for the family, as were older children who would otherwise have assisted in nursing the very young at home. The death rate was now improving, the minimum age to commence work was being increased, and the Board therefore decided, not without objections, that the nursery should close.

In the parliamentary election of 1877 there were more new faces, Mr Melly retired, but a newcomer, Mr Kenealy was adopted as a Peoples Candidate. The conservatives were represented by Mr Davenport and Mr Walton again appeared for Labour. Mr Kenealy and Mr Walton topped the poll. All was not peaceful at the election; Mr Kenealy held a meeting in the town hall which got out of hand. Since the Board had requested the chief constable to make precautionary arrangements - which he had failed to do - they claimed from the County as Commissioners of Police for the cost of the damage. Out of this ill will there came a blessing though, since in the arbitration which followed the Board learned that while all fines imposed in Burslem court were paid to the County, Burslem was entitled to a percentage which they had failed to claim, a duty which they set out to do promptly and retrospectively.

In 1876 there was a continuing problem with lodging houses, and it was reported to the Board that the Inspector has served thirty two notices on the owners in one month for contravention of the bye laws. It was suggested the offenders licences should be withdrawn since there were too many in the borough making it an attraction for tramps, beggars and thieves.

The police drew the attention of shopkeepers in the town to the act of 1851 which stated that it was their legal duty to sweep dirt on the pavement into the gutters before 9am, and a number of tradesmen were also in court for obstructing the pavement. One who was summoned was a butcher named Knight who hung a carcase outside his shop and claimed immunity since he said it was only what his father had done before him. Two other tradesmen, a draper in Market Place who had shirts hanging outside, and a boot and shoe maker in Queen Street, were all fined and warned that the penalty could be imprisonment.

1877 was a key year, in that it was the year Burslem applied for incorporation as a Borough. The application described the area as being divided into three wards, presumably Burslem, Sneyd and Rushton Grange (Cobridge). In the official application it described it as an area which had grown from a scattered village on the top of a hill, to a town of 26,000 people.

It went on to say that at present the town is responsible for lighting, sewers, paving and streets, and regulating markets. Its borrowings included £14,000 for the building of one market, it was about to erect a second covered market for £20,000; for its sewage £25,000; for drainage £8000; for a gas works £90,000 and a cemetery £20,000, achievements which entitled Burslem to a proper position. It had no borough magistrate and no power to licence public houses or beer houses, and its police were controlled from the County headquarters. They concluded, surely there is no necessity for the town of its population to have 34 public houses and 109 beer houses. Previous proposals by the Board for incorporation had been made as far back as 1869, but such had been the fears of the ratepayers of it being followed by an increase in rates, a number of members of the current council lost their seats.

The government enquiry which followed is said to have been conducted by Leiutenant Colonel Donnelly, and a successful outcome was not unexpected, since some of Mother Burslem's offspring, aspiring above their station, had already succeeded in becoming incorporated boroughs before their parent.

The Charter of Incorporation was dated 27th June 1878. The ceremony surrounding the occasion was conducted by the last Bailiff, Mr Thomas Hulme, who changed his robe of office and became the first Mayor. Speaking at the ceremony Mr S.B. Edge MP said *"Burslem was the mother of the Potteries. It was often a trait of mothers to prefer the children's advancement before their own, and so it had been with Burslem. She had watched her children, Hanley, Stoke and Longton become incorporated boroughs, and had been content to follow in their footsteps"*. The mayor reminisced that he was reminded of the time when the site of the town hall was a covered space where butter women and egg sellers met to trade.

Following the induction ceremony, the mayor, together with the six aldermen and sixteen councillors, officials and prominent citizens, went in procession to St Paul's, led by the band of the 6th North Staffordshire Rifle Volunteers and past dense crowds who lined the way. The service was conducted by the Rev. J. Price, the Vicar, and Dr Alcock read the lesson. And so an historical era concluded with the transposition of the 'Board of Health' to its new title of the 'Corporation of Burslem'. At a later ceremony, the widow of Mr John Maddock, Chief Bailiff in the year 1852/3, presented a mayoral chain to the town. The chain was in eighteen carat gold and had an ornamental medallion bearing the arms of the town. It was supplied by the Burslem firm Messrs Carryer.

The original official seal of the town, adopted about 1850, took the form of a quartered shield. The first and fourth quarter showed a piece of pottery, described as like a soup tureen without a cover. The second quarter a scythe with a fleur de lys, the scythe being a part of the Sneyd family arms, and the third quarter a Fret, part of the Audley arms. The border was inscribed with the words: Burslem Board of Health. A second seal acquired in 1878 was also quartered and crested by a wreath of colours in front of the garb, or fleur de lys, between two branches of laurel, and beneath the shield the motto: 'Ready'. The first and fourth quarter showed a Portland Vase, the second quarter the Sneyd Scythe, and the third quarter the Audley Fret. It is said that the red fleur de lys in front of the yellow garb is that of the seal of Thomas Hulme. The cost of preparation and supplying the second coat of arms was £280.

Mr Powell was the first appointment by the new borough council; that of Town Clerk at a salary of £210 per annum. He had to be found an office in the new Vegetable Market, and was personally to find a surety of £400 to be placed in the corporation's name in the Star Building Society. One of the first items to which the new Borough Council had to give attention was the granting by the Home Secretary of permission for the Wakes holiday to be altered from June to August, but so much discord arose over this alteration that in the following year the new Burslem Council decided to hold a referendum in the town on whether to revert to June. The result was two to one in favour of June, and it was agreed therefore that in future it would commence on the first Saturday after the 24th.

Mr James Maddock became the second mayor of Burslem in 1880 and in appreciation of the honour renewed his offer to build a new fountain. The proposed structure was described as fourteen to fifteen feet high on a granite base, and besides its use by the public it would have a trough to cater for thirsty dogs. Gas would be supplied to a lamp with which crowned it. The mayor and his generous gift were evidently not universally popular, since one ungrateful councillor said *"the mayor's liberality would be more effectual spent on building a ward in the hospital."* Another councillor suggested the fountain would be more popular if gin, whisky or Burton beers were laid on. Dogs had been a constant trouble and suggestions had been made that a byelaw be introduced to compel them to be muzzled!

Despite the criticisms it became a welcome addition to the towns amenities. The official unveiling ceremony was performed by Mr J. Bevis Brindley, the Recorder of Hanley. After many years, and probably dwindling use, the fountain was considered to be an obstruction and was removed and rebuilt in the precinct of Maddocks factory. Later still it was ignominiously consigned to the Town Yard. Fortunately this resulted in its preservation, and recently restored, it now stands proudly adjoining its original site, providing light but no water; hopefully a reminder of our historical heritage.

The town in this year saw the opening of the Coffee House Company's Refreshment Rooms, run on a strictly temperance basis, and incorporating a games room, and a reading room. The building was in the Market Place and called The Borough Arms, and this was presumably the later Liberal Club buildings.

The parliamentary election in this year, which embraced the revised boundaries, resulted in success for the well known and highly regarded Burslem citizen William Woodall, and another newcomer, a Mr Broadhurst who was described as a Working Man's Candidate,

There was a national slump in trade in 1881, which resulted in a general reduction in wages. The debt position was claimed to be serious. There was said to be 400 empty houses and that four manufactures had closed. This state of affairs led to a considerable reduction in the rate income, nine and three quarter percent of which was still unpaid, more than that of other towns.

There was an unwelcome visit during the year by a Doctor Barry, delegated by the government to examine the sanitary conditions in all towns. In his review, he said that the water supply was good, but the sewage arrangements were bad in places and had led to the storage of filth over a long period in close proximity to houses. Sewage was stored in some cases as long as twelve months and houses were never free from smell. He had met instances where cess pits went under floors, and others where they went under back roads. Some were of enormous size and formed part of the houses. He condemned the system in connection with lodging houses where tramps who carried diseases frequented. Massey Square, Hadderage and Adams Square had objectionable arrangements, and he suggested substituting trough closets. He preferred the water closet system but it would be necessary to appoint an instructor to advise users how to look after the closets. From this latter observation it is obvious that the toilets were installed without an integral cistern, consequently they had to be flushed by using a bucket and being communal, the inevitable result was communal neglect. The sanitary inspector's report shed light on another insanitary, but allowed practice. He said that where pigs were kept by private householders, houses for them should be a minimum distance from the human habitation. Concern was also expressed at an outbreak of typhoid in Longport, believed to be due to the seepage of sewage into the water; and the problem of the continuing high death rate among children. Figures were given of comparative death rates over the past nine years of infant deaths in twenty large towns. The overall average was 174 per thousand. In London it was 160 per thousand. In Burslem it was 190 per thousand!

One of the councillors had views on the contributory cause of the death rate among children. He said that *"It was well known how education was affecting the health of the rising generation; and equally well known that it was not intended for children to be educated as they were being, and which the nervous system could not possibly bear, consequently children had become delirious, and in that state been heard muttering arithmetical tables."* Fellow councillors were not eager to accept his dogmatic views.

Mr Snape's travelling circus requested renewal of a licence to perform in Swan Square adjoining the Methodist Chapel, but this was a forlorn hope; opposition was sufficiently strong to cause Mr Snape to agree to move elsewhere.

In this same year, the new Burslem and Wolstanton Board of Guardians premises were opened. Built in Queen Anne style and situated by the neighbouring parish offices in Moorland Road, they were probably immediately busy due to the slump in trade. The frontage of the building in Price Street stood three feet back and was surrounded by palisades. The side of the building was in Nicholas Street. The Vegetable Market, also newly completed, was sufficiently imposing to cause one councillor to suggest that it be used as a concert hall rather than for its original purpose,

Napoleon's armies never reached Burslem but the French must have must have had their eye on the town, since the Council received a Paris firm's request to be allowed to erect a stall and sell newspapers in the borough. No indication is given of the response!

An interesting society was formed in 1882 with the title of The Society for the care of Friendless Girls. It was centred in Hanley and was run by volunteers throughout the district. The Burslem representative for the society was Mrs Panter of St Paul's vicarage. The aim was to chose girls of acceptable character from poor families, following which they would be trained and placed in domestic service. They attended classes for sewing and made their own uniforms, and while so employed *"an amusing and profitable book is read, followed by a twenty minute Bible lesson"*. The matron and members of the committee visited prospective employers and arranged for payment to pay for the girl's uniform, and for a little pocket money. *"This way the girls learned to spend money to advantage."* According to the 1831 census, there were 700,000 domestics in Britain. It is thought by 1882 there were a million

The use of electricity was now gaining ground for domestic and industrial purposes and some authorities were making applications for a licence to generate and supply this new competitor of gas. The Burslem Board had not long bought out the private gas company and was loth to commit itself further, but gave notice that it would support independent applications. It was also ominous that rates were tending to rise; the General Rate for 1882 was set at 2/10, and strictures were given to the Accountant that in giving him a rise in salary to £150 per annum, a condition was that he was held personally responsible for providing and paying for any help he needed and an increase was not to asked for over the next three years.

By 1882 Burslem could be said to have become a flourishing and self-sufficient town, capable of catering for the wants of its inhabitants. The comprehensive list below shows the major shops within the town while in addition there was a considerable number of houses whose front rooms were converted to a selling area. In 1882 for instance, the total number of grocery and provision shops, which included the house shops, was given as 150; hairdressers, at that time a virtual male monopoly, was given as fifteen. There were also pawnbrokers and secondhand clothes dealers in the numerous streets of all three parishes.

LIST OF SHOP TRADERS IN THE TOWN CENTRE.1882.

GROCERS & PROVISION MERCHANTS 7.   Three in Market Place.
                                       Three in Queen St. One in St John's Square.
CHEESE & BACON MERCHANTS 4.   Two in Market Street, and two in Queen Street.
BAKERS 2.   Market Square.
BUTCHERS 3.   Two in Queen St. One in Market Place.
FRUITERERS & GREENGROCERS 4.   Three in Queen St. One in Market Square.
FISHMONGERS. Apparently none.
CHEMISTS & DRUGGISTS. 4.   Two in Market Place.
                                       One in Market Square & one in St John's Square.
CLOTHIERS. 5.   Four in St. John's Square; one in Market Place.
TAILORS 3.   Two in Market Place; one in St John's Square.
DRAPERS 7   Four St John's Square, two Market Place
                                       One Queen Street
HATTERS 4.   Three in Market Place; one in St John's Square.
BOOTS & SHOES 6.   Four in Market Place and two in Queen Street.
HOSIERS 5.   Two in Market Place. Two in Queen St.
                                       One in Swan Square.
JEWELLERS & WATCH MAKERS 4.   Two in Market Place and two in Queen Street.
TOBACCONISTS 2.   Queen Street.
UMBRELLA MAKERS 1.   St. John's Square.
NEWSAGENT 2.   One Market Place and one Swan Square.
HAIRDRESSERS 2.   St. John's Square.
WINES & SPIRITS 2.   One St. John's Square and one Swan Square.
HABERDASHERS 1.   Queen Street.

The original Haywood Hospital

Traders in Burslem in the late 19th century

PAWNBROKERS.

Baines, Mrs. E. G., 20, Nile-st.
Bourns, Mary A., 1, Port Vale-
street
Chawner, Geo., 376, Waterloo-
road, Cobridge
Elliott, J. H., 16, Liverpool-rd.
Jones, John, 11, Nile-street
Knott, Alexander, 12, Regent-
street West
Palfreyman Bros., 17, New-
castle-street
Povey, Clement D., 12, Nile-st.,
and 1, Holdcroft-street
Wilson, Hannah, 86, Liverpool-
road

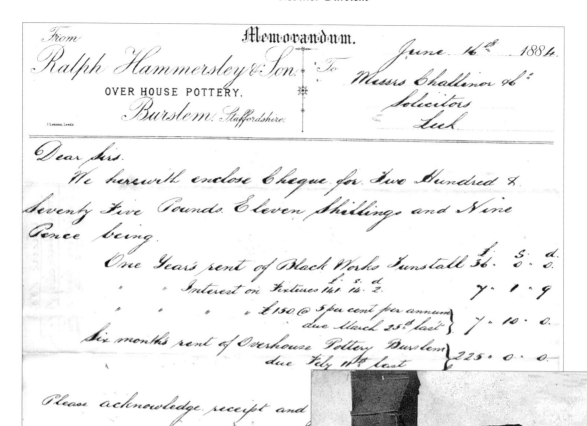

Memorandum.

From
Ralph Hammersley & Son
OVER HOUSE POTTERY,
Burslem, Staffordshire.

To
Messrs Challinor & Co
Solicitors
Leek

June 16th 1884

Dear Sirs.

We herewith enclose Cheque for Two Hundred &
Seventy Five Pounds Eleven Shillings and Nine
Pence being.

	£. s. d.
One Year's rent of Black Works Tunstall	36 . 0 . 0
" Interest on Fixtures £141. 14. 2	7 . 1 . 9
" £150 @ 5 per cent per annum due March 25th last	7 . 10 . 0
Six months rent of Overhouse Pottery Burslem due Feby 11th last	225 . 0 . 0

Please acknowledge receipt and

Ralph

The above bill features the oldest named Burslem pottery still in operation. The Over House pottery was sold by Thomas Wedgwood in 1818 to Edward Challinor, who also owned a pottery in Tunstall. He worked Over House for a time and installed new machinery. He then let it to Ralph Hammersley who was also working the Church bank pottery in Tunstall at the time.

Right: pottery workers, one carrying two saggars. This is not only a feat of strength but also risky since with constant firing saggars developed cracks, which were filled with plastic clay, but on occasion they suddenly disintegrated on being handled and caused severe cuts.

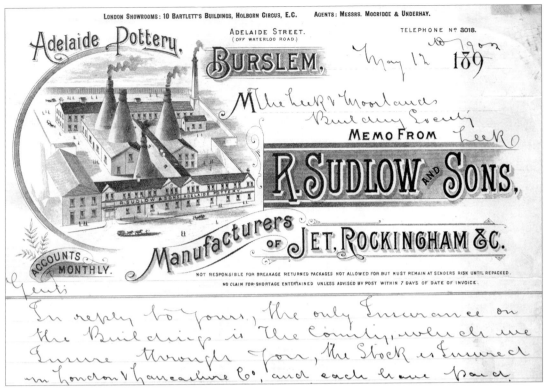

Once a prosprerous family business, this firm no longer exists, although part of the pottery buildings are still standing

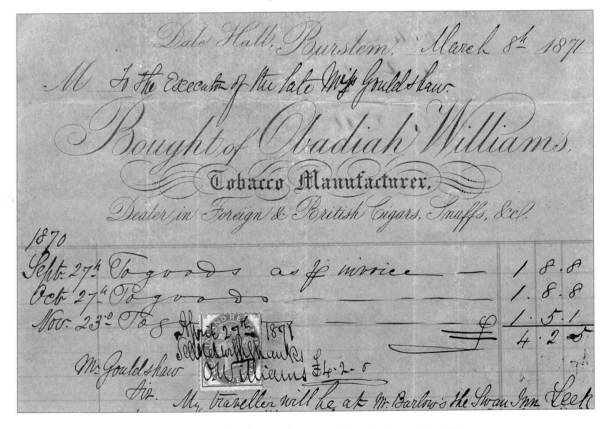

A Burslem invoice that perhaps confirms that smoking kills.

Inside and outside of a bottle kiln

Advert for Wade and Co and some of their tiling products. Several potteries in Burslem produced tiles and similar work

The following five pages show further advertisments for Burslem potteries and tarders from directories at the end of 19th and beginning of 20th centuries

Successors to the Mayer Brothers. Both firms produced artistic work which is much sought after

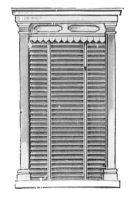

The Moorcroft Pottery at the turn of the 20th century

Part of Enoch Wood's original Fountain works used as seen here for a variety of trades but now converted into attractive appartments

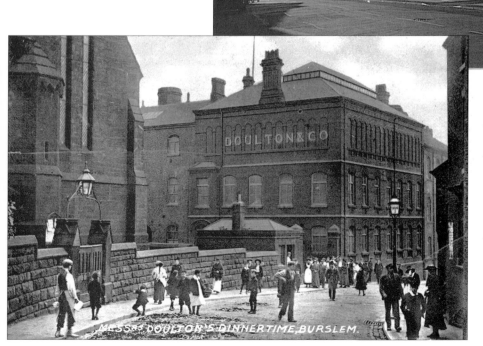

The Doultons' works at the beginning of the 20th century

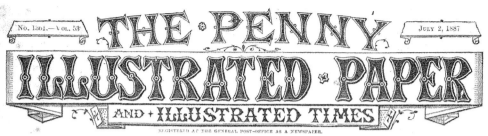

CHILDREN'S JUBILEE TREAT IN HYDE PARK: THE PRINCE PRESENTING FLORENCE DUNN TO THE QUEEN

and Florence eagerly grasping her Burslem made mug

CHAPTER TWENTY NINE: Ends and beginnings

Death of William Woodall. Victoria's Jubilee and death.   Edward the Seventh.
Birth of local Co-operative movement. Cholera. The Infectious Diseases Hospital. Burslem Park.
First Public Baths. The School of Art. Port Vale Football Club. Death of the ancient Borough.

In 1883 William Woodall decided to retire from local politics and also sever his connection with the Wedgwood Institute, an enterprise which he had cultivated with both time and money, and of whose committee he was currently chairman. Expansive tribute was paid to him in council. In response Mr. Woodall sent the following letter of acknowledgment to Mr. Powell the Town Clerk:

Bleak House.
Burslem.
9/11/1883

Dear Mr. Powell,
"Please assure His Worship The Mayor, and my other friends and late colleagues, that I most warmly appreciate, and will always gratefully remember their kindness in passing a generous reference to my withdrawal from the town council, which you tell me was adopted yesterday.
Reluctantly as I have recognised the necessity, I shall feel severance from municipal life, had I not the satisfaction of knowing that there remains many ways in which I may have the privilege of co-operating with those who are called to places within the council chamber, and that there is some reason to hope that lessons learned therein, will enable me to serve my fellow townsmen and constituents in another place, more intelligently than would have been the case but for experience so gained
Reciprocating their good wishes, I hope that the members of the council may have the satisfaction of seeing great success reward their unselfish labours for the public good, and in sincere regard and esteem for yourself
I remain, William Woodall."

In 1884, there was a mass political meeting at Cobridge on ground which later became the Burslem Cricket Club and near the home of the Sisters of the Poor. A raised wooden platform had been erected for the occasion and the principal speaker was Mr Joseph Chamberlain on behalf of the Liberals. In his speech before the thousands who attended, he criticised the House of Lords, saying *"they toil not neither do they spin"*, but while the meeting was in progress the platform supports gave way and some people, including Mr Chamberlain's daughter, fell eight feet to the ground.

The Sisters of the Poor, just mentioned, appear to have come to the Potteries around 1890 and used the Druids Hall in Hanley as a convent, but almost immediately they bought land at Cobridge to build an old peoples home. This was rebuilt early in the 20th century and even further enlarged later until it became the multi-storey building it is today. In its prime there were seventeen sisters looking after some 100 poor and ailing occupants. They relied entirely on charity and two of the nuns would be seen regularly travelling through the area in a horse drawn covered wagon, with an elderly man who had charge of the horse and accompanied the sisters for years. They covered an enormous area calling on shops, most Catholic houses and many others, and received gifts in kind or money. Rarely was a request made, they had no need to ask, for their work was so familiar a part of Potteries life and wherever they called they always left a blessing.

Mr George B. Ford was elected Mayor in 1884, and presented the town with robes of office for the Mayor, Aldermen, Councillors and Town Clerk, the mayor's robe modelled on the Lord Mayor of London.

In 1884, the Council sent a letter of condolence to Her Majesty Queen Victoria on the death at an early age of her youngest son, Prince Leopold, Duke of Albany, and expressed their feeling that, *"although the physical construction of the Prince debarred him from assuming command of fleets and armies, he was endowed with other qualifications of learning and leadership to offer the country."*

A new appointment in this year was that of Meat Inspector, evidently considered an unskilled and part time occupation since the pay was only £10 per annum for a town which now had a meat market and at least two abattoirs together with numerous butchers' shops. Evidently cattle in this age were in a healthy condition and only developed madness in response to increasing health regulations later.

Probably as a result of longer opening hours at the library, the caretaker at the Institute was awarded an increase of 1/-d a week, and since Burslem was becoming a multi-racial society it was decided to purchase Scottish and Irish papers for the reading room. Furthermore it was agreed to subscribe to the Salt Library at Stafford.

In a report to the Council in this year 1884, it was said that there were 572 houses without ash pits, and it was agreed as an economical substitute to purchase tubs at a cost of 7/6d each for the disposal of ashes and household refuse. One could assume that this was Burslem's introduction to dust bins, although that name is now a misnomer since with the demise of coal fires, dust bins have given way to refuse bins.

In 1884 a further letter was received from Miss Becker of the Suffragettes. In 1885 Mayor Samuel Oldham was to hang a sign on a public building recording in gold lettering the incorporation of the Borough. Also and with unexpected magnanimity, Miss Becker at last had her appeal recognised by a recording in the minutes that they were prepared to give their unqualified support for womens' liberation, or rights, or whatever it was that Miss Becker required. At the same meeting the council issued a notice *"Every person who shall use the dwelling house or, premises, on his or her holding or occupation, or any part thereof as a brothel, or shall knowingly permit or suffer the same to be used, or shall harbour or encourage a prostitute to reside or remain therein for the purpose of prostitution, shall be liable to a penalty of £5."*

A letter of appreciation was addressed to the Council by the Port Vale Football Club, thanking the members for the loan of the town hall where the club had entertained seventy poor old persons. Those unable to attend had received a quarter of a pound of tea and two pounds of sugar, and the remains from the meal at the town hall had gone to the Poor House to provide a tea for the children. The club derived its name from its first headquarters in 1876, Port Vale House in Scott Lidgett Road (at the time Alexander Road) adjoining the canal, and the club's first ground was a nearby meadow. In 1881 the club moved its

The famous suffragette Mrs Pankhurst seen in action about 1910

ground to the the area now covered by Westport Lake and from there in 1874 to Moorland Road. In 1885 it became a professional club under the title Burslem Port Vale and in 1886 moved to Cobridge. The club was wound up in 1907 but restarted in 1909 in Hanley on land near the Parish Church now the site of a multi-storey car park. Currently they are back again in their birthplace, on land which they bought in 1944.

In 1886 there was an outbreak of swine fever in Wellington Street, a street most likely built at the time of the French wars, but no longer in existence. The incident indicates the customary rearing of pigs on domestic premises. 1887 was the year of Queen Victoria's Jubilee and a public meeting was called to discuss arrangements for a celebration. William Boulton took charge of the organising the procession, the bell ringing,and the flying of the towns flags. The Council decided to send an address to the Queen:

To your most Gracious Majesty the Queen being your jubilee.

May it please Your Majesty, we, the mayor, aldermen and councillors of the Borough of Burslem most respectfully ask to be allowed to join in the chorus of greetings which greet Your Majesty's auspicious reign, and we earnestly and devotedly pray that the richest blessings of Heaven may be continuous to Your Majesty and your royal Family, and that Your Majesty may be spared to reign for many years yet to come over this extended, and still extending empire."

Discussion took place in 1888 on the question of the celebration of the forthcoming silver wedding of Edward and Alexandra, the Prince and Princess of Wales. The mayor proposed that the Council send them an illuminated address, but there were some members who were lacking in admiration for Edward, and one asked the mayor what it would cost, and being told approximately two guineas, he suggested the two guineas should instead go to the hospital. However on a vote being taken, the royalists won.

On the international level concern must have arisen over rumours of the removal of the American Consul from Burslem, where one as been stationed for many years. This was a vital link for Burslem who no doubt vainly hoped that by some miracle the huge trade which the Burslem potters had once achieved in the American market would return, consequently there was relief when Burslem was informed that there was no intention of the Consul leaving,

A request was received from the Lord Mayor of London for Burslem to supply a flag or banner bearing the Borough Arms to be displayed at the Paris Exhibition, but with the immediate future bleak and having overspent in the previous year, and an increase of 2d in the rates, the Council refused the request.

In February 1889, a letter was received from the town clerk of Stoke, asking for the views of Burslem on the several towns of the Potteries becoming a county. Stoke did not suggest that Burslem lead them into such status; it was not surprising therefore that the response lacked enthusiasm, despite the government urging the principle of grouping authorities nationally.

Following complaints, it was decided to print and distribute hand bills, drawing attention to The Lords Day Act, and instructed the Chief of Police to take action on the sale of sweetmeats, etc and the bawling of news vendors on the Sabbath.

Anger was expressed at the failure of Loop Line trains to keep to the time schedules, and the council were requested to raise the matter with the railway company.

A bill was going through parliament giving Electricity Companies greater freedom. This was discussed in council and it was resolved to oppose it since they had invested heavily in gas.

Despite the negative response to the Lord Mayor of London's appeal for an exhibition flag, he sent a request for a contribution in aid of his fund for the relief of famine in China, and with their customary respect for those who suffered, the council agreed to send a donation of £12.

In 1889 it was decided that Burslem needed a Refuse Destructor. Accordingly information and prices were sought and the successful tender was £1869 but perhaps this cost was frightening and there was considerable delay before the project actually went ahead. In the following year Mr J. Wilcox Edge, was appointed mayor for a second time, and to express his appreciation, he issued a public invitation to friends and burgesses to attend a celebration in the town hall. From 4pm onwards people arrived and, in addition to providing a feast, a report on the occasion said *"there was lavish entertainment comprising Messrs Morfey's band, the Burslem Glee Union, who contributed Sleep Gentle Lady and a selection from Gilbert and Sullivan operas. Madame Larcom contributed The Nightingale's Trill and other works, and Master Parker provided a violin solo, the evening finally concluding with the singing of the National Anthem."*

In 1891 consideration was given to building a college in Moorland Road for the purpose of the Technical Education Act. It was to be a commercial school to sixth form standard. Boys would not be admitted before they were twelve years of age and would leave at sixteen.

The Duke of Clarence died in January 1892 and, following custom, commiserations were sent. The Duke was the eldest son of Edward and Alexandra, and he died at the early age of twenty eight. He was engaged to Princess May of Tek; and, but for fate, would have been Edward the VIII and she his queen. As might happen in fairy tales but rarely in life, she still became queen, but as his brother George V's wife!

In 1894 Mr Tunnicliffe informed them that he was retiring from the Burslem Company of The

Burslem's third town hall was built immediately after the federation in 1910 and was named the Queen's Hall (Stoke has a King's Hall). It was thought it would enhance the choice of Burslem as the seat of administration.

Brickhouse street, at one time a popular site for cock-fighting

Staffordshre Rifle Volunteers of which he had been in command for 35 years, and he expressed his gratitude for the many acts of kindness by the governing body of the town. Certainly the town was equally indebted since the company's band had been a regular contributor to civic functions, and the council in their reply expressed their appreciation for the services the Volunteers had given them.

The adoption of Spencer Lawton as mayor in 1894 for the third time, evidently led to feeling among Council members. His election could be justified since the great occasion in this year was the opening of Burslem Park in Moorland Road to which project the Lawton family had made a major contribution. The park covers an area of twenty two acres, and was landscaped by a Mr Mawson of Windermere. It had a half an acre lake with an island, inhabited by a variety of wild fowl. The water from the lake vanished soon after the park was opened, and later equally mysteriously reappeared. The opening was a gala event; the streets were decorated from the town hall to the park and lined with sightseers to see the civic procession which included thousands of children. The main entrance gates to the park were the gift of the Spencer Lawton family.

In 1896, a request was received from the Duke of Westminster, for Burslem to open a fund in aid of the Queen Victoria Institute of Nurses which was to be established in 1897, the sixtieth year of Victoria's reign. Contribution to the fund amounted to £1065 and when the day eventually arrived, and the Council sent Her Majesty congratulations on behalf of Burslem citizens, and received a gracious acknowledgment.

In this year, the Council, no doubt realising the inevitability of competition with their current gas monopoly, applied for a licence to make and supply electricity. In the previous year, they had been urging the gas company to make the best possible arrangements for the letting out of cooking stoves and to extend the use of heating stoves, probably hoping to retain tied users.

The public baths in Moorland Road were opened in 1896. Built on land opposite the railway station, donated by the Wood family, the baths offered all the then modern facilities which included two large swimming baths, each 75feet by 60 feet, also private plunge baths and Turkish baths.

In 1897, it was at last proposed to compound the poor rate, which must have been a relief to the ratepayers who for many years had been subject to sporadic demands.

In a report to the Council on sanitation and housing there were 420 houses which had water closets with cisterns, and a larger number with slop water closets, as they were termed - i.e. bucket flushed; nevertheless there were still dwellings with cesspits where sewage was removed through the front door.

In 1898 the tramway company were asked to build a transport system from Burslem to Milton but declined, and in the discussion which followed the Council considered building the line themselves, allowing the tramway company to operate it, but this never came to fruition. In 1900 the Council, possibly in the hope of relieving the strain on finances, applied to the Local Government Board to include Wolstanton and Milton in the Burslem Borough. There had been an earlier attempt by Burslem to widen its boundaries but Wolstanton had no desire to co-operate; indeed it had a more ancient history than Burslem. Had Burslem been successful it would have doubled its existing size.

The intermarriage of the British royal family with those of the German States, appear to have kept Burslem busy with congratulations or condolences. Victoria was sent the town's condolence on the death of His Royal Highness, the Duke of Saxe Coburg & Gotha. Victoria herself died in January 1901, and the Council sent a wreath for the funeral, and condolences to The Prince of Wales in the following terms:

"We, the Mayor, Aldermen, and Burgesses of Burslem, humbly desire to tender to your Royal Majesty and the Royal Family, a respectful expression of our sympathy in the great affliction you have sustained by the death of our gracious sovereign lady Queen Victoria, whose memory will ever be held in grateful remembrance by your faithful subjects, and we also tender to Your Majesty our respectful congratulations on your accession to the Throne, and humbly assure you of our faithful allegiance, and we earnestly pray Your Majesty may long be spared to reign in health and happiness over a loyal and contented people."

This was followed by a public notice to notify all of the forthcoming proclamation of Edward's accession which was to follow in due course:

The donated gates at Burslem Park

Celebration of the civic opening of Burslem Park

An early illustration of Burslem Park

The 'vanishing lake' at Burslem Park

The Mayor is requested to read the declaration of Edward the seventh as King from the balcony of the Town Hall at 3.30.p.m. on Saturday Afternoon, and the members of the Police, Fire Brigade, Ambulance, and the Public be assembled to attend".

On the day, the procession moved to the Town Hall in the order; the Mace Bearer, Councillors, Corporation Officials, the Rifle Volunteers, the Fire Brigade, and a large number of the public. After the declaration the Volunteers presented arms and the whole company sang the National Anthem followed by three cheers. Refreshments were provided in the main hall.

This was a significant beginning of a decade, which not only saw the end of a remarkable reign, but also the end of Mother Burslem's independence and the start of a more intimate life with her sons. Like Victoria, she had a long and successful reign, and had indeed at one time been the "Empress of Ceramics".

As a further loss one of her great sons, William Woodall died in this year. At the next meeting the following tribute was made to his memory:

> This Council desire to place on record the deep regret with which it has received the news of the death of William Woodall, the most distinguished Burgess on its Burgess Roll. For several years a member of its body, and for many years the parliamentary representative of the people of this town in association with neighbours in the parliamentary borough of Stoke on Trent and Hanley, and desires while expressing its sincere sympathy with the Woodall family in the great bereavement that has come upon them, to express also its inestimable loss this town has sustained by the death of one whose earnest self denying and untiring services were always given to the town and people, in which, and among whom he had lived so long, and whose work is gratefully remembered as the chief promoter of the establishment of the Wedgwood Institute, and chairman of the Free Library and TechnicaL Institute Committee during so many years as the first chairman of the Burslem School Board, and as chairman of the late Local Board, and while expressing its deep appreciation of the great services rendered by Mr Woodall in his official municipal and parliamentary work, this Council desires to express its conviction that he will be no less remembered with grateful respect as one who was kindly helper and adviser in almost every useful and benevolent work in which the town has engaged since he first became a resident; as one whose great natural abilities, thoughtfulness, and kindness of heart has won the admiration and regard of all classes of the people among whom he so intimately moved. As one who in the widest sense, is friend and benefactor of those whom he laboured to serve, who so rapidly responded, and gave his services to any good cause, and as one whose life and example had inspired in all who had the privilege of knowing him, the respect belongs to one who loved his fellow men".

In June 1901 there was an extremely rare tribute paid by Burslem, when the freedom of the town was bestowed on three local men who had served in the Boer War. The citation read:

> The Council, in appreciation and recognition of the services during the war in South Africa by Corporal Richard Williamson, Private James Jenkins, and Private Walter Love of the first volunteers of the North Staffordshire Regiment, do hereby confer on each of them the honorary freedom of the Borough of Burslem, and do hereby admit the said Richard Williamson, James Jenkins, and Walter Love to the honorary freedom of Burslem accordingly."

1901 saw the birth of the Co-operative movement in the Burslem area, originating in the industrial areas of Lancashire. The Society was required to have two hundred members before it could be established and this was achieved by February, two hundred subscribing four shillings with a promise to raise this sum to a pound as circumstances permitted. At the end of the year the capital stood at £175, and by 1932 it had risen to nearly £1,250,000.

Immediately after its formation, No 8 Newcastle Street was the first retail outlet. People and traders came to view the shop on the opening day, and the traders predicted it would be up for sale in three months time, with the capital will have gone. In the event, sales for the first weeks trading were £68 and at the end of the first year the membership had risen to 390, and there was a dividend of 10d in the pound, amounting in total to £180. In 1903, the first of many more branches was opened at Smallthorne and by the end of this year the society was baking and delivering bread, its membership 690 and its annual sales £10,900. Such was the growth in custom, that the society was able to purchase property previously rented, and land and stabling was bought at Smallthorne to house the growing number of delivery vans.

THE BAKERY. ultimately destroyed by fire.

Early Burslem Co-op transport and the old Burslem Co-op bakery

In 1908, with a membership of 2320 and annual sales of over £44,000, it was decided to build a modern bakery at Middleport. This was opened in 1910 and from here there was a daily stream of vans up the rise to the streets of Burslem and its surrounding area. Still following the now ancient practice, somebody resorted to commemorative verse:

Forty working horse
Standing in their stalls
Forty working lads
Behind the Co-op walls

Forty working horses
Pulling with a will
Chirruped on by bread lads
To slag it up the hill

From the sale of food products, the Co-op eventually became a movement for the provision of every type of goods and services, and could boast of being Britain's biggest retailer, but it suffered ultimately from its parochial structure and was forced by the transformation in retailing style to combine in order to survive. Fred Hayward a son of Burslem, was a founder member of the Burslem Co-op and possibly the greatest expansion came in the time when he was the chief executive. He was later honoured for his work and became Sir Fred Hayward.

1902 saw the coronation of Edward VII. The proclamation was read on 9th August, announcing that the 19th, the day of the crowning, would be a bank holiday, and that all movement of traffic was to be suspended during the procession. The estimated cost of the celebrations in Burslem was £800.

The Council now went ahead with the the installation of electric lighting in the town and the design for its own generating plant. The consulting engineer's estimate for a generating station and plant was £30,666. and in anticipation the Council borrowed £26,000 in one sum, and £3,160 in another from the Liverpool & District Bank, covered by a mortgage on the Gas Works. Many private ventures also sought to break into the electricity market. One such was Rawcliffe and Company who proposed introducing a parliamentary bill to build generators and lay cables in North Staffordshire. This immediately met the Council's objection.

It was three years since Stoke had approached Burslem on the question of amalgamation, subsequent to which Sir Hugh Owen, a municipal and financial expert had been requested to review and advise on the amalgamation of the Potteries towns. Burslem had decided to take no further part in the discussion and to wait for the final proposals, and, following this, to leave it to a vote of the ratepayers. The Council wrote to Mr Geen in Stoke, one of the leaders of the amalgamation movement, drawing his attention to his long promised statement of account, also confirming Burslem's withdrawal from the scheme. The Council decided to limit the expense payment in connection with the proposed amalgamation to £25.

In 1904 the Council indicated their approval of the proposed taxation of land values; a rather contentious subject regularly on the political agenda in the first half of the 20th century.

In his report in 1904 the Surveyor drew attention to inadequate toilets at the Upper Hanley Pottery and the Alexander Pottery at Cobridge. At the first he said there were a 100 males and 160 females, with four toilets for the males, and three for the females, and there were no doors on any of them!

It was five years since the Council had agreed to install a destructor plant but only now in 1903 were plans approved for siting it in Scotia Road, and an application was made to the Public Loan Board for £11,000 to cover the cost. A further capital project considered in 1903 was the building of an isolation hospital at Stanfields. The sharing of one at Brownhills in Tunstall had long been unsatisfactory and the Council decided to give notice of their intention to withdraw from the arrangement on completion of the new hospital. The salaries they intended to pay for the initial appointments were:

Medical Attendant	£215	per annum
Matron	£50	" "
Caretaker	£65	" "

In 1904, a general rate of 3/4d in the pound was set. This was estimated to raise £20,806, but, mainly due to the Education Act of 1902, the Council considered that they would require a further £17,390, almost doubled the original estimate, and it was recommended that this be recovered in two parts on all properties exceeding £10 in value. The magnitude of these sums indicate the increased wealth of the town.

A regulation in 1905 allowed local authorities to provide food for children who were underfed and recover the cost from parents or guardian. An apparently unsolicited help was a gift of £20. 11. 6. from Pearson's fund for poor children, for which the council sent a grateful acknowledgment.

The foundation stone of the School of Art in Queen Street was laid on the 9th February 1906. The school owed its origin principally to the generosity and determination of Thomas Hulme in furthering the pursuit of art which he believed was vital to the continuing prosperity of Burslem. Thomas Hulme was born locally, his father was a pottery operative who eventually became a manager at one of Davenport's factories. His mother was a pottery paintress. His first employment was as a clerk at John Wedgwood's Woodland Pottery at Tunstall. From there he joined McIntyres in Burslem ultimately becoming co-owner of this factory along with William Woodall. He was a keen collector of pottery and paintings, his collection of which he gave to the Wedgwood Institute in his lifetime. He realised that the Institute was

The entrance to the School of Art

One of two commemorative tablets
on the face of the School of Art

Modern day Queen Street. In the
centre is the market building. The
Wedgwood Institute is in the distance

One view of the town of Burslem in the late 19th century. Not a healthy prospect!

An important local trader, various postacard views of this firm are to be found. Never likely to have experienced short-time working in the Victorian era.

Perhaps the way to keep away from the undertaker then and now? The current Burslem Cricket ground overlooking the Town. For many years they played on a site adjacent to the Racecourse

lacking in space and was determined to found a separate school of art. His name is perpetuated, and his generosity acknowledged on a ceramic tablet built into the facade of the school. Thomas Hulme was the last Chief Bailiff before Burslem became a Borough, and the first to be chosen as Mayor. He was also president of the Liberal Club, and at the time of his death lived at Dunwood Hall near Leek.

There were already many famous schools of art on the Continent, and other art schools in this district, but in Burslem, the birthplace of the local industry, all that was available was a portion of the Wedgwood Institute, and before that a dilapidated loft over the Legs of Man Inn. As far back as 1852 there had been a district meeting to discuss the establishment of a school of art for the Potteries as a whole but the government refused to fund this, having already given financial help for this purpose to both Hanley and Stoke. They offered Burslem £70 per annum to cover the services of a tutor, who in addition to teaching in the loft of the Institute, would visit other schools on a part time basis, the pupils to pay set charges.

The site for the new school, for which Thomas Hulme personally paid £8000 in 1904, was occupied by a typical Burslem pottery known as Queen Street Pottery. It had known a number of owners and tenants among them J. Edge, W.H. Adams, Cork & Edge, Cork & Condliffe and Wood & Baker, the last occupants. Further adjoining land was purchased in 1905 for which Thomas Hulme again personally paid £700. A later benefactor to the school was Mr James Maddock.

The architect for the building was Mr Absolon Reade Wood who came from a branch of the family whose name is synonymous with Burslem. In his student days he won a scholarship to Kensington School of Art but declined to go there, and was instead articled to Robert Scrivenor at Shelton. On completion of his articles he joined in partnership with J Hutchings in Hanley and later with Goldstraw.

The foundation stone of the school was laid by the Earl of Dartmouth using a silver and ivory trowel engraved with the arms of the borough. Following Enoch Wood's example an earthenware jar was placed under the foundation stone. This contained a copy of the *Sentinel* and the *Staffordshire Advertiser*, together with a programme of the event, several coins and samples of the products of the Burslem potters Maddocks, Woods, Wades, Marsdens and Bootes.

The building has a bow shaped entrance with classical pillars and terracotta embellishments produced by Doultons. The building was opened in 1907 by the then Mayor of the borough, Mr S. Gibson.

In 1906, the Council received a letter from the town's traders congratulating them on their decision to move the annual wakes from the centre of the town to Moorland Road. An interesting invitation was received at this time for the town to be represented at a conference in Birmingham to consider a government proposal that canals should be linked between all centres of industry and thence to the sea, and that they be nationalised. It was probably thought they could be revitalised for industrial traffic - something being broached today as the stagnation on the roads increases.

An invitation was received from the Rev. W.S. Lamb to the opening service at the new Congregational church in Moorland Road, the William Woodall Memorial Church.

Although there had been at least one earlier request that members of the public should be allowed to attend council meetings, this had not been allowed, but two people did impose themselves on one meeting in 1906 and were allowed to stay. Perhaps they were interested in the agenda which included the renewal of licences for six pawnbrokers, four game dealers, three petrol licences and five slaughter houses. Game laws had been cruel in the past, even poaching a hare or a rabbit could lead to seven years transportation, but gradually magistrates refused to impose such harsh penalties; it seems strange therefore that licences were still required for the sale of game - unless perpetuated as a means of raising revenue.

Some interesting figures were submitted recording the generation of electricity. In the year 1907 the number of electricity consumers was given as 130.

In 1906, the Loan Board were approached for a loan of £2000 *for "the purchase of rectory grounds for developing walks and pleasure grounds"*, the cost of which work was estimated to be £2200. This would no doubt be the small but pleasant park still in Middleport.

Another anticipated development resulted in the recommendation to buy land in Moorland Road at a cost of £5100 for a central school for cookery, laundry and handicrafts.

At one Council meeting, a report was received from the Chief Superintendent of Police with reference to Charles Key aged 16, who had broken a window while playing cricket on the recreation ground. Mrs Key attended an interview with her son who had expressed his regrets and promised to pay for the damage. By today's standards, this boy would be considered an angel. A further report by the police stated that the ambulance which conveyed bodies to the mortuary was in bad condition. Agreement was reached to have it repaired and fitted with rubber tyres - hardly likely to be noticed by the occupant. It could also be construed that this was the only ambulance which Burslem possessed, and that it was confined exclusively to moving the dead.

The Council received the annual report on the condition of canal boats which stated that 340 boats were examined, occupied by 959 persons, 557 men, 196 women and 206 children. Of the latter, attendance at school was from 32%-39%, and the observation was made that it was the exception rather than the rule. 184 of the boats captains had more than one home - presumably sailors on the ocean had no prerogative.

During 1908 there were 153 unemployed in Burslem; for their relief, it was decided to give £75 from the Mayor's Fund. The War Office had agreed to recruit 17 to 30 men for the Special Reserve, while the Borough Surveyor, the Cemetery Registrar and the Sanitary Inspector were instructed to employ only men who were members of a Friendly, Sick or Trade Society, to limit the drain on the council's resources.

The inevitability of amalgamation was affecting council work. The meetings were confined to day to day matters. It was reported that Cobridge National School would be closed for three weeks on account of an outbreak of Measles and a request was submitted that covered carts be used for the collection of road sweepings, and that shovels should be designed in some way to avoid the dust which is blown from a flat shovel on a windy day. Overcrowding was reported in East View where one house was occupied by a man, his wife, ten children, aged one to seventeen, and a woman lodger!

Burslem held a poll of the inhabitants and they voted for the rejection of Amalgamation. Mother Burslem then took steps to oppose in parliament the Local Government Board's provisional order for the inclusion of Burslem in the federation of the Potteries towns. The Reverend Stuart in his observations of his days as curate at St. Paul's said:

"I remember in my Burslem days some tentative talk about the amalgamation, but I vividly remember the keen rivalry among the towns, and the hopelessness of attempting much in the way of combined action. The mother town of the Potteries, as it is proud to call itself, was furiously jealous, and not a little contemptuous of its younger rivals, and we Burslem people had no small pride in regard to various points in which we considered ourselves superior, though now I cannot remember what those points were. The first movement for federation came from a proposal to amalgamate the towns of Stoke Fenton and Longton. This was not popular with Fenton, who thought they would suffer by being squeezed. Hanley took the view that unification of the southern towns would lead to a larger entity attempting to add the northern boroughs one by one, while the parliamentary view was of an amalgamation of them all, which was eventually forced on them by parliamentary decree"

The Burslem mayor appointed in 1908/1909 was Thomas Edwards and his term was extended to cover entry into the imminent amalgamation. His was a fitting choice and an honour which reflected the admiration of his colleagues on Burslem Council, who were aware of the vicissitudes he experienced in early life, and the spirit and fortitude which enabled him to earn the esteem of his fellow men. Scarrat says he was born in 1838 and began work at the age of eight at Davenports in Longport where he was paid 6d per week. He was later apprenticed to a 'Placer', but when he was sixteen he was orphaned and left responsible for six younger brothers and sisters. At nineteen he joined the Ovenmens Society. This was a breakaway union, formed like other sections in the pottery trade when the all embracing union collapsed in 1836. Thomas Edwards was a member for fifty years and was involved in the strike in 1865 which brought about the end of the long standing annual hiring practice. He was involved in negotiations which achieved wage increases in 1902 and 1908. He married Elizabeth Cooper, who had as a child been taken to America under the pottery union emigration scheme, and she bore them eight offspring.

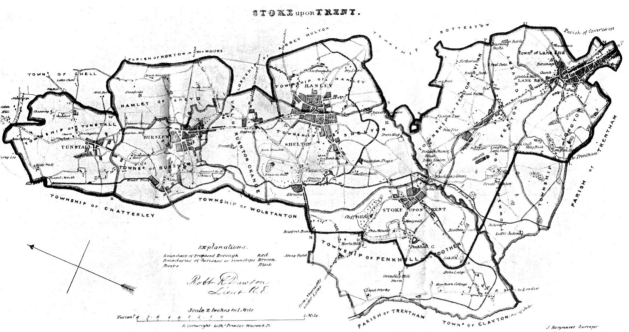

Stoke upon Trent in 1832, produced by T. Hargreaves, surveyors of Burslem, for the proposal of the new elective franchise for the Borough of Stoke on Trent

Year.	1840	1841	1842	1843	1844	1845	1846	1847	1848	1849	
Value of Exports China, Earthenware and Stoneware £'000	573,	601,	555,	629,	767,	828,	793,	834,	722,	807,	
Value of Imports											

Year.	1850	1851	1852	1853	1854	1855	1856	1857	1858	1859	
Exports £'000	999,	1,121,	1,152,	1,338,	1,306,	1,001,	1,334,	1,492,	1,154,	1,314,	
Imports £'000											

Year.	1860	1861	1862	1863	1864	1865	1866	1867	1868	1869	
Exports £'000	1,451,	1,071,	1,220,	1,341,	1,439,	1,469,	1,686,	1,666,	1,683,	1,828,	
Imports £'000											

Year.	1870	1871	1872	1873	1874	1875	1876	1877	1878	1879	
Exports £'000	1,746,	1,865,	2,142,	2,206,	1,862,	1,859,	1,771,	1,853,	1,794,	1,800,	
Imports £'000	165,	202,	263,	383,	370,	382,	399,	365,	441,	433,	

Year.	1890	1891	1892	1893	1894	1895	1896	1897	1898	1899	1900
Exports £'000	2,251,	2,165,	2,057,	1,985,	1,759,	1,992,	1,967,	1,900,	1,820,	2,042,	2,038,
Imports £'000 less Re-exports	586,	620,	623,	594,	594,	627,	743,	724,	782,	779,	777,

Year.	1901	1902	1903	1904	1905	1906	1907	1908	1909	1910	1911
Exports £'000	1,993,	1,900,	2,176,	2,106,	2,098,	2,382,	2,649,	2,344,	2,315,	2,780,	3,030,
Imports £'000 less Re-exports	758,	742,	788,	765,	789,	845,	880,	792,	735,	746,	858,

Table produced from *Staffordshire Pottery and its History* by Josiah C. Wedgwood c,1920 showing export-import trade for pottery in Great Britain

The Federation Act came into effect on March 1st 1910 and the first meeting of the new Council took place on the 31st of that month. The mace used by the new borough was that used previously by Burslem. It would be nice to think that first mayor of the extended borough also donned the Burslem Mayor's robe of office since it was fashioned to that of the Mayor of London. Attending the meeting as representatives for Burslem were:

Mr. S. Malkin.	Pottery Manufacturer.
Mr. F. Haywood.	Secretary of the North Staffs. Co-op. Soc.
Mr. H. Saunders.	Clerk to the North Staffs. Rly. & Canal Co.
Mr. J.H.Gibson.	Pottery Manufacturer.
Mr. H.K.Hales.	Trader. Burslem Stafford & Leek.
Mr. H. Finney.	President. North Staffs. Mining Federation.
Mr. T. Willet	Engineer & Ironfounder.
Mr. H.H. Saunders.	Master Baker.
Mr Wilcox Edge.	M.P.
Mr. T. Mitchell.	Occupation not given.

There were two nominations for the position of the first Mayor; Mr Cecil Wedgwood, and Mr Geen, a solicitor with a practice in Stoke, a prime and persevering figure in the amalgamation movement, but not much loved in Burslem. Cecil Wedgwood was elected and sadly Mother Burslem's future became one of an unwilling partner in a Morganatic marriage.

Appendix:

List of Mayors of Burslem from incorporation as a Borough in 1878 to amalgamation with the new Borough of Stoke on Trent in 1910

1878/79	Thomas Hulme	1894/95	Spencer Lawton
1879/80	James Maddock	1895/96	Thomas Wood
1880/81	James Maddock	1896/97	Thomas Arrowsmith
1881/82	William Boulton	1897/98	William Warrington Dobson
1882/83	Thomas Hulme	1898/99	William Bratt
1883/84	George B Ford	1899/00	Enoch Edwards
1884/85	George B Ford	1900/01	James Bowden
1885/86	Samuel Oldham	1901/02	William Lovatt
1886/87	Spencer Lawton	1902/03	William Lovatt
1887/88	Josiah Robinson	1903/04	James William Brindley
1888/89	Francis Wood	1904/05	Thomas Hulme
1889/90	J Wilcox Edge	1905/06	William Warrington Dobson
1890/91	J Wilcox Edge	1906/07	Samuel Gibson
1891/92	Robert Sudlow	1907/08	Sydney Malkin
1892/93	William Boulton	1908/10	Thomas Edwar
1893/94	Spencer Lawton		

CHAPTER THIRTY: Famous sons and daughters

Some early Sons and Daughters of Burslem who achieved fame or notoriety. Early Newspapers.

Most of the characters portrayed so far in the evolution of Burslem have been associated with pottery manufacturing or associated trades, but there are personalities who made their mark in the arts and sport, or even as myths and some of these who lived in this period must be given a place here.

One who naturally comes to mind is Arnold Bennett, the author who achieved fame for his novels centred on Burslem. His life and and works have been the subject of much research over the years and there is an active Bennett Society for the earnest admirer.

Bennett's ancestors were associated with potting in the Burslem tradition and Bennett's literary fame is primarily in his dramatic portrayal of the natives of Burslem in their struggle to cope with the vicissitudes of life, a relatively frugal existence and the nearly satanic atmosphere of an industry which produced such products of beauty and utility. His great grandfather John Bennett was a potter, but not with any claim to fame. He was said to have been the bastard son of James Brindley the famous canal engineer and there is a brief entry in the church register giving the name of the mother only: "August 31st. 1760. John, bastard son of Mary Bennett." John's eldest son, Sampson, produced eight sons and four daughters. The eldest of the eight sons was also named John. He married and was living in Pitt Street when Arnold's father, Enoch, was born there in 1842.

Enoch was apprenticed to a potter on leaving school and at 21could claim to be a master of the art. In this capacity he joined Thomas Hurd in partnership at the Eagle Pottery in Nile Street Burslem but with the regrettable but not uncommon result that the firm became bankrupt. In 1866 he married and commenced business as a draper and pawnbroker in Hope Street, Hanley - possibly having had experience of the pawnbroking business from the other side of the counter. At this address Arnold was born in 1867. As was the pattern of the age, other offspring followed at regular intervals, Frank, Fanny, Gertrude, Emily, Tantra, followed by three more who barely survived birth, and finally Septimus who did.

Enoch evidently saw no future in the shop, except to keep the wolf from the door while he articled himself to a lawyer in Burslem and set about the task of qualifying. After five years of struggle which undermined his health, he eventually succeeded in qualifying, following which a practising partnership was formed in Hanley under the title of Bennett and Baddeley. With his circumstances now improving he bought a plot of land in Waterloo Road for £200 and borrowed £900 to build a house,

The family had strong Methodist connections and Arnold's grandfather was a trustee of Swan Bank chapel in Burslem, at one time the power centre of the Wesleyans in the district, and it was to the school attached to this centre that Arnold went to start his education. From here he went to the Wedgwood Institute but along with the other boys was transferred to Longport Hall, for reasons explained in the chapter on the institute, and eventually obtained entry to the Orme School in Newcastle. Here he became friendly with H.K. Hales - who later claimed that he was "The Card" in Bennett's writings and accordingly entitled to royalties! There was no confirmation or offer from Bennett, but a riposte that if Hales was correct, then he, Bennett, was the one who should be receiving payment for the publicity which he had conferred on Hales!

On leaving school Arnold was articled to his father and collected rents for the practice. He wrote articles for the *Staffordshire Knot* and spent a deal of time with his grandparents who kept a draper's shop in St. John's Square, but evidently he had no whole hearted enthusiasm for the law, at least in Burslem, and in 1889 he left home and went to London. Here he got work in a solicitor's office and continued to write freelance articles, until in 1893 he left the legal profession entirely and became assistant editor of the journal *Woman*. By 1896 he had become the editor.

He had his first book published in 1898 and in 1900 he retired from his editorship of the journal to concentrate on literary work and plays. His output was prolific and the popularity of his work increased rapidly along with the financial rewards. His outstanding literary works are considered to be those which are centred on Burslem and its characters. Not all his output is of equal quality. He enjoyed the lifestyle in London and Paris which his success brought him, but it all made increasing demands on his time, resulting in infrequent visits to his widowed mother in Burslem in the family house in Waterloo Road.

Arnold Bennett died of Typhoid in London in 1931 (contracted in Paris) and his ashes were placed in the family vault in Burslem churchyard by his brother Frank. Following his mother's death the house was opened to visitors as a museum, but is not so now. The memorabilia went to the City Museum.

Bennett's friend of his youth, Harold Keates Hales, "The Card" in Bennett's novels, was born in Manchester in 1868 and his family came to Burslem to take over a drapery business. On leaving school he was employed by one of the potteries and at twenty one he went to America as a sales representative. On his return he soon showed he was not short of energy and ideas. In 1896 he opened a shop in Market Place for the sale of bicycles. In the same year the law requiring motor vehicles to be preceded by a man with a red flag was rescinded and Hales bought his first petrol driven vehicle. He saw a future in motor transport and opened an agency for cars - but to be on the safe side he opened a shop next door for the sale of pianos. Scarratt says that he built a garage but does not say where. He used the Drill Hall in Newcastle Street to hold exhibitions and diversifying still further he acquired a disused pottery in Waterloo Road and converted it into a skating rink. In 1910 he bought an aeroplane for £150. In 1914 he volunteered for the First World War, reducing his age by seven years. He served in Mesopotamia, Egypt and finally India where he became a personal friend of Ghandi, although he never seems to have invited Ghandi to Burslem! He visited and admired the Taj Mahal, but is said to have remarked that there was equal beauty in Burslem Town Hall - depending from which angle you viewed it.

He later wrote motoring and ballooning reviews for the *Sentinel* and in 1929 he founded a shipping agency. In 1931 he succeeded in becoming Conservative member of parliament for the northern division of the Potteries. He was vociferous in parliament in his objections to a diverse number of subjects. He objected to any restraint on motoring and had strong views on the problems of the fishing industry and Japanese competition. Whether he failed to shout hard or persuasively enough for the pottery industry, he lost his seat to Labour in 1935, and unfortunately in 1942 he lost his life in a boating accident on the River Thames. He appears to have thoroughly enjoyed his life and been a very picturesque character.

Scarratt speaks highly of a Reverend William Cook who he said was a remarkable man, three times President of the Methodist New Connection. Born in Burslem at the New Inn, kept by his parents, as seems customary with landlords the family moved several times, to the Black Boy at Cobridge, and later still to the Rising Sun at Shelton. Scarratt fails to say whether Cook went to America, but he apparently had a Degree in Divinity from an American college.

Preaching had a powerful influence in those days, and the sermons of eminent clerics were printed and either sold or freely distributed. Another respected priest of the same religious body, James Barker, was expounding views in this manner, to whose contents Cook took forceful exception. There followed a period of printed charge and counter charge which caused a temporary sensation in church circles until Barker recanted and admitted the error of his ways.

In the 1870s An interesting personality, a Madame Reymond, arrived in Burslem with her parents, Mr and Mrs Frederick Idon Holst. At a house in Waterloo Road she opened a music school, later moving to Moorland Road where her school bore the title of 'Beethoven House' offering tuition in a variety of instruments. She was of mature age when she arrived in Burslem and of a husband nothing was ever said, but among the papers she left was an official document giving her permission to marry in a district other than the one where she then lived in Denmark. That she was talented and eminent in Danish musical circles seems evident since also among her papers was a personal letter from Jean Sibelius accepting and thanking her for her offer of patronage of the North Staffordshire Symphony Orchestra which she was

Arnold Bennett, above and James Holland, right

Captain John Smith

H.K. Hales, the Card

MILLINERS—Continued.
Lear, Wm., 29, Moorland-road
Leese, Mrs. Mary W., 146, Elder-road
Lovatt, W., Ltd., 15, St. John's-square
Martin, William, 199, Newcastle-street
Pickstone, Maud, 169, Newcastle-street
Rigby, Priscilla, 207, Newcastle-street
Sandbach, E., 5, St. John's-sq.
Smith and Tyson, 2, Queen-st.
Wynne's, Market-place

MILLWRIGHTS.
Boulton, William, Ltd., Providence Foundry & Engineering Works
Kent Bros., Waterloo-road, Cobridge

MINERAL WATER MANUFACTURERS.
Copestick Bros. and Co., North-road
Podmore, John, Providence Works, 5, Furlong Parade

MINING APPLIANCE MAKERS.
Sylvester, W., Pinnox-street

MODELLERS AND MODEL MAKERS.
Williams, E. N., Moorland-road

MOTOR CAR MAKERS AND DEALERS.
Hales, H. K., 24, Market-place
Lycett, C. T., Pack Horse-lane
Owen, Arthur J., 128, Newcastle-street

MONUMENTAL MASONS AND SCULPTORS.
Barlow and Nixon, Trubshaw Cross
Ford, Walter, Moorland-road
Mellor, W. and R., Ltd., Moorland-road

MUSICAL INSTRUMENT MAKERS AND DEALERS AND MUSIC SELLERS.
Davies Bros., 10, Waterloo-road
Durber, Emmanuel, 70, Waterloo-road
Morrey, John, 15, Brindley-st.
Podmore, John, 129, Newcastle-street, and Market Hall
Shaw, Wm., 13, Newcastle-st.
Walker, Williams, 133, Newcastle-street

MUSIC—TEACHERS OF.
Cross, Marian C., 41, Louise-st.
Davis, F. A., L.L.C.M., 10, Waterloo-road
Durber, Emmanuel, 10, Maddock-street
Proudlove, Arthur Henry, 31, High-street
Stanistreet, F. W., 42, Wharf-street
Yates, Thomas, 18, Prospect-st.

NEWSAGENTS & STATIONERS.
Audley, A. M., 410, Waterloo-road, Cobridge
Barrow, James, 297, Newcastle-street
Capey, George, 357, Waterloo-road, Cobridge
Garner, Joseph, 64, North-road
Griffiths, E., 46, Waterloo-road
Harris, T. J., 6, Queen-st. & 43, Gordon-street
Holdcroft, Edward Wright, Newcastle-street
Hulme, Arthur Henry, 106, Waterloo-road
Martin, John Chas., 171, Newcastle-street
Newark, M., 15, Waterloo-road
Prince, Peter, 148, Newcastle-street
Rigby, Thos., 60, Liverpool-rd.
Ridgway, Alfred, 168, Newcastle-street
Scarratt, Cyrus, 225, Newcastle-street
Shaw, Wm., 13, Newcastle-st.
Teggin, Edward John, 49, Newcastle-street
Tipper, Esther A., Moorland-road
Tyson, Emma, 9, Moorland-road
Vaughan, T. B., 8, Moorland-road

NURSES & NURSING HOMES.
Burslem District Nursing Home, Newcastle-street; Matron, H. Burchill

H.K. Hales, the Card, above in 1910 as pilot and right in 1897 with his first car.

Below: An excursion in the early 1900s seen at the Cat and Fiddle, near Buxton

instrumental in forming in 1904 along with her star pupil John Cope. At the same time she promoted choral work in Bursiem. She was a keen charity worker and active in the peace movement at the time of the Boer War.

Her father seems to have been a craftsman, as the following extract from the *Sentinel* indicates, a copy of which was among her papers. The occasion was the visit of Edward and Alexandra in 1897 as guests of the Duke of Sutherland:

"On Wednesday afternoon January the 6th 1897 the Princess of Wales was graciously pleased to accept a gift of her own countryman Mr Frederick Idon Holst, a retired Master Cooper, formerly of Copenhagen, and now residing with his daughter Madame Raymond, at Beethoven House, Burslem.

The gift consisted of two Milk Pails made of Maple wood with solid brass hoops and handles, and the lids are most prettily decorated with a floral design excellently painted by the well known artist Wenzel Mussill. One Milk Pail bears the Danish motto "Med cud for aere Ret" (with god for honour and righteousness) and the other the motto for Wales "Ich Dien" (I serve). The Milk Pails are a very fine piece of workmanship, and were made by Mr Holst in 1872 at the time of the Great Exhibition at Copenhagen, and were originally intended for the Silver Wedding of the Danish King Christian 1X, but by some misfortune they never reached their destination.

The maker, after keeping them for many years, thought it fitting to offer them to the King of Denmark's daughter, the Princess of Wales, on her visit to North Staffordshire. Mr. Holst, who was born in Copenhagen in 1817, accompanied by his daughter and master John Cope, had an interview with the Princess at Trentham Hall where the presentation was made. Her Royal Highness thanked the donor for his thoughtfulness and was engaged in conversation with him for about ten minutes, in both Danish and English."

John Cope, her pupil, rose to eminence in his own right as an international conductor. He was of Potteries origin and from an early age he appears by parental agreement to

BEETHOVEN HOUSE, BURSLEM, *OPPOSITE RAILWAY STATION.*

School for Musical Education

ESTABLISHED 1897, BY

MADAME REYMOND, OF COPENHAGEN.

Pupil of the great Danish Masters, Nels W. Gade & Hartmann.

Tuition in following Subjects:

SOLO SINGING, PIANOFORTE PLAYING AND VIOLIN PLAYING,

ENSEMBLE — Playing on 2, 3 or 4 Pianofortes, or Organ and Piano.

LESSONS IN HARMONY.

Madame Reymond and her charity workers

Beethoven House and the letter
from Sibelius

have lived with the Holst family.   He blossomed as a protegy of Madame Raymond, and became founder and an eminent member of the Staffordshire Symphony Orchestra and he maintained a lasting and loving relationship with her until her death.

Two early characters in Burslem, both in similar business, and both situated in the Market Place, were Mary Brougham and Richard Timmis.   They were each classified as Printers and Booksellers but Mary Brougham was also listed as Parian Ear Drop Manufacturer, this presumably a woman's fashion piece - who knows it may yet be revived and become a fashion once more to the benefit of local industry.   The repute of Mary's product resulted in her selling to Queen Victoria, the Duchess of Sutherland, Jenny Lind and other prominent people.   Evidently having abundant energy she was also a sub distributor of stamps and operated a Circulating Library and a Bible Depot.   All presumably in addition to printing, and the rearing of a family of six children.

Richard Timmis was a Methodist Lay Preacher.   In addition to being a printer he was listed as stationer and bookseller.   Towards the middle of the 19th century he bought Mary Brougham's business, including the 'Ear Drop manufacture' which he continued to pursue.   He could also have been the Richard Timmis employed by the Burslem Board of Health as a part-time book-keeper Two of Timmis's daughters became School Governesses.   The Brougham premises were at a later date bought by Warwick Savage.

I have no wish to send a chill down the spine of the reader in these closing pages, but I did mention myths, and Molly Leigh was sufficient a personality to have been given the title of "The Witch of Burslem" and her story, like most others, has probably through being repeatedly told become increasingly macabre,

Molly, as a witch, was of course ugly from birth and suckled by animals rather than fed mother's milk.   She must have been an only child and when her parents died she continued to live in the cottage where she was born, her solitary companion being a black bird which was to be seen perched on a bush outside the thatched cottage, imitating other birds songs.   Apparently Molly sold milk for a living, often seen walking round the town with her pail and the bird perched on her shoulder.

Her chance of achieving saving grace and a place in Heaven was obviously through the church, but much to the anger of the rector, the Reverend Spencer, she failed to attend to her religious duties and while he could have fined her a shilling, he upbraided her personally in public and from the pulpit.   In retaliation Molly trained the bird to perch on a bush outside the Turk's Head, the favourite licensed premises of the reverend, and crow vociferously.   This eventually so incensed him that he took his gun and fired at the poor creature.   The Lord was with the bird and it flew away unharmed but the Reverend is said to have immediately developed intense stomach pains which lasted for three weeks - and presumed to be of Mary's doing.

Molly died at the early age of forty-four and the Reverend Spencer was required to take the funeral service, following which poor Molly was interred in St. John's churchyard - but the grave was in the customary direction for the repose of witches, at right angles to which the righteous are laid; presumably an ancient practice adopted to facilitate the work of the Lord at the resurrection..   Now, whether Molly took exception to this, or his funeral oration - or just read his thoughts - he was concerned when residents spoke subsequently of seeing Molly in the street with her pail, and the bird on her shoulder, singing:

> Weight and measure sold I never
> Milk and water sold I ever

Some said she had been seen in the empty cottage sitting knitting by the fire, although she would hardly need any knitwear if she had gone where the Rector had predicted.

The poor man relapsed into a state of remorse, and concerned that Mary's soul was not at rest and he the culprit, he decided that if her body was reunited with the bird her spirit would probably be at peace. But to reunite the two the body needed to be exhumed.

Now one version of how he set about achieving his purpose said that he enlisted the help of three

Molly Leigh's cottage

The gravestone and the churchyard

other clerics, one from Newchapel, one from Wolstanton and one from Stoke, and of course the sexton to do the digging. To create the right atmosphere the scene takes place at night and when the sexton had struggled with his spade to reveal the coffin, it had to be lifted from the depths. Suddenly as it reached the surface the moon appeared through the clouds and the three supporting clerics and the sexton frantically dropped the ropes and fled, leaving the Rector holding the bird. The reverend, being made of sterner stuff, hastily forced open the lid of the coffin and bundled in the bird and cage.

An alternative version is that there were those who had been visited by the spirit of Molly who pleaded with the clergy to take action to lay her ghost. Her arch enemy in life the rector, probably believing in safety in numbers, persuaded six clerics to attend St. John's church where a pig trough had been laid in the aisle. Following a period of intensive prayer by the holy gentlemen, Molly's spirit appeared in the roof of the church, but refused to come down to earth, which is not surprising considering the odds were seven to one - and among them the Rector. Finally, after even greater effort the spirit did settle in the pig trough, and this was taken to the grave which had already been opened and spirit and body were reunited. The personal cost was great; the effort entailed had been too much for three of the clerics who succumbed, while it is rumoured the remaining three sustained ill health. The rector will have joined Molly now and and it is to be hoped that they will have settled their differences, but there are those on earth as I write who show greater pity for Molly and wish to exhume her for a fresh trial and a fresh disposal, this time in a dignified direction.

There has been no further recorded instance of Molly's spirit reappearing, and alas Molly's cottage has not been preserved for pilgrimages. Neither has there been a record of anyone having seen the spirit of the black bird rising from the grave, consequently one can only assume that the rector found both to be finally at peace.

Ward tells of an interesting and influential family named Burslem who lived at Dale Hall. The family was wealthy and of ancient lineage and it is possible that through them Burslem got its name - but it is probably the other way round. John Burslem came into prominence through a strange legal case in the 16th century. It appears that there was a dispute in Leicestershire over a will in which a man had disinherited his two daughters. The claim made by the two daughters was that the will was a forgery, and one of the witnesses to it was John Burslem. In the court case which followed John Burslem was acquitted, but the case created widespread interest in view of the penalty he would have suffered had he been convicted. The penalty in law had been set in the reign of Queen Elizabeth and at the time of John Burslem's trial was still applicable to forgery under such circumstance; it included a doubling of the plaintiff's costs and damages; in addition the guilty party should *"be set upon the pillary in some market town, or open place, and have both his ears cut off. He should also forfeit to the Queen the whole issues of his lands and properties during his life, and suffer perpetual punishment."*

In 1590 John Burslem married a Margaret Ford, but he died in 1596, and as there were no male heirs, his wealth passed down the female line, some at least by inter-marriage to Catherine Egerton who married John Wedgwood of the Big House. The hall was eventually demolished and the land sold in parcels, part of it at a later date to the Adams family, and in turn part given by one of them to become the site of St. Paul's church and rectory.

A sad but interesting story, which has an indirect association with the Bennett family, is that of a young Burslem doctor in the 19th century. His name was Thomas Oliver and he had a practice in Market Place. Among his patients he was called to visit was Mrs John Wood of Brownhills Hall and here he met and fell in love with her daughter. John Wood, the father of the lass, was the son of Ralph Wood, the owner of a large pottery in Burslem, who had married Mary Wedgwood and did business with Josiah Wedgwood.

John had left his father's business and built a factory adjoining the hall at Brownhills. He evidently had other ideas for his daughter than a struggling doctor; consequently after finding the two had been surreptitiously meeting, he forbade his daughter from continuing the association. The doctor incensed by this, went to Brownhills to express his feelings. When he arrived John Wood was seated at his desk, and the two had a heated discussion which got out of hand, finally resulting in the doctor pulling out a gun and shooting the father. At the trial at Stafford, the doctor claimed that his intention had originally been to shoot himself had his plea been unsuccessful, but in the heat of the argument he lost control; however, despite the plea of his friends and colleagues, he was sentenced to hang in Stafford jail.

The report of his death was published in the *Sentinel: "on the morning he received Holy Communion at the usual hour and was taken to the place of execution, and after spending some time in prayer, he was turned off, calling on the Lord to receive his frail body, and after such dissection as the law requires, his body was given by the great humanity of the Sheriff to his friends for internment."*

The desk at which John Wood was seated when he was shot was evidently kept within the family for many years and eventually came into the possession of Absolom Reade Wood, who has been mentioned as architect for the Burslem School of Art. He found the top too small for use in his profession and exchanged it with Arthur Ellis, a solicitor in Burslem, for his boardroom table, and it was at this practice that Enoch Bennett, Arnold's father, was articled. The last Ellis in the practice inherited the desk in 1923, and in 1994 it was sent to Louis Taylor, the Hanley auctioneer and sold to a London dealer for £11,500, which, according to the *Sentinel* was five times its expected price.

Today we are inundated with news from all corners of the globe, in print, on the radio, by television, satellite and the latest, the internet, which makes it hard to believe that well into the 19th century we were only kept in touch with world events by word of mouth or print, and the cost of the latter was beyond the pocket of a mass of the population.

Scarratt tells of 'Penny Readings' which were held in Hanley Market Place in the middle of the 19th century, promoted by Mr Taylor the owner of *The Sentinel* and lasting for eight years. In this period there was a tax on newspapers, one of a number imposed to pay for recurring wars. Scarratt says he failed to find out the origin of the name 'Penny Readings', but says they were very popular and were mostly from *The Times* war correspondent, but many prominent men contributed to their success including Mark Lemon, one of the founders of Punch, Charles Dickens and the Grossmith's, father and son. The meetings were interspersed with extracts from literary works, song and instrumental music.

A paper called *The Weekly Mail & Potteries Examiner* was published by the union from premises in Brickhouse Street in Burslem in the 19th century, but the established papers were *The Staffordshire Advertiser* and *The Sentinel,* the latter still today the prime source of local news and opinions.

A paper which appears to have had an irregular publication was titled *The Public Enquirer.* It was edited by one Thomas Mullock (the father of Mrs Eliza Craik, the famous Victorian novelist who wrote *John Halifax, Gentleman),* who seems to have provided most of the content since most articles carried the same style of cynicism. Evidently at one time a reader pleaded for a subscription basis, to which Mullock replied through his paper, *"To subscribe to a journal means to obtain credit for six, twelve or eighteen months, and at the expiration of such credit the Potteries is to be travelled over continually to fetch in by instalments a few pounds..."* Religion, particularly Catholicism, was anathema to him. He insulted the Methodists and his own profession equally in the following outburst: *"I am of the persuasion that the Methodist mercenary lying and the purchased mendicity of the English periodical press cannot be equalled in any part of the globe".*

Another paper *The Staffordshire Knot* was issued on Saturdays but no information of its policy or aims have come to light.

The Potters' Examiner (see Ch 17) has been mentioned earlier as representing the unions and reporting on social problems. In 1854 a new paper called *The Potter* was issued, but this never reached the standard of the *Examiner* and in 1863 the two were amalgamated.

Bibliography of Works Consulted

The Borough of Stoke upon Trent in 1838. — J. Ward.
History of the Staffordshire Potteries — S. Shaw.
English Social History. — G.M. Trevelyan.
History of Europe. — H.A.L. Fisher.
The People of England. — M. Ashley
Old times in the Potteries — W. Scarratt.
A Sociological History of the City of Stoke on Trent. — E.J.D. Warrilow
Portrait of the Potteries. — W. Morland.
The Staffordshire Historians. — M.W. Greenslade
Industrial Archaeology of North Staffordshire. — W. J. Thompson.
Bibliographica of Staffordshire — Simms.
People of the Potteries. — H.A. Wedgwood
Domesday Studies. — Rev. R.W.Eyton
Master Potters of the Industrial Revolution. — B. Hillier.
Ceramic Art of Great Britain. — L .Jewitt F.S.A.
The Wood Family of Burslem. — F. Faulkner
Staffordshire Pots and Potters. — G.W. & F.A. Rhead.
Pottery through the ages. — R. Haggar
Staffordshire Chimney Ornaments. — R. Haggar
Concise Encyclopedia of English Pottery & Porcelain. — Markovitz & Haggar
English Slipware Dishes. — R. G. Cooper
Staffordshire Portrait Figures. — J. Hall
Staffordshire Pottery Figures. — J. Bedford.
Popular Staffordshire Pottery. — D. Seekers.
People of the Potteries, — Keele Study Group
The Pottery Trade 1660-1790. — L. Weatherhill.
Potbank. — M. Jones.
Enoch Wood's Papers. — Hanley Museum
Minutes of Burslem Board of Health. — Hanley Reference Library
Burslem News Cuttings. — Hanley Reference Library
Parish Registers of St. John's Church. — Wedgwood Memorial College
When I was a child. — Rev.C. Shaw
Stories of a Staffordshire Parson. — Rev. H.V. Stuart
English Free Churches. — H. Davies
A popular history of the Free Churches. — C.S. Horne. M.A.
Joseph Capper. — F.Harper
Tom Paine. A political life. — J. Keane
Arnold Bennett. — M. Drabble
The North Staffs Railway. — Christiansen & Miller
Keats Gazetteer — Wedgwood Memorial College
Inns and Inn Signs. — W.E. Tate.
The Folklore of Staffordshire. — J. Raven
Murder Myths & Monuments of North Staffordshire. — W.M. Jameson
James Holland — Steve Bond
Staffordshire Pottery and its History — Josiah C. Wedgwood

Future Dreams

May the love that brought us all together
On this your very special day
Go with you now, and be forever.
There for you, to guide you on your way
For marriage is a cornerstone, the base from which to build
On future dreams, before they fade and die
But marriage is not easy and the world around is filled
With those who fail no matter how they try
So be careful on this journey now, take with you into life
Love and understanding, but keep tolerance in sight
For the day will surely come when, though both of you are right
One must say "I'm sorry". While the other dims the light

Jean Jones